James Chuter Ede: Humane Reformer and Politician

TO JOAN SMITH
(1920–2018)

James Chuter Ede:
Humane Reformer
and Politician

Liberal and Labour Traditions

Stephen Hart

PEN & SWORD
HISTORY

First published in Great Britain in 2021 by
Pen & Sword History
An imprint of
Pen & Sword Books Ltd
Yorkshire – Philadelphia

ISBN 978 1 52678 372 1

A CIP catalogue record for this book is
available from the British Library.

Typeset by Mac Style
Printed and bound in the UK by TJ Books Ltd,
Padstow, Cornwall.

Pen & Sword Books Limited incorporates the imprints of Atlas,
Archaeology, Aviation, Discovery, Family History, Fiction, History,
Maritime, Military, Military Classics, Politics, Select, Transport,
True Crime, Air World, Frontline Publishing, Leo Cooper, Remember
When, Seaforth Publishing, The Praetorian Press, Wharncliffe
Local History, Wharncliffe Transport, Wharncliffe True Crime
and White Owl.

For a complete list of Pen & Sword titles please contact

PEN & SWORD BOOKS LIMITED
47 Church Street, Barnsley, South Yorkshire, S70 2AS, England
E-mail: enquiries@pen-and-sword.co.uk
Website: www.pen-and-sword.co.uk

Or

PEN AND SWORD BOOKS
1950 Lawrence Rd, Havertown, PA 19083, USA
E-mail: Uspen-and-sword@casematepublishers.com
Website: www.penandswordbooks.com

Contents

Chapter 1

Introduction

This biography began with a question, a memory, and two surprises.
The question arose in July 2016, when Theresa May became
Prime Minister, and the comment was made that she had been
Home Secretary for an unusual timespan, 'longer than any other politician in
recent times'. So I wondered who had been Home Secretary for longer, and
perhaps also who qualifies as 'recent'. That was an easy online search.

The longest-serving of her predecessors was Lord Sidmouth (previously
known as Addington, when in the Commons as Prime Minister), during the
long Liverpool administration two hundred years ago. He was at the Home
Office for nearly ten years. R.A. Cross served two terms there, under Disraeli
and then Salisbury, covering (when added together) six years and ten months
between 1874 and 1886. Apart from them, and certainly more 'recent' – just
about within living memory – the longest in office was James Chuter Ede.

As it happens, Mrs May would have been longer than that at the Home
Office had her election as Conservative leader been contested to the end.
Because she was eventually unopposed and was appointed PM sooner than
expected, her period as Home Secretary was some three weeks shorter than
Chuter Ede's.

As to the memory, I was pleased to notice two points which Chuter Ede
and I share in common, when I looked into his background. First, like me,
he originated in north Surrey – he was born in Epsom, I in Kingston. That
jogged my memory. I recall being taken to watch cricket at the Oval when I
was a small boy, some time in the late 1950s, and my mother pointing out, in
the Members' Stand, 'Mr Chuter Ede who used to be in the Government'.

As I delved further, I discovered all he had done for Surrey. I knew the
Kingston By-pass as a boy; indeed, if I walked to school I crossed it by
footbridge on my way. To me, it had always been there, but of course, it had
not – it was built in the 1920s, and Chuter Ede's was one of the minds behind
it. In addition, my elder brother told me he remembered seeing him with
the Attlees when, at Ede's expense, they reopened the stepping stones near
Burford Bridge under Box Hill in 1946.

The surprise was that Chuter Ede had been a member of Christ's College, Cambridge, which is my own college. In general the colleges of Cambridge and Oxford (and no doubt other universities) are very keen to boast about their successful former members, but I had never heard of him at all in that connection. The college has many notable alumni, but none has risen higher in British politics than Home Secretary. The college's website includes a page on Distinguished Members, but he did not feature there, and the Wikipedia page about the College did not list him in its 'Famous alumni' section. I have remedied both of those gaps in the course of my research.

That research has taken me in several different directions. I was fortunate to make two contacts early on – mentioned in the Acknowledgements at the end – and to be able to find considerable primary documentation which, though used by others before me, had never formed the basis for a complete biography, which was the second surprise. Half of Attlee's first cabinet have been the subject of biographies, but Chuter Ede is comfortably the most senior of those who have not, and particularly of those who served throughout that government's time in office.

As I started to write, one question I had to decide initially, was whether to use a cradle-to-grave approach in the biography, or to discuss it by themes. To quote Diana Souhami, a very experienced biographer, 'We don't live our lives or read in a linear fashion … the internet has so much information that it rather absolves the biographer from being a storehouse of knowledge'.[1] In her writing she has generally followed that precept, which expresses in modern form the opinion of the doyen of biographers (and of subjects of biography), Samuel Johnson, criticising those who:

> rarely afford any other account than might be collected from public papers, but imagine themselves writing a life when they exhibit a chronological series of actions or preferments; and so little regard the manners or behaviour of their heroes that more knowledge may be gained of a man's real character, by a short conversation with one of his servants, than from a formal and studied narrative, begun with his pedigree and ended with his funeral.[2]

I felt, though, that in Chuter Ede's case the internet's information was insufficient, and what was missing was a complete account of the different facets of the life of a many-sided individual. To find that out required looking into a great deal of papers which, though 'public', had been little studied, and never as a whole together. Also, when writing a political life (which is not Diana Souhami's field, nor Johnson's), it is important to know how the subject's background and experience influenced what happened next; to an extent, politics can indeed be read in a linear fashion.

That said, various themes, recurring during Ede's life, did assert themselves to justify being written about. First, his was a passage from a Liberal background to Labour politics. That was a voyage taken by several politicians in the early twentieth century, though in a variety of ways. A well-known case is Charles Trevelyan, with an entirely different background from Ede, though one notes they both became experts in the same specialist field of education. It is interesting to enquire how Trevelyan's achievements and failures influenced Ede, whom he encouraged and who succeeded him as the Labour Party's expert on the subject. So Ede became the person Attlee recommended to be Butler's junior minister in the War Coalition, and whose 'special thing' (in Attlee's words after he decided to place him at the Home Office) was education.

Ede eventually became a member of a Labour cabinet which included several who had migrated from the Liberal tradition, but Addison, Stansgate and Jowitt had, like Trevelyan, come from professional or landowning families and a privately educated background. They did not make the move until the 1920s, doing so partly in the light of the factional strife within the Liberal Party, when Asquith and Lloyd George went their separate ways, while others like Churchill joined the Conservatives. Ede had already shifted to Labour earlier.

The inference is that, with his experience of the trade union movement, he concluded it was the Labour Party which provided the better vehicle for promoting the interests of those working in his particular field, and hence of those – the pupils and students – for whose benefit education was designed. However, this took a form which was not doctrinaire, partly because Ede's liberal background had taught him the degree of tolerance and composure needed to pursue his reforms, both in education and as Home Secretary. It has proved to be well worth studying how a 'person of a liberal turn of mind' and 'never a very good Party man' (both self-descriptions, more than forty years apart), whose contemporary heroes were – perhaps improbably – Campbell-Bannerman and Attlee, could have achieved what he did.

Linked to that, a further significant theme is the influence of Nonconformity, and in Ede's case particularly Unitarianism, in the radical politics of the time. It is worth noting how proud he was always to declare himself a 'Nonconformist', with its implication of rebelliousness. The view that truth is not constant, but develops from age to age, might in some contexts be linked to the Marxist heritage of Socialism, yet for him it was inherited as one of the principles of the dissenting faith, and his Unitarianism took this one stage further. I was pleased to discover how the speeches and talks which this elderly politician gave, to Unitarian audiences in Britain and North America, illustrated the tradition in which he saw himself – from Cromwell, Milton and Bunyan, through Fox and Cobbett, to the Labour reformers of liberal disposition in his own time. This is a less well-known aspect in Labour history, and I have not had space to analyse or quote from these speeches in great detail, but it might provide a profitable field for a further researcher following on from what I have written.

Among the other themes which may make this life worth investigating, the most significant is perhaps the role of the Home Office in regard to civil liberties. When he stepped down, Ede referred to 'the traditional liberal policy of the great department for which I was responsible', but describing the Home Office tradition in that way is a challenge to anyone familiar with the career of Sidmouth, its longest-serving Secretary of State, and several of Ede's own predecessors in the twentieth century. However, he was conscious he was the successor of Robert Peel, and more recently Samuel Hoare, and he lived to collaborate with Roy Jenkins, though not quite long enough to see him as Home Secretary. When we look at his years in that office, it turns out that the balance he had to make between safeguarding individual liberty on the one hand, and his task of maintaining strict law and order on the other, was a 'double duty' which he recognised. In some ways, that is as interesting as the actual legislative and administrative reforms which he initiated. He is the supreme example of a Home Secretary in office for an extended time, who wrestled successfully with these issues, and his life justifies being examined for this also.

Finally, there is the devout Christian politician and his attitude to war. In a 1960 BBC interview he stated 'I'm a pacific person but I'm not a Pacifist. I joined the volunteers when I was 17 … and once a soldier always a soldier.'[3] That was during the Boer War, and in 1914 he offered his services as soon as he could. He then became one of the founding fathers of the British Legion, and of course had no hesitation in supporting the Second World War when it became inevitable. In his days as a senior Unitarian, he was sometimes faced with a majority in his faith who argued for nuclear disarmament; according to one of them, he was unembarrassed about his support for nuclear weapons, trying to 'sit on the fence' when he could.[4]

I trust themes such as these will emerge from this biography, even though, in presenting Ede's life, I have started at the beginning, and proceeded chronologically to the end. If on occasions that means I have jumped from one subject to another, and then back again a short time later, I hope the reader will be patient and understanding. If, conversely, I have seemed to be addressing questions like 'What was he doing on Thursday 29 January 1942? – and then what on Friday 30 January?' in too much pedantic and trivial detail, I hope to be pardoned for that also. I do believe it is important to get an idea of the routine (monthly, weekly, and sometimes even daily) of what Ede was doing in his jobs and, particularly where we have his own diary as a reference, that gives an excellent idea of what life was like for him.

Having said that, I consider this an 'introductory life'. I want to introduce Chuter Ede to readers and researchers, in the wish that some will be interested enough to enquire more into the archives than I have been able to do. Most of his diaries have never been transcribed, still less published, and the papers he left merit much more time than I have given them. I hope others may take up what I have started, and bring into more detail a life which, in my view, deserves much further study, for Dr Johnson also said in the same essay that 'there has rarely passed a life of which a judicious and faithful narrative would not be useful'. He believed that everyone can find other people similar to himself, from whom he can learn, and that we all have so much in common that we can recognise how the lives of others bear on ourselves. The life of Chuter Ede has taught me much about myself, and perhaps will do the same for other readers.

It should also help to teach us how Britain reached the position in which we are now. For so many of the fields covered by Chuter Ede remain important issues today – British national identity, immigration and refugees, the environment, penal policy, civil liberties, policing, Parliamentary representation, and how best to provide opportunities in education, are examples. There is great misunderstanding about the Education Act 1944, which needs correcting. Hence it is essential to grasp the role played by Ede and his colleagues in the mid-twentieth century, in order to appreciate what has happened since.

One final comment – when writing I have had to decide how to refer to my subject, James Chuter Ede. The custom is to use a surname only, certainly as far as a male subject is concerned, and nowadays often for women too. His closest associates seem to have called him 'Jim', but many of those who knew him addressed him as 'Chuter', in the days when surnames were widely used among men. I decided that, as Ede was his surname, until he changed it in his last few months, the best course was to call him that. In a few places, where it is necessary to distinguish him from other family members, he is 'James' or 'Jim', and in a few others I have used his longer name where it felt more appropriate, but generally he is 'Ede'.

Chapter 2

The Early Years

In February 1961, the elderly James Chuter Ede, a Member of Parliament for more than twenty-five years, out of Government office for nearly ten, was approached by the Oxford historian Alan Bullock. Bullock was seeking to learn Ede's recollections of the period when he and Ernest Bevin had worked together as Government ministers, first in Winston Churchill's War Coalition, and then in Clement Attlee's administration from 1945. Bullock had already published the first volume of his huge biography of Bevin, and was now preparing the second, covering his five war years at the Ministry of Labour. It would not be published until 1967, after Ede's death, but Bullock benefited from the reminiscences about their work he was happy to give. In 1983, a final volume would eventually appear, dealing with Bevin's last years, when Foreign Secretary, while Ede was Home Secretary, nominally a post which took precedence over Bevin's. Bullock's entire work is nearly 2,000 pages long, and took him twenty-five years. Ede's life deserves the same detailed treatment, but has never received it. It is not getting it now, but a shorter introduction to his life is well warranted.

It starts in the part of England south of London. The names 'Ede' and 'Chuter' are found particularly there, so it is no surprise that a man named 'Chuter Ede' and his forebears should come from Surrey.

James Ede (senior) was born on 16 August 1840, in Epsom, the son of a miller who, with his wife, carried on a baker's and grocer's in the High Street. The family was aware that one of his ancestors had been hanged at Lewes for smuggling.[1] From what little we know about his parents, George and Elizabeth Ede, we can say that George died in 1850, when James was still a boy of about ten, fortunately after his mother had shown prudence by becoming a member of the Twenty Pound Burial Society.[2] She carried on with the retail business, while young James continued his education at Ewell Academy, where he was given a geography book two years later.[3] He then trained as an assistant at the London store of John Budgen – a name that remains in groceries to this day – and later took the family enterprise over from her.

The registers of births from around 1840 show that there was an average of twenty-seven children named Ede born each year in England and Wales, of whom over 75 per cent came from Surrey or its adjacent counties (there was also a group from around the east of Cornwall, comprising virtually all the rest). By the early 1880s, when James Ede's eldest son was born, the number of births had increased to about fifty annually, reflecting the 80 per cent increase in the country's population over that period, but the pattern was the same. Nearly 80 per cent were from Surrey or its neighbours, with most of the rest from Cornwall, and fewer than 10 per cent from elsewhere. A less common name is Chuter, and it is even more local; around 1849, there were nine Chuter births a year on average, all of them in or adjacent to Surrey, many of them from around Farnham, and by the early 1880s, the number had increased to about fourteen, but only the odd one was from elsewhere.

All Surrey images reproduced by permission of Surrey History Centre.

Grandfather James Chuter, from the *Epsom Advertiser* 1906 Christmas Annual. (© *Surrey History Centre*)

The reason for selecting 1849 is that Agnes Mary Chuter was born on 15 May that year, also in Epsom. Her father, James Chuter, born in Farnham himself, was a local builder, though he apparently liked country pursuits, as he became Master of the Surrey Draghounds in 1873,[4] and her mother Ann Hannah Chuter. James Chuter had set up the development business of Chuter Brothers with his two brothers. They lived in Epsom High Street, with a builder's yard stretching along the back of the street beside the railway bank.[5] After the Epsom Local Board of Health was set up in 1850[6] – the first parish in Surrey to set one up[7] – he became a member of it, and was vice-chairman for over twenty years.[8] He then joined its successor from 1894, Epsom Urban District Council, totalling more than thirty years' service on the two authorities.[9] His grandson, James Chuter Ede, recalled that he fancied his chances as the UDC's first chairman, mainly for the honour of being an ex-officio magistrate, though he did not get the post.[10] He claimed to have known William Cobbett, and was a follower of his independent political ideals.[11] His eldest daughter, known as 'Mary', received her education locally, being given a textbook, *Hall's First French Course*, as a prize in 1861,[12] which her son, James Chuter Ede, would keep throughout his life.

We can guess that the Edes and the Chuters knew each other, as Epsom was a fairly small town in those days, and it is likely that they became acquainted, at least in the course of their respective businesses. Elizabeth Ede died in 1875, when her son James was thirty-four, and was buried on 11 May in Epsom Cemetery; her gravestone is still recognisable today, though the wording is very hard to make out. James carried on the bakery alone, until he and Mary Chuter married, on 24 November 1881. He was 41, she was 32. They continued to live over the shop in Epsom High Street, which became their children's first home.

The Edes were Nonconformists in religion, and some summaries of the life of their son Jim, whose career we are following, describe them as Unitarians.[13] That is to say they did not adhere to the established Church of England, believing in the essential unity of God, rather than the Trinity of the Catholics and most other Protestants (though over the years the term 'Unitarian' has acquired various meanings in different situations). The Unitarians themselves, on the other hand, claimed that in fact Jim settled on their faith when he was about twenty, and that seems more likely. He certainly worshipped in a variety of different churches during his life, most of which would be described as 'Nonconformist', though he attended Anglican services on occasion. He gives us a clue about the doctrine he inherited from his parents, as he once said in Parliament,

> I am not a Free Churchman. I am a Nonconformist, and there is a substantial difference between the two. As a Nonconformist I reject the authoritarian conception of religion … if I challenge the right of [Parliament] to pass an Act … contrary to my religious belief, I must be very careful that I do not attempt to impose my views on other people. That is the philosophy on which I have based my attitude.[14]

Epsom has a modern United Reformed Church, in Church Street – near, as it happens, both the Baptist and Anglican churches – and the family worshipped at the old Congregational Chapel then on the site. Mary taught in the Sunday School, while in 1903 James Ede became the full-time caretaker of the Congregational Hall.[15] She was 'a very staunch Nonconformist Radical, and there was no doubt she regarded an interest in political affairs as one essential of a good citizen'.[16] In politics, James and Mary supported the Liberals, which is common among Nonconformists, as was their passion for learning and education that their children inherited. Though their son would later say that nearly all shopkeepers in small towns then were Liberals and Nonconformists,[17] they would have been in a political minority in Epsom; four years after they married, the town became a separate

Parliamentary constituency, elected a Conservative member, and has done so at every election since.

Within a few weeks of their marriage, Mary found she was expecting her first child, and he was born in Epsom on 11 September 1882. He was given the names of his maternal grandfather, James Chuter, with 'James' for his father also. His mother prayed he might be a missionary,[18] though that did not come about, at least in the literal sense. He was followed a year later by a sister, Agnes Elizabeth, known as 'Lizzie', on 15 December 1883, and then quickly by two other children. A brother George Noel, was born on Christmas Eve 1884, and his name given to recognise the season, Noel, was the one by which he was known. Finally, a second sister, Constance Ellen, called 'Nell' by her brother James, followed on 30 March 1886.

Young James – 'Jim' – was told the very next day that he was starting school, according to comments he made more than once in later speeches.[19] As 31 March was three-and-a-half weeks before Easter in 1886 – on 25 April, Easter was as late as it can be – he probably did not actually start school that day, just before the vacation, but he may well have been told that he was starting a few weeks later. He was five months short of his fourth birthday, which suggests he was recognised as having a precocious talent of some type; he certainly knew his alphabet already.[20]

West Hill Infants School was located on the road going out of Epsom towards Oxshott, a few hundred yards from the High Street. The headteacher was Miss Llewellyn,[21] and the building had been constructed, probably some time in the eighteenth century – nobody knew for sure – and had been used as a stable, including in 1780 for Eclipse, the greatest racehorse of the age. 'It was a very old Church school', Jim liked to say, but at some stage around 1830, 'when the building was no longer fit for housing bloodstock, it was turned into an infants' school'[22] – 'an elementary school for educating the children of the poor in the principles of the Established Church',[23] though still under the auspices of the Epsom Grand Stand Association. Epsom being a centre of horse racing ('Home of the Derby', the signboards tell the modern traveller), he implied the local priority was racing rather than education. The school was on a restricted site, insanitary and badly lit.

The description he gave of the school – following a sanitary inspection thirty-seven years later, from which he concluded little had changed – was

that the school is rat infested, that the wall behind the big cupboard has not been repaired or cleansed for years and is in a dilapidated, filthy, and insanitary condition and the floor-boarding rotten, that an old pot gulley with its foul contents is in the lobby, that the woodwork behind the three wash basins is dilapidated and foul, and that the waste pipes from the basins are untrapped; and that the sanitary inspector alleges that these conditions give rise to nuisance and endanger the health of the children and staff.[24]

He would continue to ask questions in Parliament about the school for years to come, until eventually it was replaced. From 1886 to 1890, however, it was the school he knew.

When he was eight, Jim Ede received a prize (*The Giants and how to Fight Them*) for his regular and punctual attendance at Epsom Congregational Sunday School, and about the same time he joined the Epsom National Schools in Hook Road, to the north of the town. 'I was taught in a class of 90', he said later;[25] for how long that applied is unclear, but he felt that was a fairly typical class size at the time for a school of this type. The school was not entirely free, for '9d a week was demanded for his education'.[26] 'National' indicates it was an elementary school run by the National Society for Promoting Religious Education (ie, Church of England education), which had been set up in the early nineteenth century, with a view to having a Church school in every parish in England and Wales. It did not achieve that, but it went a long way towards it, and one was established in Epsom. When universal education had been made compulsory, under the Education Act 1870, School Boards had set up 'board schools' where there was no local provision but, where a suitable school was already in situ, this was reckoned to suffice; board schools were intended only to fill in the gaps. So the Epsom National Schools were what was available for children like the Edes, even though they were not adherents to the Anglican Church. Epsom was a 'single-school area', like many others, and the existence of such areas was a grievance to many Nonconformists and Free Churchmen, which Jim Ede would have to address in due course. Around this time, James Ede (senior) went to Epsom Town Hall, taking his young son with him, to press for a School Board to cover the Epsom area,[27] but this had no effect for the boy, who spent his years to age thirteen at the Church school.

Fortunately it was a 'higher grade' school, that is, one in which the pupils could continue beyond the compulsory school leaving age (which was 11 from 1893, and twelve from 1899), which eventually enabled him to stay until he qualified for secondary education. A consequence of this, he recalled, was that he attended cookery classes, unlike his sister, whose elementary school was not higher grade, so he passed his notes on the subject to her, so she could use them.[28] He was conscious, as he would continue to be, of the divisions in the education system, which benefitted some pupils and disadvantaged others.

Ede would later on speak of his amusing recollections of life at the school. In 1890 he was examined by one of Her Majesty's Inspectors at Standard I. The children were drawn up on three sides of a traditional British army square, and the HMI walked round the outside. He was the baldest man he had ever seen, 'with a protuberance on which grew three hairs. This was before the time of regulated ventilation, and the draught caused the three hairs to wave about.' One boy read from a book, until the inspector pointed at Ede and told him to go on with the reading, but there was only one book so he went on reciting it, as he knew it by heart. The HMI said he had failed, but the headmaster remonstrated that he was the best reader they had, and suggested the inspector found him something else to read. He produced a copy of *The Daily Telegraph* from his Gladstone bag. 'The devil looks after his own, for it had been my job to read each day to my father the leading article in the *Telegraph*. I passed.'[29]

A further incident at school occurred at standard III during another inspection, when the teacher had prepared the boys in detail about the visit, down to the likely arithmetic questions, and what hand signals he would give about spelling words in a dictation. When the HMI eventually asked the children, 'Who was born at Huntingdon?', Jim ventured the reply, 'Oliver Cromwell', and the inspector passed the whole school in geography. Next day the headmaster, Mr O'Connell, picked Ede up by the collar, put him on a desk, called him 'a model of erudition and publicly presented me with the sum of a penny'. That was the least he deserved because, having been passed, the school was granted 2/6d per capita, and the head – who was paid by results – was rewarded with £40, together with 60 per cent of the grant to the school. As for the penny, 'I did something that boys nowadays cannot do – I spent it on my way home, a farthing at a time'.[30]

Ede's childhood was a happy one in a secure family. He later looked back with fondness on his trips with his father to sell his bread to the gipsies on Epsom Downs,[31] and one wartime Christmas he recalled the seasonal celebrations when they were still living over the shop. The best dinner service would be produced, with heavy cut glass tumblers. They would dine on a very large turkey, bought from Hall and Davidson, millers in Ewell, plum pudding, mince pies, and desserts including nuts and fruits, and then play 'harmless games' like Ludo and Halma. The drinks, however, were simply ginger beer and lemonade, the Edes being teetotallers, as Jim would remain, almost, drinking very little alcohol at any time in his life. The next day, Boxing Day, till he was about thirteen, they would go to a party given by James Hailes, a local violin teacher; Mrs Hailes and Mary Ede were cousins. 'We were very happy. The world seemed so secure in those days.'[32]

Ede did well at his elementary school, because in 1895 he was entered for Dorking High School for Boys and, he explained later:

I sat as a candidate for one of the … junior county scholarships. There were 32 scholarships on the list and I passed number 32 on the list. I was only three marks ahead of number 33 and I am sure it was the peculiar Surrey method of addition that resulted in my getting into that position.[33]

With his scholarship, he started there on 11 September, his thirteenth birthday. The school, in Dene Street, just off the High Street, had been only recently founded, and was less than ten years old; it merged with the Girls' High School in the 1930s and, after a further merger in the 1970s, is now called the Ashcombe School, its current site being in Ashcombe Road, Dorking. In his time, the founding headmaster was there, a priest, the Revd. Henry Roberts. Ede retained a pride in his school, noting in his diary on his fifty-ninth birthday that it was forty-six years since he first started there. The journey to Dorking is not difficult, only four stops on the train from Epsom, and in fact the nine mile distance can be cycled in less than an hour, though this does involve a climb over Box Hill. Ede's later career, and comments he made about he walks he loved to make in the area, indicate he got to know the part of Surrey between Epsom and Dorking quite well, although he spent only three years at the High School.

Like so many whose schooldays are behind them, he was left with amusing memories of his years at Dorking. Meeting in 1942 a man named Sanders from the neighbouring village of Shere, after not seeing each other for 44 years, they spoke of the time they had been classmates, and Roberts, the headmaster, teaching the geography of Holland, asked Sanders the names of the principal towns there. 'Damn!' the boy muttered. 'Yes', said the head, 'Amster or Rotter?'[34]

He also told Parliament[35] that he had been punished at the school for reading *Treasure Island*. The book was considered 'a blood', and the 'penny blood' was 'a desperate work of imaginative adventure', inveighed against by magistrates as causing juvenile delinquency. Robert Louis Stevenson had indeed first published the book as a serial in a children's magazine, around the time of Ede's birth, and Ede regarded it as 'the bloodiest blood of all', though he disagreed with the views of the justices, particularly when, forty years later, he found himself handing out *Treasure Island* as a school prize. However, 'I sometimes warn a boy who gets it that it is a book that needs to be read with discretion and its examples followed with great care.'

During his time at Dorking, the family suffered at least two bereavements. His grandmother Ann Chuter died in the summer of 1897, and was buried in Epsom Cemetery. Then, more poignantly, Lizzie Ede, the older of Jim's two sisters, died of typhoid on 22 March 1899, when she was fifteen. She was also buried in the town's cemetery, six days later, and in the same grave where her grandmother Elizabeth Ede had been laid fourteen years before. Lizzie's name is also just readable on the tombstone. March 22 would be another anniversary which Ede would remember.

In March 1899, at the age of 16, Ede left Dorking High School, joining the London School Board as an apprentice teacher. His college work was carried out at the Pupil Teachers' Centre in Battersea, while he worked half a day in the classroom. Before the year was out, he was elected as the junior representative for Battersea to the London Pupil Teachers' Association Executive, in 1900 was re-elected, and became senior representative for 1901 and 1902.[36]

We can get an idea of Ede's energies around this time, by looking at his other activities. He joined the Second Volunteer Battalion of the East Surrey Regiment in 1899 – the year the Boer War started. Some of the East Surreys went to fight in South Africa, though it is unlikely there was any question of this with an underage Territorial (as they would soon be known) like Ede. Attending for duties at the Barracks in King's Road, Kingston, would have been the main activity of someone in his position, and he remained in the volunteers until he went to university four years later. He also put together an Epsom Congregational Church Cricket Club, of which he was secretary, and the committee included his fifteen-year-old brother Noel. A fixture list was printed,[37] showing the team played seventeen matches during the 1901 season, starting on 4 May with a match against J Chuter Ede's Eleven. Notes penned on the fixture list under the words 'Score', if they record his own batting, show Jim had few claims as a batsman. The highest score for the season was 19, with an average of seven. A newspaper profile a little later makes him out to be more of a bowler:

> Ede, in a Mafeking hat and brown shirt, with his long, brown and white arms swinging like windmill sails, careering madly down the pitch, cheered by an admiring little crowd, whose hero he is, is a familiar and exhilarating sight in the Recreation Ground on long summer evenings.[38]

The sentiments sound rather overflowing, as though the writer ('ENM') was someone suspiciously close to him, but his interest in cricket is clear, and it would continue for life.

In March 1901 and February 1902, he won a prize in the London Pupil Teachers' Debating Contest, as we know from a notebook[39] he kept for a couple of years, marked on its first page with his name and that achievement. The little book contains notes for the YMCA debating class, as well as a long account of the life of Oliver Cromwell, Ede's hero throughout his life. On 17 and 24 November 1900, letters appeared in the *Epsom Advertiser* signed by 'Oliver Cromwell', and we can assume Ede was the writer, since he pasted them in this book. Early in 1902, Canon Arthur Hunter spoke to the YMCA on Church schools, which started a debate in the press between Ede and him about the Anglican financing of education. He was starting what he would continue, a career of argument in words, both spoken and written.

It was during 1902, according to the Unitarian account,[40] that Ede learnt about the Unitarian faith, rather than having assimilated it from birth as central to his family's Nonconformity. On his way to classes he happened to pass the bookshop near Essex Hall, the Unitarian headquarters, and bought some cheap pamphlets, which convinced him that this was the creed in which he believed.

On 4 October 1902, he proposed a motion at a debate at Toynbee Hall in the East End, sponsored by the London Pupil Teachers' Association, that 'Free Trade is a Necessity for this Country', winning a further prize (the two previous debates having been on 'Imperial Federation' and 'Payment of MPs').[41] Free trade sounds a characteristic subject for a Liberal, and by now he was active in the Epsom and District Liberal Association, of which by 1903 he was Secretary. The address on his membership card was Hawthorne Villa, the family having moved the short distance from the High Street shop to Hawthorne Place, across the railway line in Epsom. He also joined the Epsom Liberal Club and, as its Assistant Honorary Secretary, gave a lecture on 'The Housing Problem' on 17 April 1903, at which the seventeen-year-old Nell was present – his sister was starting her career as one of his closest supporters. He was a member too of the Epsom Literary Society, to which he delivered a lecture on 17 February 1903 on the 'Garden City Project', at the King's Head Assembly Rooms in Epsom. His interest in the environment, as it would today be termed, had already commenced.

The organisation in which he was the most active speaker was probably the Independent Order of Good Templars (IOGT), part of the temperance movement which originated in North America. On 23 April 1903 he addressed a temperance demonstration at the Congregational Lecture Hall, in Station Road, Epsom, for the local United Temperance Committee, and there are several flyers in his notebook for meetings of the IOGT at which he was a speaker, starting with one on 6 July at the Town Mission Hall in Epsom High Street.

As a pupil teacher, his report books show he was considered unaffected and sincere, perhaps a bit earnest, but a top-rate trainee,[42] even though the head of the Centre, Thomas Huitt, did make some criticisms. In January 1901, he received a highly creditable report from his headmaster, Arthur Baker, at Basnett Road School, off Lavender Hill, near Clapham Common, where he spent the four years of his training.[43] This was close to his Battersea base, which had been transferred in 1888 from Surrey to the new County of London. Unlike Ede's own school in Epsom, it was a board school, not a Church school. One of his supervisors, E A Saltmarsh, described him as 'a student of most conspicuous ability, likely to do good work in the world.' Baker's leaving remarks describe how 'he has loyally served the London School Board during his apprenticeship. With the training he will get at Cambridge, he will make a thoroughly good teacher' – for the young man had been granted a scholarship to continue his studies at university.

In 1903, James Chuter Ede was admitted as a pensioner at Christ's College, Cambridge. He matriculated, to use the academic term, on 29 July,[44] shortly before his twenty-first birthday, in advance of the term starting in the autumn. To do so, he was led to the University Senate House by Harris Rackham, a classicist Fellow of the College.[45] His status as a pensioner is significant, in view of his shortened career there – from the College's point of view, he was a fee-paying undergraduate, without any scholarship assistance from the college's endowment, although he was supported by Surrey County Council. He had gained a Surrey scholarship in March, an event which justified a long write-up in the local paper.[46] The same newspaper article which glorified his bowling at cricket mentioned he had won a medal as one of the team which won a trophy, listed his achievements in science:

Among other certificates he holds … Theoretical inorganic chemistry (advanced and elementary), practical inorganic chemistry (advanced and elementary), mathematics (stages I and II), geometrical drawing, and theoretical mechanics (elementary).

It acclaimed his time as a pupil-teacher:

Among his fellow students, fellow workers, and the boys at Battersea he is deservedly popular, for his congeniality and, not least, for the quaint, old-world charm of his personality. The boys at Basnett Grove (*sic*) will lose a warm friend – a friend that it will be difficult to replace … Mr Ede is well known and much esteemed in Epsom and neighbourhood …

> He takes pains pleasantly, on examinations thriving well … He is an elocutionist of some considerable excellence, an amusing singer, a fair pianist, a temperance advocate, a politician, a cyclist, a chessman, a lay preacher of much power, a Sunday School teacher much loved, a citizen soldier, a wide and deep reader, a sound thinker, a clear speaker, a hard hitter, a man of deep religious convictions, yet having nothing of bigotry, a 'true-born son of earth and heaven', a loving brother, an exemplary son, and a warm friend. We wish him every success. The world has a task and a place for him.[47]

Within the gushing style, much of description of Ede would in the fullness of time be proved accurate.

Shortly before he went up to Cambridge, he carried on with his public speaking engagements. On 2 September 1903 he was at a temperance meeting of the IOGT in Ewell High Street, and the following day he was in Leatherhead, giving a lantern lecture, under IOGT auspices, on housing problems. On 15 September he gave a further lantern lecture at the Congregational Hall in Epsom on 'The Struggle for Religious Equality', a subject which would stimulate him throughout his life. The next day, he was chairing an IOGT meeting at the Parochial Hall in Ewell. He was in touch with the *Westminster Gazette*, which hired out lantern slides to illustrate talks such as his, for 10/6d a time, with a returnable deposit of the same amount, the modern equivalent of about £60 (with £60 deposit), so these were clearly well-planned events. An indication of the reputation he was developing is that, on 24 September, he was asked by the Liberal Party if he would address election meetings, whenever the next elections were called. But he declined that invitation, knowing for the next few years he would be busy in Cambridge, where his family sent him off to, with their good wishes. At his death he still had the bible given him by his parents, sister and brother for the occasion.

Cambridge had set up a Day Training College in 1891, part of the movement to establish teacher training in the British universities, at the time when the demand for qualified staff was increasing after education had become compulsory.[48] Its aim was to supplement the work of the residential colleges of education, by providing training to students able enough to read for a degree, in an environment which was not restricted to one religious denomination (which many of the existing colleges were). It was also intended to provide a more rigorous, academic introduction to teaching than that provided by the pupil-teacher system popular in the nineteenth century, under which Ede had already been trained. In many respects, this movement was being led by the new municipal universities, but Oscar Browning, an idiosyncratic Fellow of King's College, had ensured that Cambridge followed, and he became its Principal from 1891 into the first years of the new century. Browning did so in the face of apathy, sometimes verging on hostility, from the boys' public and grammar school heads, for whom practical training was considered unnecessary for their staff, or even reducing the status of well-educated men to that of elementary school teacher.[49] So Ede learnt early on the attitudes his career would need to challenge. The extravagant *Epsom Observer* article said that his scholarship would enable him to read for a degree as a non-collegiate student but, if that was so for anybody, it was not the case for him. Generally, students joined a college, and studied for a degree in their subject, but were attached also to the Day Training College, and Ede's scholarship was to enable him to develop his professional skills through study there.

Most of the information about his time at Cambridge comes from comments he made later in life, or documents he left among his papers. Christ's in the nineteenth century had a reputation as a free-thinking and radical college, and it founded a College magazine in 1886,[50] which continues to this day. However, there is no mention of Ede in the magazine regarding any sporting or academic associations, and neither does the college hold any material about him in its Fellows' papers.

We do know that his tutor was the Revd. James William Cartmell, a 60-year-old Fellow, who had come to Christ's,[51] where his family had connections, as a scholar in 1861, and had joined the fellowship in 1866, three years before he was ordained. His academic field was German, and he had been active in establishing the modern and medieval languages Tripos – that is, the subject of an honours degree – in 1878. He would spend his entire adult life in Cambridge, dying there in 1918.

The Master of Christ's at the time was John Peile, a classicist who developed a career in comparative philology, though he is most remembered for his researches into the history of the College itself. This resulted in a detailed account, which would be largely (though not totally) finished when he died, still in post as Master, in 1910, and published in 1913. He also produced a *Christ's College Biographical Register*, listing the members of the College over the centuries, in which Ede features briefly.

This six-line entry lists Ede's name, the name of his father, and details of his birth. His schools are described as 'National, and Dorking High'. His date of admission and tutor are included, along with the information that he resided six terms. By 1913, when the *Register* was issued, he was described as a member of Epsom UDC from 1908, and vice-president (president-elect) of the Surrey County Teachers' Association in 1912, residing at Hawthorne Place, Epsom. From the perspective of ten years later, therefore, his career was looked upon as being fairly unexceptional at Cambridge, with a few elements of the public service which the university would expect of its members, as standard conduct in their later life.

Cambridge at the time had recently experienced major changes as a university, without which Ede's student experience might have been very different, even if he had been accepted there at all. In 1871, Parliament passed the Universities Tests Act, a significant reform measure, partly under pressure from colleges such as Christ's. For the first time, Nonconformists such as Ede, and those of all faiths, could be admitted to the universities without the rigorous requirements for a religious test. In addition, the study of natural sciences had been adopted as a Tripos in 1851. By 1903, therefore, he could enter the University as a science undergraduate on his own merit, though it seems that laboratory provision was lagging behind what was properly required.[52]

By modern standards, Christ's would have seemed a small college, with no more than fifteen Fellows, and undergraduate numbers having only recently reached two hundred. While many of the prominent Fellows in the late Victorian period – including Peile himself – were specialists in history or languages, it seems by the end of the century to have developed a strength in the sciences, particularly the life sciences. The proportion of undergraduates reading natural sciences had risen during the period to 10–15 per cent, far more than in the university as a whole. Among the biology Fellows was Francis Darwin, one of the sons of the most famous scientist to come from Christ's, Charles Darwin – also from a Unitarian background – who had been an undergraduate there around 1830 (though he had taken an ordinary degree in Divinity). In addition, the fellowship included Sir Arthur Shipley, a distinguished zoologist, whose memorial in the College Chapel Ede visited many years later, recalling 'Shipley, who was my tutor'.[53] That does not contradict Cartmell's role; he would have been Ede's moral tutor, looking after his progress generally, while Shipley was College Tutor in natural sciences, taking the part nowadays described as 'director of studies', in charge of his tuition in the particular subjects he was reading. Shipley would go on to follow Peile as Master of the College, and then Vice-Chancellor of the University.

At Cambridge, science undergraduates typically start by reading a range of subjects, gradually narrowing them down in each successive year, and it is not known which sciences Ede studied, though he did once comment that he had been told while at Cambridge the atom could not be split. In fact, that would have been a commonplace in school physics or chemistry at the time, and is scant evidence of which disciplines he studied. Then, he continued, 'someone from my own college went to America and split it'.[54] (It is unclear whom he meant, as most early work on nuclear fission was done in Europe, not America, and none of those leading the Cambridge effort was from Christ's. The most likely candidate is Robert Oppenheimer, an American who spent a couple of graduate years at the College, before moving to Germany and then back to the US, where he later helped develop the atom bomb, which of course involved nuclear technology.)

Sport had developed greatly at the University in the late nineteenth century, and it was important at Christ's. A recent undergraduate of the College has concluded 'that some form of participation in a college sport was expected of the majority of students', from his review of college magazines of the time.[55] He notes that in 1899, four years before Ede's arrival, the football club complained, in justifying its poor season, that there 'are not enough men who play soccer', blaming 'those people who prefer to deliberately slack instead of joining in the College games'. Furthermore, the amount of sport played was substantial – in the first four weeks of May 1893, the cricket team played on thirteen days, more games than the team nowadays would play in two seasons.

In 1896, Gilbert Jessop had been admitted to Christ's, a cricketer who would, arguably, become the greatest English batsman between the time of WG Grace and Jack Hobbs. He remained for three years, distinguishing himself at University and College level, and playing football also. So there was a distinct tradition of sporting activity at the college. As for Ede, though he had organised a team in Epsom, and though he followed cricket throughout his life in Surrey, there is no evidence of his involvement as a player while at Christ's, but he certainly knew about their star cricketer. In his seventies, Ede kept a copy of the list of College members sent to him in 1954 and one single name in the list is circled – Gilbert Jessop.[56]

Another recent member of Christ's was Jan Smuts, a highly gifted Afrikaner from the Cape Colony, with all-round academic talent, who gained a brilliant degree in law before qualifying for the Bar in London, and then returning to South Africa, despite the college's attempts to retain him. He then, however, became one of the Boer War leaders opposing the British and, by the time Ede arrived at Christ's, the college was not so proud of him. Some forty years later, Ede was amused to learn that Smuts, by now an Honorary Fellow, was cheered by the students, who rose to applaud him, when he joined them to dine in the

Hall at Christ's;[57] he was by then appreciated for his contribution to the Allies in both World Wars. Eventually, after Smuts's death, we shall see Ede would quote him in one of the many speeches he made during his year of office as President of the General Assembly of Unitarian and Free Churches.[58]

Ede came into contact at Cambridge with men who would go on to positions of influence. It seems that he joined the University's Nonconformist Union, whose President at the time was EA Benians. He would eventually become Master of St John's College, and wartime Vice-Chancellor, whose death Ede recorded fifty years later.[59] Ede's activity in politics included membership of the Cambridge Union,[60] of which he was 'Not a very distinguished member; in fact I recollect on one occasion the note in *Granta* was Mr Ede, Christ's, also spoke – and was dull.'[61]

It also led him to join the Liberal Club (CULC), of which Oscar Browning was the founding Treasurer, and where he came across the imposing presence of John Maynard Keynes. Keynes was nine months younger than Ede, but had joined King's College a year earlier, in 1902, as part of his gilded career at Eton, Cambridge and onward, a forceful contrast to Ede's less privileged background. Many meetings of the Club took place in Keynes's rooms at King's, giving the impression that he dominated Liberal politics at Cambridge. Ede recalled[62] that, when Keynes was secretary of CULC, he discovered that the price of the club's dinner at the University Arms Hotel was higher than that of the Pitt Club, the up-market members' club in Cambridge, of which Keynes was also a member. When Keynes, who would go on to be president of CULC, queried this, he was told that the hotel had to charge more, because the members were nearly all teetotallers, and so provided little ancillary income when they dined. The Pitt Club members, by contrast, consumed a great deal of wine, which helped to subsidise the meal – no doubt Keynes among them. Ede would have sympathised with the temperance issue, Keynes with the economic one.

The Liberal Club would have given Ede an exposure to the prominent politicians of the time. Though the Conservatives were in office, it must have been clear that the tide was shifting, even if Campbell-Bannerman's landslide at the next election, which would so impress Ede, was not expected. One MP who visited to speak was Richard Haldane, an Opposition front bencher, who would eventually follow Ede into the Labour Party (and achieve high office before him, becoming Ramsay MacDonald's first Lord Chancellor). Ede commented that CULC 'treated our speakers with respect'.[63]

When he was not at university, he continued as busily as before in his activities in Surrey. Back for the Christmas 1903 vacation, he lectured to

Leatherhead Congregational Church Young People's Social Society on New Year's Eve, his subject being John Bunyan, another of his Nonconformist heroes. He cut out and pasted in his scrapbook the report of a lecture given in Epsom on 2 December about John Milton, a Christ's graduate himself.[64] In the following long vacation, on 13 September 1904, Ede gave an illustrated talk on Cromwell at the Lecture Hall of Epsom's Congregational Church, relying on the account of John Morley's *Life of Cromwell*, published in 1900, and no doubt on the notes he had himself made some four years earlier. A newspaper account of this lecture has survived, some 900 words long,[65] thanks either to the particular detail in which journalists then wrote, or to the speaker's own use of a press release; only a few extracts can be quoted, but they are instructive:

> Already (in 1620) England was beginning to feel the first strokes of the coming struggle. Learning had increased, religious foundations had been shaken, and men were beginning to realise something of 'the homespun dignity of man'. Revolutions were fertile soil for pamphleteers. Cromwell had been a strenuous supporter of the rights of the poor … The Presbyterians proved little more tolerant than the bishops. After the declaration of war, Cromwell continually urged the need for liberty of conscience … Charles made terms by suggesting an enquiry – then, as in more recent times, the refuge of a Government in distress, but the army did not favour the open mind in legislators … It was difficult to justify [Cromwell's] action in expelling the Rump. It started him upon … ruling … more and more arbitrary as events crowded on one another. To the Little Parliament he made a noble plea for liberty of conscience. Cromwell was too conservative to like the radical policy of this body. The sturdy individualism of the Calvinistic faith … was proved a broken reed in the constructive work now in hand … His aim was to place himself at the head of enlightened Europe, and his name made the stoutest of continental tyrants tremble … Cromwell was an Independent and a Statesman … the lofty spiritual gaze of Milton [was] beyond the multitude, but in Cromwell they could see the amalgam of saint and sinner of which they were also composed … he kept his faith in God and himself undimmed. In an age of bigotry he made it the one aim of his life to secure liberty of conscience'

While some of these points may be open to challenge by students of the Civil War and Protectorate, they illustrate several of Ede's themes throughout his life.

Back at university, his college celebrated its 400th anniversary in 1905, and he attended a dinner held in the Hall on 9 May, along with another 100 fellows and students,[66] where a loving cup was passed round the diners.[67] The likelihood, however, is that on the whole he concentrated dutifully on his studies, living frugally, bearing in mind that his local authority scholarship covered his fees but not any other living expenses. During the vacations, he worked to augment his funds as a clerk in various jobs, including for Surrey County Council's Education Office,[68] with some supply teaching in Surrey elementary schools, though work in this one profession for which he was qualified was unavailable outside term time. In the end, he stayed at Cambridge for two years, but then had to give up his place through lack of funds, without taking his degree.[69]

According to the account of John Strudwick, who would come to know him well in their activities in the National Union of Teachers in Surrey and the County Council, 'his grandfather wanted to make his stay at the university conditional on his training for the Church',[70] but he resolved to remain as a teacher. That would have been his namesake, James Chuter, his last surviving grandparent, already a very old man, but with still nearly ten years to live, in relation to one of the Nonconformist Churches. Ede later said he had considered becoming a minister, but having at Cambridge come across WB Selbie, he chose politics instead.[71] Selbie was minister at Emmanuel Congregational Church in Trumpington Street, the obvious place in Cambridge for a man with Ede's religious background to worship. When he went on to be the influential Principal of (the nonconformist) Mansfield College Oxford, from 1909, Selbie's main objective was to educate future preachers, and his well-known comment on sermons by his students was 'that would not save the soul of a tomtit'.[72] Ede may possibly have received such comments under Selbie's tutelage; he was already teaching before his move to Oxford. Perhaps the young student took a message that the religious life was not for him, but with the result that a source of funding was withdrawn. However, it built up his determination for action in politics – Cambridge, he said in his last years

> was far too expensive for me – my money ran out before I could complete the course. One of the things I have managed to achieve in my life is that no child should ever suffer that indignity. Now, every young person who goes to the universities has a sufficient assurance of financial help to be able to get through.[73]

He retained his affection for Christ's. The 1954 list of College Members which highlights Gilbert Jessop contains details of some 5,000 people. It is marked in pen with small rings around the dates of Ede's contemporaries there, some 120 living and 30 in the obituaries, presumably those he remembered, as well as a line by those whose addresses were in Surrey or (a more limited number) on Tyneside, near his constituency. In his speeches, he was often at pains to mention other Christ's men, such as Smuts, but in particular John Milton, whom he especially admired. When *Country Life* published two detailed articles on the College, he kept the copies among his papers,[74] and he visited there, corresponded with Christ's[75] and, it is believed, attended reunions there into his old age.[76]

Nonetheless, he had to return to Surrey, to a post teaching in an elementary school, though his continued studies to become a teacher were recognised. His Teachers Registration Council registration certificate (number 66,000 on the register) cited the source of his professional training as the Cambridge University Day Training College.[77]

Chapter 3

First Political Steps

After James Chuter Ede left university in 1905, he took up a post at the Ewell Church of England School, where he taught for about a year. He would later say that his teaching career started on 10 February 1906, when he also joined the Surrey County Teachers' Association (which became part of the National Union of Teachers),[1] but his teacher's registration document states he was at Ewell from 1905 to 1906, when he moved to Mortlake. There is some evidence that he also taught at Tolworth Council School, perhaps between his time at Ewell and Mortlake.[2] More probably, he was there on a temporary basis after leaving Cambridge, before he spent a few months at Ewell,[3] close to his family's Epsom home, and then took the post in Mortlake. He was certainly at Ewell in the summer of 1906, as a photograph[4] exists of him dated 2 August, with a group of some seventeen boys, as well as his father James Ede, described as 'Visitor', on a trip to Box Hill. The boys are equipped for cricket. From then on, however,

Ewell Boys' National Schools visit to Box Hill, 2 August 1906, with Ede in white hat (centre),and his father in boater. (© *Surrey History Centre*)

he spent all the rest of his active teaching career in Mortlake, until 1914, by which time he was the senior assistant there.[5]

In the year 1906, the General Election occurred, for which Ede had declined the Liberal Party's invitation to speak at public meetings. He was caught up in the enthusiasm, being invited to the National Liberal Club to hear an address from the party leader, Campbell-Bannerman, newly appointed as Prime Minister; as usual, he pasted a record in his scrapbook.[6] The invitation must have recognized his own position in the party, and he soon became identified as a potential candidate. He retained an admiration for the new PM, 'a plain steadfast man',[7] who had led the Liberals to their greatest victory, and whom he compared to Clement Attlee, who would do likewise for Labour – 'Like C-B Attlee was perfectly straight. He stood by a man even to his own hurt. I asked no more than that from my leader.'[8] We shall see that, at the time of Attlee's greatest triumph, Ede's thoughts would return to the victor of 1906.

Teaching at the time was, as ever, hard work and not well paid. In the words of A.J.P. Taylor, classes at the time were 'grotesquely large', and would remain so till the 1930s.[9] Ede's first class at Mortlake was 73 children, and he never taught a class of fewer than fifty-five, the annual pay for which started at £90, rising in increments of £5 to a maximum of £130.[10] Those were the Surrey scales, this being before national rates for teachers were established (in London they were in the region of £160, but some authorities would have paid less, a typical figure in the counties being just over £100[11]). They equate to between £10,000 and £15,000 in current (2021) terms of retail prices (wage inflation has of course increased by more). When he gave this account of his teaching days, he added laconically that, some time in the next seven years, the maximum was reduced from £130 to £125. On another occasion, he quoted his pay as 6/- a day, with a day's pay lost when the school closed for a Sunday School excursion – 'quite an insufficient salary'.[12] It was no surprise that a politically active teacher in this environment would develop an interest in trade union affairs, as well as in educational reform.

While his career was developing, that of Lilian Williams, a teacher from Devon, was doing so too, and bringing them into similar circles. She was six years older than Ede, and had started her teaching career in Teignmouth in 1894, an eighteen-year-old training under the pupil-teacher system, while he was still at elementary school in Epsom. Shortly after, as her own registration document shows, she moved to Epsom herself, to teach at East Street Church of England Infants' School, in Hawthorne Place, close to the Edes' home, moving in 1906 to The Junior Council School in the town, and a year later to Hook Road Girls' School there. At what stage she came across her younger colleague can only be speculated, but his activities are likely to have been noticed, even if it would be another ten years before they made a partnership together.

One of the first provisions proposed by the new Government was an Education Bill, formulated in response to concerns about the Conservatives' Education Act, passed four years earlier. This 1902 Act had transferred the powers of the School Boards to local authorities, in itself reducing the influence of the Nonconformists, and beyond that had given those authorities responsibility for Church schools, which as a result were now being supported by public funds. The Church schools were predominantly Anglican, and a minority were Catholic; few were Nonconformist. This had been a major point of contention, causing the Act to take more than twice as long to debate than the 1870 Act which first set up the School Boards.[13] Ede visited the Commons to listen to part of the 1902 debate, and in particular noticed the young Liberal MP, Charles Trevelyan, argue that the education system needed to address the country's problem of having Europe's worst-educated children. When Trevelyan was President of the Board of Education, and Ede a backbencher supporting him, he was able to remind him of that, and exhort him to legislate further.[14]

The denominational controversy caused such an impression on another young MP, Winston Churchill, less than two years into his long career, that forty years later he was reluctant to pursue any further educational reform which would stir up religious debate; and, in the short term, Nonconformists' concerns about the 1902 Act were one of the reasons they had supported the Liberals in large number in 1906, so contributing to the landslide victory. So the new President of the Board of Education, Augustine Birrell, introduced a Bill which would have ended state-support for the denominational schools.

By April 1906 Ede was sticking more cuttings in his scrapbook about Birrell and his Bill, and writing in the press about it, from the viewpoint of a Nonconformist and a strong believer in the professionalism of teaching.[15] The President had 'the desire, not to please any dignitary of any church, but to secure for every child a teacher who was a teacher and not an impecunious bookworm nor an unemployed nursemaid'. The Bill would replace run-down Church schools with new, publicly-funded, non-denominational ones. He did not expect all voluntary (that is, Church) schools to:

> come into ratepayers' hands ... Some are hardly worth taking as old bricks. They were built in the dark ages between 1798 and 1870, when the monitorial and pupil teacher system was in full force and they are absolutely unfitted for the scientific method and capable teachers of

today … A speedy death awaits those schools which attempt to survive as charitable agencies for the distribution of dogma.

Ede felt Birrell should have gone further in one respect, as the 'work of women for English education cannot be over-estimated … They toiled early and late … on the old School Boards and now they are to be denied direct election on to the governing bodies, about whose work they know so much.' Later on, his approach to gender equality in education would be inconsistent, but as early as this he recognised it as an issue.

Birrell's Bill passed through the Commons, but was rejected in large part by the Lords, and was eventually withdrawn. This first step in the confrontation between the Government and the House of Lords could only encourage Ede's activities in the Liberal Party, which led to his nomination as a candidate for Epsom Urban District Council in 1908, supported by the Epsom and District Working Men's Association. He was elected, the youngest councillor in Surrey,[16] and the Christmas Annual of the *Epsom Advertiser and Observer* featured his photograph, describing him as the youngest member of any Urban District Council in the country. It added that 'his stock has done much public work for the town', a good tribute to his family – though who wrote it is an interesting point; a copy of the 1906 Christmas Annual (both are in the Surrey archives), which includes a fine photo of grandfather James Chuter, is annotated with the remark that most of the articles were written by James Chuter Ede.

According to a profile written when he was Home Secretary, Ede 'began his political career bicycling on glowing summer evenings from one Surrey village green to the next, offering radical doctrine'.[17] While that bucolic picture fits well, we have seen that it had all started some years earlier, before in April 1908 he achieved elected office. Although Jefferys and Evans state that initially he considered himself 'in a minority of one',[18] the following year[19] he sought re-election along with a colleague, James Weir Gow, a plumber who lived in Miles Road, Epsom, not far from his own Hawthorne Place home. They were both proposed by old James Chuter, who had himself served for the council in the past.[20]

There was considerable press coverage, considering the relatively minor significance of the contest, with Gow and Ede arguing for the publication of the auditor's report on the Council's affairs, while the council chairman, J Templeton, opposed this on the grounds that it would cause harm to a council official. Ede was also keen to tell his electorate that Epsom had no intention of annexing the Parish of Ewell, something that would subsequently change before he helped to bring the two together as a borough. In the heaviest poll ever recorded in the town,[21] he was at the head (907 votes), with three others elected, Gow coming a close third with 745, following J Tryon, another retiring member, achieving 755. Templeton, with 480 votes, lost his seat. In 1911, Gow and Ede put up a further candidate, Thomas B Johns, to support them. By now, with his activity in the area, Ede had in April 1909 issued Volume 1, No 1 of *The Epsom Liberal Monthly*,[22] and by 1910 had become secretary, and then honorary agent, of the Mid-Surrey Liberal Association.[23] It is easy to guess who would have written most of the articles in the *Monthly*, but it is unclear whether there were any further issues.

This was the time when, at the national level, the government's difficulties with the House of Lords had reached a crisis, principally because of Lloyd George's 'People's Budget'. Ede took a local role in this, writing a press article about 'Epsom Land: an Absurd Anomaly', his main targets being the rating of shops and the property acquisitions of Lord Rosebery. Though a former Liberal Prime Minister, Rosebery opposed the Budget, in particular the proposed land taxes, which would affect him as a major landowner in the Epsom area, where he had come to live and pursue his racing interests. Ede issued his article, with a press release, embargoing it until 30 September 1909, when he saw it published with detailed calculations of the effect of taxation on land. Though in Liberal politics, Rosebery was now far removed from Asquith, the new Prime Minister, and his colleagues such as Lloyd George. The problems which the government faced from him were starting to show Ede that the Liberal Party could not be entirely relied upon to champion the cause of the people.

On Epsom Council,[24] he chaired the Recreation Grounds Committee for a year from 1908, became Chairman of the Electricity Supply Committee in 1909, and of the Baths Committee in 1912, when he was re-elected to the Council unopposed. He represented Epsom on various bodies, including the first Town Planning Conference at the Guildhall, the Royal Sanitary Institute, and the Incorporated Municipal Electrical Association. He was credited with saving £550 a year by amalgamating the Poor and General District rates and, on the Electricity Supply Committee, helped to make a substantial profit from what was an almost bankrupt business.

With his work in Mortlake, and his duties in Epsom, he was a busy individual, but he ensured he did what he could to join the two together. In July 1910, he took a party of Mortlake boys on a trip to Box Hill, as he had done at Ewell previously. They walked to the station at East Putney, took the train to Epsom, and walked on from there.[25] That was an energetic outing – the walk from Mortlake is over two miles, and from Epsom to Box

Hill more than seven. The round trip involved perhaps seven hours' walking. He was ensuring the boys from the London suburbs would see the Surrey countryside which he was determined to enjoy and preserve.

At the same time as he was teaching, and active in party politics, Ede was working within the Surrey County Teachers' Association on trade union affairs, trying to link the two. He attempted to secure representation on Epsom UDC for trade unionists, and was criticised in the press for stirring up 'class prejudices and class hatreds', as an 'ignorant and reckless tub-thumper'.[26] In 1912 he became Vice-President of the SCTA[27] and, next Easter, represented the Surrey teachers at the NUT National Conference, speaking on the need for the Government to require local authorities to pay adequate salaries under an agreed scale. In his conference speech, he told the story of the Home Office requiring Surrey County Council to include a fair wages clause in a building contract, because the bricklayers and carpenters had 'a great and powerful union'; surely the teachers should have a union strong enough to press the government to do the same for them. However, '"Lloyd George" was a generic word covering a multitude of departmental iniquities', and within 'eight miles of Charing Cross' – presumably in the Surrey suburbs – 'there were women ... working in the schools for a less salary than a London borough council paid its road sweepers.'[28] He was becoming critical of the Liberal Party establishment, and by that summer his efforts had made him President of the SCTA, the youngest person to be chosen for the post, and the first from an elementary school.[29] The article introducing him in the *Surrey Teachers' Quarterly* added that one of his 'chiefest regrets is that there are only 24 hours to the day'.

Early in 1914, Epsom's County Councillor, E.B. Jay, was elevated to Alderman, and with the support of the Liberal Party and the Epsom Working Men's Association, of which he had become Secretary, Ede decided to go for the vacancy on Surrey CC. This was a major step, as he was a Surrey employee, which prevented him from becoming a council member. He had to resign his post in Mortlake, and take a gamble on both his electoral chances and his financial future. He had no time to give notice to his employers, and had to pay one month's salary in lieu, which he borrowed from a friend, A.E. Baxter. On his election papers, no longer employed as a teacher, he described himself as a 'tutor', though he is unlikely to have had much work tutoring. His one opponent was John Hatchard Smith, an architect who now chaired Epsom UDC.[30]

Baxter[31] was a teacher at Queens Road School, Wimbledon, and he safeguarded Ede's position as a representative of the SCTA, which had been pressing for the County Council to have teachers represented on the Education Committee. He became President of the SCTA himself in 1916,[32] and would go on to work with Ede in one Parliamentary election after another, not least when he won Mitcham in 1923, driving him from place to place – for Ede never drove a car. He may well have been one of the colleagues who provided him with 'a small salary', in the words of John Strudwick, another of his later SCTA supporters.[33] Strudwick described Baxter as 'a teacher champion of progress' in Wimbledon.

On polling day, 4 April, Ede was elected Epsom's County Councillor by 1,046 votes to 414. He retained for the rest of his life, among his papers, the poster announcing the result. His teaching career had come to an end, and would in fact never be resumed, though his eight years' work, and his time training before that, would prove essential experience for so much of his future contribution to politics. For a short while at least, he kept in touch with his school in Mortlake; a photo exists of him with some of the staff and boys on a boating excursion on the Thames, repeating one that had happened in July 1913.[34] When a photo of the Thames appeared in The Times on 4 August 1941, he noted that he had been there with the Mortlake party on that day in 1914.

He was welcomed to his first council meeting on 12 May 1914, making a maiden speech at the first opportunity. The meeting was to consider the finance estimates and Budget, and he spoke in support of a motion disapproving the use of council funds for capital expenditure; application should be made for consent to borrow. He also argued that Surrey teachers' pay, being less than that in London, was insufficient to attract recruits, and raised particular concerns about the Hook Road Council Schools in Epsom, where Lilian Williams was working. There were several newspaper reports of the meeting,[35] and he was complimented on his diplomatic approach, devoting his attention to the details of expenditure. This contrasts with the story told that, at his first council meeting, he spoke on every item, so the meeting was delayed well beyond its normal duration, as he was trying to defeat Surrey's policy of not having teacher representation on the Education Committee. Perhaps that was on a subsequent occasion, Strudwick, who reported it, having heard of it only much later. Whenever it was, the Chairman eventually passed a note to Ede, agreeing to appoint him to the Education Committee if he would stop this course of conduct. A note came back, 'you cannot keep me off', and his appointment duly went through.[36]

A few months later, a new job became hard to avoid, as the Great War started, and he joined the army.[37] On 7 November 1914, he signed his attestation as 20047 James Chuter Ede, a member of the National Reserve, Epsom Company, becoming a member of the No 2 Supernumerary Company, 5th Battalion (Reserve) of the East Surrey Regiment, the unit in which he had indeed been a reservist for a few years as a younger man. His attestation (that is, his commitment to serve if called upon) states that, already belonging to the National Reserve, he would now serve for one year – 'or for the duration of the War (provided His Majesty should so long require your service)', implying 'whichever is longer', and that is of course how it turned out. Importantly for him, he was enlisting as a volunteer, as conscription would not be introduced till more than a year later. He was medically examined, and declared fit to serve as a local guard in the Supernumerary Companies, which were responsible for guarding key points, such as railway bridges. Having done this until 18 August 1915 (as a lance-corporal since 19 November 1914), he was promoted to Sergeant, his Army form declaring his character to be very good. He was then discharged at Woking, so that he could enlist in the Royal Engineers as number 113194, the Territorial contract being different from that of the regular Army. His transfer papers describe his occupation as 'Member of the Surrey County Council'.

He wrote to his mother on 5 September, saying that:

> I do not think I am constitutionally a soldier. I do not love fighting for its own sake ... Still I find here measuring myself against the other Sergeants where we are all unknown that I can hold my own quite easily & that I have been deputed to carry out more responsible duties than any ... I do not face the unknown with fear ... In good time we shall meet again to talk and laugh over the jests of chance.[38]

He was in France by 7 September 1915 and, as far as is known, served there in the RE for the duration of the War, as part of the Special Brigade – the RE's Gas Section[39] – retaining his rank of sergeant throughout. The Brigade's first action was at Loos, later in September, so it is very likely he took part in that.[40] The 1915 Annual Report of the Christ's College Club included a list of its members serving in the War; his own entry referred to the 5th East Surreys, and he altered it to Royal Engineers, dating the entry 1 June 1916.[41] Around that time, he was at Aire-sur-la-Lys and Roquetoire, near St Omer.[42] Nell had a photo of herself made into a postcard, which she sent him 'With best wishes from your affectionate sister', addressed simply to 113194 Serjt JC Ede, Depot for Special Brigade, RE. In 1916, the *Surrey Mirror* reported he had returned to England and, at a County Council meeting, the chairman 'amid hearty applause welcomed back Provost-Sergt Chuter Ede ... They were very glad to see him that day.'[43] For Christmas 1916 he came back to Dorking High School for the end of term, where 'Provost Sergeant J Chuter Ede' presented a prize to the commander of the smartest section in his old school's officer training corps.[44] However, becoming an officer was not for every old boy of the school, as he himself twice applied for promotion during the War, having sought support from Surrey's Lord Lieutenant, whom he knew as a colleague on the County Council. When interviewed he was asked how much private income he could devote to his commission and, being unable to give the correct answer, was unsuccessful.[45]

He kept himself busy with his outside interests, corresponding with the NUT in England, and on 23 March 1917 writing and producing 'Charles Montmorency VC', an 'Original Mellow-Drama', to entertain the troops at the 'Theatre Militaire, Sumwarinfrans', with some 30 of his comrades in arms.[46] In November that year, he was again on leave, speaking at Epsom Technical Institute on 'English Education after the War' to the Epsom and Sutton Association, an address which he had already given to soldiers in YMCA huts in France. He also participated in County Council activities, including a discussion on the Education Bill being piloted through Parliament by the President of the Board of Education, Herbert Fisher, appointed after Lloyd George succeeded Asquith as PM. Fisher had intervened to have him granted this leave.[47]

Most importantly, while on leave, he married Lilian Williams on 14 November 1917, at the Congregational Church in Epsom. He was 35, and she was already 41, described as an Assistant Mistress in an Elementary School, living at 78 Miles Road. His address was still at Hawthorne Place, with his rank described as Sergeant, Royal Engineers (County Councillor for Epsom). As we have seen, Lilian came from Devon, having been born in Plymouth on 10 February 1876, and Ede would later joke, when discussing the suitability of Dartmoor for an emergency Borstal, that he knew the moor's climatic conditions well, as he had done much of his courting there.[48] In fact, Lilian had been in Epsom since she was 18, and her father Richard, an accountant, was now dead. She had become a Surrey girl, and would live there for the next thirty years, the rest of her life, joining the County Council herself for a period. She was a competent musician; when Robert Evans was researching Ede's work in education, he spoke to Mrs Russell, who in the 1990s was living at 78 Miles Road, and she recalled being taught the piano by Miss Williams. After the marriage, Jim moved into the house in Miles Road but, as with many wartime marriages, they were soon parted by his duties in France.

During the Great War, Ede's political sympathies were changing. His criticisms of Rosebery have been noted, as well as a cutting remark about Lloyd George, and these were part of a growing disillusion with the Liberals, moving him towards the Labour Party (like several others at the time). The Liberals were arguing amongst themselves, and he was doubtful about whether the Party could satisfy the trade unions and organised labour, of which he was a representative. Serving in the ranks during the War 'convinced me as it did a good many people that the idea that there is a special body of persons born to lead, is quite a mistake', though he also claimed to have joined the Labour Party as early as 1914,[49] which seems unlikely in the very year he was elected as a Liberal councillor. He said[50] that his unhappy experience in applying for a commission made him conclude that officers with new ideas were not getting justice; in contrast, in the French army, 'nobody worried if a man shaved', and independent thought was encouraged, unlike in the British establishment. I suspect Lilian may have influenced his move towards Labour also. Once it was likely the war would be coming to an end, and that a General Election would then be held, it was suggested, around the end of 1917, that he stand for Parliament as a Labour candidate, presumably hoping to have Liberal support also.

However, he was beset by problems. Ian Macpherson, the Under-Secretary for War, stated in the Commons on 22 January 1918 that if an election was pending, and a soldier was adopted as a candidate, special furlough would be granted so he could promote his candidature. On 4 July, H.S. Jones, the Secretary of Epsom Labour Party, wrote to Ede, asking him to apply for leave to return home to address Party members and some affiliated organisations, between the end of the month and 17 August. Although he applied for leave on 11 July, immediately he received Jones's letter, and he understood his application had been sent forward with a recommendation for approval, he had to reply on 28 July, that he had had no answer to it. He had sent two telegrams to Lilian, so she knew the situation, and could keep in contact with the Labour Party. By 3 August he was writing to Jones again,[51] saying matters were unchanged, he was unclear whether he could get back even to start the adoption process, and had his doubts whether, once the election was called, he would be allowed home to contest it. In those circumstances, he would not have a chance effectively to be selected and to fight the seat, and so he had decided not to be a candidate.

He was clearly unhappy about this. His letter mentioned 'good reasons why one voluntarily enlisted early in the War might aspire to sit in the Parliament that would deal with the reconstruction of the civilisation the British army

… will have saved.' But, importantly, he was still having doubts about where his sympathies lay:

> Everyone's political opinions must have been modified on many subjects during the past four years and I confess frankly that the time has had a considerable educative influence upon me. Never a very good Party man, and now less inclined to mould my ideas by others' patterns, I have felt lately that when we met in conference my views on one or two topics … might be in sharp conflict with the opinions held by some at least of your members.

Somehow, however, his doubts were overcome. On 8 August 1918 he was back, speaking to a meeting of supporters at the Cooperative Hall in Leatherhead, with another meeting scheduled for 15 August, the press report describing him as prospective candidate.[52] By 31 August the papers were able to report that he had been adopted as such, at a meeting of about 100 delegates,[53] and he had issued a short pamphlet, with his photo in uniform on the front, setting out the agricultural wages award for Surrey, effective from 2 September, as The Labourers' Guide, by 'Sergt J Chuter Ede RE, County Councillor for Epsom and Prospective Labour Candidate for Epsom, now serving in France'.[54] This looks suspiciously like something put together by his wife and friends back home; clearly it was aimed, under the guise of a factual information sheet, at raising his profile among the farmworkers who were an important section of the electorate for him. Clearly, too, there was no doubt he was standing for election.

Lloyd George did not waste time. Three days after the armistice on 11 November, it was announced that the poll would be held on 14 December. Neither did Ede delay; on 17 November he addressed a printed letter to the 'Naval and Military Voters' of Epsom, headed with his photograph above 'Labour Candidate, Now Serving in France', addressed from 'In the Field, France'. Its salutation was 'Gentlemen', though for the first time there were women among the electorate and candidates, but few among the naval and military voters this was addressing. The theme of his campaign was clear – he had enlisted voluntarily and had served overseas, and the sacrifices made by his comrades must not have been to no purpose, but must be recognised with proper opportunities for work:

> what chance shall we, who will be thrown into the competition at the time chosen by the Authorities, have, unless WE NOW SAFEGUARD OURSELVES by ensuring that this great resettlement shall be controlled by those who know from actual experience what our feelings are?

THE HERO OF THE BATTLEFIELD IS SOON FORGOTTEN.
The LIGHT BRIGADE at BALACLAVA was glorified in immortal
Poetry: The survivors DIED IN THE WORKHOUSE. Wartime's
artificial prosperity *for every one but the fighter,* its huge profits, its high
wages, have hitherto been followed by a deep poverty.[55]

Jobs for the war veterans, housing, education, councils to settle labour disputes
and wages, and opportunities for young people – these comprised the list of
policies for which he was standing.

He ran his campaign, partly in Epsom, and partly from abroad. On 4
December, he made a speech confirming his loyalty to the Epsom area and,
when he was not there, he corresponded with constituents by post. To a lady
in Ashtead he wrote about education:

> at present the child of a Worker leaves school at the age when the child
> of the Rich is just commencing his education and, at the Age when
> sound Education has the greatest effect … education requires to be so
> arranged that admission to all State-Aided Schools from the lowest
> to the highest shall be obtained by capacity to reap advantage from
> the curriculum, abolition of all fees and the grant where necessary of
> maintenance allowances.[56]

Ede was, in many ways, arguing for a 'country fit for heroes', which
unfortunately for him and many other Labour candidates was the promise
on which Lloyd George was himself campaigning, and his Coalition
Government endorsed candidates of whom it approved. The 1918 election
is accordingly known as the 'Coupon Election', and those candidates with
the Coalition coupon, few of whom were Labour, were returned in very large
numbers, especially in England. Epsom was a strongly Conservative seat,
Labour had never previously contested it, and the Liberals had often left
the Tory candidate unopposed. The sitting member was not standing again,
but his Conservative replacement, Rowland Blades, received the coupon and,
even though Ede may have benefitted from a lack of any Liberal candidate,
took nearly three-quarters of the vote:

Blades	Conservative	13,556
Ede	Labour	4,796

Blades's career would be more distinguished in local government than in
Parliament, though he did eventually receive a peerage, taking the title
'Ebbisham', an early name for Epsom. His defeated opponent returned to
France, awaiting his discharge from the Army.

On 20 February 1919, Ede sailed from Boulogne to Folkestone, where he was demobbed that evening from the Royal Engineers with the substantive rank of Sergeant.[57] He could resume his activities on Surrey County Council and the SCTA. No longer receiving army pay, he faced the same financial difficulties as previously, though initially with a working wife, and these were eased to an extent by his appointment as Assistant Secretary of the SCTA. In reality, this must have been a form of sponsorship for him on the County Council, as it provided an income of some £400 a year,[58] and continued for most of his remaining career in local government and in the Commons, until he was a Government minister. No other local association of the NUT outside London paid any of its officers.[59] It may not have been a complete sinecure, but his main duty was to represent the union on the County Council, and later in Parliament. Indeed, Strudwick believed that, as time went on and the Secretary Lance Rawes advanced in years, Ede took over more and more control of the SCTA, and gradually overshadowed Rawes, though always referring his own decisions to him for confirmation. He used his Labour Party contacts to get politicians, including one President of the Board of Education, to speak at the Association's AGMs.

For many years, the SCTA provided him with a secretary, Eileen Grant, who worked at his house, an arrangement which ended only in 1940, around the time of his first Government post. To find the £400, members' subscriptions were raised by 1/-, while income was also obtained from the sale of *Surrey Teachers' Quarterly*.[60] It was not a huge amount – perhaps equivalent to about £17,000 today – but it would have contributed well to their living costs, particularly when Lilian's pay as a teacher was added. She, however, gave up her job in 1919, so they must have been able to live on his income alone. In 1922, the SCTA went further, and under Baxter's guidance took out a superannuation arrangement with the Prudential for Ede.[61]

He soon took up fresh appointments, in the manner he would throughout his life.[62] He became a member of the Epsom Board of Guardians, which administered the Poor Law, for a three-year term starting in 1919. He was chosen to be President of the Epsom branch of the National Federation of Discharged and Demobilised Sailors and Soldiers, which merged into the British Legion in 1921 – when he duly became President of the Epsom (West Street) Branch. He presided over the Epsom Trades and Labour Council and Epsom Labour Party, and joined the Labour Party's Advisory Committee on Education. He was a member of the Surrey Insurance Committee.

He also took on one significant responsibility in June 1919. A local property in Epsom, Woodcote Park, had become a convalescent hospital for Canadian soldiers, and large numbers of Canadian troops were now stationed there, waiting to be shipped home after the end of the War. They were bored, and impatient at their transport being delayed. Tension had developed between them and the Epsom people, in particular the local soldiers returning from the fighting. On 17 June, following a fight in a pub, two Canadians were arrested by Epsom police and, when the news spread to the army base, some 300 or 400 of their comrades stormed into the town to release the two from the police cells. The result was a riot in which, among various injuries, Police Sergeant Thomas Green was killed.

When Green's inquest was opened, Ede was on the jury, and was chosen as its chairman. Though adjourned at the time, it was reopened on 25 June and concluded five days later, after six of the Canadians, arrested the day following the incident, had been committed for trial by magistrates in London. At that time an inquest could name those they considered guilty of homicide, and the jury's verdict was manslaughter against the six men and one other – a young bugler who had allegedly blown a signal to egg the rioters on, and whom Ede had insisted be brought before the coroner. In the event, all seven were found not guilty of manslaughter at the assizes in July, though five were convicted of riotous assembly and sent down for twelve months (the bugler was acquitted on all charges). In fact, they were all released in November or December 1919 and, barring one who died soon after, were quickly sent back to Canada.

From the inquest reports, it is clear that Ede suspected the authorities (both British and Canadian) were covering up many details, and trying to play down the incident, to avoid a murder trial, and to prevent putting the relationship between the two countries at risk. That has also been the conclusion of a recent researcher into the riot.[63] In line with his non-partisan approach to practical matters, Ede had been in touch during the affair with Rowland Blades, his election opponent, who had been briefed by Churchill at the War Office. From his point of view, it must have enhanced his view of the crucial role played by the police in the community, and provided him with useful practice for the work he would have to carry out on the magistrates' bench, and indeed eventually as Home Secretary.

Epsom held Peace Celebrations on 19 July, starting with a parade at the Clock Tower in the morning, and ending with a dinner, which Ede attended.[64] His first Christmas home was well celebrated, with the family coming to the Edes' house at Miles Road. They had a turkey, and the incident he most recalled was that the oven proved too small for the bird, so an arrangement was rigged up and it was 'slung perpendicularly'.[65] The games of Ludo and Halma from his childhood were replaced with cards, generally Nap.

Then in 1920 he was chosen to be Chairman of Epsom UDC, a post he held for two years,[66] and he was appointed a Justice of the Peace for Epsom, remaining a magistrate until he reached the compulsory retirement age which he himself imposed as Home Secretary. For much of his career, though, his appearances on the bench of magistrates could only be infrequent. As Chairman at Epsom, he was able to boast that houses built under his leadership were from 2/- to 3/- a week cheaper than houses built by other Surrey authorities within the Metropolitan Police area.[67]

At the County Council, with his command of education as a subject, he 'in time became the unofficial Director of Education for the County',[68] according to his colleague John Strudwick, and his presence there meant that representation of teachers on the Committee became no longer vital. He ensured that, for the first time, a County Education Officer was appointed, the highly-respected Haig Brown, but there was no doubt Ede was the chief, for the twenty years from 1919. He led Surrey's decisions about teachers' salaries, after the Burnham Committee, newly established by Fisher, proposed four different zones of payment – London in Zone IV, and cheaper parts of the country in Zones III to I. The Education Committee considered its view on where Surrey should fit in, and he suggested the SCTA should accept Zone III status, until his colleagues granted Zone IV salaries to their teachers in the London suburbs. He was a member too of the Education Development Committee that implemented Fisher's Education Act, in which he had taken such an interest, reorganising the county's elementary schools so that, at age 11, pupils could move on to senior schools. This was started in Mortlake itself in 1921, and gradually spread out over Surrey in the next few years.[69] He never became Chairman of Education at Surrey; according to Sir Edward Britton, General Secretary of the NUT after Ede's death, who knew him for many of his latter years, he felt it could conflict with his position in the union.[70]

Before 1920 was over, Ede was to make a return visit to France and Belgium. He reached Boulogne, and left there on 6 August, touring the battlefields for the next two and a half weeks. He was at Wizernes on 8 August, on the Menin Road on 14 August, at Kemmel Hill and other sites the following day, and the next he was in Ostend. He watched HMS *Vindictive* being raised. This was a cruiser which had been deliberately scuttled to block a passage during an unsuccessful raid on Ostend in 1918. On 17 August he was at Passchendaele and Menin, and the next at St Eloi and other places, before reaching Ypres on 19 August. He continued his trip round Belgium, until he returned to France on 22 August, and so back home. We know this detail – and much more – because he wrote it up in three articles for the *Wallington and Carshalton Times*, the first of which must have been sent home from his travels, with the last published on 2 September. He does not indicate which of the sites he visited were ones in which he had worked as Sergeant in the Royal Engineers, but many would have brought back memories.

His choice of newspaper for these articles is interesting. To age 37, most of his frequent correspondence in the press had been in the Epsom or Kingston papers. Carshalton and Wallington are several miles from Epsom, and in an area with which he had had little previous connection. However, he had encouraged Surrey to use land in Carshalton (as well as Banstead) to build housing estates for resettling ex-servicemen,[71] complementing his British Legion work. In addition, they were in the Parliamentary constituency of Mitcham, which at some point in the early 1920s Ede identified as a potentially winnable seat. He and Lilian would eventually live for several years in Mitcham, and there is a little evidence that they obtained a house there before he became a candidate, not merely after his eventual success in the constituency.

Then, in November 1921 James Ede, Jim's father, died. Like others in the family, on 30 November he was buried in Epsom Cemetery. Whatever the sadness of the occasion, and despite his son's regret that his father did not live to see him as an MP, he reflected later that 'fate was generous to take him before the disastrous nature of the Peace was known'.[72]

In 1922, Ede's term of office on the Epsom Board of Guardians came to an end but, busy as ever, he involved himself in setting up a Surrey Secondary Teachers' Association, as a separate local branch of the NUT.[73] This was intended to represent Union members in technical colleges, technical schools and grammar schools, sending delegates to the SCTA, along with the local branches. He was also chosen to be President of the Dorking High School Old Boys' Association;[74] he was already the most distinguished old boy, and so he remains, though its successor schools have had some well-known pupils. At this stage, with the War behind them, the future still looked promising for the country, and for Jim and Lilian Ede also, with Mitcham in their sights.

Chapter 4

The Member for Mitcham

Mitcham is in the southern part of the London conurbation, south of Tooting and Wimbledon. Since the reorganisation of Greater London in the 1960s, it has been part of the London Borough of Merton, but it is in the historic county of Surrey, and in Ede's time it was still a Surrey urban district. Until the Great War, it had been included in the Wimbledon constituency, but it had then become a constituency of its own, joined with the neighbouring urban districts of Beddington and Wallington, and Carshalton (all now in the Borough of Sutton). It bordered on the Epsom constituency, which Ede had fought in the 'Coupon Election' of December 1918, immediately after the armistice. It had then elected Thomas Worsfold, standing as a Conservative in support of Lloyd George's coalition. In 1922 the majority of Conservative MPs, against the advice of their leader, Austen Chamberlain, had decided to break up the coalition, their leader Bonar Law became Prime Minister, and another General Election had been held, at which Worsfold was re-elected in support of the new government. Though Ede may have started nursing the seat, Labour did not fight it.

Ede had no particular connection with the area but, as it is no more than ten miles from either Epsom or Mortlake, and with his work in education on the County Council, he would have been well known to the Labour Party when, in February 1923, Worsfold resigned, and a by-election was called for 3 March. Ede was duly chosen as Labour candidate and, with the party's support, fought a vigorous campaign, canvassing methodically, and visiting gipsy groups and outlying settlements in the area. His election literature centred on 'Housing First', rather than education.[1] He was again supported by his teacher friend, A.E. Baxter, who had lent him money to help him first join Surrey County Council, and in Baxter's schoolroom in Wimbledon, they worked out a plan for fighting the election. Baxter went to each of Ede's meetings, driving him from place to place, 'feeding me with meat juices and rabbits', as Ede recalled when Baxter died nearly twenty years later.[2]

On this occasion, there was no doubt that the women in the electorate were significant; for a circular put out to voters presented on its front page a 'Message from Mrs Ede to the Women Electors', with Lilian's photo above

Jim's. The 'Message' concentrates on housing, taxation of tea and sugar, 'things that the poorest must buy', and the welfare of children. With stress on his Surrey background, he was 'the man who has given fifteen years of his life to fighting for the welfare of the people, and especially the children, of this county'. The leaflet is headed 'Labour Election News, No 1' but, dated 1 March, it can hardly have been the first of a series. It included a long extract from *The Times*, in which Austen Chamberlain criticised Sir Arthur Griffith Boscawen, the Conservative candidate who had voted against his advice in 1922, but had then lost his seat in 1922 and, as Minister of Health, was trying to re-enter Parliament. It went on to record Boscawen's voting record on taxation, welfare and pensions, highlighting his support in 1920 to increase the duty on beer, and reduce the duty on sparkling wine.

A letter from Lilian Haste, described as Ede's old schoolmistress, was included, her address given as Doyle Road, Balham, and Brixton Central School:

> Do you remember what I used to tell you, that you were born to be a Member of Parliament? Shakespear (*sic*) says 'There is a tide in the affairs of man, which taken at the flood leads on to fortune.' This is the flood of the tide for you. Take hold of it and 'good luck'.

There was also a jingle, the 'ABC Guide to Mitcham Electors', along the lines of:

> E is for EDE, Labour's champion today;
> F the big FIGHT – come and join in the fray.
> G's for the GOVERNMENT, wrapt in tranquillity;
> H for their HOUSING schemes, gems of futility.

At the end, beside a sample election form, and as part of a comment about housing, is a short passage from Ede with a twinge of defensiveness:

> Although I am an abstainer myself, I am as much opposed to compelling other people to abstain, as I should be to their compelling me to drink. I do not believe in the class legislation involved in closing public-houses on Sundays, while leaving the rich free to use their wine cellars unchecked.

This sounds like a response to criticism that he would be opposed to the use of alcohol, which may have come from other candidates.

When election day came, Ede won by 833 votes. His cause was helped by an Independent Conservative intervening, who split the Tory vote with the Government candidate, Griffith Boscawen. Nonetheless, Ede might well have thought his own vote had been reduced by the Liberals, who also fought the election. The result was:

Ede	Labour	8,029
Griffith Boscawen	Conservative	7,196
Brown	Liberal	3,214
Catterall	Independent Con	2,684

The victor would later describe the result as 'sensational'[3] and, if the press coverage is anything to go by, that is the right word.

Polling had been on a Saturday and, as soon as the result was announced on Monday, the *Evening Standard* had a photograph of Ede in the centre of its main front-page story. His own comment focused on housing, while Boscawen announced, 'We have been "done in", by rank treachery and nothing else', aiming his fury at Catterall. The *Evening News* published an editorial headed 'The Message of Mitcham. "Wake Up!"' The morning papers on 6 March continued the story. In the *Daily Graphic*, 'Lady Griffith-Boscawen Cries over Mitcham Result' was the caption above a photograph of the defeated Conservatives along a balcony and, below it, another of the Edes raised up on the roof of a car, Jim standing and waving to the crowd. 'Houses First' was the moral of the occasion for the *Daily Sketch*, where the leading photo was of the Edes surrounded by the crowd and a lone police escort. Even *The Globe* in New York carried the news on its front page; a copy was sent to the new MP, with congratulations, by James Ede, of Baldwin Street, Newark NJ, and the comment 'Thought you might appreciate this'. A cousin perhaps, or just a namesake who had made contact?

'Government Wobble' was the headline in the *Daily Mirror*, above several photos of the candidates and the cheering crowd; on the first inside page, five articles analysed the result and its consequences. One of these was headlined 'Sir A Boscawen Resigns as Health Minister – Mr Neville Chamberlain as Probable Successor', accompanied by a photograph of Chamberlain – and so it turned out.

Triumph at Mitcham – a newspaper report. (© *Surrey History Centre*)

Boscawen retired from politics, and Chamberlain, only recently appointed Postmaster-General, took his place as Minister of Health, his next step to becoming Chancellor of the Exchequer and eventually Prime Minister.[4]

As for local papers, *The Surrey Comet* on 10 March published the result, following it with the 'Career of Mr J Chuter Ede', running through his achievements to date, and confirming he had already taken his seat on Tuesday 6 March, to a fine welcome. 'He has a singularly alert brain, is rarely caught out in debate, and frequently scores at the expense of speakers who have not taken care to verify their references', it went on. Then *Punch*, on 14 March, included a short item in its Charivaria column, stating that the 'resignation of Sir Arthur Griffith-Boscawen as Minister of Health only goes to show that there was one Cabinet Minister who could take a hint'.

The Edes then moved from Miles Road into his new constituency, living at Tamworth Farm House in Mitcham, where they stayed for several years, even after he had been defeated as MP there.[5] Tamworth Farm is on the main London Road, north of the centre of Mitcham, in the direction of Tooting and Wandsworth. While the farmhouse itself no longer exists, the area is to this day called by the name Tamworth Farm, and allotments cover what must have been much of the old farm's fields. The area is known for the farm's (and one of Mitcham's) main products, lavender and other aromatic plants and shrubs, and a large children's day nursery, run by Merton Council, and called the Lavender Nursery, also occupies the spot.

By 14 March, Ede was asking a parliamentary question of Chamberlain, in his newly-appointed role, about a new site for Reigate and Redhill Hospital, an issue related more to his concern for Surrey than for the Mitcham constituency. He then kept active, asking written and oral questions on a range of matters. On 22 March 1923 he was asking Sir Samuel Hoare, the Air Secretary, whether more housing might be built as part of the development on Croydon Aerodrome, part of which was located in the Beddington part of his constituency. Then, on 29 March, he made his maiden speech, and his subject was appropriately education.

It was the afternoon of Maundy Thursday, and Sir John Simon, then the deputy leader of the Liberals, and out of office (as he was throughout the 1920s), raised the subject for the adjournment debate, immediately before the Easter recess. Simon made a broad sheet of criticisms about the state of education and the role which the Board of Education, then under the presidency of Edward Wood, the future Lord Halifax, was playing. According to Simon, the objectives of the Education Act 1918, named once it was passed as the 'Fisher Act', were not being adequately pursued. As we see in the next chapter, that was probably a fair comment, though one of its main provisions, increasing the school leaving age to 14, had indeed been implemented, as Simon conceded.

As is expected of a maiden speech, Ede's tone was less critical than Simon's, instead patiently making a few comments about the condition of schools as he had experienced them, though there was no doubt he was unhappy with the state of affairs. He explained that he was a product of 'the public' (ie, the maintained) school system, but had reached 'one of the old universities', without any detail of which one, or of the circumstances of his leaving. He had achieved that through parental sacrifice and public funding, so he claimed to know of what he spoke. The first point he then made related to poor school buildings, which he followed by a critique of the limited way opportunities for secondary education were provided. His other points covered the 'dilution' of staff in elementary, and particularly in infant, schools, and the relation of the Board of Education to local authorities.

As regards buildings, he recalled his own West Hill Infants School, the very old building of unknown provenance, where Eclipse was stabled, and which later was no use for stabling bloodstock, so was converted into a church school. He had been a manager of that school, and had handed it over from the Epsom Grand Stand Association to the county. The two local authorities wanted to replace it, and he felt the Board should ensure children now 'are taught in a building better than a disused stable'. After these amusing comments, he went on to cover the overcrowded schools of Surrey, following their welcome increase in pupil numbers.

On the opportunities for secondary education, he picked up a point made by Simon, to the effect that the minimum quota, of 25 per cent of maintained school places which should be free ones, had in many become in effect a maximum as a result of changes in regulation. Mitcham County School was, Ede said, the first school to which the new order was applied, and it was a prime complaint of his poorer constituents whose children were excluded. As chairman of Epsom County School for Girls, he told of his experience admitting worse performing fee-paying children, when better performers had applied for free places but were denied them.

As evidence of the importance of infant education, and thus of having well-qualified infant teachers, he told another anecdote from his past. He recalled that, at age four (and presumably in Eclipse's rejected stable), he had to sing a solo, and performed so badly that his teacher, an underqualified young woman, heard a crow outside, which she claimed made a better performance than his. So 'I have lost all interest in singing', whereas at the infant stage we should seek to encourage children in whatever their aptitudes may be. Last, as to the Board's approach to local authorities, he cited a gift of land in Surrey for use in field study. The Board refused to recognise it for grant purposes, or to accept that pupils attending there would be at school for the purposes of the law, despite its high educational value, and its worth as an experiment the Board should have been encouraging.

The maiden speech was a good example of much that would characterise Ede's career. His reliance on personal experience and on local knowledge, his concentration on education (at least until his surprise elevation to the Home Office), and his calm illustration of points with humour – all these would be found again and again during his parliamentary career. He was politely complimented by the next member to speak (as is the convention for a maiden speech), an elderly Scottish Unionist with a background in education, on just these points. His speech was followed by several other members from different parties, making a range of comments about the shortcomings of the education system, and Wood, in summing up, also courteously congratulated him on the issues he had raised. On the substance of what Ede had said, Wood pleaded lack of funds on poor school buildings, pointed out that the 25 per cent ceiling on free places was not imposed if it had already been breached before the new regulations came in (which was hardly the point), and denied that the youngest children require the best teachers. Wood's replies, to the many issues raised by members, do not give the impression that he was on top of his brief.

On his return from the Easter recess, Ede was involved with the Committee Stage of the Army and Air Force (Annual) Bill, making a couple of interventions. In one, he told of his unsuccessful interviews for a commission during the War, and the conclusions he had drawn. In the next part of the debate, he argued (interestingly, in view of his later experience at the Home Office) against the death penalty for cowardice.

He also raised points on agriculture and housing, giving examples of the state of homes both in Mitcham ('the poorest urban district in the richest county in England') and in Epsom, where he chaired the Housing Committee. In addition, he spoke on behalf of War veterans, contrasting the lack of adequate housing with the sacrifices they had made in battle, and also expressing concern for the lack of educational grants for the children of those who had lost their lives.

On May 1923, the Prime Minister, Bonar Law, having been diagnosed with throat cancer, submitted his resignation to George V. He was hardly able to speak, and told his PPS, JCC Davidson, to let the Palace know he would prefer not to be consulted about his successor.[6] The King decided to invite Stanley Baldwin, the Chancellor of the Exchequer, to form a Government. Wood remained at the Board of Education, and Ede continued to press the case of West Hill Infants School, listing the dilapidations, rats, untrapped waste pipes and filth, and again noting it was used as a stable some 150 years previously. Lord Eustace Percy, who had been Parliamentary Secretary for Education under Bonar Law, but had been moved to be Chamberlain's deputy at Health by Baldwin, was nonetheless asked to answer on Wood's behalf. When assured by Percy that Wood was in contact with the LEA, Ede pressed for speedier action, 'as the school has been condemned ever since I was in it 37 years ago'. The same day he was arguing for a removal of duties on educational films, basing his argument on the ignorance of the wider world of many primary age children, even in places as close to London as Surrey. He was supported in this by another teacher, Morgan Jones, a Labour member from South Wales.

July 1923 was a month of particular activity, according to the record in Hansard. Many of his local concerns were about Epsom as much as Mitcham. He continued his interest in housing matters, speaking several times about restrictions on mortgage interest, and asking questions about new homes being built. He also returned to writing published pieces, this time issuing *Housing in Surrey*, a long introduction to the 1922 report of the county's Chief Medical Officer of Health. The report was not party political, but Ede's commentary was. He pointed out that Surrey was the richest county in England, by rateable value per head, and quoted William Cobbett, 'the greatest man Surrey has produced', who stated that in Surrey 'every prospect pleases'. However, Conservative actions in the county had undermined all this, with houses erected for the well-to-do, not the disadvantaged. In John Milton's words about building peace following the Civil Wars, 'War has made many great whom peace makes small', and the fine words about building homes fit for heroes had been forgotten.

He also went on pressing points about servicemen's pensions, and settling ex-servicemen in smallholdings, and about levels of unemployment. Above all, however, he pursued with his interest in education. With no fewer than forty-nine mentions in Hansard (including oral and written questions), more than twice as many as between March and June, it was almost as though he recognised the Parliament did not have much longer to sit, and he wanted to show how busy a Member he was.

A plea went up from Ede on 17 July, common among novice MPs. The House was sitting late debating, as it happened, the Education (Scotland) Bill, and immediately before the evening's adjournment, he complained that if the sitting went past 11.30 he, like other Members who lived in the suburbs, had no further train to catch till 5.18 am. They had to go to a hotel, or walk the streets and risk arrest for loitering – so, 'if we have a night sitting we really should have one'.

When the Universities of Oxford and Cambridge Bill came up for debate, he involved himself in the proposal that women should be awarded full membership at Cambridge. He was unsuccessful, though only after he had challenged the assertion that Cambridge was founded by men, by calling to his aid Henry VII's mother who had founded two colleges (including his own), and the foundresses of Clare, Sidney Sussex and other colleges. It seems that he was chosen to speak last on the amendment, and was called by the Deputy Speaker in preference to Jack Jones, the Labour MP for Silvertown in London's East End. Ede did not forget Jones; when he died in 1941, shortly after resigning from the Commons, he recalled Jones had said to him, 'Shake hands. That was the best speech of the day.'

He sometimes got involved in certain pieces of legislation outside his usual remit. The Oyster and Mussel Fishery (Seasalter and Ham) Provisional Order Bill proposed to confer on a private company exclusive rights to fish in a small part of the Thames estuary, and Ede joined the objectors. His comment was that the same arguments were being used on this provision as had been used to support Enclosure Bills in the early 19th century, recalling how, ten years previously, he had had to read through Parliamentary documents from the consideration of those bills.

Ede's last activity in the House was a question on 2 August to Wood about over- and under-staffing of elementary schools and, later that day, Parliament adjourned until 13 November 1923 for the long autumn recess. By the end of the recess, Baldwin had decided on a general election. There was no further business for the House of Commons and, after the Lords had dealt with outstanding matters, Parliament was dissolved. The election was held on 6 December, and this time Chuter Ede was faced in Mitcham by a single opponent, a new Conservative candidate, Richard Meller, a locally based barrister with a record of unsuccessful attempts at election to Parliament.

Again the main election material featured a message from Lilian, with her photograph, to the ladies of Mitcham, stressing the Labour policy on the 'Women's Questions – on Food, Housing, Education, Wages, Equal Rights and Privileges for Women and Men, and on the Evils of War'. On the front page, too, was Ede, a brief letter from him, and a record of his Parliamentary activities – 'Out of 335 Divisions in the House of Commons, Mr EDE took part in 327' – and a quotation from *The Times* – 'Mr Chuter Ede, in his nine months' possession of the seat, has worked hard and well and is greatly respected in the constituency.' To emphasise the point, the remaining three pages list every speech and Parliamentary Question from him, with the occasional gloss where he could derive credit – 'We are obliged to you for the active interest which you took in our proposals', the Underground Railway Company was quoted as saying on one matter. Finally, to stress the female dimension, it records Ede's inclusion in the 'White List of Candidates' drawn up by the Non-Party Organization of Women, which entitled him 'to the work and vote of women electors'. Their message included:

> Beside your support on other points, we have to thank you for your splendid speech on the Universities of Oxford and Cambridge Bill, supporting the admission of women to full membership of Cambridge.

How many voters, of either sex, would have read all the detail and been duly impressed, must be doubtful. At any rate, the message did not get through in sufficient numbers.

Baldwin's main motive for calling the election was to give himself a mandate, as having become Prime Minister during the middle of a Parliament he had not led his party at an election. In particular he wished to change his party policy, to reintroduce protectionist tariffs – it had been an undertaking by Law (who died in October) that another election would be called if such a change was made. However, with a loss of some eighty-six seats, Baldwin saw his majority disappear and, though the Conservatives were still comfortably the largest party, it was clear that they could not form either a coalition or minority Government with the support of any other party. The Liberals, united (at least temporarily) under Asquith, made it clear they would support a minority Labour Government, though not join in a coalition with Labour, and the King invited Ramsay MacDonald to become Prime Minister.

The Labour Party had increased its representation in the Commons by some forty-nine seats, but that figure was net of a dozen losses, of which Mitcham was one:

| Meller | Conservative | 10,829 |
| Ede | Labour | 9,877 |

The majority was 952, with the vote split 48 per cent to 52 per cent. Meller would retain the seat until his death during World War II, and Ede's Parliamentary career was over, after nine months, during only five of which the Commons had been sitting, and just as the Labour Party was forming a Government for the first time. He could not know whether he would ever sit there again.

Chapter 5

A Surrey Tynesider

Sir James Yoxall, a former Liberal MP, who had been General Secretary of the NUT since before Ede started in the profession, announced his retirement in 1923. Ede applied for the position, around the time of his election defeat.[1] He claimed to have been interviewed over the years for every full-time office in the union, always without success. The successful candidate on this occasion was Frank Goldstone, who had been a Labour MP for a short while until, like Ede himself, he had failed to get elected in 1918.

So Ede continued his work on the councils at Surrey and Epsom, for the SCTA and other bodies, while living in Mitcham, and nursing the Parliamentary seat in expectation of a further election. MacDonald's hold on office was insecure, and in the autumn of 1924 his Government lost Liberal support on a matter which it considered one of confidence. MacDonald asked the King to dissolve Parliament, and an election was called for 29 October. Ede was once again adopted as the Labour candidate in Mitcham.

By this time, his election address was able to list an even more extensive inventory of appointments. These included membership of the Surrey CC Agricultural Committee, the Wimbledon, Mitcham and Epsom War Pensions Committee, and the Surrey Voluntary Hospitals Committee. On Epsom UDC, he was Chairman of Finance, and on the Labour Party Advisory Committee on Education he was Chairman of the Policy Subcommittee. He was a Governor of four county schools, in Mitcham and Sutton for boys, in Wallington and Epsom for girls. Some of his councils and committees would have met monthly, others once or twice a term, and he would probably have been required at least monthly for his duties on the bench – all told, he must have had to devote two or three days a week to his public and political offices, before finding time to fight a Parliamentary seat. His duties as Assistant SCTA Secretary cannot have been many, although the conclusion at the foot of the list: 'The Labour Candidate. The Hardest Working Member you have ever had' would have looked appropriate.

On this occasion the first part of the election leaflet dwelt on the government's record in foreign affairs – MacDonald was his own Foreign

Secretary – with particular reference to 'resettlement of the world', to France and to Russia. Housing and tax reduction followed, with only a small reference to education. Credit was taken for a reduction in unemployment, while efforts to secure rent reductions had been frustrated by the Conservatives. Labour had proved itself fit to govern, and its future policies would include restricting profiteering, bringing the coal, transport and electrical industries into national ownership, and reforming the Poor Law. A particular reference to women concluded with the aim of making the 'HOMES OF ENGLAND THE SHRINES OF A HEALTHY, HAPPY FAMILY LIFE' (capitals as in the original).

Richard Meller was standing for re-election, and was comfortably part of a Conservative landslide. Baldwin, already leading the largest party, achieved a majority of more than 200, with Labour reducing its number by 40 seats, and the Liberals suffering even greater losses. The election was marred by the publication, in the days immediately before the poll, of the Zinoviev letter, a fake which suggested the Soviet Union was planning to subvert Britain and its politics. Whether or not it affected Labour's vote, it certainly helped drive towards the Conservatives those many Liberal voters who were wary of Socialism. There were no other candidates in Mitcham, but in these circumstances there were few sympathetic Liberal votes to help Ede and, even though he received almost as many votes as the previous year, the small majority against him increased to over 6,000:

| Meller | Conservative | 15,984 |
| Ede | Labour | 9,776 |

Though he and Lilian remained living in Mitcham, he began to realize he needed to look elsewhere for a winnable seat.

Continuing his work in local government, Ede was raised to the office of Alderman on Surrey County Council in 1925. This co-opted position meant that he no longer had to stand for election regularly, and entitled him to use the title 'Alderman' in front of his name, in whatever context he was operating, not merely on Surrey CC. He used it in Epsom, and also in South Shields.

Among those who got to know Ede and his work in education in the 1920s was a mathematics teacher at Woking County School for Boys, Ernest Luery, some six years his junior. Luery was active in the SCTA, and would go on to be its President in 1943,[2] when Ede himself was at the Board of Education. Amongst the papers in the Surrey History Centre are some notes written by Luery, apparently for a talk he was giving about his memories of Ede, in the late 1960s or 1970s (he lived to be over 90). He noted that Ede did not trouble about his appearance, typically wearing heavy shoes and cycle clips, and that Lilian had asked Luery to have a word with him about this, as he had told her he was too busy to be bothered about how he looked. Luery said that in fact he never spoke to him about it, but that she nonetheless felt he had begun to look smart, and afterwards dressed for the part he was playing.

One of the things which impressed Luery was Ede's memory, particularly for the schools in Surrey. He knew every one, its age and surroundings, its state of repair, and the type of children who were in its classes. It was partly because he worried the County Council so much about all the deficiencies that he was voted on to the Education Committee. In his Union work, Luery recalled the particular care which he would put into its planning. Throughout its early history, the NUT relied on local organisations, led by a few active members,[3] and Jim and Lilian filled this role in Surrey. They would visit in advance the place chosen for the NUT Conference each year, and book rooms in one hotel for the entire Surrey delegation, of fifty or sixty people, while other counties would have their members scattered about. As a result, he could discuss the agenda with the Surrey team, hold whist drives in the evening and go for country walks and coach trips when the conference was not in session.

In 1928 the Conference was held at Llandudno, and the delegation stayed at One Ash, the former home, by then a hotel, of John Bright, the Corn Law reformer and advocate of free trade. Ede told Luery how much he admired Bright and his colleague Richard Cobden. Another year, the Conference was in Cambridge, and the delegation dined each evening in the Hall at King's College.

In 1926, Ede secured his adoption as prospective Parliamentary candidate for South Shields, a borough on the south bank of the Tyne, a few miles east of Newcastle. It had a long tradition of returning a Liberal MP, though the sitting Member, Edward Harney, had first been elected in 1922 with a majority of only 35 over Labour. Ede had a contact there, Cuth Barrass, a local teacher and activist in education, with a fine war record. Barrass had picked out Ede as a man of promise and experience – a 'rising star', to quote one of his successors as MP – who, not being local, could stand above the quarrels in the Shields Labour Party. Coal mining was a local industry, and bitterness against the established parties continued after the collapse of the General Strike in 1926. During the strike, Ede made a point of coming to South Shields, but was hampered by the interruption to the railway services. So he took the train for part of the journey from Surrey, and walked the rest.[4]

It is not clear how much of it he walked, but the incident stayed in the local mind when election day came.

By the time the South Shields Labour Party and Trades Council produced its annual report for 1927, it could note that 'Our prospective candidate, Alderman J Chuter Ede JP, has admirably co-operated with the Party and Council in all our activities. At Public Meetings he has expounded the Labour Policy with the effectiveness which creates confidence and support.' A fair prospect for Ede, though far from certain, winning the constituency would surely require the effort he was making. By now, though, there were signs that, despite his unflagging appetite for work on many bodies, he recognised the need to cut back. Surrey was taking up a significant amount of his time, and in 1927, having not lived in Epsom for four years, he stood down from the Council there. By this time he had served the town as Chairman of the Epsom Downs Committee, where one of his aims was to prevent encroachment on to common land[5]. Disputes about access to the Downs had been running since the 19th century; the Open Spaces Society, which Ede would later lead, kept a file of legal papers and pleadings on the subject.[6] This was in line with the environmental protection causes he would take on with broader scope in Surrey, particularly during the next ten years.

Several educational developments from the mid-1920s onwards followed on the school-leaving age being raised to 14 in 1921, and the 'reorganisation' of schools called for by Fisher's Education Act. The Consultative Committee (set up in 1889 to advise the government on education) was now chaired by the energetic Sir Henry Hadow, the Vice-Chancellor of Sheffield University; it produced a series of reports, in particular *The Education of the Adolescent* in 1926, which called for all-age elementary schools to be abolished,[7] in favour of a break in schooling at age eleven and separate secondary schools. Most elementary schools had been built when children finished education at 11, and their buildings were inadequate for older pupils.[8] Ede recognised the need to take action, and the following year the St Helier estate was started, an overspill development built by the London County Council, but within Surrey, some three miles south-west of his home in Mitcham. By the time the estate was completed around 1933, Surrey had had to build thirteen new schools, in the reorganised pattern,[9] the SCTA having advised on the school buildings there. Before then, in 1929, Ede's Educational Development Committee reported that new 'central' schools were in operation in Barnes and Walton, setting the pattern for Surrey, and then for the country as a whole.[10]

In 1928, Ede joined the London and Home Counties Joint Electricity Authority (LHCJEA), the main power company covering the south-east until electricity was nationalised when he was in the cabinet. It was, though, already a formative nationalised industry, being a public sector body put together by local authorities. He represented Berkshire, Buckinghamshire, Essex, Hertfordshire and Kent, as well as Surrey itself.[11] With his knowledge of Surrey and outer London, and his background studying science, this was a very suitable appointment for him, and one into which he put considerable effort. In addition, he became Chairman of the Surrey County Valuation Committee in 1928, and the same year saw Lilian elected as County Councillor for West Mitcham.

The Board of Education in May 1928 issued its Pamphlet 60, *The New Prospect in Education*, informing LEAs how it expected the Hadow proposals to be implemented. It defined the task of providing facilities for pupils over 11 as 'a readjustment of the existing elementary system'. This met with opposition from Ede and others, and at the NUT Conference in April 1929 he proposed that all post-primary education should be classed as 'secondary'; the term 'elementary' was becoming offensive to him. It was clear that the general reaction of teachers to Hadow was in favour of multilateral secondary schools for the older children.[12]

In 1929 the 1924 Parliament had to be dissolved. Baldwin called the General Election for 30 May, a few months early. Ede was prepared for the fight at South Shields – though not, one imagines, for the death of Edward Harney, the outgoing MP, a couple of weeks before polling day. He found a reliable agent, Ernie Gompertz, who would stay with him throughout his time at South Shields. A little younger than Ede – he would not disclose his exact age, but a registration search shows he was born in 1888 – Aaron Ernest Gompertz came from a Dutch Jewish family, and had been in South Shields since he was twelve. Like Ede, he was married without children, a teetotaller who did not smoke. Unlike him, though, he was a vegetarian and, more importantly, had been a conscientious objector in the Great War, imprisoned for three years in Leeds, at a cost to his health;[13] as Ede said, 'I'm a pacific person but I'm not a Pacifist', which was certainly correct.[14]

In addition, Gompertz's background had been in the Independent Labour Party, where he was an admirer of Keir Hardie, whom he was proud to have brought to South Shields before the War. At a 1950s Party Conference, he would form a small group with a few others who had fought with Hardie. There was no Liberal component in his Socialism. His attitudes were more pugnacious that Ede's; he was described as 'a fanatical teetotaller', while Ede had no wish to be evangelical to others about not drinking. He had been arrested at open meetings, and had a reputation as a street-fighter. He served for many years on the local council, taking his turn as Mayor in 1953, and held the post of Secretary of South Shields Labour Party and Trades Council from the early 1930s till after Ede's last election, besides many other local positions. He is credited with doing more than anyone else to build up South Shields' Labour Party – he was 'Mr Labour', according to a later MP for the town.[15]

Their relationship would always be slightly formal, Ede addressing letters to him as 'My dear friend', though with some others he would use their first name – Morrison was 'my dear Herbert'. Gompertz's letters would start 'Dear Friend Ede'.[16] There was no doubt about the effectiveness of Gompertz's work for his MP, however. He was reliable, and loyal to a member who would most of the time be absent from the constituency. He also appreciated the enigma that this Surrey man was the right person for South Shields:

> Although a man from the South, he seemed to understand instinctively the sufferings of the North and did more than was realised to make the southern people aware of what was happening. He went to the people who counted and told them what he had seen and what ought to be done,

was his eventual epitaph on Chuter Ede.[17]

To replace Harney, the Liberals quickly chose as their new candidate Harold Robson, whose father had once been Liberal MP for South Shields, generally popular for his radical support for industrial legislation and trade unions,[18] who became Asquith's Attorney-General and then a Law Lord. Unusually, the Conservatives decided to contest the seat also. Their candidate, William Nunn, did not attract many voters, but may have split the poll in a way which made the difference for Ede. In this campaign, as he would do later, he issued small cards, about 9 by 4½ cm – similar to cigarette cards – with on one side his photograph and the injunction 'VOTE FOR EDE X', and on the reverse his message to the electors. The message in this instance came from the Labour leader, Ramsay MacDonald, addressed in person to 'Alderman J Chuter Ede, JP', regretting his absence from the House after his previous work there of 'outstanding value', and ending that South Shields 'will not only secure a capable and industrious representative, but will materially strengthen our power in the next Parliament' by choosing him.

South Shields did indeed achieve that for him, though by only a whisker. The result was:

Ede	Labour	18,938
Robson	Liberal	18,898
Nunn	Conservative	7,110

a majority of 40 in a turnout of 45,000. Labour's percentage was virtually unchanged from 1924, but Robson's fell significantly from what Harney had achieved when he had had no Conservative opponent. Also, Ede was 'the right candidate for Shields because he was dead centre … he got Liberal votes', according to one Labour supporter.[19] He himself gave a more humdrum account of his success; at a presentation when he was finally giving up the seat, he said '21 pretty nurses' put him in at his first election.[20] Nationally, Labour had gained more than a hundred seats, and the Liberals a few, so Baldwin was no longer leading the largest party in the Commons (though the Conservatives secured more votes than either other party). It was clear that he had to resign.

With such a slim majority, Ede ensured his presence was noticed in South Shields during the next months. In July 1929 his interest in the British Legion led him to take part in its Memorial Service there, in South Marine Park. Then, on 13 September he was part of the official party visiting the North East Coast Exhibition in the town.[21]

At Westminster, MacDonald was asked to form a government again, but at this stage it was too soon for Ede to expect a place in it. The Education portfolio, which would most have interested him, went to Sir Charles Trevelyan, who had held it briefly during MacDonald's first ministry in 1924, when he had secured greater expenditure on education from the Treasury. Like Ede, Trevelyan was a Liberal who had moved to the Labour Party during the course of the Great War, though starting from a far more privileged background. He received a deputation from Labour's Education Advisory Committee in July 1929, of which Ede, with the historian R.H. Tawney, was part. The main subject discussed was raising the school-leaving age from fourteen to fifteen, to which Trevelyan was sympathetic, but he had great difficulty convincing the party as a whole that this was feasible.[22] While today it might seem obviously beneficial, some poorer families would have seen it as delaying by a year the time when their children could contribute financially, and it would have met opposition from parts of the Conservative Party mindful of the interests of employers. Also, some found it hard to justify as a spending priority at a time of austerity.

During the 1920s there had been an attempt within the party, led particularly by Tawney, to develop an education policy based on a free and universal system of education, ideally to age fifteen, without the social class distinctions which characterised English schools. Trevelyan had done little to further this in his first term in office, preferring the view that education was a field which should be kept out of politics, of which he convinced his

Government colleagues. Following his discussion with the EAC members, he gained agreement from the cabinet in July 1929 that there would be an Education Bill, to include raising the school-leaving age in 1931, on 1 April (an appropriate date, as it turned out). However, MacDonald and, among others, his Chancellor, Snowden, were not convinced of the urgency.

Ede naturally took part in the debates on his subject in the Commons, putting the standard case for a liberal education which went beyond mere instruction in practical skills for working life, and for equality of provision, because problems

> in the past were relegated to a very few people … If we are to have a democracy capable of shouldering this great burden, … it can only be done through giving to the children of all classes of the community a greater opportunity of entering into those great heritages of literature, of art and of beauty that should enrich the lives of the community.[23]

The question of the school-leaving age was also raised later in the year[24] by Sir Donald Maclean, a veteran Liberal who had led his party in the Commons for a short while after the Coupon Election of 1918. He was in no doubt the Government should get on with its Bill to implement the change. Trevelyan accepted the point, proposing to introduce a Bill by Christmas, six weeks later. Ede spoke last in the debate, a couple of hours after Trevelyan, making two points. First, keeping fourteen-year-olds in school for a further year would delay their entry into the depressed labour market and, with a bulge of children going through the schools, would give the benefit of extra education to a particularly great number of children. Secondly, he recalled the Education Act 1902, when he had watched, from the Gallery, Trevelyan and others praise that measure as establishing a municipal secondary education system; the awaited Bill would give every child over eleven 'a full higher education'. Maclean's motion was agreed without a vote, though the path to a full secondary education would be a much longer one than all hoped.

Ede also played an active role in other discussions in the House, one of which he was particularly proud being on the Blasphemy Laws (Amendment) Bill on 24 January 1930. In his view, 'we are discussing the greatest thing this House can discuss' – liberty of conscience, and reconciling the principle of not using secular means to defend religion, with the belief that the authority of any Government comes from a divine source. He called to his aid 'the great address which John Milton delivered to this House in 1644', without mentioning its name – 'Areopagitica' – and stated the central Nonconformist belief, that what 'Milton said is still true. Truth does progress from age to age.

We hold in scorn today the men who imprisoned John Bunyan, but it was the same spirit which protests against the repeal of this [blasphemy] law that sent John Bunyan to prison.' He criticised the religious tests being given to teachers:

> I recollect being called up for a headmastership and, after many attempts to find out what my religious persuasion was, at last the vicar, who was in the chair, thought he would discover it in this way. He said, "Would you, if you were appointed, play the organ on Sundays?" I said, "No, but if the sermons are good I will blow it." Through the sporting nature of the offer he discovered that my theological convictions were not of the kind that he required

and he concluded with a loud call:

> realise that liberty never harmed this nation. We have made great and risky experiments in liberty. We made one last year when we extended the franchise to women ... under 30, and the results excellently justified the step we took, though they may not have pleased the immediate authors. Liberty, as Milton said, 'the nurse of all great wits,' has been one of the things that this nation has been proud to give to the world, and this last vestige of theological intolerance is one that we can honour ourselves if today we take the first step towards removing it from the Statute book.

This was so close to the core of his belief, that he had the speech printed in several copies, for circulation to those who might be interested. Over the years, several unsuccessful attempts were made to dispense with the laws against blasphemy, so Ede had every need to keep up the pressure – the offence of blasphemy was eventually abolished in 2008, more than forty years after his death.

An incident from this time which remained in the common memory occurred when the Bishop of Durham, Hensley Henson, in whose diocese his constituency lay, made remarks about the idle ways of the local working class. Ede wrote a public letter, with sharp references, in a rebuttal of what Henson was saying. Soldiers in the war paid in blood for the mistakes of their officers, and:

> workers paid in hunger and cold for the mistakes of those who marshalled the Peace. The men and women your Lordship condemns are idle, like those in the Parable of the Vineyard, not from choice, but because no one thinks he can make a profit out of their toil.[25]

The unemployment problems of the working-class areas, particularly far from London, would continue throughout the years until the next war.

Among Ede's papers in the Surrey History Centre is a press cutting, without date or reference, illustrated by a caricature of him, under the title 'MEN WE KNOW – Ald J Chuter Ede MP'. It described the widespread popularity he had attained in South Shields, despite his narrow majority of 40, and put its finger on one issue for him:

> It is not always easy for a South-country man to adapt to Tyneside ways, but Alderman Ede appears to have surmounted this obstacle. He believes in keeping in close touch … and at frequent intervals he makes it his business to be among his constituents. 'Canny Shields' has grown to like its first Socialist MP … A native of Epsom, Alderman Ede has taken a prominent part in public affairs in Surrey,

where, it concluded, he is a JP.

In fact, one can say as an aside that it was often expected an MP would not come from the same background as his constituents. Even today, that is common enough, though Ede's most recent successor at South Shields, Emma Lewell-Buck, believes there are more regional voices in the Commons than previously – including hers. This, she feels, makes for a more vibrant Parliament, representing the country better. A Tynesider herself, she has reported problems being understood in the House: 'Hansard would often ask for clarification. I type my speeches out in full now, to make Hansard's job easier.' She gets surprise from some in South Shields, that their MP sounds like them.[26] That would not have been Ede's experience, and in his day South Shields would have found no issue in having a member with duties at such a distance from each other, even if it was uncommon.

However, when in 1930, Ede was appointed Vice-Chairman of Surrey County Council, he became concerned about either the conflict of interest this would place on him, or else the pressure on his time. As the press article implied, it was unusual for an MP representing a seat in the north-east to hold high office in a county authority south of London, and there was the prospect that he would soon be elected chairman of the SCC. Nonetheless, he had been elected by South Shields as Alderman Chuter Ede, in the full knowledge of his other commitments, and that was recognised locally. So when, on 13 May 1930, he wrote to his Chief Whip explaining his dilemma, and proposing to resign by taking the Chiltern Hundreds, he was told that he should certainly not give the Liberals the chance to regain a highly marginal seat. It is interesting to see where his priorities lay, and how important he considered his local authority work to be. In the end, though, the Whips and the NUT General Secretary, Frank Goldstone, between them convinced him to stay on, pointing out the work there was to be done on education in Parliament.[27]

He had certainly found work to do in Surrey, as the Norbury Park estate, which sits across the River Mole from Box Hill, had come on the market. This was close to the route that Ede had taken every day to school in Dorking, and where later he had led his own pupils to discover the Surrey countryside. He and Lilian would take walks there themselves, which during WWII he would describe in his diaries. It seemed likely to be bought for development, which Ede could not contemplate. He managed to induce Willcocks, one of his wealthier colleagues on the Council, to guarantee some funding, and get Surrey CC to agree to pay £20,000 towards the purchase price of £97,000. They started a public appeal for more donations, but this raised little, and eventually the house was sold privately and the parkland financed by the sale of other land for a by-pass round the neighbouring village of Mickleham.[28]

Although Surrey was the centre of Jim's and Lilian's life, with visits by him to South Shields from time to time, they did manage to take holidays, and it is clear from his photograph albums that a favourite destination was Cornwall. The thousands of photos which he left behind,[29] some stuck into albums, others loose or in envelopes, some with captions or dates and others without, are testament to his enthusiasm as a photographer. Pictures of him on country walks generally show him with, round his front, the strap of a bag which doubtless contained a camera, and at least one photo is of him standing and taking a shot with this apparatus. Places in Cornwall feature importantly at this time, with the dates of the two years he was in Parliament before the Labour Government fell, 1930 and 1931, and even more are of the Thames or of his beloved Surrey.

Trevelyan made two attempts at introducing an Education Bill, each resulting in withdrawal of the measure. In October 1930 he made a third attempt, to which his colleagues agreed to give priority. He needed to address the question of how Church schools would fit into a landscape of education to age 15, a question which would challenge his successors, including Ede himself. The Anglican and Catholic schools were concerned they did not have the resources to meet the expenditure needed to keep them in good repair and, when he agreed with them an arrangement granting financial assistance if they accepted more LEA control, the Nonconformists were concerned. Their complaint was the old one, that their children might need to go to state-funded schools which taught religion in a way with which they disagreed.

It was not long, however, before Trevelyan's attempts to get his Bill through Parliament collapsed, through opposition from Catholic Labour MPs who wanted better funding for their schools, from the Conservative opposition, and finally from the House of Lords. Anyone who expected the school-leaving age to rise on 1 April 1931 had been fooled, and Trevelyan resigned in March. Though the Government pressed on with the measure, and threatened to overrule the Lords, it was killed when the Labour Government was replaced that August.

Rumours persisted, however, that Ede would not be staying loyal to South Shields. While he was there at the end of January 1931, he had to write a letter to the local paper, denying that he would retire from Parliament, as some of the London and other papers had suggested.[30] In fact, he went on pressing causes close to his interests, both abroad and at home. Back in South Shields on 27 February, he spoke to a public meeting at the Imeary Street Hall, condemning the British concession in Shanghai, where there were 836,000 Chinese without a representative on the Municipal Council, which had rejected a proposal for factory regulations. He said Labour would not tolerate the British armed forces being used to perpetuate labour conditions there, which amounted to 'tyranny and slavery'.[31]

A subject such as that, overseas, was an unusual cause for him; more typical, nearer to home, the following week he accompanied a deputation from Tyneside to discuss relief from unemployment, and especially the allocation of naval contracts.[32] Local mayors, town clerks and several other MPs were involved, as concern continued about high unemployment and the depressed economy. Next, Ede and Sir Alexander West Russell, the MP for Tynemouth, both accompanied a deputation from Tyneside to Herbert Morrison, the Minister of Transport. They joined two local authorities they represented, which lie opposite each other at the river mouth, and were keen that cross-river facilities over the Tyne should be improved.[33] Financial stringency prevented this getting any positive response, and the first Tyne tunnel would not be approved till during World War II, and built only several years after. On a more personal note, but no lighter for the Edes, their house in Mitcham was, a few days later, broken into by intruders, who entered by the bathroom. They left the same way, chased by their Airedale Terrier, Pogo, and Lilian was able to make a statement to the press about the incident.[34] This may in fact have not been the only time they were burgled.[35]

Shortly before his resignation, Trevelyan had decided to investigate the educational standards of private schools, and asked Ede in December 1930 to chair a departmental committee on that subject.[36] There had been what Ede called 'a crop of scandals' in private schools, about which questions had been raised in Parliament.[37] He was joined in this by two Conservative MPs, Michael Beaumont and Victor Cazalet, one Liberal, Graham White, and two other Labour members, Leah Manning and Dr Alfred Salter. A few others from the world of education were involved, including Maurice Holmes, a rising civil servant at the Board of Education. The committee took a wide range of evidence, and managed to present its report in less than two years, though by the time it did so in 1932 it was to a new President of the Board, in a new Government, and Ede, Mrs Manning and Trevelyan were all out of Parliament.

The political crisis caused by the economic depression came to a head in the summer of 1931, with a budget crisis and a split in the government. MacDonald offered his resignation, but was convinced by the King and others to form a National Government, bringing the Conservatives and some Liberals into his team. Most of the Labour Party was deeply shocked, and the majority disowned MacDonald and his relatively few supporters, who were proposing spending cuts which would affect working people, and the unemployed, most of all. Ede sided with the majority, and in particular he fought the National Government's proposal to cut teachers' pay.[38] His personal thoughts were not recorded, but he must have felt his loyalties were to his supporters in South Shields, and to his Parliamentary colleagues; they felt they were being betrayed by the Prime Minister, elected to oppose the domination of Conservatives who, in their view, had done much to cause the depression. The Tories were now the majority in the Government, even though MacDonald, calling himself 'National Labour', remained at its head.

So Ede went into opposition, writing to Gompertz from his Cornish holiday that he would return from Penzance to Mitcham on 29 August, and would make an early appointment to visit South Shields. He said the government should meet the situation created by the banks with a Socialist programme, and that attacks on wages and social services would merely aggravate the situation.[39] He had to defend the seat at the General Election, called by MacDonald for 27 October 1931. On this occasion, the Conservatives did not put a candidate forward in South Shields, and the Liberals chose Harcourt Johnstone. From a strong Liberal family background, Johnstone was a supporter of Herbert Samuel's group of free-traders, who were induced to support the National Government even though the Conservatives wanted to introduce protectionist policies. Ede warned his constituents that a Tory majority, under whatever name, would destroy free trade, increasing difficulties for shipping, a local industry. Johnstone had been in and out of Parliament over the years, and had fought several seats with varying success. On this occasion, he took the great share of the Conservative voters from

1929, and probably many who had not voted at all then; for, while Ede's own vote increased by nearly 2,000, he was beaten by 30,528 to 20,512.

This time, 51,000 votes had been cast, compared with 45,000 for three candidates previously. Even though Ede's share of the poll had reduced by only 2 per cent, he had been defeated comprehensively, a result experienced by Labour throughout the country. Nearly 90 per cent of the Commons supported the National Government, whose MPs were overwhelmingly Conservatives; the Conservative Party had taken well over half the national vote. Labour, even including its allies, held only 52 seats. All the Labour Cabinet ministers who had not joined MacDonald were defeated, apart from George Lansbury. Arthur Henderson, who led Labour into the election, lost his seat, Lansbury took on the role of leading the party in the House, and succeeded Henderson the following year.

Ede did not give up on South Shields. The Constituency Labour Party's 1931 accounts show that he made 'grants' to them that year of £39 – perhaps worth £2,500 today – out of total income of £288. For the moment, though, his activities were in London and Surrey. His committee's work on private schools had been suspended for a while by the political crisis but eventually, as he himself put it, on 'restoration of animation our labours continued'. The evidence it received confirmed the huge range of 'private', 'independent' and 'public' schools' in the country, with a corresponding diversity of standards and conditions. Some of the worst cases were dire. The reader of the report[40] learns of absurdly small premises, teachers elderly and ill who should have long before retired, very large numbers sharing WC facilities, and so on. As the only duty on parents, under the successive Acts from 1876, was to ensure a child received 'elementary instruction in reading, writing and arithmetic', it was almost impossible to take action against them for poor education. If a child could write his name and add a few figures, any magistrates, giving the most restricted construction to those words, would dismiss a case. The type of child who attended a private school was likely to have picked up enough of the three Rs at home, even if the school taught him or her nothing at all.

Ede and his colleagues found that reputable schools agreed that parents should be 'protected from the charlatans', but were concerned about their own independence if there was any sort of public control. He was surprised to discover they also feared such control might prevent experiment, and was pleased to find none of them could produce an actual example of any experiment in their schools. Occasionally a prosecution would succeed, where the parents of the dullest pupil in the school were chosen as an example, and then the school might fold because other parents took their children elsewhere. However, he said, the teacher could then sing, 'Tomorrow to fresh fields and pastures new', once more quoting his beloved Milton, though this time the poem 'Lycidas'.

Some private schools were occasionally inspected by the Board of Education, but this had happened to no more than 1,300 out of some 10,000 which existed, teaching around 400,000 pupils. Those which agreed to be inspected were generally those of high efficiency and standards, and the number of inspections had decreased since the Education Act in 1918.

The committee concluded that duties should be placed on each of the parties involved in private education. Every school should register, be open to inspection, teach the three Rs, and conform to laid-down standards. Parents should ensure their children attend a school so registered, or a State school, and receive instruction in the three Rs; the committee could not agree whether merely sending a child to school was adequate to meet this requirement. The LEA's duty was to register schools, inspect them, and take proceedings where necessary. The Board of Education should receive reports on schools, and inspect those that needed inspection, the Courts having the power to order closures and enforce their judgments. Trevelyan, though now out of the Commons, wrote to congratulate him 'both on the tenor and quality of the report, and on the success in obtaining what is practically a unanimous report'.[41] These were all noble challenges, and Ede would carry them round in his planning. It would take many years, though, before the proposals were enacted.

Ede used his committee experience to speak on the subject of private schools. On 7 May 1932 he was in Kendal, for a meeting of the Westmorland NUT. He told them his concern was that 'when children reach eleven, we split them into groups of little snobs'.[42]

He now tried to divide his time between South Shields and Surrey, visiting Tyneside in October 1932, to speak in support of Labour candidates in the municipal elections on 1 November.[43] As to Surrey,[44] in 1931 his experience on the bench had seen him become the first elementary schoolteacher appointed a Deputy Lieutenant for the County (after which he ensured the initials DL appeared after his name). In 1933, he was elected unopposed back on to Epsom and Ewell UDC, which had been renamed and enlarged to include Ewell (despite his own protestations to the electorate twenty-five years earlier) and various rural areas around the two towns. He was immediately embroiled in a contentious decision of whether to widen the High Street in Epsom, the cost of which many ratepayers opposed. Ede's view was firmly that the new Council should go ahead to seek a grant to do the widening, and 'ensure that Epsom had its place as the capital of mid-Surrey'.[45] While in the Commons, he had helped pilot the Surrey County Council Act 1931 through Parliament, giving evidence on some of its planning aspects. Beside his Parliamentary duties, he had served two years as Vice-Chairman of the County Council, under the chairmanship of A. Leycester-Penrhyn who, as chair of the school managers, had appointed him many years before to teach at Mortlake School. It was now time to take the chair himself, and on 26 April 1933 the Council elected him.

His appointment attracted considerable coverage in the local press, both the *Surrey Comet* and *Epsom Advertiser*[46] devoting long columns to his praises and biography, in words similar enough to suggest a press release had been issued. The Epsom (West Street) Branch of the British Legion, of which he was now President, presented him with a gold watch to commemorate his election. He used his love of country walking to keep an eye on Surrey; the Southern Railway put on rambles in the county and elsewhere, and he kept records of those in which he was involved.[47] Many of his duties now were ceremonial, such as opening the new library in Merton, where he was given a leather-bound edition of *Pepys's Diary*,[48] but he took on other functions as well. He was elected in 1934 to chair the Electricity Authority, of which he had been a member for seven years (and finance committee chair for two),[49] which was a role where leadership flowed from the top, unlike a local authority with its majority leader and ceremonial chairman. Lilian, as well as acting as Chairman's lady, was re-elected to her Mitcham seat on Surrey CC in March 1934, for what would in fact be her last term. They worked together on the environmental protection of the Surrey countryside, and for Christmas 1934 sent out a card, illustrated by a photo he had taken of the Devil's Punch Bowl, near Hindhead, the highest village in the county, from 'The Chairman of Surrey County Council and Mrs Chuter Ede CC,' who 'wish you Happiness this Christmastide and Prosperity in 1935', the address being the Chairman's Room, County Hall. He must have been pleased to sign, on the Council's behalf, the River Wey Improvement Order[50] in May 1935. The Wey, which flows through Surrey from its south-west corner, past Godalming, Guildford and Old Woking, and into the Thames below Weybridge, was regularly inclined to flood, a problem tackled by him and his colleagues on Surrey CC.

A couple of months later, he was representing the County Council at the opening of the Guildford and Godalming Bypass, carried out by the Transport Minister Hore-Belisha.[51] The planning of this originated with Ede, as it had for the bypasses built during his era around Ewell itself, as well as Kingston, Sutton, Egham, Caterham and Leatherhead. At his death, John Strudwick credited him with providing Surrey with more bypasses round its towns than any other county, and with Surrey's coming earlier.[52] This was all part of his commitment to keep the ancient towns and the countryside as free as possible from the increased traffic which drove through the county, in addition to a particular concern of Hore-Belisha, keeping the roads safer.

In the summer of 1935, he wrote a report for the Institute of Municipal Treasurers and Accountants on a subject he knew well – cooperation between county councils and district councils. By now, however, he was getting more occupied by matters in South Shields. Other constituencies may have expressed an interest, but he decided to stay loyal to the Labour Party there, with support as ever from his agent. Ernie Gompertz had been keeping the campaign going during the early years of the National Government; in 1933 he told the press that Harcourt Johnstone had attended only 77 divisions out of 148 in the Commons – he was 'only a half-time member'.[53]

MacDonald had remained in office since the 1931 election, but he was nearly 70 and his health was weakening. He too had a background as a Unitarian preacher[54] but, unlike Ede, he was a pacifist, opposing the War in 1914, and struggling for disarmament while in office. Germany's developing militarism under Hitler crushed his spirit. It made sense for him to hand over the premiership. The realistic successor was Baldwin, already twice Prime Minister and the leader of by far the largest party in Parliament and the National Government. He took over in June 1935, and decided to get a personal mandate by calling an election a year early. The date was set for 14 November. George Lansbury, who since the 1931 rout had led Labour in the Commons, was ready to fight it despite being 76 himself, with Clement Attlee as his deputy. Attlee was the only other Labour MP with ministerial experience, apart from Stafford Cripps, who had for a few months been Solicitor-General.

The South Shields Party adopted Ede as their candidate, and they set to work to unseat Harcourt Johnstone. They produced a poster which the Liberals had issued in 1931, asserting in bold capitals 'There is no destitution test. Vote for Johnstone and truth in politics.' This was copied into a Labour handbill with its description as 'a Poster issued by Harcourt Johnstone in 1931 when National Candidate. The election was won on this untruth. Beware of similar tactics this time. Down with the Means Test. VOTE FOR EDE X.' It was a risky approach. At first sight its message is not altogether clear, and it was calling another candidate a liar. In addition, it is unlikely that the handbill had made the difference between success and failure last time, but Ede and Gompertz must have decided that the point would be understood.

The main document for the election was a detailed address, featuring an attractive photo of Ede with the request that it be put in the window, a list of fourteen public meetings which Alderman Chuter Ede JP DL would address – he seems on occasions to have been in three or more places at the same time – and a description of the candidate as 'Formerly MP for So.

Shields and Mitcham, Chairman of Surrey County Council, Chairman of the London and Home Counties' Joint Electricity Authority, Justice of the Peace, Deputy Lieutenant, etc'. There was no disguising that he came from the other end of the country, but that did not signify when it came to listing his qualifications. His letter inside concentrated on opposing the 'destitution test', supporting the League of Nations (and in particular opposing Italy), preventing rearmament, and 'national planning', which included extending education, though that was not a central theme. He criticised the destruction of free trade and the encouragement of nationalism abroad, which he said he had warned about if there was a Conservative Government; and he berated the way the Government had been treating the poor. Though there was again no Conservative candidate, it was clearly aimed at Johnstone and his support for the Conservative-dominated Government. Another candidate had appeared, however – Frederick Burden, a young Londoner who was standing on a National Labour ticket, and so would have been equally tarred with the National Government's brush.

Another handbill was issued, with a photograph of Ede being raised in victory by the crowd, going back to his first election in South Shields. Its caption was "Victory for EDE 1929. Make sure of Victory, 1935, by Voting for EDE X'. They were keen to remind the voters he had been there before, he had remained loyal to the town, and things had not changed. For the Party as a whole, though, there had been a major change. The elderly Lansbury, a longstanding pacifist, had come into conflict with the Party, particularly over Italy's threat to Abyssinia, one of the main points which concerned Ede. His opposition to sanctions was denounced by the Party Conference in October 1935, under Ernest Bevin's leadership, and he realised he could not lead it into the election. He resigned, and Clement Attlee was hastily appointed as caretaker Party leader.

Chapter 6

In South Shields to Stay

When the party under Attlee fought the 1935 election, they must have hoped that the difficulties of the last four lean years were behind them. In numerical terms, they made a significant stride but, starting from such a low base, its impact was small. In South Shields, Ede received 1,500 votes more than in 1931 and, though not quite achieving an absolute majority, won the election comfortably, with his two opponents splitting the Government support between them:

Ede	Labour	22,031
Johnstone	Liberal	12,932
Burden	National Labour	10,784

The intervention of National Labour had given him a majority of over 9,000 but it is fair to conclude that, even without that, Johnstone would have lost. Both the defeated candidates would go on to political careers elsewhere, Harcourt Johnstone as a senior Liberal in Churchill's War Coalition, and Frederick Burden as a long-serving Conservative after the war. As for Ede, he was back in, and would remain so for good.

Nationally, Labour secured 38 per cent of the vote, a good percentage, greater than in any previous election, and trebled their Parliamentary seats; but even with their unreliable allies in the Independent Labour Party, that amounted to no more than 158 MPs. The Conservatives had a very comfortable majority on their own, besides being supported by some National Liberal and National Labour Members. Baldwin's government was not seriously damaged by its losses. For Attlee, though, it was a personal triumph, and within three weeks he was elected as Labour leader on a permanent basis, a result which would have a major impact on Ede's career, the two men working together for the rest of their lives.

Tyneside was still suffering the effects of the depression of the earlier years, and the Labour victory in South Shields was reflected next door in Jarrow, where Ellen Wilkinson, another MP who had lost her seat in 1931, had been returned at the general election, though with a much narrower majority than Ede's, in a two-way contest. On the debate on the King's Speech, she laid into the government for its record on unemployment benefit and the means test, their effect on maternal mortality, the burden of the rating system, the history of decline in the shipyards and steel industry in Jarrow, and the need for overall economic planning in Tyneside. She was followed a little later by Sir John Jarvis, Guildford's newly-elected Conservative MP, who had been High Sheriff of Surrey. He told how he had got the people of Surrey to contribute a small fund to Tyneside, to create jobs and improve living conditions there, with Ede starting a halfpenny collection among the Surrey schoolchildren to provide playgrounds in Jarrow.

Ede spoke next, congratulating Jarvis on his maiden speech, and to support Wilkinson, arguing against the 'policy of isolation' which made each disadvantaged locality responsible for its own poor relief, while prosperous areas like Surrey carried a much lighter burden. John Jarvis, Lord Eustace Percy (a Northumbrian who had moved to Surrey):

> and I live in a county where the poor rate is 1/2½ in the £, and the chairman of the county finance committee never presents it to the county council without alleging that it is going to bring about the speedy ruin of the richest county in England. I live in a house rated at £60 a year and, when I have paid £3/12/6 for public assistance, the law says that I have discharged my duty towards my fellow citizens who have to come upon public assistance for the means of subsistence. If I paid a poor rate in my constituency, instead of paying £3/12/6 I should pay £15/7/6. If I lived … in the borough of Jarrow, or any other part of the administrative county of Durham, I should pay £27 instead of £3/12/6.[1]

It was a message which would reverberate in Jarrow a few months later.

Attlee did not need him immediately on the Opposition front bench, which was perhaps just as well, bearing in mind his duties on Surrey and Epsom Councils, in addition to his constituency. He carried on with his official duties as Chairman at Surrey, such as opening Raynes Park Boys Secondary School in November, the same month as the election.[2] He was attending a similar opening the following 10 September at the South Shields High School for Boys, where he joined his old opponent Bishop Henson on the platform.[3] The boys, who came there from two former schools in the town were given an extra week off while work in the building was finished, but the ceremony went ahead on the appointed day without the pupils. On 28 February 1936, Epsom and Ewell presented a petition to the Privy Council seeking borough status for the authority,[4] a matter which would consume much of Ede's time the following year, and then, on 28 April, he was elected for a fourth term to chair the County Council.[5] He saw the passage that year of the private Epsom and Walton Downs Regulation Act, which secured open access to the Downs on which he watched the Derby each year.[6] He described his involvement as part of a 'happy cooperation with the Grand Stand Association and the owner of Walton Downs'.[7]

A further contribution to preserving the environment of Surrey then occurred. Burford Lodge, an eighteenth-century house on the edge of Box Hill, came on the market with eight acres of grounds, and conveniently the Joint Electricity Authority, of which Ede was Chairman, was looking for a property for its own use. The National Trust already owned other land nearby, and he was able to ensure that Burford was taken over on 4 July 1936[8] by the authority, which used it for repairing and testing meters, and overhauling cookers.[9] So he could use his varied responsibilities towards the different aims he was pursuing, both in local amenities and conservation. In 1937, in his capacity as chairman of the Electricity Authority, he invited the Surrey County Teachers' Association council to meet at Burford Lodge.[10]

Open spaces generally became an interest of his in Parliament at this stage. In February 1936 he asked a question of the Minister of Agriculture about the state of commons and manorial wastes subject to public rights, and the prospects of a Bill in Parliament. He received a letter from the Secretary of the Commons, Footpaths and Open Spaces Preservation Society, congratulating him on this, and it is clear he was already cooperating on this subject with the Society, of which he would become a leading member later on. He would follow this up a year later, in January 1937, with a question to which his supplementary comment was that commons were rapidly becoming incapable of maintenance because of building operations. The Society's files include a note stating he regarded many commons as 'suburbanised', where they became waste land surrounded by houses.[11]

In October 1936, Ellen Wilkinson followed up her appeals in Parliament for Jarrow by leading 200 marchers from her constituency to London. The Jarrow March has become the best-known of the protests of the 1930s against the conditions of the poor, but it was consciously limited to Jarrow, so there was no reason for Ede to get involved. It set out with a blessing from the Bishop of Jarrow, who was criticised by his superior, Bishop Henson of Durham, whose view was that it was designed in the interest of the Labour Party rather than the unemployed, though in fact the party's attitude to the march was ambivalent. Ede did, though, make a point of attending the House on 4 November, when Ellen Wilkinson presented the petition from Jarrow and spoke briefly about the situation there. When Walter Runciman, the President of the Board of Trade, spoke casually about unemployment in Jarrow improving, and there being every hope there would be increased demand for Tyneside shipping workers, Ede made one short comment: 'the Government's complacency is regarded throughout the country as an affront to the national conscience.' He received a little support from Thomas Magnay, the Liberal member for neighbouring Gateshead who sat in support of the Government, but the attitude of Runciman, also a Liberal, must have confirmed Ede in his decision to leave the Liberals nearly twenty years before.

In the early part of 1937, the Edes moved from Tamworth Farm House, their 'house rated at £60 a year' in Mitcham, to Tayles Hill, a building of some substance near the centre of Ewell. Their connection with Mitcham was now distant, and there is a suggestion that the burglaries they had suffered there induced them to move.[12] Built in the early nineteenth century, Tayles Hill is a three-story house, a substantial villa once owned by Edward Coates, an earlier MP active in Surrey local government at the start of the twentieth

century, and then used as a military hospital in the Great War.[13] It is still standing, divided into flats, and with a plaque placed there by the Borough to celebrate its fiftieth anniversary in 1987, recording that James Chuter Ede lived there from 1930 to 1964. In fact the first date is wrong, as his solicitors were corresponding with him in Mitcham until the end of 1936, and at Tayles Hill by April 1937. The date of 1964 records that, while Lilian would live there for the rest of her life, he did eventually move out a few months before his death.

In March 1937, Ede finally retired after four years as Chairman of Surrey County Council, receiving tributes in the press.[14] According to a later profile in *The Spectator*, a generally Conservative journal, 'he was one of the most successful chairmen it has ever had'.[15] While he remained there as an Alderman for another dozen years, Lilian retired from her seat in

Picture of Lilian Ede, taken by her husband, a keen photographer. (© *Surrey History Centre*)

Mitcham, where of course she no longer lived. At Epsom and Ewell UDC, where the petition to the Privy Council had been successful, he was chosen as prospective Mayor for the new Borough, being the only member who could date his service to as early as 1908,[16] and Lilian was now more available to work with him, in what was to be the busiest year of all for the town. He also kept himself occupied with work for the Electrical Authority, writing a piece in the *Financial Times*[17] explaining the British Joint Electrical Authorities, their constitution and their impressive work. He had been elected to chair the industry body, the British Electrical Development Association, for the 1937 year.[18] His ideas were developing about the form that nationalization could take, if ever there was a Government committed to it, which could hold office for long enough to implement it. This was two days before passing on the chair at Surrey, so he was identified as Chairman there as well as of the London and Home Counties JEA. From 1937, the Christmas cards would send greetings from 'The Chairman of the London and Home Counties Joint Electricity Authority and Mrs L.M. Ede'.

He also provided an article to *Helios*,[19] an electrical specialist journal, on 'Placing of Modern Industry'. It is a piece with a cynical thrust:

> Town Planning in administrative practice consists in the 'developer' showing what is the worst use, aesthetically and hygienically, he can make of his land and the Authority considering if it can afford the necessary compensation to cause him to desist,

but it had a positive theme that, with the electricity grid now in place, energy could be moved for use anywhere in the country, rather than industry being localised near the source of coal. So there should be Government strategy to place or resuscitate industry in places which were physically suitable for it, which is good for both the depressed regions and those which need to be preserved for their beauty:

> The national conscience is affronted by the spectacle of areas deprived of their industries and left to rot, where elsewhere tracts that were a delight to the eye and a refreshment to the soul are turned into wildernesses of bricks and smoke.

The one policy would benefit both Tyneside and Surrey, in other words. He cited his own Electricity Authority's example of good practice:

> The coming of the electricity supply system into the Dorking rural area was much resented by some who thought that an overhead wire, no matter how carefully screened, must be a desecration. The … Authority

have not merely been able to overcome that prejudice. They materially helped in the preservation of the foreground of Box Hill

by buying and using Burford Lodge. Industry could be 'healthy, wholesome and clean' because of electricity – though now we might point out that he was speaking of power derived from coal, as a Tyneside MP must. The problems of fossil fuels were not an issue then. In this article, he was using the term 'environment' in its modern sense: 'Life which can be so great must have some environment more noble and inspiring than the nineteenth century mill or mine.' In support he called on three Cambridge men, GM Trevelyan, the brother of his Parliamentary colleague in the education debates, and perhaps predictably, two from Christ's: 'General Smuts has told us that mankind has struck its tents and is on the march', and

> I am reminded of the warning Milton gave his contemporaries of the judgment posterity might form on their conduct: 'They will see that there was ... an opportunity afforded for the greatest achievements, but that men only were wanting for the execution.

This time, this quotation came not from 'Areopagitica', but from *The Second Defence of the English People*, a call for a country of civic idealism and freedom of thought.

Another article he submitted to *Bus-Bar*, the magazine of the Electricity Authority's Social Association,[20] though this was on the lighter subject of 'Some Historic Aspects of the Coronation', for 1937 was a coronation year.

The evidence from Ede's papers is that he was confidently a royalist (his attachment to Cromwell notwithstanding), who preserved commemorative editions of newspapers on royal events. He also kept photos of himself with Queen Mary, Queen Elizabeth, and the young Princess Elizabeth before her accession. His portrait painter recalled he told him that, when passing through Windsor as an elderly man, he informally called in on the Queen.[21] He did not leave us his thoughts on King Edward's abdication of December 1936, a year after his return to Parliament, though many years later he would make a caustic remark about the Church's role in the affair. When King George VI and Queen Elizabeth took the place of Edward, he excitedly attended Westminster Abbey for their Coronation on 12 May 1937, as an MP and representative of Epsom, and would be able to use the experience when a Privy Counsellor involved with arranging the next Coronation.

After that, it was the Surrey local authorities which took up his time. On 16 June, he was made a Freeman of the Borough of Wimbledon,[22] and his duties in Epsom included opening the Epsom Central Council School (now known as Rosebery School). On 15 September he attended the incorporation as a Borough of Beddington and Wallington,[23] which he had briefly represented when that area was part of the Mitcham constituency. Its 'Charter Mayor' was Sir Richard Meller, who had defeated him years before in Mitcham, and was still the area's MP, and this provided a blueprint for his own local authority, which was itself to receive its Charter as a Borough.

The day set for the Borough celebrations was Wednesday 29 September 1937, Michaelmas Day as Ede would later note. The Edes went early to Ewell's Garden of Remembrance and the Epsom War memorial, where Lilian laid wreaths. There was then a procession through the streets to Nonsuch Park, part of the grounds of Henry VIII's old palace, long since demolished, which the new Borough, along with Sutton and the Surrey and London County Councils, had purchased to retain as undeveloped Green Belt.[24] On the border between Epsom and Sutton, they welcomed Surrey's Lord Lieutenant, and processed the five miles back to Epsom High Street by horse-drawn carriage. In a long ceremony, watched by 10,000 people, the Lord Lieutenant presented Ede, as Mayor, with the Charter, and the Bishop of Guildford led a service. A luncheon with 300 guests was held at the Grandstand on the Racecourse, where the Lord Lieutenant proposed the toast to the Borough, to which Ede responded. Among those present was his mother Mary, now 89 and blind for seven years, in what would be her last public appearance.[25] Her son gave a lyrical description of the fame of Epsom salts, and listed the achievements since he returned to the enlarged Council – a new Fire Station and Town Hall, commencing new public baths, widening the High Street, and in particular the environmental work at Nonsuch together with the purchase of Epsom Common. Apart from the ancient boroughs of Kingston, Guildford and Godalming, he considered Epsom to have had the longest experience of local government in the county, and it was now catching up with other towns in Surrey.

There was a pageant of historic tableaux round the town, depicting incidents such as the Romans building their roads, physicians testing the quality of Epsom spring water in 1619, Charles II visiting the wells, Pepys on the Downs, Lady Castlemaine selling old Nonsuch Palace (which she had acquired from Charles in a racing bet) and the founding of the Derby. Ede then went to the formal opening of Nonsuch Park by the London County Council Chairman – a further opportunity for a speech from him. When the Borough had chosen its coat of arms, depicting horses' heads (for the races) on a green field (for the Downs) and water (for the springs of Epsom and Ewell),[26] its motto was 'None Such', a phrase Ede emphasised in his messages to the townsfolk.[27]

The church bells pealed out in the evening, and the celebrations, with dances and funfairs, then carried on through Thursday and Friday, and over the weekend. By the end of it, the Edes had visited several schools, including the Church of England Boys' School in Hook Road, as his old school was now called; there he gave another speech. He was wearing new mayoral robes, funded by collections from schoolchildren, typically a penny each; he had himself donated the new mace to the Borough.[28] He had drafted a small booklet for the local children about the new Borough, and included descriptions of its parks and open spaces 'to promote the health and happiness of the inhabitants and especially of the children ... To how many have you been? ... Try to visit each of them.' A booklet published in 2012 to celebrate seventy-five years of the Borough reported that all still existed as parks, barring one which had become allotments.[29] His legacy to the area survived, and his new designation, Charter Mayor of Epsom and Ewell, was a title permanently his, quoted for the rest of his life among his other honours.

One of the more incongruous duties Ede had during the remainder of his term was to attend the banquet of the Epsom Sutton & District Licensed Victuallers Protection Society, at the Connaught Rooms in London, on 19 October 1937.[30] There he responded to the toast to the ladies and visitors, though what he might have drunk or said on the occasion, not designed for teetotallers, goes unrecorded. While Charter Mayor, he 'carried out with commendable zeal and distinction the onerous and exacting obligations of that important office, being graciously assisted therein by his Wife as Charter Mayoress', in the words of the motion subsequently awarding him the Freedom of the Borough, and eventually, when his duties came to an end, he left the Council of Epsom and Ewell for good. He had been a member there for more than twenty years, covering nearly thirty years with a break in the middle.

At the national level, Ede kept in touch with developments in the educational world, in particular the report from the Consultative Committee of the Board of Education chaired by Sir Will Spens, the long-serving Master of Corpus Christi College, Cambridge. This covered secondary schools with, as its title said, 'Special Reference to Grammar Schools and Technical High Schools'. It was a large committee, of nineteen members, one of whom was Shena, Lady Simon, a Labour politician from Manchester with a special interest in education, and its work had been going on since 1933. Sir Henry Hadow had produced the last of his Consultative Committee reports in 1933, when he was over seventy, and had since died; Spens had taken on his role. The problem the report addressed was the small proportion of elementary school pupils being selected to go on to secondary schools which, even in 1938, was still about 10 per cent, with the rest remaining in all-age elementary schools or transferring to 'senior' schools, which were not providing a proper secondary education. They were divided by class, and the system was not doing its best for the pupils. In Germany twice as many went on to higher education, in France more than twice, and in the USA almost ten times as many. Even Scotland had a much better record.

There was in some circles support for a system of common secondary schools for all, though most thought aptitude and intelligence should be the criteria for choosing how different children should be treated. In some ways ahead of its time – it recommended 'adoption of a minimum leaving age of 16 years, which is now the rule in Grammar Schools', which 'may not be immediately practicable, but in our judgement must even now be envisaged as inevitable' (though we know was eventually achieved only in 1972) – the Spens Report concluded that arrangements for education had ceased to correspond with the structure of society and the economic facts. However, it was persuaded by the view that, because of the different aptitudes of children, there should be a diverse provision of secondary school types. There should be grammar schools for academic children, technical schools for those with more practical aptitudes, and 'modern' secondary schools – a new concept – for the rest. 'Parity of esteem' should apply between the different types of school but, while the Report accepted in principle the benefits of all secondary age children being educated together in 'multilateral' schools, as they were then called, they 'could not advocate the adoption of multilateralism as a general policy' for a number of reasons.

This was not by any means universally welcomed in academic, trade union, local government or Labour Party circles, but it subsequently became the dominant view[31] and was prevalent among educational administrators and civil servants. Shena Simon may later have regretted she had not held out more forcefully for the multilateral system, doubting whether parity of esteem was realistically possible, but she seems to have had doubts, like the rest of the Committee, about the practicalities and the cost. Ede, however, initially from his viewpoint as a backbench MP, was formulating the view that multilateralism should be the aim wherever this was possible.

On the international front, Ede was aware of the tensions building up in Europe. Generally, he took much more interest in domestic than in foreign matters. For instance, in 1938 there was talk of a 'Popular Front' of politicians from several parties to oppose the Chamberlain Government's appeasement policies towards the Nazis and the European dictators. Though Stafford

Cripps and others advocated this, the Labour Party as a whole was lukewarm. In South Shields, Gompertz discouraged any involvement, partly because of the Front's links with Communists, and Ede did not dissent from this. When Ellen Wilkinson wrote a memorandum sympathetic to the Front, he commented discouragingly about making any alliance. Labour should remain a socialist party, a 'strong united opposition' rather than in 'a weak coalition which always tended to break up'.[32]

However, what was happening abroad could not be ignored. When Cripps was for a while expelled from the party for pressing for the Front, Ede wrote to the party in London and South Shields in January 1939, criticising the decision. He had been getting concerned about Europe, having visited Austria for a month in 1937.[33] So, two days after the Austrian Anschluss on 12 March 1938, he was on his feet in the Commons calling for more action from the Government, warning them that Czechoslovakia would be next. Sure enough, the Germans took over the Sudetenland, part of Czechoslovakia, in the autumn, and on 10 November Ede was speaking in support of Churchill and Eden, attacking the Government's attitude towards the Nazis, adding his concern for the vulnerability of Tyneside in a war. On 15 January 1939, he spoke at a large demonstration in Newcastle City Hall, in support of Spanish Republicans.[34]

Partly on the strength of his speeches in the House, he was elected to the Opposition front bench in 1938,[35] and was starting to be able to put his views on education, and areas such as penal policy, into practice. So, on 2 February 1939, he asked a question of Kenneth Lindsay, the Parliamentary Secretary, who confirmed the Board of Education would press ahead with the Spens recommendations, to the extent they did not involve high expenditure.

Before that, on 29 November 1938, the Home Secretary Sir Samuel Hoare introduced a Criminal Justice Bill, intended to abolish or modify several of the harsher punishments which the courts could inflict, and Ede spoke immediately after Sir Archibald Southby, the MP for Epsom with whom he had sat as a JP. Unlike Southby, he welcomed the proposal to abolish corporal punishment, and scorned the idea that the cinema was a cause of increased delinquency. He welcomed the Bill, a cross-party measure, ending his speech with the hope that it would live long as a monument to Hoare, unlike the foreign policy associated with him, a reference particularly to his 1935 pact with Pierre Laval, which opened Abyssinia up to invasion by Mussolini. Ede also showed himself a supporter of abolishing capital punishment, at least for the present; on 16 November he had voted in favour of a motion to that effect. The Bill did not in the end include that change and, as it would turn out, it was still before Parliament in September 1939, and was dropped as a measure when the attention of everyone was diverted to the outbreak of war. It would eventually be Ede who, at the Home Office, introduced very similar measures, with Hoare's support in the Lords, after the war had ended.

For there was no doubt that a war was now feared. Back in his constituency, on 10 July 1938 he paid tribute, at the South Shields British Legion, to the soldiers of the Great War, noting that it was now a 'grim hour'.[36] This recalls a bracketed query in his *Helios* article, that placing industry in the right place might 'make the western ports capable of much they were unable to do in the last (or is it only the latest?) war'. The possibility of a further war was becoming a realistic threat, if that question about 'latest' can be taken in its apparent sense. Surrey County Council was starting to look at air-raid precautions. On 25 April 1939 it appointed Ede to a special committee in charge of the matter[37] and, on 5 May, he and Sir Richard Meller were together representing Surrey at the first meeting of the London Regional Civil Defence Council.

That May was a busy month for him, one of both sadness and honour. On 13 May his mother Mary died, two days short of her 90th birthday, and her funeral took place at the Congregational Church four days later. She was given an obituary of a full column on the front page in the local paper,[38] well over a thousand words, besides the description of the funeral. Its fulsome tribute concentrated on her lively interest in Epsom and local government, as well as her Nonconformist faith:

> Blessed with a retentive memory and a gift for vivid phrasing, she delighted in recalling the many episodes she had witnessed, and in which others in her family had played a part. She was an entertaining conversationalist. She imparted information with a sense of humour always happy in its play. She followed the successes of her friends and their children, with real sympathy and ready admiration. Envy was completely unknown in her. In moments of perplexity and difficulty she was a wise and cheerful advisor. She felt very keenly, and with the only sense of personal loss she ever mentioned, the low standard of girls' education in her youth, and wholeheartedly rejoiced in the present wider opportunities.

The emphasis on education and local government, together with a quotation from Bunyan later on in the obituary, suggest it was at least in part composed by her son Jim.

Epsom Borough Council had met on 16 May, when the Mayor had paid a tribute to her and to the 'illustrious son' of both her and Epsom, and had stood in silence to her memory. That same day, Ede had been chairing the bench at a special Police Court in Epsom, dealing with several defendants charged with betting offences.[39] Customers in the White Hart pub and the Spread Eagle Hotel had been seen taking part in illegal betting, and they and the licensees were appearing before the justices, and various fines were handed down. As a racing town, Epsom had its sympathies with gamblers, which Ede himself shared, though he scarcely bet himself and would always have taken the view that the law needed to be followed. He would later help relax the law relating to betting, believing it a 'folly', not an evil.

The honour which came to him in May 1939 was the Freedom of the Borough of Epsom and Ewell, voted by the Council at a special meeting held the same evening as their tribute to Mary Ede.[40] He was the first Freeman of the new borough, and the Mayor, H.W. Cushine, picked out two places in the town where Ede's name featured:

> Firstly it is one of the first on the scholarship honours board in the old National School in East Street, which illustrates his great endeavour. Secondly, it appears on the honours board at the Town Hall, both as a past Chairman and as Charter Mayor, representing its achievement.

He ran through Ede's early struggles on Epsom UDC, working on developing the town's water supply and negotiating the first open spaces, and the control of Nonsuch Park and the Epsom Downs. Cushine and Ede had together been founder members of the British Legion. The deputy mayor, Charles Shaw, had previous shown his affection for Ede by giving him in 1937 his father's copy of Morley's *Life of Cromwell*, from which he had often quoted over the years. Shaw, who had been Mayor of the Borough for six months in 1938, now added his own words about him, regretting his late mother had not quite lived long enough to know about his new honour, joining instead Ellen Ede as a family member who had helped to further his career. It was a remarkable coincidence that three different stories – Mary's death, the Police Court trials, and the award by the Borough – should all have occurred in a few days, consuming most of the *Herald*'s front page.

Ede was admitted as a Freeman of Epsom and Ewell at a dinner given to honour him, and also for Shaw who received a badge recognising his mayoral term, at Epsom County School for Boys on 5 June. The Town Clerk recited the resolution of 16 May, which described once again his background and career in Epsom, his term as Charter Mayor, his work on the Electricity Authority, his special interest in education and the British Legion, and his achievements over Nonsuch and the Downs. Everything he had done, during the last thirty years or more, had been rewarded, and it must have felt a triumphant time. However, in the country, war was coming close, which might have undermined so many of these achievements. His brother Noel Ede was active in the International Friendship League, and is credited by some with having founded it around 1931, with a view to ensuring the countries of Europe would understand each other better and the old enmities would be replaced by peace. It was not of course to be. Within three months of the dinner in Ede's honour, the Prime Minister Neville Chamberlain announced that Britain was at war with Germany.

To being with, the war was 'phoney', and the tasks of many of those in Parliament carried on much as before, with Ede speaking particularly on educational matters. So on 5 March 1940, a debate chosen by the Opposition for a Supply Day with education as its subject, he was the frontbench spokesman chosen to sum up for Labour. Children had been evacuated, and he was particularly concerned about the poor schooling many of them were getting, criticising Kenneth Lindsay for the Board of Education's failure to get children back to school. It was a strong performance, leaving Lindsay exposed, on this and other grounds. Ede mentioned the endowments of schools such as Eton, where none of the poor scholars, for whom he argued the funds had been entrusted, came from an elementary school background. He ranged also across religious education, the employment of those under twelve, and the health of the evacuee children, but it was re-establishing full-time education for them to which he gave most emphasis.

Sticking mainly to his own specialism, he played little part in the debates about the war which resulted in Chamberlain's downfall but, when it happened, his opportunity had come. Aged 57, and with a lifetime of experience in teaching, union work and local administration, he was more than ready to take on responsibility within government at a national level.

Chapter 7

In the Coalition

On 10 May 1940, Chamberlain resigned as Prime Minister, and Churchill was appointed in his place. Among his junior ministerial appointments, on 15 May he selected Ede, one imagines on Attlee's nomination, to be Parliamentary Secretary to the Board of Education. Amongst the Labour MPs, and probably among all Members, he was supremely qualified for that post. He wrote to Sir Frederick Mander, the General Secretary of the NUT, on 20 May, confirming that the Board was 'a Department with whose broadest aims and highest purposes I am in complete agreement'.[1] Concentrating on this job meant shedding other positions, and he resigned as Chairman of the Electricity Authority,[2] and took unpaid leave from his post as Assistant Secretary of the Surrey County Teachers' Association.[3]

MR H RAMSBOTHAM O.B.E, M.C, P.P.

The President of the Board of Education was Herwald Ramsbotham, newly appointed by Chamberlain in a ministerial reshuffle in April, and for the moment Churchill kept him in post. Ramsbotham had been a Conservative MP since 1929, and served in various junior posts in the National Government under MacDonald, Baldwin and Chamberlain, until his elevation to the Cabinet in his new job. His Parliamentary Secretary had been Kenneth Lindsay, a former Labour supporter who had been elected to Parliament in 1933, backing MacDonald under the National Labour label; this background would count against him when Labour joined

Contemporary caricature of Herwald Ramsbotham. (*By permission of Professor Oliver Ramsbotham*)

Churchill's coalition. We have seen Ede criticise him in debate, and he had also strongly done so in print, accusing him of tolerating 'wilful and flagrant breaking of the law concerning the employment of children.[4]

Views on Ramsbotham vary. While some, such as Barker, imply he was a relatively inactive minister,[5] in Brian Simon's opinion he was already beginning to espouse educational reform in the winter of 1939–40.[6] The following winter, he certainly encouraged his Department to prepare a discussion document on the subject, called *Education after the War*, generally known, from its colour, as the Green Book.

There were several important issues at the time regarding educational change.[7] The school-leaving age was fourteen, and there was widespread support (particularly from Ernest Bevin and others in the Labour Party) that this should be raised to sixteen, with fifteen as an interim arrangement. After the failure of Trevelyan's attempt in 1931, the Education Act 1936 had in fact provided it should be raised to fifteen, effective in September 1939, but the War had prevented that, and many building programmes needed to achieve it were behind schedule.[8] Next, there was a desire to abolish the parallel systems of elementary and secondary schools in the State sector after the age of eleven, a cause which Ede considered very important. Related to that was the question of whether there should be separate schools for pupils with different aptitudes. The Spens Report had argued for the tripartite system, with secondary grammar, secondary technical and secondary modern schools, while others pressed for multilateral, multi-bias or common schools; today's more current term is 'comprehensive', and in discussions on the issue in the late 1940s, the words began to develop distinct meanings, but at this stage the terms were fairly interchangeable. A fourth issue was whether, and if so how, to assimilate the 'public' schools (that is, the independent or private ones) into the national system of education, or indeed whether to abolish them completely. In addition, the 'dual system' of State and religious schools operating side-by-side was causing concern.

The dual system had resulted from the decision in the nineteenth century, when elementary education first became compulsory, for state schools only to fill the gaps where there was no other adequate provision for schooling, which in many cases meant that where a church school existed, no other one was set up. This put the Church of England in a position where it could bid to control much of the school system, with the Catholic Church also having a strong influence in some areas (particularly in urban centres with a significant Irish population). After 1902, the church schools were often financed, at least in part, by the rates, but this did not normally cover upkeep of the buildings, and many were in disrepair. There was widespread pressure to end the system, supported not only by educational specialists, but also by Nonconformists who found they had no realistic option but to educate their children at an Anglican school. The Hadow Report had recommended in 1926 that these arrangements should be reorganised (along with raising the school leaving age and providing secondary education for all children), but little had been done.

The Green Book grew out of work done by an informal committee of civil servants and schools inspectors, which had started meeting in November 1940, under the encouragement of Sir Maurice Holmes, by now the Permanent Secretary to the Board of Education. Holmes was an Oxford-educated barrister, who had not practised, having taken a temporary placement at the Board of Education (his father being an influential school inspector) while waiting to join chambers, and never left. He had worked his way up through the Board, stopping only during the Great War when he reached the rank of Lieutenant-Colonel. He had become Permanent Secretary at the Board two years earlier, and developed a reputation for quiet and discreet work in his field of education.[9]

Ministers were not involved in the Green Book, so neither Ramsbotham nor Ede played a major role in drafting it. In fact, Ede does not seem to have been very busy in his new job, at least in Westminster. During 1940 and until July 1941 he answered fewer than a dozen Parliamentary Questions on behalf of the President, and took part in three debates, mainly about wartime arrangements being made for children, and particularly those being evacuated. He was involved with only one piece of legislation, which came before the Commons in May 1941.

There were pressures for change coming from those involved in education, including the churches, who were concerned with post-war reconstruction, and it is clear that comment in the press was one of Holmes's motivations to get his civil servants working on the issues. R.A. Butler seems to have attributed the active mood for reform to the effect of a letter which appeared in *The Times* on 21 December 1940, though Evans argues that the mood must have predated that.

In the new year, on 22 January 1941, Ede received a visit from Harold Laski, Labour-supporting professor at the London School of Economics.[10] Attlee had asked the two to meet, so that Laski could raise various points about education after the War. One of his issues was that of multilateral schools, commenting that the Spens Committee had really been sympathetic to the concept, but had been reluctant to recommend them in view of the vested interests against them. He also suggested Ede get the Board to seek more publicity for educational topics, and sort out the inconsistent approach of LEAs to financing grants for students. Later events, when he was Prime Minister, would show that Attlee found Ede a much easier colleague than Laski; perhaps he pointed Laski towards the junior minister to defuse unhelpful comments from him.

The following Monday, 27 January, Ede was in Leeds, where he presented prizes and gave a speech at Leeds Modern School. The report of this illustrates his opinion that education in England had been too much stratified socially, and segregated young people into narrow groups, giving them a class outlook and association only with those of similar abilities. Churchill had said the privileges available to only a few should be more widely shared, and the Board of Education intended to further that policy. The leaving age should be increased to fifteen, and the system of education for those over eleven should then be recast.[11]

His visit to Leeds was one of many which he made to different parts of the country during the late winter and spring of 1941, meeting education authorities to find how they were coping. It is not possible to establish every place he visited, but one example was Carmarthenshire, where he noted the secondary schools were quite full; in Ammanford, where there was a large secondary school, children were being taught in a mining college and other buildings, because there was not room in the schools themselves.[12]

The one legislative measure he advanced was the Public and Other Schools (War Conditions) Bill which, having passed through the Lords in March 1941, received its second reading in the Commons on 1 May. It was aimed at helping schools 'meet special difficulties and embarrassments', as Ramsbotham put it, arising from the wartime conditions. Many independent schools had had to carry the cost of evacuation, and had suffered loss of income from reduced numbers. The objective was to permit their funds to be used, subject to government approval, for purposes outside those of the trusts under which they were run, for no longer than the duration of the War. After the President had introduced the Bill, much of the debate was taken up by MPs wanting to criticise the public schools generally, which the Speaker tried to restrain. Ede summed up, accusing Aneurin Bevan, one of the dissidents, of arguing that in no circumstances must endowment funds be diverted. Ede was at pains to mention one of his frequent concerns, that he wanted ancient endowments restored to their original purpose, giving more children from poor backgrounds the opportunity to attend public schools; but the Bill was limited to the exigencies of wartime, and this was not the place to reform a major part of the country's education system. The second reading was easily passed.

The Green Book was presented in draft to Ramsbotham on 13 May. Its main proposals included raising the school leaving age as soon as possible (and without the exemptions for children with a job, permitted by the 1936 Act), establishing primary and secondary as successive stages in education, reforming and expanding the State secondary schools, with a 'common code' of education for all (though in different schools according to the pupils' aptitudes), and abolishing fees in all of the schools. On the religious question, it included denominational education. Much of this derived from the Hadow Report of 1926 which, as we have seen, argued for significant reform leading to distinct secondary education for all. However, Ramsbotham indicated there were some proposals with which he disagreed, and partly for this reason its circulation was restricted. Nonetheless, he made several speeches about this during the summer of 1941, and then issued the Green Book to a number of recipients, on a supposedly confidential basis, though its wide 'restricted' circulation became something of a joke. (It seems that Ede himself was not at this stage included.[13]) He announced that it provided a good basis for action about education post-war.[14]

That discussion was taken up by a good many parties, from whom the Board received more than fifty responses. A summary of those from the LEAs was published in June 1941,[15] a report which mentioned Ede's own tribute to the 'extra work that is being done by Education Authorities all over the country, often in the face of extreme difficulties'. An indication of the views of Ede's own authority, Surrey, was given a year later in a report on the Education Committee's proposals, accepted by the Council:

> The Surrey proposals accept the basis of the Hadow report that there should be a break in continuity of a child's school life at the age of 11 … All Secondary schooling is to be free … What is firmly established is the raising of the school leaving age to 15 without exemptions at the end of the war and to 16 without exemptions as soon as possible thereafter.[16]

It was at this time, on 14 July 1941, that Ede began to keep a diary, on a detailed, almost daily, basis. These comprise some thirteen notebooks, and amount to hundreds of thousands of words. They shed light on his leisure activities as well as his daily routine; he often starts the day by mentioning which train he took from Ewell – or, if he was in the car driven by 'Wiltshire', who it seems was a friendly neighbour, what mishaps befell the vehicle –

and the route he took to Whitehall, Kingston or wherever. The diaries have been used by many historians and biographers to illuminate the period, and on the major personalities in politics during the War years (for they essentially run only to 1945, with brief later reappearances). Those writers, of course, concentrate on their own interests, which may be different from ours. One publication has been based on the diaries, an extract of entries, with introduction and notes, edited by Kevin Jefferys. *Labour and the Wartime Coalition* is an extremely thorough work of scholarship, and an excellent source of detail but, as its title indicates, Jefferys' concern is with the workings of Churchill's Coalition Government, particularly from the viewpoint of its Labour members, and hence his selection of entries concentrates on that. Naturally, the personality of James Chuter Ede, the diarist himself, and the issues surrounding education and his work at the Board, show forth to an extent, but those are not the main areas which interest Jefferys, as they are for us. On the other hand, the diaries provide us with an excellent account of what interested and occupied Ede day by day.

Ede's own comment, when he finished the second volume on 12 December 1941 (that is, after less than five months) was:

> I have tried to set down daily just what happens without any colouring due to personal feelings. This is not easy, and I am only too conscious that in many matters it is quite impossible. The events recorded as occurring on any one day are not necessarily in chronological order with respect to that day, but in every case actually took place on the day to which I have assigned them.

It would be valuable if a researcher could transcribe and annotate them all, but that is an exercise very different, and much more protracted, than writing a life of the diarist. They are of considerable interest precisely because Ede does add colour from his personal feelings. Much of my account in the next pages is based on these diaries; where I mention a date and no other authority, you may normally assume they are my source of information.

This was a fortuitous time to start diarising for, on 21 July 1941, Ramsbotham was removed from his post of President of the Board of Education. The reason, according to some commentators,[17] was that his enthusiasm for a widespread debate based on the Green Book upset Churchill, who wanted no government efforts directed at anything but the war. His ideas, based on the Green Book, might have had a disturbing effect in Conservative circles, which the PM could not risk. Another writer states simply that Ramsbotham 'was not a Churchillian'.[18] Whatever the reason, the two did not gel, and Ramsbotham was soon to be given a peerage, as Lord Soulbury, with a subsequent career much involved in the independence of Ceylon, where he eventually became the last British Governor-General. On 21 July he told Ede that he was sorry he was going, and 'said we had worked well together'. His replacement as President of the Board of Education was Richard Austen Butler.

R.A. Butler – 'Rab', as he was widely known, and I shall often call him – had little experience of educational administration, and certainly none in the state sector. As a boy, by his account,[19] he had expected to get a scholarship to Eton and, on failing this, did not seek a place there, refused to attend Harrow (a school with which his family had connections), and went instead to Marlborough, after which he read Modern Languages and History at Pembroke College, Cambridge, with great success. After a brief spell teaching at Cambridge, he became a Conservative MP at twenty-six (and would hold his seat at Saffron Walden from 1929 to 1965), a Parliamentary Private Secretary at twenty-eight, and a junior minister a year later, in 1932.

So he had considerable experience, but for most of the thirties, and until July 1941, he was at the India Office or the Foreign Office, in both of which areas the government had to deal with fierce opposition from Churchill. This was not an obvious qualification for promoting the cause of state education, nor one for getting a sympathetic ear from the Prime Minister. Indeed, he may have been chosen precisely because he was likely to stick to the administrative tasks related to evacuation – or perhaps because he did not see eye to eye with Eden, Foreign Secretary since December 1940.[20] He was not yet forty, and the most interesting point for us is the relationship he forged with Ede, who was twenty years older, had been involved in education since before Rab was born, and knew the subject through and through. Apart from their time at Cambridge (which in Ede's case had been brief and considerably less distinguished), they had virtually nothing in common. They would, nonetheless, achieve much together.

Initially, though, Ede thought his own position might be in danger. On 20 July he recorded his fear that he might be moved to 'make room for a displaced Tory', and he was surely relieved this did not happen. Then, on the afternoon of 21 July, he was told Butler would be at the office from 3.30, and said he would be available, but the message did not get through; Ede waited till after five, to be told Rab had gone. The next day, though, the new President sent him a note, arranging a meeting, and saying 'I shall rely very much on your experience.' He remained to support Butler, who quickly saw the value of a deputy 'senior in age and experience'. Around the time they both retired from the Commons, Butler gave a speech recalling that, at one of their first meetings, he had been greeted by Ede with the 'double-dutch' questions, 'Do you realise what a difficult task you have? Are you ready to discuss before lunch the abrogation of Cowper-Templeism in the secondary schools as defined in the Spens report?'[21] By reference to the principle banning denominational teaching in local authority schools, Ede gently told him how much he had to learn.

They agreed that each should share all the other's correspondence which they wanted to peruse, and did so, developing an understanding that they would exclude purely party matters. Butler wrote later that Ede had 'been himself a teacher', a remark described by Evans as 'an almost dismissive understatement',[22] though I prefer to see it as testimony of his appreciation. 'I was very lucky, to have this consistently loyal and wise friend as my chief lieutenant'.[23] That was doubtless so; on 15 August 1941, Ede noted that Rab had had to ask, 'What is an elementary school?', and that he had 'not yet grasped the difference between elementary and secondary'.

While these developments were happening, Ede was still busy with his local authority work, especially where it concerned education. On 19 July he met Epsom youth leaders, who were pressing for the Board to have a Youth Department, to provide ideas of projects in which young people could be active, and who were dissatisfied with the standard of history teaching. He then took the Mayor of Epsom's car to watch a sports match between the Armed Forces and Civil Service.

On 23 July he was presiding over a meeting at Epsom Town Hall on juvenile delinquency, and two days later was at a Surrey CC committee in Kingston, noting that evacuee children were streaming back to London. On 26 July he travelled to Brighton, where there were various meetings on education, and on 29 July was in Kingston again, at a Surrey CC meeting.

On 30 July, Lilian came up to Westminster, where she and Jim had tea in the Strangers' Dining Room, and then went on to a reception at the Savoy Hotel, put on by Lord Kemsley, the newspaper

Richard Austen Butler, with whom Ede worked during World War II and beyond.

proprietor, and Lady Kemsley, to meet Dorothy Thompson, a well-known American journalist. Ede noted that a pleasant feature of the day was the genial manner in which the police at the Commons greeted Lilian.

The first weekend in August 1941 was spent partly in walking on the Downs at Epsom. This was their regular refuge from the pressures of the week, provided the schedule permitted it – though often it did not, as we can see from the number of weekends spent visiting South Shields or other places, or carrying out engagements. On this occasion, Friday 1 August had partly been consumed by meetings at County Hall in Kingston, though then Jim and Lilian had taken tea at the Mitre Restaurant, and gone on to the Empire – presumably the ballroom in Leicester Square – where they had been invited to a private show, watching dancers from the Dorchester Hotel. After their weekend back in Epsom, Nell Ede called her brother, to report war damage that had been caused to their properties at 172 East Street and Hawthorne Place; the damage had been financially assessed, and in Jim's view the assessment for Hawthorne Place was excessive.

Ede's familiarity with education from the local authority viewpoint, and his frequent discussions with those on the ground, would have fed into the help he was giving Butler, who had quickly started to develop his ideas about education. On 31 July 1941 Ede told him that he felt an Education Bill could be ready in time for the 1942–43 session of Parliament, and while Rab agreed they should be ready with a timetable, he expressed caution on some points, such as whether some Conservatives might resist raising the school leaving age to sixteen immediately. He wanted to consider the problem further.

An indication of the pressures they were under came on 5 August, when Ede had a visit from 'Mrs M.A. Hamilton', whom I assume to be Molly Hamilton, a writer who had been Labour MP for Blackburn during MacDonald's 1929–31 Government, and was now working for the Ministry of Information (though Hamilton was her maiden name). She had produced notes on the Green Book, which she wanted to discuss. She regarded a school-leaving age of sixteen as inevitable. 'So did I, in the distant future', Ede told her, though that was presumably not the answer she was seeking. She wanted all children to go through the State system free, while he said that parents who could pay more should do so, though he was able to reassure her that he would enquire into how the endowments of the public schools were being used, wanting them not to be available for beneficiaries whose parents could afford the fees. From his diary comments, it is clear he felt the public schools were asking for the impossible; they wanted a grant like that given to the universities, but with no public control over them.

A couple of days later, he met Dr G.F. Morton, an old Cambridge associate, who was finishing off his career as Headmaster of Leeds Modern School, where Ede had distributed the prizes in January. Morton was not at his college, Christ's, so perhaps they read natural sciences together, or were both members of the Liberal Club. They lunched at St Ermin's Hotel in Caxton Street, close to his office, where he noted the Attlee family were at the next table. It is intriguing to speculate, by comparing Morton's career, how the loss of Ede's third year at university might have changed his entire path in life. Had he completed his course, and left with a Cambridge science degree plus a teaching qualification, might he have been swept into the grammar or public school system, and never become involved in NUT or County Council work? Would he then have been commissioned straight into the army in the war, and possibly not survived (as many officers did not) – or if he had, might he have left the army with leadership experience, to put him straight on the path to posts of head of science or headmaster in a major school, such as where Morton finished his career? Would he have moved from his Liberal position towards Labour at all? There is nothing unworthy in such a career, but it would have been a very different one, and probably never have made him a public figure. There is little purpose in hypothetical history, but we might conclude that leaving university early could in the end have dictated the course of his life.

Morton, who was due to retire the following year, wanted to serve on a committee looking into boy emigration to the British dominions. He was no doubt wanting to see what influence Ede could use to achieve that, an instance of the calls made on him to advance people, though one to which little exception could be made in this case. A further attempt to pull strings – one rather less innocent – occurred on 8 August 1941, when one of Ede's contacts discussed with him the failure of his granddaughter to get into the North London Collegiate School. In response, Ede telephoned the school, and got the head mistress out of a meeting, attempting to get the matter fixed.

At the same time, he was preparing a paper he was to deliver to a Co-operative school conference. This involved a trip to Bangor in North Wales, again taking up considerable time on the railway. He left Ewell at 8.24 on 10 August, a Sunday, reaching his hotel in the early evening, and presenting his paper on the Monday. He then managed to take some time off, to visit Anglesey and take part in a game of bowls. After another night away, he caught a train back on Tuesday morning, and noted he was back home by 5.30 that afternoon.

Of all the issues relating to education at the time, there is little doubt that the trickiest related to religion, and to the 'dual system' which, as we have seen, had characterised arrangements since 1870. As soon as 23 July, Butler had spoken to the Archbishop of Canterbury about five points which the churches had developed together earlier in the year, namely that:

- A Christian education should be given to children at all state and voluntary schools.
- Religious instruction (RI) should become a full, though optional, subject in training colleges.
- RI should not be restricted to the first or last lesson of the day.
- HM Inspectors should inspect religious teaching as they did other subjects.
- All schools should start the day with an act of worship.

The Archbishop, Cosmo Gordon Lang, was now nearly eighty. He had been a bishop for forty years, originally with a somewhat radical reputation, though was now a more conservative figure. His talk with Rab was to prepare them each for a meeting on 15 August 1941, when Butler and Ede received the Archbishops of both English provinces and of Wales, and a group including a high profile Methodist, Scott Lidgett, and others from the Free Churches, thirty-three people in all. They pressed the government to support the five points, and Ede advised Butler not to make any commitment about them which might be independent from other reforms.[24] Butler took that advice, and subsequently attributed his success at resolving the religious question to doing so.[25] Ede told the meeting that, with public sympathy for religious education running high, it was the time to reach agreement. Archbishop Lang continued to press the case for RI to be a compulsory subject, but this was resisted at this point, and he was in any case to notify his retirement in the autumn. Holmes had described Lang to Ede before the meeting 'as an old cynic who didn't come for the religious issues in the matter at all'. When Rab surprisingly asked the Archbishop to end the meeting with a prayer, he 'said it was the first time he had ever been asked to pray in a government department. He mumbled a collect.' Ede's final shot was, 'I gathered ... no prayers were offered when he and Baldwin brought about the abdication.'

Ede's personality is generally characterised by a humble modesty, but his diaries show he did take pride in his achievements. On 16 August, his father's birthday, he mused about his parents. He felt fate had been generous to his father, by taking him (in his early eighties) before the 'disastrous nature of the Peace' had become known, but he regretted he had not seen him become an MP; his mother had lived to see that, but sadly she had been taken a year before Jim became a minister of the Crown, though in her case she would have found the Second World War 'a terrible trial'. That Saturday, he went on to a bowls match at Ewell, where in a speech after tea he waxed lyrical about life and the war struggle to those attending. On Sunday, it was to Chertsey, to inspect the Epsom and Ewell Officers' Training Corps and attend a church parade with the cadets.

The Edes took a holiday in Brecon at the end of August, taking trains each way, and finding rewards in the Welsh countryside, just as they did in Surrey. It was a 'restful, happy holiday, certainly equal to the best we have ever previously had'. Work did not let up entirely, though. He kept track of political and war news in the papers, and did occasional pieces of paperwork. He noted that the hotel charged him less than he had expected, 16/6d a day – a little less than £50 today.

He was straight back to education work on his return. Problems included an expected failure in the supply of bottles for school milk, and the provision of mugs for all children in consequence. He was discussing a 10 per cent increase in grants to the LEAs, with a particular stress on providing school meals – the Board was hoping to get a million children into the school meal system. At lunchtime on 3 September he and Lilian went to Downing Street, where they were entertained by the Churchills, along with his Labour colleague, the First Lord of the Admiralty, A.V. Alexander, and Kenneth Clark, Director of the empty National Gallery – the paintings having been sent for safety in Wales – who was working for the Ministry of Information, all with their wives, and three other guests. They lunched in the new basement dining room, recently reinforced against attack. Churchill announced that this was the largest party held in the room. Ede was taken with Mary Churchill, the PM's youngest daughter, who was joining the ATS a couple of days later, to start training for anti-aircraft work. He in turn amused Churchill who, criticizing the Admiralty and speaking about gun capacity, asked what 9 times 23 was; Ede quickly answered 207, at which he was told, 'My Professor Lindemann' – his scientific adviser – 'would have wanted a slide rule for that!'

The next weekend he was on his travels again, this time to Merseyside. He was collected from Lime Street station on the evening of 5 September and, driving to his hotel in Wallasey, noted how badly bombed that town was. The following day, a Saturday, he visited the town and some of its schools, making a speech he had prepared during the week. With the mayor and others he went to the cinema, and noted a conversation he had with the town clerk's teenage son, worried about his Cambridge career, his military service and post-war prospects. Ede took the train back on the Sunday, and saw some evidence of the bombing in Coventry as he passed through.

Meeting at the Board again on 8 September, he learnt from Butler that, in his view, the experiences of evacuation had removed many of the objections to residential schools. While that might have helped the task of integrating the public boarding schools into the national system, Rab's regret was that those schools were not distributed geographically, so it would not be possible to use them as some had hoped.

Another lunch at St Ermin's found Ede at the same table as a man called Davidge, one of the Surrey town planning officers, with whom he had a useful conversation, combining his local authority and educational concerns. He was a firm supporter of effective town and country planning, believing that public ownership of land – both municipal and national – should increase, but otherwise with owners left in possession, subject to very effective public control. He stressed to Davidge the importance of remembering education in the early stages of planning the country's reconstruction.

Further special pleading came on 11 September 1941 from a governor of Cranleigh School, Sir Douglas Hacking, who was concerned that the Admiralty might take over the school premises. Ede knew something of Cranleigh, having been a governor himself while Chairman of Surrey CC between 1933 and 1937. While he did what he could to oblige, he recorded that the school had a mortgage secured against its buildings, but that these were valueless except as part of a school in operation, and that the governors had failed in their attempt to get power to mortgage the capital of its scholarship funds. He was pessimistic about the school's future, and thought it might have to consent to being taken over. In the climate of the time, many public schools were considered candidates for acquisition by the State, bearing in mind their financial position, deteriorating since the Depression, but in fact most of them recovered in the 1940s, and Cranleigh survived and prospered.

Ede then made one of his relatively rare visits to his parliamentary constituency in South Shields. His diaries are the only source we have to clarify how often he made this trip, but in view of the length of time involved, and his other commitments, it was not very frequently; in those days, of course, constituency demands placed on MPs were far less than are expected today. When he went, it was normally for a weekend, and his agent, Gompertz, a South Shields Councillor, would arrange for a series of engagements about local affairs, leaving hardly any time for meeting constituents, which nowadays might be considered the main purpose of a visit. There might be a single constituents' 'surgery', to use the modern term – or there might not be. He had no home in his constituency, as would be normal today; he booked into an hotel. He was, however, seen as someone who, a Cambridge-educated southerner, added respectability to Labour locally. So he was received in some state, the stationmaster at South Shields literally laying out a red carpet when he knew their MP was on the expected train.[26] Ede seems to have visited South Shields five times in the year between September 1941 and August 1942, and there is no reason to suspect this was other than normal, even bearing in mind it was wartime and he had ministerial business to occupy him.

On this occasion, Gompertz had been in London on the weekend of 9 August. Ede had gone into town to meet him, to plan the constituency visit; they also discussed school meals in South Shields. When the day came, he went with Lilian on the Friday, 12 September, catching the 9.50 train from King's Cross, and reached the constituency in time to have tea with the Mayor; they would have had to change trains at Newcastle. He then attended a meeting of the Council's Education Committee until 7.30, went to their hotel, and had dinner there, while a dance for soldiers and the ATS was in progress. On the Saturday morning, he received a deputation from the local Temperance Council, and then met an officer from the Ministry of Labour named Jamieson. They lunched at a restaurant, where the food was 'very plentiful but coarse' – was this a comment on rationing, or northern tastes from a southerner, or both? While Lilian called on Mrs Gompertz, he went to the Labour Hall to see some constituents. He learnt that three South Shields men on air raid precaution duty had lost two or three weeks' pay, through being ordered to return to mining, for which they had then been declared unfit, and he agreed to press for payment of this. He then received a deputation from First Aid Posts and Rescue Squads about their conditions, finishing at 5.30 in the afternoon. On the Sunday, he and Lilian took the morning off, and walked around the town, before having lunch. He was then driven to a party meeting, noting that his car knocked down a small boy, whose father refused any help. So Ede left his card with the man, and reported the accident to the police. The party meeting went well, as far as the war and the government were concerned; there were no signs of defeatism, or distrust of the country's leadership. However, there were clear local antagonisms among the members. They next went to Newcastle, where there was a meeting at City Hall, addressed by Clement Attlee, who was in town; one suspects that was the reason for choosing this weekend for the trip. They stayed at an hotel in Newcastle, from where on Monday 15 September they caught the 9.50 train, reaching London at 4.32 that afternoon – with his usual attention to detail, Ede noted it was 22 minutes late.

Back at the office, he had a quiet week, though on 17 September he met his Surrey colleague John Strudwick, who wanted to know the chances of the denominational issues being settled. They also discussed the possibility of a war bonus being paid to teachers. Strudwick then drove him to a meeting of the Sutton and District Teachers' Association, where Ede spoke on the subject of fifty years of education in the district.

On 19 September 1941 he made an overnight trip, via Derby, to Burton-on-Trent, where he opened a Junior Technical School. Burton is a brewing town, and Ede was offered a bottle of Bass which, as a virtual teetotaller, certainly abstaining at work, he politely declined – which caused the Mayor some surprise. The two teased each other about their respective towns. The Mayor said the famous product of Burton would be emblazoned on windows throughout the world, but Ede replied that the only one more famous came from Epsom, where there was a well (in the grounds of the place where his own father was born) whose product was known worldwide, and whose name did not need to be on windows. That evening he took the opportunity to address the local Teachers' Association, and he got home the following day, a Saturday, when he and Lilian went up on Epsom Downs again. On the Sunday, he was on a further overnight trip to Newport, in Monmouthshire, to address a meeting there.

With some satisfaction, he was able to note the following week that the three South Shields men, whose case he had taken up when they lost pay, were to be paid by the colliery the difference between their miners' wages and their unemployment benefit.

In September, Ede outlined the Board of Education's thinking about educational reform to Attlee, while Rab approached Churchill. Butler's efforts were not rewarded. He had decided the Green Book covered too narrow a canvas, and that, as well as the religious problem, two other issues needed addressing, first the relation of education to industry and training, and secondly the public schools. On writing to the PM on 12 September, he received a reply the next day, to the effect that they could not contemplate a new Education Bill during the war, and it would be a mistake to stir up the religious and public schools questions.[27] Butler claimed not to be dismayed by this, but it was clear that Churchill was expecting them to deal with the problems of wartime and do little else. As an illustration of this, the sole memorandum which Churchill quotes in his war memoirs as sent to Butler asks how many boys 'leave the public elementary schools at 15', going into industry, employment, munitions, the cadet corps, and so on.[28] Attlee, on the other hand, told Ede that the government should decide what it wanted to do and put an Education Bill together – partly to challenge a proposal from Rab that a Select Committee should be set up.

One committee established at this stage was chaired by Sir Cyril Norwood, the President of St John's College, Oxford, and previously headmaster of Marlborough when Butler was a pupil there, and then of Harrow. The remit of his enquiry related to the curriculum and examinations in secondary schools (indeed, its members were constituted as a subcommittee of the Secondary School Education Council) but, as we shall see, two years later Norwood made recommendations which went far beyond his brief.

After further committee meetings at County Hall in Kingston on 26 September, and a further discussion on the perpetual subject of juvenile delinquency, Ede went on his next excursion, this time to Devon. One of HM Inspectors, Dr Platts, met him off the train at Exeter, and drove him to Torquay, where he inspected a school, and spoke to representatives from LEAs in the county. He looked at a school in Newton Abbot, which was being used for evacuation purposes, but was closed for potato picking, on 29 September, noting it was the fourth anniversary of Epsom and Ewell's incorporation as a borough. At Dawlish, he spoke to the session of a course on Rural Life for Teachers.

As is clear, his work kept him more than occupied in London, in Surrey, and in the range of places he visited in England and Wales, with only occasional contact with his constituency. This must have been particularly difficult when news came, as it did at the start of October 1941, of an air raid on South Shields, in which he first heard that some fifty had been killed. That number was later reduced to twenty-seven and, a day later, to eleven, though with ninety-seven injured. A power station had been hit, and the railway line from Newcastle cut. The final report made it clear that North Shields had suffered a heavier blow, but another raid two nights later hit the Town Hall at South Shields, cutting the railway again, and damaging two ship-repairing yards. This time there were seventy fatalities, with 300 injured. All Ede could do was write a letter of sympathy to the Mayor. It must have been frustrating to know what was going on at such a distance, but be able to do little to support those on whom he relied for his place at Westminster.

In October, there was discussion about government duties being reorganised, and on 8 October Butler told Ede 'he must retain me as Parliamentary Secretary in the Commons. I knew the administrative side of the work; I had contacts which he regarded as valuable; he could not face a debate without my help.' He protested that he was not in love with office, and would do anything he was asked in the Commons, but in 'no circumstances would I go to the House of Lords'. That sounds an interesting comment in view of his ultimate destination in politics, but his arrival in the Lords would be well over twenty years later, in at least extremely different circumstances, of genuine retirement in old age.

Surrey matters took priority again at the weekend of 11–12 October. First, he drafted a letter to the Lord Lieutenant, recommending a number of new magistrates. Then Lilian and Jim were driven in the Epsom Borough car to lunch at the Town Hall, where he addressed the inaugural meeting of the Epsom Auxiliary Youth Corps. Among the guests was the Olympic runner, Harold Abrahams, who was employed at the Ministry of Economic Warfare. When the habit of timing speeches (and sometimes holding a sweepstake on their length) was first initiated is not known, but it was a new and amusing experience for Ede, to be told by Abrahams that he had spoken for 16 minutes and 11 seconds – 'the first time I have been checked by a stop-watch', though an occurrence frequent enough for the athlete, of course. On the Sunday, the Edes entertained a friend to lunch, and then took the train to Box Hill station, from where they walked to Leatherhead, passing under the extension to the town's by-pass, where it crosses the River Mole, at the time carried by

Tayles Hill, Ewell, the home of the Edes for most of their later lives (as it is now, with later addition to the left). (© *Stephen Hart*)

a temporary bridge constructed by the Canadian Royal Engineers – a project to keep the troops occupied.

On 13 October 1941 Ede had another meeting with Harold Laski, which covered teacher training, public schools, the school-leaving age, and multilateral schools. They both agreed they believed in the multilateral schools, and Ede 'thought in the small towns of England the multilateral school would find itself'. Laski said the Labour Party would accept a school-leaving age of only fifteen, as long as a date for increasing it to sixteen was fixed, within a period of three years at the most. Ede was more realistic; the amount of rebuilding would require a five year period as a minimum.

The diary's lyricism about Surrey, and pride in his achievements, reached a peak on 8 November. He and Lilian took a bus to Mickleham Corner, on the side of Box Hill, and then took a long walk through the countryside. There was autumn tree-felling going on, and he recalled the verse, 'Woodman, spare that tree', which he misattributed to Wordsworth (it is in fact by a rather lesser poet, an American, George P Morris). They looked at the 'meadows at the corner of where the Headley Road runs into the main road', which had been preserved for all time, as they had been sold with severe restrictions against development, and the 'beautiful surroundings of the Mole, in the preservation of which I can claim to have taken the leading part. But for my energetic action', he said, a speculative builder named Ansell would have taken it, and it would have been vandalised like the amenities on the Leatherhead to Guildford road in the villages of Fetcham and Great Bookham. They went on to Druid's Grove, noting that, with its surrounds, it had been bought by Surrey CC, and was managed by the Box Hill Management Committee, the National Trust having declined to take it because of the insufficient income it produced. In fact the Trust had already owned some land in the area for over twenty years, and bought more during the rest of the century. The entire area is now part of the Surrey Hills Area of Outstanding Natural Beauty, which was designated in 1958, doubtless with Ede's approval, while he was still in the Commons.

Chapter 8

A Strategy for Education

Back in Parliament, on Tuesday 18 November 1941 the debate on the King's Speech was subject to a proposed amendment, that greater recognition should be given to the role of religious education. At Butler's request, Ede responded to this debate, while Lilian and a friend were in the Gallery, though he said he had to jettison half the speech he had rehearsed with Butler. He covered many of the Archbishops' five points, by assuring the Commons that the President of the Board was supportive of the religious lobby, though enacting the necessary legislation to implement them was another question. He pointed out that nearly all schools did start their day with an act of worship (though varying in quality), and expressed a fear that, if RI was made compulsory, some schools might lower their standards, rather than raise them. His main thrust, however, was that the Board took a positive approach to the issues. Butler phoned him that evening to express his gratitude.

That Saturday, 22 November, the congratulations continued. Though it was a typical working weekend, with a train journey to Dartford, to address a rally of Youth Service workers meeting at a girls' county school, Ede heard a eulogy on his speech broadcast on the radio from Major Maxwell Fyfe. He said that, to MPs who remembered him 'as the wielder of a humorous bludgeon on the Opposition benches', Ede's performance from the government box 'was an education in itself'. Maxwell Fyfe would shortly become Solicitor-General, and then go on to follow Ede as Home Secretary ten years later, before rising to be Lord Chancellor, but at this stage he combined being a Liverpool MP with a post as a legal officer in the army. Ede had also read a complimentary leader in *The Times*, mentioning both him and Butler, and encouraging them to produce a large scheme of educational reform.

A problem to this was, nevertheless, the lack of agreement among the parties, and even sometimes within the same church, on how the 'religious question' might be resolved. The Green Book had proposed that there should be a common approach to RI, with reserved teachers to cover the topic, and Lang favoured that, though he made it clear that some of his bishops wanted a more denominational approach to the subject. Many Nonconformists wanted at most non-denominational teaching in the Anglican schools their children often attended, while the Catholic preference was to retain their own schools and give a firmly Catholic education. As to the politicians, many Conservatives were strong supporters of the Anglican position (or one of them), some Labour MPs were sensitive to the Catholic stance, in view of their local vote, and others on both sides wanted to end the dual system completely, in line with the general approach of the educational professionals. At the same time, all the churches pleaded financial problems when it came to keeping their schools in good repair (though it was questionable whether that was accurate in the case of the Catholics, in view of the church's wealth, and its employment of those under vows of poverty). The churches were looking for assistance.[1] It was clear that improving buildings was one of the requirements for improving the country's education.

On 26 November Ede and Butler went to lunch with the Polish ambassador. Ede was due to sit next to a Polish academic, but he was ill, and instead in the next seat was Lord Cecil of Chelwood, son of Prime Minister Salisbury, who had been an MP in 1923, before he left the Commons in disillusion with the Conservatives. Cecil did not initially recall Ede from that time. He politely asked if he spoke Polish or English, and Ede put him right by answering that he spoke no Polish, and his English had been criticised at times. He reminded him they had sat opposite each other, during their few months in the House together, when Cecil had defended the Home Secretary, Bridgeman, who had been challenged in the House for breaching the Statute of Praemunire. Cecil, who had already won the Nobel Peace Prize for his work with the League of Nations, commented, 'How far off all that seems'. Ede would hear from Cecil again, when he himself had become Home Secretary.

On the first weekend of December 1941, Ede paid a visit to Barrow-in-Furness, where he stayed with the Town Clerk, his wife and newly-born daughter. He commented that the only help they had was from a family billeted on them – the mother of the family did the cooking and some housework. The Town Clerk was also giving hospitality to the manager of a local steel works whose home had been destroyed. After dinner, they met the Mayor and others, and then looked in at a ball with which the Local Youth Committee was closing its Youth Week. The next day he went to Duddon Hall in the old county of Cumberland, to where a nursery school had been evacuated. Returning to Barrow, he addressed the Youth Week's final rally, a 'great audience of keen young people', and went back to London the following day. In the dark early morning, the train was subject to a blackout, with blinds down, as far as Preston; there he discovered frost on the ground as far as Warrington, and after that, snow.

It is interesting that, even when he was in the North of England, less than 100 miles from South Shields, there was, it seems, no question of his combining a constituency visit with his ministerial duties. He could see the tribulations of the ports and shipbuilders, selected for bombing by the Germans, in Barrow and Merseyside as much as on the Tyne, where he knew similar things were happening. South Shields was, nonetheless, out of reach.

Just before Christmas, Ede was able to assure John Strudwick that a handicraft teacher, whom he wanted to be regarded as on war service as a munitions worker, would exceptionally be granted that status. Then, on Christmas Eve, he noted it was his brother Noel's birthday, without any further comment, and he reviewed the problems of the shortages which the country was suffering. Lilian had used the first of her clothing coupons on some stockings, and there was difficulty getting books. They could find a bottle of sherry, to break their abstinence for the festivities, but it cost 14 shillings, while before the war it would have been 5/6 – perhaps £40, as against £15, today.

The Prime Minister had gone for Christmas to the USA, newly joined as an ally after the Japanese attack on Pearl Harbor on 7 December 1941, and Jim and Lilian were able to listen on the radio to Churchill and Roosevelt lighting the Christmas tree in Washington. She had made a plum pudding, which they ate after a chicken bought locally, and he recalled Christmases of old, in terms I have already described. Civic duties imposed themselves quite quickly; on 29 December, Ede was sitting on the Bench as a JP. The most interesting case, he found, was that of 'Fred', of Upper Court Road, Epsom, charged with stealing two tons of sugar from the Epsom Grandstand, in use as a Ministry of Food store; a diary footnote records that Fred was discharged at the Quarter Sessions, where he managed to establish an alibi.[2]

Immediately in the new year Ede paid another weekend visit to South Shields. The next days were taken up with routine problems, some arising from the wartime conditions. Sir Percy Hurd, the MP for Devizes, had written to him about a rural school in Aldbourne, for which no cleaner could be found, and which had therefore closed. Ede and Butler thought the senior girls at the school might have to be persuaded to do the cleaning on a rota. There should be no exceptions, though some would surely object strongly – not presumably on grounds of sex stereotyping, but because they would not see it as their duty.

The main subject which 1942 brought to the fore was the public schools. The Bishop of London, Geoffrey Fisher, who chaired the Governing Bodies Association, arranged to bring his committee to discuss these with Butler on

14 January, and sent a note to the Board in advance. Ede commented on this on 9 January, and four days later produced a note with his observations on the position of the public schools.[3] Together with G.G. Williams, the Principal Assistant Secretary responsible for this area, he resisted the Bishop's proposals regarding the dangers of external control on the independent sector, and the consequent suggestion that the Board centrally should provide scholarships to public schools. He was aware that, in Surrey, both Kingston Grammar School and King's College School had sought help from the County Council in times of financial stress, and that Charterhouse was now negotiating about forming a Junior School. As he had said before, the corollary to state financial help was more state control. He was wary of the subject weakening the political cooperation in the Coalition, considering what he could sell to the Labour Party, and thought little of the argument that parents value education more if they have paid for it themselves. From Rab's viewpoint, though, the Conservative Party 'would be up in arms unless a boy could get into a public school on payment'. Fisher's proposals would have covered preparatory schools also, which Ede saw as private businesses that should not be supported with state funds.

While these discussions were going on in Whitehall, Ede was also focusing on the other questions of the day in Surrey where, on 19 January 1942, he attended the County Education Committee's Future Policy Committee, which agreed in principle that the school leaving age should rise to fifteen, and then to sixteen as soon as possible, and that, rather than different types of school, there should be a single multilateral school provided for all. This ran counter to much thinking at the Board, as well as that of the Spens Committee and others, including some Unions, as Ede knew already, and would find out in more detail shortly.

The same month, Rab saw a delegation from the Workers Educational Association, pressing him for 'common schools' (ie comprehensives which would incorporate the private schools) and, having learnt that the Liberal Party also supported these, he asked Ede (and Holmes) on 26 January for their views. While Butler felt there was much to be said for such schools, he doubted that Parliament would support them. Ede's reply[4] was that the case was unanswerable 'in an ideal world in which lice and skin troubles had been eliminated', but do we have 'the moral right to compel a parent to send his child from a clean, healthy home to a school where lousy, scabrous children attend?' In practice, one school in an area develops a reputation (perhaps unfounded) as a 'posh' school, and hence becomes more popular. Preventing all this would involve significantly reducing parental choice. The issue was a social and political question, not just an educational or financial one.

After a further visit to South Shields on the weekend of 23 to 25 January, Ede found himself two days later at the funeral at Wimbledon Cemetery of A.E. Baxter, 'my stalwart supporter' and friend for over twenty years, who had helped him so much in his early days in local and national politics. He believed Baxter had come to South Shields for every election he fought there. The Surrey County Teachers' Association was represented there by John Strudwick and another official, W.H. Spearing, and they had a discussion about pay at the Surrey Evening Institute.

Although Butler normally seemed sanguine about his abilities to move the religious issue forward, he sometimes had his doubts. On 29 January 1942, Ede described him as 'despondent', asking if they could not by-pass the issue. Ede replied that 'we could not. The bad state of the Church school buildings blocked all educational advance.' Asked on 30 January whether they were 'justified in pursuing negotiations without the PM's consent' to legislation, Ede argued strongly in favour of drafting an Education Bill, whether or not it became possible to introduce it. He realised there were difficult problems to resolve – particularly relating to the dual system and the state of school buildings – but resolving them was essential to make any progress.

While these concerns were being addressed, a strange incident happened to Ede, which might have risked his own career. On 4 February 1942, he was summoned to meet Churchill. Butler warned him, before he went, that 'his Gestapo' had told him Ede was to be given a post in another Department. He told Rab he would try to dissuade the PM, 'if I was allowed to speak', which Butler described as 'very noble', saying he would probably be bullied, and getting Holmes to give support. When he arrived, Churchill told him he was appointing a Minister of Production (who was in fact Beaverbrook) and in consequence was shuffling his ministers; he would like Ede to move to the Ministry of War Transport where, as deputy to a minister who was in the Lords, he would have responsibility for the brief in the Commons – a small promotion, therefore, with more prestige. With kid gloves, Ede explained that education had been his life's work, delicate negotiations were in train and, if a new Parliamentary Secretary had to start from scratch at Education, the work might be put at risk. He was grateful for the PM's recognition, and was of course at his disposal, but felt he could contribute best if he stayed put.

One suspects that what swung the matter in Ede's favour was Churchill's admission that Butler himself had wanted him not to be moved. The PM had intended to bring Philip Noel-Baker into the government, by giving him Ede's post, and seems to have agreed on that with Attlee, whom he now tried, without success, to reach by phone. While they were waiting for

Attlee to be reached, time passed, and the two men discussed Russia, Libya, Pearl Harbor, whether Japan should be bombed, and indeed education. The Prime Minister was pleased the public schools were getting attention, and said that 60 per cent to 70 per cent of places should be filled by bursaries, not by examination alone – the ruling class must be reinforced, not chosen by accident of birth or wealth, but 'by accident of ability'. Eventually the phone conversation between those involved occurred, and it was settled that Noel-Baker would go to War Transport and Ede stay at Education. According to Ede, Churchill 'shook hands & said he knew I only wanted to serve the cause & the country', so his stand had worked. He received support when he lunched, in particular from Ernest Brown, the Minister of Health, who led the Liberal Nationals in the Commons after 1940, when John Simon had moved to the Lords. He was also flattered by Butler himself – when Ede said he thought he was the only man to refuse to move from the Board, Rab countered that he was the only one who had resisted Churchill's wish to move him, an even greater distinction.

The next trip away from London was to Stoke-on-Trent, on 15–16 February 1942. Ede went with Florence Horsbrugh, a Scottish Conservative who was his opposite number at the Ministry of Health, by the Sunday train. They discussed a plan which was afoot, to replace Churchill as PM with Stafford Cripps (that, of course, came to nothing), and next day met the 'unimpressive' Lord Mayor and the Town Clerk, before visiting a small house converted to a war nursery. The building was small, stuffy and cold and, despite the bright young teacher in charge, 'the children had dull eyes'. Then on to a school with nursery classes, where the rooms were large and airy, and the children 'responsive and bright'. Ede was able to use his own classroom experience to pick up details and to confirm, or develop, his ideas of what best practice in education should be – and then to pass this on to his colleagues. Before returning to London, they lunched with the Lord Mayor, off exquisite chinaware supplied by the great firms in the Potteries, and had a conference with other local authorities in the area.

Although Ede was suffering from a bad cold by the time he got back, and spent some days in bed, he was able to appreciate a letter from Fred Mander of the NUT, to whom he had written reporting the job offer from Churchill, saying he was thankful he was remaining at the Board of Education, although 'it may be that you have "missed the step" on the way to much higher office'. Mander's speculation would turn out to be wrong.

Recovered by the weekend of 21 February, Ede joined the annual meeting of the Surrey County Teachers' Association, and prevailed on Butler to speak there. It was held in Sutton, at the West Boys Central School, chaired by W.H. Spearing, and in the course of the debate he opposed a Communist resolution about the future of education. He went with Edward Britton – a future General Secretary of the NUT, but then the local delegate from Guildford – to collect Butler from the station, in time for lunch together, and then heard Rab's speech.

On the religious question, Butler called a meeting on 26 February, with Ede and Holmes, as well as R.S. Wood, the Deputy Secretary to the Board, and William Cleary, the Principal Assistant Secretary in charge of the Elementary Education Branch. Ede insisted that, if the Churches were given all they wanted on the religious question, there would be no settlement in other important areas, such as making higher education a duty of LEAs, and raising the school leaving age. It would also be harder to deal with the 'Part III Authorities', a number of the larger municipal boroughs and urban districts with responsibility for elementary education under that Part of the Education Act 1902, alongside the counties and county boroughs which covered all state education under Part II. This was an anomaly Ede and others desired to end.

As Ede's thoughts developed on these points, he exchanged notes with Butler, Holmes and Cleary, which resulted in a document known as the White Memorandum, for which Rab in his memoirs gave Ede the main credit. This offered alternative approaches, under the chief of which the Anglican Church would hand over control of its schools to the LEAs, in those areas where there was a single school. The LEA would then have to keep each school in good repair, and have full use of the buildings, other than on Sundays and at other times when they were not required, when the school would be at the Church's disposal; the LEA would control staff appointment. RI would be to the Authority's agreed syllabus, with no denominational instruction or reserved teachers. Where more than one school existed, the Church would have this option, but alternatively it could seek a grant of half the building costs, finding the rest itself, and retain control of RI, which could be denominational, as well as of recruitment of teachers.

This was a solution which appealed to Nonconformists like Ede, as it would ease their problem of parents in single-school areas. It was also approved by the teachers, such as those in the NUT, who disliked appointments made on a sectarian basis, and were keen to maintain (and extend to secondary schools) the Cowper-Temple Clause – the provision in the Education Act 1870, named after its sponsor, which banned denominational teaching in board schools, and had been perpetuated in subsequent legislation. Many on the Liberal and Labour side of politics followed those views. Between Ede and the NUT there was mutual support. George Thomas, a Methodist Welsh teacher, who would subsequently become a Labour MP, cabinet minister, and Speaker of the Commons, said fifty years later that the NUT 'leaned on Chuter for much advice. They wanted to get as much into the Act[5] as they could'. At a meeting in which he participated on 19 March 1942, with the Association of Education Committees, Ede proposed the two options to address the religious issue, and felt his solution was well-received. Shortly after, he explained to Maurice Holmes that his own party colleagues would expect him to demonstrate advances in his own field, in the face of doubts as to whether their presence in the coalition was correct.[6]

For the Church of England, however, it was a different matter. It had been announced on 23 February that Archbishop Lang was being replaced by William Temple who, as Archbishop of York, had already been playing a major role in the discussions, and who was a known Labour sympathiser and a likely reformer. Ede, though, when told on 21 January that Lang was retiring, said he had been disappointed by Temple in the meetings they had held, and would have preferred Bishop Garbett of Winchester for the Primacy (Garbett in fact became Archbishop of York). Temple was sent a copy of the White Memorandum on 1 April, the very day he was officially in his new post, but it was soon clear from talks with him, which Rab started on 9 April, that the Church could not go along with the idea that the village schools would cease to be Church schools, and Bishop Fisher (who would in due course become Temple's successor) wrote in strong terms to Butler against it, causing some offence to Ede.[7] Rab, a Anglican Conservative himself, quickly saw that it would not succeed. Nonetheless, he worked for several months 'with much patience and experimentation' to find a solution, or at least a compromise, which would satisfy all interested parties, and here the mutual goodwill between Temple and the Ministers was crucial. In the discussions, to produce the solution (eventually presented as part of the Education Bill), Ede took a back seat, though he was by no means an absentee.

Further trips away from London took place during the weekends of 28 February 1942, to Wolverhampton and the Black Country, and 14 March, to Gloucester, and we then find an amusing entry in Ede's diary for 17 March. He asked Geoffrey Lloyd, a Birmingham Conservative who was Minister for Petroleum, if he could have 'petrol for my motor boat'. Lloyd's response was that he would get it only if used for essential purposes, which must have put it out of the question. Ede kept a boat on the Thames, and there are many photos of him wearing a flat naval cap, which mostly date from the post-War period, but he had acquired a boat in the 1930s,[8] and probably recognised he might joke about fuel supply, but would have to sacrifice his hobby for the duration of the War.

His next visit away was to Derby, on 21 March, where he met the Deputy Mayor, the Head of Amber Valley Camp School (to where Derby School had been evacuated), and others including the Bishop. He spoke to the school, and handed out prizes, but was particularly struck by the Bishop's view, with which he did not concur, about selecting bright children very young. They should 'start Greek at eight', said the Bishop, leaving Ede concerned about the attitude in some quarters over selection in the education system. He had the consolation that, Derby being a railway town with fine connections, this was only a day trip, but he stored the conversation in mind till he saw Rab and repeated it to him. Butler 'said the Bishops were stupid. He despaired of the Bishops. I said too many of them came from Oxford. He said it would be a good thing to abolish Oxford.'

A new experience for him, though one which is routine for a politician today, occurred on 27 March, when he gave a radio broadcast. His subject was 'the registration of girls'.[9] He had prepared a script in advance, and he went to the BBC that afternoon to discuss and practise it. He took 3 minutes 27 seconds – after the incident with Abrahams he must have been used to a stopwatch – and was told it sounded like reading. He accepted the professionals' suggestions for a second try, and was then told three times in the recording room that his voice was too soft. The microphone was moved nearer, and he made the final recording, taking 3 minutes 31 seconds. When it was played back, he was astonished at his voice, as were many at that time when they first heard themselves. The broadcast was due to go out at 9.00 pm, but was moved to the 6.00 news; Lilian heard it and said he had come through well. The next day, a Saturday, he went to a funeral in Guildford, where several people said they had heard it, and he sounded as though he was talking to them in the same room.

Before and after the appointment at the BBC, Ede spent time with Fred Mander. Mander said that they should spend more time together, to which Ede, perhaps unhelpfully, said it was not his fault they failed to do so; after two interviews in 1941, Mander had not kept in touch with him. Bailey[10] has suggested that, with little evidence that they did keep more in touch after this, it may be symptomatic of Ede's character that he was not good at maintaining contacts with the NUT or with other organisations which might have furthered his objectives.

A further prize-giving took place at Banbury School on 31 March – or, more accurately, presentation of certificates, prizes having been suspended for the duration of the War. At lunch, Ede typically drank ginger beer, while the others had beer. He was amused to note that when he said 'a few seconds of glory was purchased by a year's hard work … I used to think it really wasn't worth while,' the pupils, led by the girls, broke into hearty applause. He liked, as he said on other occasions, to be on the side of the underdog.

Ede's path crossed again with his Cambridge colleague – if that is a fair description – Maynard Keynes, who on 1 April became Chairman of the Council for the Encouragement of Music and the Arts (CEMA). This was a Board of Education position, although credit for the appointment was given to Butler personally by both Ede, who described it as 'a great score' when it was announced,[11] and by Keynes's own biographer.[12] CEMA had been set up by the Board in 1940, was working hard to keep the performing arts going in wartime conditions in distant parts of the country, and would eventually develop into the Arts Council of Great Britain when Ede was in the Cabinet in 1946 (though by then Keynes would be dead).

In April 1942, the NUT held its Annual Conference in Westminster, and on 9 April Butler spoke to it on the non-religious aspects of the proposed reforms, with Ede (and Lilian also) in the audience. These were well-received, but Ede noted that Mander, the General Secretary, who 'eulogised' what Rab had said, had made a speech a couple of days earlier, attacking the idea of multilateral schools, and the associations of secondary teachers who supported it. Mander alleged that they did so for their own selfish ends, whereas his own Union could not do so, because it would greatly reduce the number of posts as headteacher. On 10 April, a proposal was made to Conference by, amongst others, John Strudwick in favour of multilateral schools but, despite Strudwick's speech, this amendment was narrowly voted down. As Bailey has said, this left Ede 'without a clear lead for the common school from his sponsor union'.[13]

He made a further visit to South Shields from 17 to 19 April 1942, and the following weekend, on 25 April, he completed notes he was writing about the implications of the new scheme to address the religious question. For every child, he was saying, there should be, first, a good general education in a building hygienically sound, secondly the possibility of receiving instruction in agreed Christian faith terms in an atmosphere his parent does not distrust, and thirdly the right to receive instruction in the faith of his parents in the place associated with that worship. On those principles lay everything he felt he and Rab would, or could, achieve on the matter.

Although on his brother Noel's birthday on Christmas Eve Jim had done little but make a diary note, they did occasionally come across each other. On 2 May, when as it happens he was going to Epsom Foot Clinic to have a corn out, Jim saw Noel at a stall in the town, selling Communist literature. They had a chat, and Jim learnt that he sold about two pounds' worth of pamphlets each week, but Noel regretted that he could not get a good variety, as most went for sale in factories. Jim bought two pamphlets for 5d, and went on his way. One would not expect Epsom High Street to be a good prospect for a Communist street-seller, although the swing against the Conservatives in this safe seat three years later would be more than 15 per cent, so perhaps Noel Ede could see the direction in which opinion was moving.

On 6 May Ede was writing to Butler[14] about the vexed subject of clothing and footwear for children inadequately supplied with them, a problem which particularly attached to evacuated boys and girls. Though initially Government departments were reluctant to get involved with what was clearly a parental duty, the Board of Education was coming round to the position that it would have to take action, if it were given the powers. He and Butler both felt it should be included in an Education Bill, if there was one in the next year or so, but Ede was arguing that it was urgent enough to justify a separate statute if necessary (it was in the end included in the 1944 Act).

Air raids were a constant concern, in Epsom and elsewhere, and Ede was on the rota for ARP duty. On 8 May, Lilian woke him at 2.00 am, having heard a siren in the far distance, it being his night for duty. The alarm that time was not near enough for him to need to take action. On 14 May, he discussed ARP with Ernest Brown and Lord Woolton, the Minister of Food, who, like Ede, had visited Barrow. The people there had told Woolton that without the help of the barrage balloons the Germans would never have found the town. Brown, on the other hand, supported having balloons, arguing that, but for them, the aircraft carrier HMS *Illustrious* would not have been kept safe at Barrow. Ede supported Brown; whatever the situation in Barrow, on the Tyne the accuracy of German bombing was reduced significantly, owing to efficient barrage balloons over the shipyards.

The religious question had by now found its way into the popular press. The 17 May edition of *Reynolds News* contained a comment article headlined 'Vested Interests of Illiteracy'. It complemented Ede and Butler for the strong progressive line they were taking on educational reform, but warned this was being obstructed by those (mainly religious interests) who insisted on retaining slum schools, and by private schools, which were determined to profit from the spread of illiteracy and snobbery after the war. It congratulated the LEA in Sheffield, where both parties had got together to reach a progressive plan. Ede was amused enough by the article to cut it out and stick it in his diary, commenting that it was a 'curious misunderstanding of our RI scheme'.

Ede was one of the team who met Church of England clerics on 5 June 1942 to discuss the religious issues.[15] He had already advised Butler on 6 April about the views of the Nonconformists, in a memo Rab marked as 'Interesting', and on 18 May had met Dr Yeaxlee, one of their representatives. On 20 May he had a confrontational meeting with the Bishop of Woolwich (they shared experiences in Surrey), whose attitude was 'uncompromising'. The Bishop claimed 250 of his clergy had said they would not relinquish their right to appoint teachers, and Ede told him there were nothing like 250 Church schools in his diocese.[16] So he was able to use his experience in education in Surrey to criticise the Church schools and their reluctance to reorganise schooling, although at the June meeting the Anglicans explained their opposite viewpoint. Rab took the opportunity to quote statistics about the number of schools on the blacklist of buildings, and the Church representatives agreed to review things further. 'Little that was new emerged', in the words of Gosden. Yet Butler used this to start a continuing negotiation with Temple, which laid the steps to a successful resolution of the religious question. He would say that 'the threat of the White Memorandum' – 'Ede's scheme' – 'coupled with a recital of the grim facts about … buildings … soon produced results'.[17] Though Ede did not play a major part, his three requirements for each child's education were without doubt at the forefront of Butler's mind.

Ede had meanwhile made three further visits to different parts of the country. On 30 May he travelled to Gainsborough in Lincolnshire, via Retford, staying at the Sun Hotel. He had been there in 1941, but noted that the White Hart Hotel, which he had used then, had been damaged by a blast. He visited a Youth Leaders' Course at the town's technical college, where he spoke, and was applauded, with the boys whistling their delight. Next day being Sunday, he walked to church, smugly noting that he arrived before the parson and his wife who took the bus, and spoke on 'Youth in the Present and Future'. He also addressed the Unitarians at their chapel, celebrating its 280th anniversary. His subject was 'Liberty to Know, to Utter and to Argue', always a theme close to his heart. He referred to Cromwell and Milton and how, on 14 June 1643, Parliament (having abolished the Star Chamber and its edict against printers) passed an order 'for the regulating of printing', against which Milton produced a 'learned and impassioned defence of the liberty of the press' in November 1644. That was his polemic 'Areopagitica', to which Ede would return frequently in his speeches.

On 3 June, he gave out prizes at Bolton School, and on 12 June he went with Lilian to Newtown in mid-Wales, via Wolverhampton and Shrewsbury. They had a number of pleasant walks there, but he was still on duty to speak to an audience of about 200 on education. He also spoke to Clement Davies, the local MP, about the resources available for education, noting that in Montgomeryshire the local rate produced so much lower a figure than in Surrey that financing the schools was inevitably affected.

He was, of course, also carrying out duties in the House of Commons all the time it was sitting. On 16 June he was charged with winding up the debate on the education estimates, and referred to his conversation with Davies. He took questions, and summarised the debate, on the range of issues which were of concern, in particular the religious question and the public schools. He was pleased by the subsequent press coverage. The *Manchester Guardian*[18] applauded him for trying to think out a strategy for education, noted that the Board was appointing various committees to enquire into the different subjects, and that Ede had taken up the issue of religion, but concluded it was too early to forecast the policy which would emerge. The *Church Times* was pleased he had put up a stout defence of denominational teaching.

On 20 June 1942, having reviewed these articles, the Edes went with a friend for a Saturday drive round Surrey. In view of the curtailment of petrol he felt it might be their last glimpse of the Surrey countryside for a long time. Again he was able to congratulate himself, when he saw Redlands Wood, near Holmwood south of Dorking, which he had persuaded Surrey to save in 1934. Then they went on to Epsom Common, which he helped to buy, and in addition the Dorking, Mickleham and Leatherhead bypasses with whose layout he was associated.

The next weekend he travelled to South Shields again. On Thursday 25 June, he saw Gompertz, who was in London for a Trades Council gathering. Gompertz complained at being removed as a Food Emergency Officer, and felt other officers would resign in protest. It is clear Ede had to confront considerable needle within his local Labour Party, the detail of which cannot be known at this distance of time. There was also a threat of the Whitburn Colliery being closed, near the coast to the south of the constituency, and Ede asked for more information about this before his visit, which he started on the sleeper train the Friday night. When he arrived, he discussed Whitburn, and met constituents with their problems. On the Sunday, he walked around the town, and then went to the Presbyterian Church with the Council and gave an address. He met the local Communist party, advising them not to press for a meeting about the pit closure – in fact the colliery stayed open till the late 1960s. He then went into Newcastle where, before catching the overnight sleeper back, he addressed a congregation of 400 to 500 at a further service at the Church of the Divine Unity. His theme was again 'Youth in the Present and the Future'. He was keen that the country's Youth Service should not develop into a youth movement, as in continental Europe – he was thinking particularly of Nazi Germany – as youth should not march in step together. The purpose of education, he said, was to make 'everyone … a full and active citizen', which involved young people to be encouraged to think for themselves as individuals.[19]

Around this time, Rab wrote a report on educational reforms for the Lord President's Committee – the group chaired by Sir John Anderson and subsequently Attlee, which dealt with business not connected with fighting the war. His own Conservative colleagues were unenthusiastic, but on 13 July 1942 he told Ede he did not share their views – and indeed, Butler's impatience with old-style Conservative backbenchers was one of his motivations for driving his reforms through. It was clear, however, that the course of the war would determine the prospects of early legislation. By 7 August Butler was able to report that he would submit a paper arguing for the education service as a public benefit.

In the course of Butler's discussions with the Archbishop, he was told of proposals being formulated by the National Society for Promoting Religious Education, which had established many of the voluntary Church schools (Ede had of course attended an elementary 'National School' in Epsom in the 1890s). The National Society were thinking of suggesting that RI on an agreed syllabus might be introduced in Church schools as long as the school could supplement it with denominational teaching, and the LEAs could appoint teachers provided there were adequate reserved teachers, approved and qualified to give that instruction. When Ede was told about this, he was not sympathetic, and on 21 July he wrote to Rab,[20] arguing against the suggestion of reserved teachers, and of more than one denominational lesson weekly. He set out his own proposals, stating many were conditions to be met before he could recommend it to any of the political or religious interests with which he was connected.

Ede was determined that the clergy should not be conceded a right of entry to Council schools, and said that a clear-cut scheme was preferable to what he considered the ill-defined proposals of the National Society. He felt the National Society should examine the White Memorandum, and say what modifications would make it acceptable to them. In his view, there should be an agreed syllabus for RI in all Church of England schools, and legislation to implement this should be promised. The religious tests for teachers should be abandoned, except in regard to reserved teachers; as for reserved teachers, these should never include the school head, and they should be limited to a defined proportion of the staff. Respecting the schools themselves, there should be a survey of them all, to eliminate redundant ones (which should be repeated every five years), though regard could be made to maintaining a reasonable variety of types of school when redundancy was considered, and where an LEA required a school to be brought up to standard, this should be required in a specified time. It is clear from these proposals, and others which he minuted, that Ede felt the time had come to take a tough line on the approaches of the religious groups, and the inconsistent arguments he was hearing. He was holding the position for the Nonconformists, the Labour Party and the NUT, and was resolute in seeing it maintained.

Around this time, Ede took the step of producing an index to his diaries, which had already filled four volumes in one year. With his usual thoroughness, he noted he started on Sunday 12 July, and by Tuesday 14 was on volume 2. It is interesting to speculate what his purpose was, both in writing them, and in then indexing. He might have been doing it just for his own benefit, to keep a record of what he felt was an exceptionally interesting time, with the war and him in a government office which he believed might be the peak of his career. Alternatively, he might have been writing for posterity, hoping that some day his diaries would be of general, or at least academic, interest to those concerned with life in the early 1940s. Perhaps he knew of other political diarists, such as the American 'Chips' Channon, who sat as a Conservative, or the National Labour MP Harold Nicolson, and thought he might compete. Channon asked that his diaries be not published till sixty years after his death, a wish that was honoured partially, and with that anniversary having arisen in October 2018, it would be interesting to have full transcripts of accounts from two such different personalities.

As a change from his indexing efforts, Ede travelled to Darlington on 15 July, where he met the Chairman and Secretary of the Education Committee (noting that Haughton, the Secretary, had been at his college, Christ's), together with an HMI. They visited schools together, looking at nursery classes and feeding arrangements. Darlington, he found, was feeding 30 per cent of its schoolchildren. He mentioned to the chairman that one school had no mechanical domestic appliances for the girls, but several electrical machines for the boys. He then went to a training college, where he gave a speech, and had dinner hosted by the Mayor. The Town Clerk was interested in discussing RI.

That same month, July 1942, Butler and Ede decided to address the issue of the public schools by appointing a committee chaired by Lord Fleming, a Scottish judge, who had been a Conservative MP and Solicitor-General for

Scotland in Baldwin's early governments. Rab recognised that the position of the independent schools could be an obstruction to getting agreement from the Conservative Party to educational reform. Although much thinking at the time favoured integrating the public schools into the state system by some means, Ede could not ignore Butler's statement that the Conservatives would insist on access to a public school by payment. He recognised too that these schools wanted a public grant, but with no public control. It is a well-known procedure to side-line a problem by passing it to a committee to consider, and Butler himself was to concede that, through the appointment of Fleming, 'the first class carriage had been shunted into the siding' by him.[21]

Chapter 9

Ready to Proceed

On 7 August 1942, Ede discussed the possibility of an Education Bill with Butler and Holmes, arguing that it should be introduced in the next parliamentary session, in view of the Labour Party's need to be seen to be achieving reform in some field. The context for this was the preparation of the Beveridge Report, arguing for significant improvements in social services, but at what was considered a very high cost. Rab was responsive to Ede's view, of course, and indicated that, from his perspective, he could argue that the Beveridge Report, when published shortly, would propose welfare changes costing some £650 million annually, whereas benefits to education could be achieved for £100 million a year – an argument likely to appeal to many Conservatives, if they felt some reforming measures were needed. Ede then told Butler privately of the possibility that some Labour MPs might disown the coalition, and it would be hard to know which Labour ministers, if any, might remain in government. The President's reaction was to pray that Ede himself would stay on, as his knowledge of the religious issue was essential; but the answer was not entirely reassuring – 'I said I might not be asked to stay & if I was, the answer would depend on the circumstances of the break.'

The Report of the Beveridge Committee, *Social Insurance and Allied Services*, was not in the end published until nearly the end of the year, and its implementation would have to await action from Attlee's government after the war. Rab saw his opportunity and acted. He spoke to the junior Health Minister, Florence Horsbrugh, along with her ministerial head, Ernest Brown, on 5 September 1942, about the options for social services and education. According to Ede's diary, Rab intended this as a party discussion between two Conservatives, but Brown, the Liberal National leader, butted in. He prophesied 'a big blow up' at the end of the year because of the expenditure needed to implement Beveridge's scheme, and Rab's conclusion was that an Education Bill would be approved, to show the Government was actively pursuing social legislation. It has indeed been well argued that reforming education was a Conservative project designed specifically to eclipse the threat posed by Beveridge.[1]

Ede now reached his sixtieth birthday. Conscious of his age, he decided to resign from the juvenile court panel of the Epsom bench. In the Justices of the Peace Act seven years later, when he was Home Secretary, the Government took the view that 'somebody of a parent's age is better able to deal with naughty children than is somebody of a grandparent's age', as Lord Jowitt put it.[2] That was Ede's own view in 1942, though 'I was very unpopular with some colleagues and found that I was very much in the lower half of the list as regard ages, but ... it is necessary that the ages of magistrates serving on the juvenile court panels should be kept reasonably low'.[3]

Later in September 1942, Ede decided also to leave the Labour Party's Administrative Committee, which consisted of Labour ministers and some backbenchers, and of which he had thus been a member. Questions had been raised by George Daggar, a Welsh MP, about the Committee's constitution, and how it could be dominated by government ministers. To show his good faith, that ministers should ensure they did not become a majority, he stated on 30 September he would not seek re-election. He attended the next few meetings, finally leaving on 20 October, having told Butler a few days before that, depending on the elections for the new Committee, there might be trouble if there was no social legislation in the King's Speech. Butler had written to James Stuart, his Chief Whip, telling him he might want legislation on education, and Stuart's reply was sent to Ede, saying he would bear it in mind. This was still a touchy subject; Butler had told Ede that, when Morrison had asked for 'controversial legislation' to be resumed, he caused concern to both Churchill and Stuart. Many Conservative backbenchers did not want any legislation, Butler had been told, but Ede warned the Labour Members would be obstreperous if there was none.

Ede was also having to deal with education issues in Surrey, and in October 1942 he was at a meeting of the Education Committee, trying to address the problems of bringing the public schools into the national system. He told his colleagues, 'We do not at the moment control effectively the method of entrance to some of the schools, including two of the biggest boys' schools. Unless these schools are willing to co-operate this thing will be a complete "flop"'.[4] It is unclear which two schools he had in mind, but the presence in Surrey of Charterhouse, Cranleigh, Epsom College, St John's Leatherhead, Reed's Cobham, KCS Wimbledon, Kingston Grammar, and several other independent schools would have been significant for him.

After the election of the new Administrative Committee on 21 October, Ede spoke to Ernest Bevin while they were lunching in the Commons. Bevin said he was going to write to Butler, asking for an Education Bill, and would also 'stir up the War Cabinet'. Ede's account of the exchange was that he 'said some Tories might prove difficult', but Bevin 'replied that a good kick in the pants occasionally did them good'. It was clear that a favourable wind was being blown by supporters from different quarters, and the following day Ede was encouraged by Pethick-Lawrence, the Parliamentary Party Chairman, agreeing that, if a settlement on the religious question was near, speedy legislation was needed, not least to undermine opposition from some Conservatives. Pethick-Lawrence used the ingenious simile, which he attributed to Richard Denman, the National Labour MP for Leeds Central, that 'a religious settlement should be treated like a bottle of port wine. It should be consumed immediately after uncorking.' Presumably Ede had to take the accuracy of that image on trust.

As the autumn proceeded, a solution to the religious question was discussed with a series of delegations from the different groups concerned. On 9 October, the meeting was with the NUT, and Ede took a leading role, explaining that some 9,000 Anglican schools were likely to take the alternative of being 'controlled', to use the term eventually introduced, by the LEAs, whereas if the suggestion in the White Memorandum had been followed – that no Church schools in single-school areas should be supported – there might have been no more than 4,000.

Butler then wrote formally to Anderson, as Lord President, proposing an Education Bill, and chased this up with a complaint on 27 October that he had not replied. Anderson said he thought the Board of Education should proceed, asking for a paper on the following Monday, 2 November. This brought about a meeting on 28 October at the Board, of Butler, Ede, Holmes, Cleary, and the Chief Financial Officer D du B. Davidson. Discussion centred on the financial implications of their proposals.

Ede had come to this meeting having just spent time with a former Chief Inspector of the Board, who invited him to the Athenaeum and told him his view that all the Secretaries to the Board since Sir Robert Morant at the turn of the century had been averse to popular education. He attributed this to the Treasury deliberately choosing Secretaries who would be disinclined to promote any social services, which had become a permanent Conservative attitude. Ede does not record his reaction to this, but he must have come well-armed to the meeting with Rab and the civil servants.

Holmes had himself arrived with a paper prepared for Butler's presentation the following week, but Rab was concerned about proposing, as two separate points, making secondary education a duty of LEAs, and abolishing fees in secondary schools. His political antennae sensed that the fees would be an issue for some Conservatives. Ede recorded that he saved the day by proposing that the points were combined in the same paragraph, so that one proposal made secondary education a duty 'and in consequence abolition of fees in secondary schools administered by LEAs'. That obtained Butler's approval, as the policy on fees would seem inevitable to the Conservatives.

By 31 October 1942, Butler was able to tell Ede that he had seen the first draft of the King's Speech, and that there was a paragraph in it about education. However, before much more could proceed, he had to convince Churchill about their proposals, and on the evening of 3 November they had an inconclusive phone conversation, in which it became apparent the Prime Minister could not understand Butler's scheme. Rab took a copy of it round to Downing Street, and saw Churchill along with Stuart and Lord Wolmer, who was Minister of Economic Warfare. Wolmer, who was related to the Cecil family, and had recently joined the upper House as Lord Selborne, was able to give Churchill his approval of the education measures, confirming Lord Salisbury and Lord Cranborne would also agree.

Butler told Ede the next day that the Prime Minister was mollified by this, since he did not want to upset any High Church Conservatives. However, there was no promise about an Education Bill in the King's Speech, merely a general paragraph on the subject. When Rab had raised the range of issues with Churchill, his reaction to an increased school leaving age had been, 'Ought to have been done years ago – helps to solve unemployment.' Butler also told Ede of his presentation of the proposals that day (4 November), which was positively received, both by different shades of Conservative opinion, and by Labour, William Whiteley (the Labour Chief Whip) stating that the TUC would be satisfied. There were, however, further discussions to be carried out. Arthur Greenwood, the new Parliamentary Party Chairman, was asked to meet Cardinal Hinsley, the Archbishop of Westminster, to discuss the Catholic viewpoint on educational issues, and Ede had to tell Butler at the end of the month that he did not believe this had happened.

Between that November and January 1943, Ede was involved in a number of meetings with Catholic leaders, either along with Butler or deputising for him. Thus on 1 January he met Bishop Brown, to discuss the contribution which might be made to the buildings of the Catholic schools. Archbishop Hinsley was himself a conciliatory figure, but he was not well, and he died in March 1943 which, in the view of some,[5] set matters back. In the end, the Catholics remained dissatisfied with the new arrangements offered, and Butler and Ede proceeded with the Education Bill without their support on the religious question.

For on 18 December the Lord President's Committee eventually gave Butler its consent to his preparing an Education Bill. By his account, Herbert Morrison gave the only doubtful comment, about the value of educational reform, while the Chancellor Kingsley Wood was seeking more detail on finances, a job Rab was asking Ede to take on. Attlee himself seemed disappointed that the Bill was not to cover a wider field, including public schools and teacher training, each of which the Board had passed to other committees to consider.

At the end of 1942, Ede noted in his diary that he had experienced 'one of the great years in the history of mankind', with a change from depressing news of Japanese expansion, the collapse of France, the fall of Tobruk and the Soviet insinuation that Britain was failing its allies, to news which 'became outstandingly cheerful', as an American landing in Africa was expected, and the Russians had struck 'tremendous hammer blows'. As for his own career, he felt he had gambled in February 1942 when he declined to move from Education, but he 'had to fight hard to keep the educational cause in the forefront of political interests'. He was disappointed that 'I have not been helped as much by the interests dearest to my heart as I had hoped', a reference to the Nonconformists failing to press the case for the White Memorandum – 'perhaps it is asking too great ... insight ... to expect them to understand the politicians' difficulties'. This raises again the question of how far Ede kept in touch with the NUT and the Free Churches, being not a particularly sociable person – not 'clubbable', as we might say today.

In the new year, a subject Ede was discussing within the Board was the future of the Part III Authorities. He had been corresponding about this for some months with the local authorities and William Jowitt, the Paymaster-General. While his colleagues were agreed that the authorities' powers should cease, there was uncertainty how to achieve this. On 11 February he came up with a suggestion that arrangements could be made, along the lines of the poor law provisions when boards of guardians were abolished by the Local Government Act 1929, which would divide counties into smaller areas with their own committees.[6] His own experience in local government, which Butler and many civil servants lacked, was proving very valuable in progressing the reforms, and on this subject he took the lead. 'I am much obliged', Rab wrote on Ede's note.

The war was certainly impacting on his work. The Ministry of Works was persistently pressing for a reduction in the educational building programme, owing to the shortage of labour in construction. This was hard to reconcile with the need to provide schools with adequate air raid precautions. When a further demand was received early in 1943, Ede wrote to the Ministry on 19 February, pointing out that reducing work on shelters was not feasible, owing to bomb damage recently suffered at schools. The restrictions might lead to double-shift working in schools, which would reduce the supply of married women for industry, and would aggravate problems caused by the return of evacuees, which was making new building even more necessary in some areas.[7]

In February 1943 eight Parliamentary by-elections were held, all in vacant Conservative or Ulster Unionist seats. As part of the coalition, Labour did not contest them, but in five of these there was a strong showing by candidates described as Independent Labour or Common Wealth, and Northern Ireland Labour won Belfast West. In the view of Simon,[8] this alerted Conservatives in Westminster to a belief in the country that they were not interested in reforming legislation. This strengthened the hand of the progressive minority of Tory reformers, and helped Butler develop education as a Conservative project to eclipse the Beveridge proposals, which in turn assisted Ede to convince his Labour colleagues that there was value in being part of the government.

In March 1943, Rab, knowing he still had to convince Churchill to proceed with an Education Bill, paid a visit to Chequers, which he described in amusing terms in his memoirs.[9] Ede was not involved in this episode, but its result was a much more positive approach from on high to the possibility of an Education Bill. Work on a White Paper could continue, though at the same time Ede could also contribute to the Board's operation by using his local authority experience. He wrote two minutes to Butler,[10] pointing out the lack of coordination between some housing authorities and local education authorities. With plans already being made for the country's reconstruction, working together was essential to ensure schools were planned where houses were to be built. In some areas this was done well. Elsewhere the housing and education departments, even under the same council, did not communicate with each other. Ede was able to draw his colleagues' attention to an issue which those outside local government might have missed, and they took action to ensure better coordination.

A further by-election took place on 8 April in Eddisbury. This constituency, which covers much of southern rural Cheshire, had been represented by a Liberal, R.J. Russell, since 1929, though Russell had, along with Simon's Liberals, supported the National Government when it was formed, and he was unopposed (with Conservative support) in 1931 and 1935. Russell was a dental surgeon, well on the conservative wing of the Liberal party, and the

Liberals who opposed the National Government had expected to oppose him, if an election had been held in 1939 or 1940. As it was, he remained in the seat till February 1943, when he died. At the by-election, National Liberal and Independent Liberal candidates split the vote, and the seat was won by J.E. Loverseed for the Common Wealth Party.

Common Wealth, which was contesting many elections at the time, was an alliance of left-wing groups and some former Liberals, generally seen as to the left of mainstream Labour, which had never contested Eddisbury. Ede described Loverseed as 'standing on an advanced left platform', and his majority was only 486 over Peacock (the National Liberal candidate), in a turnout of over 18,000, so it might have seemed that his success owed much to the Liberal split. However, in Ede's view most of the Independent candidate's votes would have gone to Common Wealth, and the result indicated a trend to the left in the electorate. Aware that nobody reaching twenty-one since mid-1939 would have been on the register, and those over twenty-five who were in the forces would not have voted, he described the result as a portent. Though Loverseed would, after moving to Labour, lose the seat in 1945, and though Ede would not expect the result which occurred in the General Election that year, a portent indeed it was. In addition, the more immediate impact of this and other by-election results, was to strengthen the desire of some Conservatives to be seen to implement socially reforming legislation.

By 13 April, Rab's information was that he, Anderson and Kingsley Wood hoped to see Churchill a couple of days later; he was encouraging about the prospects of an Education Bill, though drafting it was becoming a problem. Butler and Holmes were arguing about this, and in the end it was decided to publish a White Paper initially, which would set out what the Government intended.

The same month, April 1943, the Fleming Committee on public schools produced an interim report, at Butler's urging, which unfortunately was the subject of internal disagreement. The majority favoured abolition of all fees in (state) secondary education, which accorded with the Labour Party view, and that of Ede himself; the Committee's members included Harold Clay, of the TGWU, who chaired the Party's education sub-committee, and G.D.H. Cole, the Fabian academic and writer. However, a minority proposed that fees should continue to be charged in direct-grant secondary schools, and on 21 April Butler told Ede this disappointed him, since it would stupidly make trouble in the Conservative Party. Ede was able to joke that such was the Tory Party's 'inherent characteristic'.

On 27 April, he was writing to Butler about school fees. He felt that neither group on the Fleming Committee really understood the nature of the changes being made to education; the idea that public schools would lose independence if they received State funding had been a great hindrance to establishing a widely available system of secondary education. He also took the chance to expand on his educational policy for the future:

> The post-War Britain may well find itself subjected to social strains far more severe than those which were felt … prior to 1939. … A broader based secondary education, with its various institutions genuinely open to a wide range of aptitudes and to which admission can be obtained by individual ability to profit will be a greater cohesive force than any other. … A suspicion that the ability of the parent to pay reserves for the child a particular place, and places that child outside the craftsman's class, will be socially disastrous.[11]

Ede's conviction that education was necessary for citizenship, as well as for vocational and academic purposes, is well illustrated here – and there is every reason to believe that Butler took a similar view.

On 6 May Ede met a number of Anglicans, whose reaction to the discussion was to contact Archbishop Temple about their concerns, particularly about the privileges they felt the Catholics might get. Temple wrote to Butler later,[12] but he replied that the White Paper would answer the points of the group 'who had not impressed the Parliamentary Secretary'. The President was clearly confident in Ede's judgement, as well as in Temple's relationship with them both. On 27 May the Archbishop sent a letter to Butler, recommending an experiment in North Wales being run for the benefit of evacuated children from Bethnal Green. This was led by John Raven, whose father was known to Ede as the Master of Christ's College, and Temple said how interested he was in making the great boarding schools open in the future to suitable children, independent of their parents' means.[13] That matched the sympathies of both Ede and Butler.

A very pleasant surprise occurred for Ede on 11 May 1943. He was in bad shape, having woken up dizzy, and then vomited, but had eventually taken a late train to the office. There he received a letter from Cambridge's Vice-Chancellor offering him an honorary MA degree, for his great services to education. When he spoke to Rab about this, the President already knew, having been briefed by his father Montagu, who was Master of Pembroke College, as well as Mayor of Cambridge. Ede heard from Butler that

> Cambridge was very chary of giving honorary degrees, but they wanted to recognise my work … This is an honour quite beyond any I have ever hoped to receive for my work. I clearly must be a 'late developer'. I went

to Cambridge years ago; today I get a degree! Such an interval must be a record.

It happened that he had an appointment at Cambridge that evening, speaking at Trinity College to a packed meeting, mainly of women, on Reforms in English Education.

None of this, though, was what he felt was his main achievement. On 19 May, he read in the *Evening Standard* an interview with Dick Coppock, a trade unionist and new chairman of the London County Council, and he mused[14] about the time when Coppock would join him in Surrey, they would lay out maps, and talk together about Surrey's share of the Green Belt. A good deal of such visiting had happened while the Green Belt negotiations had been going on, which Ede felt might 'together with the Norbury Park acquisition (not a Green Belt purchase) … prove the most enduring of my life's work … Nonsuch Park, the Chantries, and Ockham Common would be pleasant memorials'.

Surrey, then, was very much the centre of his ambitions and thoughts. He still sat on the Epsom Bench as a magistrate when he could, dealing often with cases which sound banal relative to his other work. On 22 February he had dealt with the case of a Canadian military lorry driver who had driven the wrong side of a lamp post – a natural risk with so many drivers from allied countries unused to driving on the left – and knocked down a woman cycling, who had ended up in hospital – fined five pounds, with £2/2/6 costs, after the man's officer had helped his defence. Next, a fine of ten shillings was imposed on a former French master at Epsom College for cycling on a footpath, and a gipsy was fined forty shillings for using insulting language to a farmer. Now, on 24 May, he had to deal with three conscientious objectors who refused to do agricultural work. They ended up, as second offenders, with three months' hard labour, after Ede had taken part in a theological discussion with them about the merits of war.

Back at the House of Commons on 27 May 1943, Ede and Butler received visitors from the Association of Education Committees – Alderman Cropper, its chairman from Chesterfield, and Sir Percival Sharp, its secretary. They were pressing for some local interest to be retained in any new structure for education, preferably retaining a role for the Part III Authorities. While Butler and Ede would make no commitment about this, the discussion clearly helped develop Ede's thinking.[15]

So producing the White Paper was important for Ede, aware as he was that on 25 February the National Executive of the Labour Party had proposed to the Board of Education seventeen points on which it wanted action. These points are worth listing:[16]

1. School leaving age to rise to fifteen immediately after the War, and to sixteen within three years.
2. A common code of regulations for all secondary schooling of all pupils over eleven.
3. Maximum class size of thirty.
4. Public schools, and others not grant-aided, to be brought within the general system.
5. LEAs to develop nursery infant schools for children of two-seven, and nursery classes for those of two-five.
6. Compulsory medical and dental services for all children, free of charge.
7. Junior colleges for part-time continued education for young people of sixteen-eighteen, with compulsory attendance of two days, including day release from work.
8. Minimum standards of juvenile employment.
9. LEAs to provide accessories, including clothing, and free transport.
10. A single type of Education Authority, for all primary, secondary and further education.
11. The Board of Education to take over educational functions of other ministries.
12. Abolition of fees in maintained and aided schools.
13. Free midday meals in all maintained and aided schools.
14. Calculating the Board's grant as a percentage of each LEA's expenditure, distributed to provide efficient education and iron out inequalities.
15. Full access to universities and colleges independent of means.
16. The Youth Advisory Council to be reinforced, and to recommend development of the youth service.
17. Teacher training colleges to be part of universities, with those in the Armed Forces encouraged to enter teaching.

During the week beginning 14 June 1943, Ede was attending the Labour Party Conference in London, and was able to confirm that most of these points were included in the White Paper.

In fact, only two issues were not covered by what had been drafted, the minimum standards of employment to be laid down and enforced by LEAs (8), and the widened remit of the Board (11) – those would have encroached on other ministries. The Conference unanimously passed a resolution supporting the seventeen points on 17 June, although there was some opposition to dual control on the religious issue. Labour's National

Executive made it clear they wanted a good Bill, and soon, to put an end to the country being two nations with different school leaving ages. A definite date for a leaving age of sixteen was needed.

Early in June, the Edes made their trip to Cambridge for his degree ceremony. First he met Montagu Butler, acting in his capacity as Mayor of Cambridge rather than college head, so they could discuss a proposal for the Borough and Cambridgeshire County to form a joint Education Committee. There had been some disputes about how this could be implemented, which Ede used his good offices to try to resolve. They walked around the Guildhall, where he had last been in 1905. They stayed at the University Arms Hotel, and next day went to Christ's, and looked around the chapel, where he saw the memorial to his old tutor Shipley. Back in his hotel room, he changed into the morning coat, waistcoat and striped trousers which he had worn for the Epsom Charter celebrations, and they were driven to Queens' College, whose President was Vice-Chancellor. At lunch there, they were joined by, among others, the University's Public Orator, the Senior Tutor of Christ's, the Mistress of Girton College, and the Chairman of the Borough Education Committee. Ede spoke about Cambridge of forty years previously, of Shipley, who knew every surreptitious method of climbing into college, and of Fitzpatrick, his host's predecessor as President of Queens', who as Dean of Christ's had sat next to Ede at the 400th anniversary banquet there. They then went to the Senate House, where the honorary degree was conferred, the Orator speaking in Latin which Ede did not understand. They were met at the Senate House by Harris Rackham, the retired Fellow of Christ's who had taken him there to matriculate forty years earlier.

The following week, Ede received from Guthrie, the Public Orator, the text of the speech which he had failed to follow, and he copied it into his diary, both in Latin (with a number of errors) and in English, though the demands of real work once more had to take priority. On 28 June, he was again having to argue the case in regard to the religious question. The Anglican Church Assembly had resolved that any Church school should have at least one teacher appointed to give denominational teaching, however small the total staff number – the Board was proposing that in schools with only one or two teachers, this should not be required. Ede opposed the Church's argument,[17] once again saying he could not commend it to any group he might influence – the Free Churches, or the LEAs, and certainly not the NUT, who he felt might resolve to abolish the dual system completely. His language showed he was close to despair of a settlement – 'walking on a knife edge with sheer precipices on either side … some people seemed to enjoy shaking the rope'.

Butler added to the mixed metaphor, 'We shall have many slips twixt cup and lip', he said soothingly.

At last, on 6 July 1943, Butler was able, with support from Ede and Holmes, to present the education White Paper, entitled *Educational Reconstruction*, to Attlee and his Lord President's Committee. It received wide support, not least from Kingsley Wood, who surprised some of his colleagues by confirming the financial side of the proposals could be covered within government priorities. Ede suspected Herbert Morrison was again a reluctant voice, who might have wanted the project postponed, but once it was clear that would not happen, Morrison 'said he was all for educational advance'. The Committee agreed to minor amendments, in particular clarifying that it was the structure of education being changed, not its content, after which it should be sent to the War Cabinet, with a recommendation it should be published as soon as possible.

Butler attended the cabinet meeting on 13 July, and was thrilled to report the White Paper had been accepted, with only two words changed. He said Churchill had talked at length about the Education Act 1902 and, when the religious issues were discussed, said he was prepared to tell Parliament how much the religious lobby (particularly the Catholics) were getting – if a free vote defeated the proposals, 'the most generous example of religious toleration in the history of the world would be destroyed, and the great measure of educational advance with it'. It was clear the Prime Minister had been brought well onside. Ernest Bevin would subsequently claim credit for this, by convincing Churchill that it was hard to find the skills needed for the services and munitions works.[18]

Three days later, Rab could present the White Paper to the Commons, where he confirmed his conversations with all the interested parties and, in answer to a question, his achievement of closer agreement than had been achieved before, resulting in the White Paper which would be available in print later that day. Anthony Eden, in his capacity as Leader of the House, confirmed there would be a chance to debate the proposals, perhaps a fortnight later, with a Bill being introduced, probably in the autumn. Ede was pleased with the reaction, and learnt from Rab that Joseph Tinker, an elderly miners' MP with interests in Catholic education, had assured him the Catholics would be satisfied with the proposals if the position on denominational education in the White Paper could be held.

At this point, a further issue arose on which Ede, with his local authority background, was able to make a major contribution. He argued that, while it was right that every LEA should be required to appoint a Chief Education

Officer, it was not good enough to leave that to the authority alone, as Holmes felt. Appointing and dismissing the officers, as well as their pay scales, should be subject to the consent of the Board of Education. Butler's sympathies on this point seem to have been with Ede when he sought his views, but on 20 July it was the Parliamentary Secretary who put the case most strongly.[19] He knew that some of the Chief Officers in post were not up to the job, certainly of introducing all the new arrangements, including those for secondary education, and all new ones appointed must understand what the Board required and have the Board's confidence. This in turn found its way into the Bill.

Also on 20 July Ede attended the Party's Administrative Committee, to discuss the White Paper. He was able to show how far the seventeen points were being addressed, and the meeting agreed the Party's requirements had been substantially met. The Committee also discussed the religious question, excluded from the points, without reaching a firm conclusion. Ede noted that Tom Williams, his opposite number at Agriculture, 'said the scheme was sound, the religious compromise reasonable, and' (most importantly) 'the Party would do well to get it passed during the lifetime of this Govt.' Williams's concern was to avoid a repetition of the events in 1931 when, it will be recalled, Trevelyan's attempts to raise the school leaving age were thwarted by Parliament.

Next day, 21 July 1943, a meeting of the Parliamentary Labour Party discussed the notice of a motion to be debated in the Commons at the end of the following week, Thursday 29 July. Despite its simple statement that the House welcomed the Government's interest in education, Ede found that some MPs had remarkably decided the White Paper did not show any such interest. He, however, was clear – 'I said the White Paper was the greatest State document ever issued on education.' He was congratulated on his efforts, and there were cheers for the end of the Part III Authorities.

A Welsh MP, William Cove, who like Ede was sponsored by the NUT, was leading the critics. On 22 July *Tribune* published an article by him, alleging the Conservatives were dominating educational advances. Butler excitedly told Ede the article by Cove would assist his efforts with his own party colleagues, as it helped him show the proposals were Conservative ones, and Ede responded that, in view of the Tory majority, Butler needed to propose the measure, as 'if it was suggested that it was to any large degree my scheme it would be killed'. He was, characteristically, playing a sharp political hand, and mentioning, but understating, his own important role. Bailey has concluded from all this that it illustrates Ede's junior position, despite Rab's confirming his part would be acknowledged, and that his hard work on the White Paper, and later the Bill, enabled considerable potential for advance which had, though, to be underplayed.[20]

When the House debated the White Paper on 29 July, Butler opened at 12.45 with a long speech, in which he paid tribute to those who had collaborated outside, but also to those who assisted him personally, and 'particularly my Honourable friend the Parliamentary Secretary'. He ran through the historical background, and then started on the proposals, making it clear that he hoped to see some multilateral schools, though he was also open to the idea of separate grammar and technical schools. He then discussed the religious questions at some length and, though the Catholics' reservations were raised, it was clear the House was not deterred by them. After Rab finished covering other topics, Ede noted that he had been cheered both on rising and on sitting down. Several MPs spoke at length, though he was generally unimpressed, and was himself not called upon to do anything but intervene with short clarifications, before the debate was adjourned at 7.00 pm.

It continued the following day, until at last Ede was called to sum up the debate. He promised to keep it short and, compared to some, he did. He covered a range of issues which had been raised, including the Part III authorities, referring to the time in 1902 when he had attended the House to listen to the Education Bill being debated, as well as the private schools and the medical services. With a nod towards Cove, who had spoken about his own misgivings, he halted as soon as the time for the debate was up, and the resolution, to welcome the reform, was agreed without a vote.

Among the proposals of the White Paper was a statement that the three main types of secondary school were grammar, technical and modern, while conceding that providing different education under one roof might be combined – but there

> is nothing to be said in favour of a system which subjects children at the age of 11 to the strain of a competitive examination on which not only their future schooling but their future careers may depend … children at about the age of 11 should be classified, not on the results of a competitive test, but on an assessment of their individual aptitudes largely by such means as school records, supplemented, if necessary, by intelligence tests, due regard being had to their parents' wishes, and the careers they have in mind … the choice … will not be finally determined at 11 … At … 13 or even later, there will be facilities for transfer.[21]

These words would stay in Ede's memory. Shortly before he finally stood down as Labour spokesman on education, he quoted them in an article describing the party's policy for the 1955 election, criticising the Conservative support for the 11+ examination. One can well envisage the pen of James Chuter Ede writing them in 1943.

However, the same week that the Commons were debating it, the Norwood Committee published its report. It had been formally signed in June 1943, and welcomed privately by Butler, and then made public in July. While the Committee's remit was ostensibly to report on secondary curriculum and examinations, there had been much controversy while it was doing so, as to whether it was exceeding its terms,[22] and in the outcome it stated firmly that there were three types of pupil, who needed three types of school. In recommending the tripartite system, and supporting its statements with little or no evidence, it went well beyond its task, but in view of its timing, it created an approach to secondary education which became a main thread of administrative thinking. In the longer term, this thinking affected opinions about the Education Act 1944, which made no reference to a tripartite structure (or to comprehensive or multilateral schools). It is unlikely Ede was impressed by this.

As the autumn drew on, the position of the universities was also consuming the time of the ministers. Butler had for a while believed that they should come within the remit of the Board of Education, a point on which Holmes dissented, and on 17 September Ede joined them both, and several other of their officers, to meet thirteen vice-chancellors.[23] Rab, with his detailed knowledge of how the universities operated, took the lead on this subject, though the result of the meeting was largely to report back and consult further. This was not a matter on which there was any significant progress while he and Ede were at the Board.

As regards the White Paper, the objections of the Roman Catholics had not disappeared, of course, and much of the autumn was taken up in trying to deal with them, in a way which did not upset the Free Churches and Local Education Authorities. Many Catholics felt the proposals gave insufficient aid to denominational schools, and favoured unduly the requirement for an agreed RI syllabus. On 29 September 1943 Ede, after taking Butler around Tyneside, accompanied by Percy and Trevelyan, both local magnates, went with Rab and Maurice Holmes to Ushaw College, which was then a Catholic seminary, not far from his own constituency near Durham. Butler's own memoirs date this to December though, as Gosden argued, it must have been earlier.[24] The purpose of the visit was to meet the northern Catholic bishops, whose main aim, Rab's account implies, was to overawe the men from government, and show there would be no let-up with their demands for better terms in the Education Bill. They were wined and dined on the college's own sheep, and Ede unusually 'had a glass of very good sherry'. After that he asked for mineral water, and was given 'brownish' water from a well.

They were then shown round the chapel, and he was overawed. From its far end, the crucifix looked as if the white figure was floating in the air, as the black wood of the cross was indiscernible in the shadow. They passed a mural of figures holding a headsman's axe – Thomas More and John Fisher. Ede noticed the arms of Christ's College, which Fisher had helped found. 'Chuter Ede told me he thought he was going to faint',[25] remarked Butler, while he himself was left feeling he had not handled the bishops well. He described the history of the voluntary schools since 1870, and how government aid to them had increased. Though they found the bishops reassuring, they were told it was their Catholic supporters who could not be controlled on the issue. The party 'left with only a good dinner', was the conclusion of Butler's biographer.[26]

A few days later, on 5 October, Butler told Ede that Holmes had been working hard to find a way of meeting the Catholics' objections. Ede had concluded that it would be difficult to find anything the Catholics would accept without offending the Free Churches and the education authorities. On 7 October, Rab reported to him that, at a conference organised by the Conservatives, some attendees had advanced the Catholic position, and even had boys outside handing out leaflets in support. In the end, however, he was not prepared to change the White Paper's proposals, and he seems to have been confident that, having got the balance right between the parties, they could push on with their proposals. Bevin had pressed Ede not to concede anything more to the Catholics. Together, Butler would handle the Conservatives and the Anglicans, while Ede would look after the Labour Party and the Nonconformists. They were ready to proceed with an Education Bill.

Chapter 10

The Privy Counsellor gets his Education Act

By October 1943 Chuter Ede had largely completed his work on dividing of LEAs into districts, in order to deal with the problem of the Part III Authorities. On 6 October he wrote to Rab,[1] suggesting what functions district committees should have – such as some budgetary control, supervision of building work, recommending the appointment of assistant teachers, and consultation with the LEA on policy. His ideas were passed to those drafting the Bill.

On 29 October, the next issue being argued was whether the Board of Education should be changed to a Ministry. The Board had been set up by the Board of Education Act 1899, at the same time as the school leaving age was raised from eleven to twelve, as the department responsible for education, replacing a split responsibility of two departments. By 1943, it was unclear why the term 'Board' had been used at all, though some ministers thought it was worth keeping; again, Morrison was a reluctant voice about making a change. Ede and Butler pressed for the change, but eventually settled for keeping 'President' as a title, but with clear powers of a Minister.

After further discussion about the Catholic position, the Lord President's Committee told Rab to send the draft Education Bill to the Government's Legislative Committee. The Bill had been largely drafted under the supervision of Sir Granville Ram, the First Parliamentary Counsel to the Treasury, and Ram had indicated that no other Bill was anything like ready to be presented. Considerable time and discussion had gone into preparing it; as long before as 24 February, Ede had been reworking Ram's draft, which initially provided for three types of secondary school, a 'differentiation which is in direct contradiction to all I have been trying to do'. In May Ede was concerned that Ram 'doesn't understand our ideas', and was resisting his attempt to leave the wording to the professional draftsman. Just before they submitted the draft, Butler and Ede spoke to a meeting of Anglican churchmen about the religious settlement, and on 18 November they were able to plan the passage of the Bill. James Stuart was prepared to impose the whip on his Conservative members, and had agreed with Butler that the

Second Reading should take two days, immediately in the new year, after the recess.

No doubt Ede was involved in other ministerial duties, beyond planning the Bill. On 19 November 1943, he joined Ernest Bevin and Malcolm McCorquodale, the Conservative Parliamentary Secretary at the Ministry of Labour, for a meeting to discuss conscripting schools' kitchen and domestic staff. Those involved included the Headmaster of Winchester and the High Mistress of St Paul's. Ede records Bevin musing unfavourably about the public schools, as represented by such people, and on teachers generally, whom he considered 'a spoiled lot', and whom Ede had to defend as 'great men in many cases'.

In mid December the Education Bill was published. Unfortunately for Ede and Butler, Churchill had just gone down with pneumonia, and Attlee's statement to the Commons about the Prime Minister's health on 16 December took priority over the First Reading in the London papers, which nonetheless summarised and commended it. After the recess, as planned, Rab was able to open the Second Reading debate on 19 January 1944, the day after Churchill's return to Parliament from his sick leave.

Ede had taken the opportunity, a week earlier, to comment on the draft of Butler's speech, which he considered disjointed, and criticised for describing the policy as 'modest'. He was still concerned about the religious issues, and that Rab, vacillating on them, was not convincing enough. However, on the day his presentation of the Bill seems to have been successful, and he was supported by John Parker from the Labour benches. Parker was an Oxford-educated Fabian, who had represented Romford since 1935, and would go on to be an MP until 1983, finishing as Father of the House. A younger contemporary of Butler's at Marlborough, he had been selected to speak in support by Arthur Greenwood, though he anticipated there might be a struggle against snobbery, class-consciousness, and 'violence of enthusiastic sectarian protagonists'.

There was certainly no letting-up from the Catholic and High Church lobbies. Sir Patrick Hannon, the Conservative member for Moseley, went on at length, in a speech which both supported and criticised the Bill, until he fizzled out, and others indicated their desire to amend it at the Committee Stage. Richard Stokes, the Labour member for Ipswich, who would later serve alongside Ede in Attlee's cabinet, put in more sober terms the desire to have Catholic teachers in Catholic schools, as a minimum, once those schools were part of the whole system. Ede intervened in Stokes's speech, to clarify how the school managers would be appointed.

The following day, 20 January, the debate continued until, an hour before the adjournment was due, Ede started to wind it up. His speech covered he range of points which had been made during the two days, and led to the Bill being given a Second Reading without opposition. Ede finished his speech with a quotation from Tennyson's 'In Memoriam', though according to Hansard he did not identify it as such, presumably inferring that most of his audience would recognise it. The Bill was then committed to a Committee of the whole House of Commons. This was an unusual decision, and has been attributed to a desire by the Government to keep Members of Parliament occupied – presumably there were fears that both Conservative and Labour backbenchers might find alternative issues on which to cause trouble. In Rab's words:

> The beauty of the Bill, as [the Government Whips] saw it, was that it provided endless opportunity for debate on issues which ... were not vital to the war and which would keep members thoroughly occupied without breaking up the Government.[2]

As we shall see, though, trouble was not avoided entirely, and at one point the Government might have fallen as a result.

Ede recorded that he was given a generous round of applause, with congratulations from the Treasury Bench, and subsequently a warm compliment from Butler himself. Rab repeated that congratulation the next day, when a meeting at the Board noted that Ede's contribution had not been mentioned in radio broadcasts. They discussed further whether there should be compromises on religious or other issues, and the general view was against any.

An interesting interlude at the time occurred when Ede and Attlee were invited to a dinner of the County Councils Association, whose chairman, Dr Maples, wanted his executive to meet the Labour leader. Attlee joked that he was a Surrey man, like Ede, though he had never managed to become a county councillor (in fact he had stood for the LCC, unsuccessfully), and he did think that all MPs should have experience in local government. One of Ede's neighbours at table said he was impressed, by a man he expected to be 'a colourless person incapable of leadership', which gave Ede the chance to laud Attlee's qualities, as straight and loyal, comparing him with Campbell-Bannerman from the turn of the century – the comparison he made more than once in his diaries.

Meanwhile, the religious issues arising from the Education Bill resonated in the country. Sir Cooper Rawson, one of the Conservative MPs for the two-member seat at Brighton, resigned in January, and his party nominated a candidate, William Teeling, who was expected to be unopposed, as the other Brighton member had been in 1940. At the last minute an Independent was nominated, who claimed to support Churchill. The Prime Minister denied this, calling it 'an attempted swindle' and, when B.D. Briant, the Independent, suggested Churchill had not used those words, a further message made it clear he had indeed, and they were intended. As an Irish Catholic, Teeling was asked if he intended to wreck the Education Bill, despite standing as a Conservative, and Ede mused that some in Brighton may have voted against him because they suspected he would not support government policy. In the event, Teeling won the seat, did not wreck the Bill, and had a Parliamentary career of twenty-five years for which he received a knighthood.

On 28 January 1944, Butler and Ede got the House to agree to authorise expenditure arising from the Education Bill. On 8 February they started to proceed through the Bill, clause by clause. Clause 1, which reconstituted the Board of Education, took up considerable time, and featured an amendment that the Board should be renamed a Ministry, and the President its Minister. This had of course been the subject of much discussion within the Government for some time, and the amendment was withdrawn on Butler's undertaking to look at the matter. By March, as we shall see, the nomenclature had been changed.

The following day, the House considered Clauses 4 and 5, regarding the Central Advisory Councils for Education, and started on Clause 6, which covered Local Authorities, both subjects which provoked considerable debate. The two CACs (for England and Wales respectively) were proposed 'to advise the Minister upon such matters connected with educational theory and practice as they think fit', and questions referred by him, unlike their predecessor committees, which were purely for consultation by the President.[3] The dispute was over whether they should be broadly representative of national life, including some with experience in education, as was proposed, or should have direct representation of particular interests. Butler successfully held his ground on this.

The Local Education Authorities were to be the county and county borough councils for each area. This seems straightforward enough today (as amended to reflect local government changes over the years), but it caused considerable concern in 1944. Parts II and III of the Education Act 1902, enacted after local councils had been established throughout England and Wales in 1889, had replaced the School Boards with LEAs. It will be recalled that the counties and county boroughs were the LEAs for all state education, under Part II, while many of the larger municipal boroughs and urban districts had responsibility for elementary education under Part III. As the Bill was to abolish elementary education, the function of the Part III Authorities (more than half of all LEAs) was to become redundant.

There was considerable debate about this. The Part III Authorities were of varying size and competence, but some were large and well able to administer the new educational arrangements, and abolishing their role would cause a loss of much experience. This had already been an issue when proposed by the White Paper,[4] and Ede had expressed some sympathy with the arguments against removing their duties for education. On 9 February, Butler and Ede dealt with a series of amendments, based on the solution Ede himself had floated in 1943 – joint boards should be made available for areas where combined administration was most appropriate, and 'divisional executives' where it was suitable to split an LEA into smaller areas. Provisions for these were included in the Act's First Schedule, and it was decided they should be debated when the House addressed the Schedules.

The next day, 10 February, Ede was lunching when, his diary reports, Ernest Bevin spoke to him, criticising Herbert Morrison. As we have seen, Bevin was one of the strongest supporters of the educational reform among the senior Labour figures. Ede felt he contributed more to the Education Bill than anyone outside the Board itself, being readily prepared to advise about it and make suggestions.[5] While his dislike of Morrison was well-known, it does seem that Morrison was the least enthusiastic. Bevin accused him of taking the civil servants' views on everything, resisting handing over factory inspectors to the Ministry of Labour and approved schools to Education. Morrison, he said, was keen to retain the title 'President', while in his view Education should have a Secretary of State. 'The department which dealt with the whole of the young life of the nation ought to be given the highest position.'

The Commons proceedings then started with a petition being presented by Davie Logan, the Labour member for Liverpool Scotland, protesting against the financial proposals for Catholic schools as set out in the Bill, and asking for provision in the Bill to remove 'these injustices'. Logan was a well-established MP, already in his seventies, who would continue to represent Liverpool for twenty more years, till he died at 92; he came from an Irish nationalist background. His petition was in the name of the Liverpool Archdiocesan branch of the Union of Catholic Mothers, backed by 94,000 signatures. It was clear that the government, and particularly its Labour component, was going to experience much opposition, organised by the Catholic church, on the question of religious schools.

The Bill's Committee Stage continued on 15 February 1944, with a further session about the LEAs and Part III Authorities. Butler was buffeted by members looking to support the Authorities in their own patch, but held firm against this 'local patriotism', pointing out that he and Ede had visited the main areas in England where the issue arose, and held public meetings. His approach was the best one in the interests of the new system of education. The clause was successfully agreed, without a vote, though only after the most prolonged debate on any part of the Bill.

Clauses 7 and 8 were then dealt with. The former, subsequently described by Dent as 'the most important in the Act', divided the statutory system of education into 'three progressive stages to be known as primary … secondary … and further education', with LEAs having the duty (not merely the power, which Part II Authorities had in regard to secondary and subsequent education) to provide all three. This was widely approved; much of the debate covered whether there was adequate coverage for nursery and infant education, and Ede responded for the government on the points made.

During this debate, a discussion took place which would prove interesting, in the light of later issues about the tripartite system of schools. The Committee was debating the requirement on LEAs to provide sufficient primary and secondary schools, and in particular 'such variety of instruction and training as may be desirable in view of their different ages, abilities, and aptitudes'. Ede explained firmly that the duty being placed on each LEA was to provide schools of a wide variety. Grammar schools had been mentioned in the debate, but other schools would also be needed, including those 'with a strong technical side', and rural schools leading to agricultural college. He hoped that not too many stipulations would be made at age eleven, for he had learnt from 'the troubles of the last forty years' that selection could be made too early.

Clause 8 prescribed the detail of the LEAs' duties, and Ede had to deal with amendments proposed on matters as varied as playing fields and class sizes.

As all MPs had had experience of one educational system or another, there were several references in this discussion to their own background, as pupils and in some case teachers, which prompted Ede to state:

There have been several autobiographical references in the course of this debate, and I would like to say that I was taught in a class of 90. The first class I had when I left college was 73, and the smallest class I ever taught before I left the teaching profession, for its own good, in 1914, was 55 in number.

The words 'for its own good' were a typical case of Ede's self-deprecating humour, which was followed by a member interjecting, rather more pompously, 'There are 614 here'. Ede continued that 'when I was first certificated it was said that the head teacher could be regarded as the equivalent of 35 pupils, every certificated teacher responsible for 60. That was how I came to have 73 – I had my own 60 and a third of his 35. There was a similar allowance for each other type of teacher.' He convinced the House that smaller class sizes, and in particular a maximum limit of 30, should not be a statutory requirement, but rather an objective, supported by an increase of teachers and a massive building programme (Dent was later to point out that over 7,500 new schools had been built by 1966).

Rab then proposed an amendment, that children should be educated in accordance with the wishes of their parents, so far as is reasonable. This was in response to wide lobbying on the issue, but this, together with the rest of the debate, meant that Clause 8 was not completed by the end of the sitting, which had been extended by an hour. Ede was 'very disturbed' by the slow progress, though Rab 'professed himself satisfied', and the debate continued the next day, 16 February.

Once Butler's amendment about parental wishes had been accepted, Clause 8 was eventually agreed, Ede's main contribution being to confirm that providing boarding provision, where appropriate, would be an LEA duty. Clause 9, which gave LEAs the power to run schools outside their own area, and dealt with nomenclature, was quickly agreed, followed by lengthy speeches on Clause 10. This provision (which eventually became Section 11 of the Act) required each LEA to submit a development plan with its proposals on how to achieve sufficient schooling in its area. Initially the debate concerned the time-frame permitted to the LEAs for this, and in the event most authorities found the permitted twelve months too short. Ede's main contribution was to resist a proposal that all urban and rural districts within a county would need to be consulted about its development plan, and the timescale for objections to the plans. He also dealt quickly with Clause 11 and part of 12, covering respectively the orders which the Minister would then issue in response to a development plan, and the consultation required in establishing and discontinuing schools.

There was then a pause until 24 February 1944 before the Bill was considered again. In the interim, two by-election results had come through, at Kirkcaldy and West Derbyshire, both of which were encouraging for Labour. In particular, in West Derbyshire an Independent Labour candidate stood against the Tory, the Marquess of Hartington, unopposed by official

Labour under the Coalition parties' agreement, and had won convincingly. The new MP's father had, between 1918 and 1923, held the seat, which otherwise had been taken for many years by family nominees of the Duke of Devonshire. The retiring MP had resigned when, Ede mused, he ran away with another married woman, deserting his wife who was the Duke's sister – thus convincing the voters that leaving the Duke's family required surrendering his family seat. More seriously, he told Butler that the electoral truce would be very hard to continue, because it might not survive Labour's conference at Whitsun.

On 24 February 1944 consideration of the Bill continued, with further discussion on Clause 12, together with 13, which covered discontinuance of schools. Butler and Ede again shared the task of speaking for the Government, and their efforts resulted in provisions that notice must be given, to the public and the Minister, of proposals to establish or continue a school, with set timeframes for objections. Ede was able to illustrate how this would work, along with a development plan, by recalling his experience at Surrey County Council, when the LCC started to build the St Helier estate, and the Catholics asked for two schools to be built to serve what they expected their numbers on the new estate to be. That was near his old constituency of Mitcham, close to his heart in 1944, as he was made a Freeman of the Borough of Mitcham that year.

Next, the debate turned to the thorny issue of the schools themselves. Clause 9 had given names to 'county' and 'auxiliary' schools – respectively those established by a local authority and those maintained by other bodies (in effect, church or otherwise endowed schools) – and clause 14 classified the latter into 'controlled', 'aided' or 'special agreement' schools. A short time was devoted to this, before the House had to adjourn, with the Clause taken up again on 25 February. While Ede played his part, the day was dominated by Butler making several long speeches about his religious settlement. Rab said firmly that many denominational schools were not up to the required standard, and insistence on that standard was causing the government to incur a great deal of odium. He had been faced with difficulties for two years, and was guided solely by the interests of the children and the future of education.

The compromise was reached, which distinguished controlled schools – the financial obligations for which fell on the LEA rather than the governors – from aided (and special agreement) schools, the governors of which took responsibility for capital expenditure to keep their premises to government standards, as well as any repairs to the exterior of buildings, but with half the cost provided from Whitehall. In return, the controlled schools were required to follow an 'agreed syllabus' on religious education, not distinctive of any particular denomination, as for the 'county schools', so perpetuating the Cowper-Temple principle from the 1870 Act. Butler said later that Archbishop Temple had 'grasped at' this proposal from him and Ede when it had been put to him.[6] The aided schools (and the special agreement schools, few in number, which had already entered into agreements with their LEAs under previous legislation) were entitled to provide religious instruction distinctive of their denomination. In controlled schools, most governors would be appointed by the LEA, in aided schools by the church. In practice, the Roman Catholic schools would largely opt for aided status, while most Anglican ones (and such Nonconformist ones as there were) would become controlled, those Nonconformists and others who hoped the dual system would end being disappointed. These provisions would shortly be debated in March.

At the end of the day, Clause 14 was agreed, and the Commons left the Education Bill for two weeks. On 3 March, Butler attended a meeting of the Lord President's Committee. He was able to report back to Ede and their civil servants that a decision had in the end been taken to change the President of the Board's title to Minister of Education. This was still against the wishes of Herbert Morrison, but he was absent, and Ellen Wilkinson (Morrison's deputy at the Home Office, presumably standing in for him at the meeting) had tried, without success, to argue the case for keeping the title of President. Rab reported also that Henry Brooke (who would one day follow both Ede and Butler as Home Secretary) had spoken to him about amendments to give greater power to Anglican dioceses, and to oblige Young People's Colleges (intended to provide part-time education for those aged fifteen to seventeen, after the school-leaving age had increased) to provide religious instruction. Ede and the others said that both of these would cause needless difficulties, but interventions along these lines were expected.

It was 9 March 1944 before the Bill came before the House again, but that day eight Clauses were covered. Clause 15 concerned transferring schools to new sites, and substituting new schools. Ede dealt with amendments proposed, largely about the notice and consultation to make such changes, by referring, as on other occasions, to his old infants' school – on a restricted site, insanitary and badly lit, an eighteenth century stable turned into a school when no longer fit for bloodstock – as an example of the straightforward type of replacement which the clause would cover.

Clauses 16 to 18 covered the governance of schools, retaining the distinction between managers in primary, and governors in secondary, schools, which disappointed a number of members, not least on the political left. Willie Gallacher, the Communist MP for West Fife, and D.N. Pritt, the Independent Labour member for Hammersmith North, both thought the term 'governor' was inappropriate, suggesting managers could be appointed for all schools. Ede explained that the machinery existing for creating the governing body of a secondary school was more than was needed for management of primary schools, as it had already been for the elementary schools. (In fact, 'governors' is the term more usual today, and the one I am normally using to cover both bodies.) Clauses 19 to 21 provided more detail on this, and about the use of school premises, which Butler was able to look after, and following short discussion, Clause 22 was deferred to the next day.

On 10 March a further six Clauses were addressed. Clause 22 placed on governors in aided schools control of determining the secular curriculum (while in other schools that was a duty of the LEA). This caused considerable concern – some MPs felt governors would have too much power to change a school's character, others that, if the aided schools were almost exclusively grammar schools, this provision

Ede collected many caricatures of himself. (© *Surrey History Centre*)

would undermine the equal status of grammar, technical and modern schools (even though that distinction was not in the Bill). Rab dealt with these points, though it was Ede who made himself available to address how teachers would be appointed and dismissed, under the next clause, numbered 23.

A further interlude then took place, with an attempt to amend this clause to prevent a woman being dismissed from teaching on getting married. This was proposed by a Conservative named Hamilton Kerr, chosen by his friends to move it, he said, because 'I am a soured and seared bachelor, broken on the wheel of life', but it was supported from all quarters. With more schools, and an increase in pupils continuing to a higher age, considerably more teachers would be needed, and the requirement for married women to retire not only deprived the profession of them, but also put off prospective recruits to teaching, if they thought their careers might be cut short. Married women had kept many schools going during the War, and might have particular skills in caring for children. Gallacher also referred to women's special skill in teaching domestic science, which from today's perspective seems a worrying stereotype, though he redeemed his speech by arguing the principle of equality between the sexes, and striking out 'the old tradition of the inferiority of women'. Women MPs, unsurprisingly, supported the measure, including Conservatives such as Lady Astor and Thelma Cazalet Keir, a keen feminist and a 'Tory Reformer'.[7]

While there was resistance from the civil servants, Ede's support was clear, if expressed in unfortunate language. A marriage bar resulted in a headmistress being typically single and middle-aged, 'who has led a life of repression' and 'has to deal with young and good-looking assistants'. With secondary education extending to older pupils, the most suitable head will not be 'a sex-starved spinster'.[8] Butler was persuaded by this, and by the argument that after the war a teacher shortage was expected. He promised to insert an amendment to cover the point. The change proved highly significant for the teaching profession in the post-war years, with Dent commenting that only one in twenty full-time women teachers at maintained schools in 1939 were married, while by 1960 nearly half were. As we shall see, though, the Act was not entirely a triumph for the principle of gender equality.

On Clause 24, the House for the first time had to divide and vote. The issue here was the requirement that every school day should begin with a collective act of worship. This was already standard practice, and whether it should be made compulsory was a contentious point, particularly with teachers. Butler was accused of having given in to Archbishop Temple and other Church leaders. A number of MPs on the political left forced the division, but they were easily defeated. Ede was, however, prepared to amend the clause from requiring 'a collective act of worship' to 'collective worship', to reflect the reality of schools where the space was not available for the whole school to assemble together.

Under Clause 25, in county schools collective worship would not be distinctive of any particular religion, and Clause 26 provided the same for auxiliary controlled schools, though Butler and Ede conceded to them the right to give denominational instruction twice a week, if parents requested it. As for the aided (and special agreement) schools, Clause 27 permitted their governors to arrange for entirely denominational religious teaching. In the words of Stuart Maclure, 'The Roman Catholic interest never accepted the financial settlement for voluntary school building, but in general the religious clauses aroused less acrimony than past experience had led many to expect'.[9]

It was becoming clear that the Bill was not making as quick progress as might be wished, though Ede recorded on 13 March that Rab, suffering a bad cold, had told his team he was not despondent about it. His greater concern was that some of the points made by Henry Brooke might be taken up by the bishops in the House of Lords, though that did not in fact turn out to be a problem. Ede, however, pressed the case for more time for the Bill, writing to Butler that he feared problems with local authorities failing to budget properly where they were affected by arrangements for the Part III Authorities changing, and also with the possibility that the Labour Conference might end the electoral truce, and put in jeopardy the Bill as a compromise, cross-party measure.[10] Butler spoke to the whips and, on 14 March, it was eventually decided the Committee Stage must complete before Easter, which fell on 9 April 1944, sitting on two (and if needs be, three) days a week.

Nonetheless, it was not until 21 March that the Bill was considered again. By this time, an amendment raising the school-leaving age to sixteen (rather than merely fifteen) within three years, had been drafted, under the driving force of Mrs Cazalet Keir, with cross-party support. On 16 March, Ede met five other MPs, as the Party's Committee on Education, to discuss this, and we can infer he was unhappy. When the House met again on 21 March, various Clauses were despatched quickly, but the main debate was on Clauses 31 to 33, concerning special educational treatment and the compulsory school age. Special treatment for pupils with disability had been uneven in the past,[11] but the Bill would require each LEA to ascertain which children required it, for children to be medically examined, and for the authorities to address 'any disability of mind or body'. Ede dealt on his own with the points raised about this, which were generally suggesting that the provisions were insufficiently forceful. He promised to consider stronger wording, though in the end the matter was overlooked.

Then came the question of compulsory school age. Clause 33 defined this with a maximum of fifteen years, effective from the date this part of the Education Act would come into operation – which would be 1 April 1945 – but with a provision, in a subsequent Clause, for the Government to postpone this for two years at the most. Mrs Cazalet Keir's proposal required this age to rise to sixteen twelve months after the Act's effective date, with a maximum period of postponement of three years. The problem was that virtually all who spoke agreed that sixteen was the ideal age, but from the Government's perspective this was unrealistic. Butler dealt with this on his own ('I went out for lunch', Ede recorded) and, when the argument was pressed to a vote, he won by 172 votes to 137. Ede then took a further proposal about individual children having a personal school-leaving age of sixteen, which he disposed of by showing it was unnecessary, and a cheerful Rab told him he now hoped to get the Bill through in line with the timetable. In the outcome, the Bill set the age at fifteen, with the objective that it would then rise to sixteen, though this would not happen till 1972.

The next clause taken that day imposed a statutory duty on every parent to cause their child 'to receive efficient full-time education suitable to his age, ability and aptitude, either by regular attendance at school or otherwise.' Ede considered this crucial, later recalling that 'the word I fought for … was aptitude, and it would be a complete social revolution … if parents carried out that duty'.[12] An attempt was made to amend this Clause 34, to the effect that children between seven and twelve would have to receive their education at a State school, but Ede opposed this, arguing for parental freedom to choose education outside the state (mentioning the problems caused recently elsewhere in Europe by a state monopoly on education), subject to the requirement that the government could inspect private schools and refuse to licence them where they were inadequate. This also went to a vote, but only six members opposed him.

Ede also covered much of Clause 35, which dealt with parents who neglect their duty, supported by Butler, who responded in regard to Clauses 36, about compulsory attendance at special schools, and 37 and 38, regarding the offence of failing to secure regular attendance. They both took the lead on Clause 39, respecting the duties of LEAs for further education, before the House called an end to the debate for the day. Two days later, Thursday 23 March 1944 (the debate was being kept off Friday business), saw a quarter of the entire Bill (in terms of numbers of clauses) discussed.

Some of these dealt with further education and 'young people's colleges', which would provide part-time and day-release courses for all those up to age eighteen. Ede played the leading part in responding to speeches here, but with hindsight that seems of little importance, since the plans for the young people's colleges were never implemented. The next Clauses established the School Health Service, one of the major advances of the 1944 Act, and provision of school meals and milk, which were both covered by Butler.

Ede, on the other hand, took the lead on Clause 51, by seeking an amendment to impose a duty on LEAs to provide facilities for recreation, and social and physical training. This had been first drafted as a discretionary power for the LEAs, but Admiral Sir William James had argued that was not good enough; it must be a duty. James was the grandson of John Everett

Millais, whose first call to fame was as the boy in the painting of 'Bubbles', but had now recently retired from a long naval career during and between both world wars, including as commander-in-chief at Portsmouth, the city he had then been elected to represent as a Conservative. Ede cited his own experience, as a schoolmaster and a pupil, of schools where it was hard for children to get adequate PE, and often only on gravelled playgrounds – after 'having to pay for footwear for four children, my father used to say that playgrounds were laid down ... by ... the leather industry'. LEAs should plan for playing fields, as the Surrey and London County Councils had recently done in Surrey.

Ede also covered the clause empowering the LEAs to provide free transport, and largely those altering the law in regard to employment of teenagers to take into account the rise in compulsory school age, exempting auxiliary schools from rates, and preventing endowments from being used for relief from rates. Next, he addressed the registration of independent schools (and complaints about them raised in the course of inspection), the only part of the Education Act which would affect the independent sector at all. Rab dealt with provisions for determining disputes and questions.

In the course of the debate on Clause 67 (complaints against independent schools), a significant tribute was paid to James Chuter Ede. Kenneth Lindsay, the National Labour politician who had been Ede's immediate predecessor at Education, and (it will be recalled) had been criticised by Ede over employment of children, now sat for Kilmarnock as a 'National Independent'. He said:

> It does not fall to many of us to preside over a Departmental Committee and then to take part in the Debates on a Bill which puts the recommendations of that Committee into legislation. It must be a very peculiar sense of satisfaction to [Ede]. He did a very fine job on this work many years ago.

Lindsay had often to state that the right moment for legislation had not arrived, but Ede had seen it through. In reply, he thanked Lindsay, saying it

> is a matter of some satisfaction to me that ... at any rate I have been able to play my part in bringing this matter on to the Statute Book, because the revelations laid before my Committee were such as to convince us that a substantial number of children in this country are being most shamefully ill-treated in the matter of education in the worst of these independent schools. Other independent schools are among the best in the country.

On that happy note, the debate was adjourned to 28 March, when the biggest conflict relating to the Education Bill arose.

The first issue that day was the extent to which fees could be charged by LEAs (Clause 59). Rab dealt with several points here, 'very effectively' in Ede's view, though in one case only after a division. Ede then covered ten further clauses, about school inspections, authority for private schools to make arrangements with LEAs for ancillary services such as their health service regarding medical inspections, and empowering LEAs to give financial assistance for pupils, to conduct educational research, and to accept gifts for educational purposes. A further measure, close to his heart, required a Chief Educational Officer to be appointed by each LEA, with the Ministry's consent to each individual shortlisted; he had argued that good CEOs were essential to make the Act work, and had convinced his colleagues that the Whitehall veto was necessary, based on his experience with police authorities appointing chief constables[13].

When Clause 82 was called he went out to tea, leaving Rab to deal with Mrs Cazalet Keir's proposal requiring the Burnham Committees to abolish different pay scales for male and female teachers. Equal pay had been an issue for many years, particularly for the National Union of Women Teachers, which claimed to have asked a number of women MPs to raise the question at this stage[14]. So she was supported by a succession of MPs, both on the Conservative side (such as Nancy Astor and Peter Thorneycroft), and from the radical left (Jimmy Maxton, for one). Butler opposed this, but he was clearly 'on the spot', as he put it. His grounds were that the Bill should not be 'a stalking horse for people's political views', that it would upset the authority of the Burnham Committee, and would have financial implications for the Treasury. He and Ede discussed resigning if the amendment passed, one of a number of points which Howard[15] cites as evidence of the close working relationship between them, and of Ede's loyalty to Rab. In fact the Committee approved equal pay by one vote (117–116). Churchill and Attlee did not take part, though Anthony Eden, Leader of the House as well as Foreign Secretary, did. He said the government would consider the result of the vote.

This was the only major defeat Churchill's War Coalition ever suffered in the Commons, and the Prime Minister, refusing to accept any resignations, called a cabinet meeting at 10.00 that evening. He insisted that the amended clause be struck out, and was prepared to make the issue a matter of confidence. He said he feared the Germans would announce the vote 'as a sign that Britain was war weary and that the Government no longer had their support'.[16] He told Butler he felt the equal pay principle was perfectly good, but 'in the wrong place. The amendment is like a potato in a gooseberry pie', according to Ede's later account of the PM's words[17]. There was considerable dispute in both major parties; in Labour those opposed to equal pay included the trade unionist Bevin and the NUT. 'Not his finest hour', is Adonis's conclusion about Bevin on this occasion.[18]

At noon the next day, Churchill announced the government's decision, and that evening Attlee spoke to the Labour ministers, indicating he was not prepared to continue unless he received strong support from the party. A number of MPs on all sides objected – Mrs Cazalet Keir asked if all amendments were to be confidence issues because, if they were, there was little point in the House discussing measures in Committee. But the Government would not budge. On Thursday 30 March 1944, the Clause was returned to the Committee, and Butler had the amendment deleted, even Mrs Cazalet Keir agreeing to vote against her own amendment, having no option but to support the PM in this vote of confidence. On this occasion, Churchill and Attlee made sure they took part in the division.

It seems strange to think that, just a few weeks before the victory in Europe was complete, Churchill's government might have been brought down by a decision on equal pay for women teachers, and it has to be wondered whether he would have indeed have broken up the Coalition and resigned had the House not come into line. At root, it seems that the union of Labour members, Tory reformers and others of a feminist inclination were wanting to make a point, which today seems beyond dispute, while the government did not want any distraction from its main business. With the subsequent decision to set up a Royal Commission on Equal Pay, both sides were eventually satisfied.

Ede then took over again from Butler, who must have been emotionally exhausted, and dealt with clauses regarding compulsory purchase of land by LEAs, local enquiries on the Minister's behalf, provisions consequential on cessation of functions by former authorities (and protection of rights of their officers on war service), and compensation for those affected by the statute. Butler, however, took over the debate on Clause 92, empowering the Minister to intervene if an LEA or governors failed to discharge their duties. The Bill was then adjourned to 4 April.

By this time, the House was speeding through the Clauses. Comments on the financial and supplemental provisions were responded to by both Butler and Ede, as each matter required, though one gets the sense that Rab was relying on his Parliamentary Secretary for much of the detail in the points they covered. Clause 108, on the Commencement of the Act, provided that Parts I and V (addressing the central administration of the new Ministry of

Education and the supplemental provisions) would come into effect on Royal Assent, Part III (with the limited provisions about independent schools) at a date to be appointed, and the rest on 1 April 1945. Ede was asked when he intended to implement Part III, and he gave an evasive reply, citing a lack of inspectors for independent schools (the answer would in fact turn out to be October 1957, when Ede would write a commemorative article about it). Then the Chairman announced that the final original clause (Clause 111) stood part of the Bill, and it was greeted with a resounding cheer.

There were, however, several further clauses to be added. Butler introduced a financial one, and it was on this that Ede made his comment that Butler 'commissioned me to see the leaders of the Free Churches', making his distinction between a Free Churchman and, as he was, a Nonconformist, hence his rejecting the authoritarian conception of religion, and the right to impose his views on others. 'That is the philosophy on which I have based my attitude to the religious Clauses of the Bill, and I speak as one who was a Nonconformist child in a single-school area. Think where I should be if I had had a board school in my parish.' The distinction between Free Churchman and Nonconformist was one which stayed with him, and he would return to it later in life.

The next clause he proposed, which became Section 54 of the Act, dealt with the power of the LEA to take action where a pupil was 'infested with vermin or is in a foul condition'. It received no challenge. After that came clauses exempting school buildings from building bye-laws, and empowering LEAs to make grants to universities to improve further education in their areas. Butler accepted a clause authorising an LEA to defray members' expenses. Various other proposed Clauses were withdrawn, many after clarification from Ede about the government's view. Though a 'very trying day', wrote Ede, few MPs were inclined to challenge the government again.

Even that was not, however, the end of the Second Reading. The Schedules to the Bill had to be considered, and 5 April was taken up with these, and in particular the First Schedule. This raised again the question of which authorities should be LEAs, and which should not, bearing in mind the proposed abolition of the Part III Authorities. Butler let the debate continue for a considerable time, before he intervened with a long speech himself, and then Ede took over, resisting some proposals and moving other amendments of his own, to facilitate local joint arrangements for LEAs where appropriate. The Schedule empowered the Minister to constitute a 'joint education board' for two or more small local authority areas, and LEAs to set up schemes of divisional administration. This compromise was eventually accepted, after an extended period of time, so that, on the Wednesday of Holy Week, the Bill passed its Committee Stage and Second Reading. The target of completion by Easter had been met. At the end of a Parliamentary Party meeting that day, Arthur Greenwood congratulated Ede on his work on the Bill, and he was able to record that their principal difficulties had been overcome, with no major concessions made.

The week after Easter, the NUT held its 1944 conference at Central Hall, Westminster, where a discussion on the Bill took place among members and officials of local education committees. W.P. Alexander, Sheffield's Director of Education, offered what he described as his solution to grouping secondary children – 15 per cent should be educated at grammar schools, 10 per cent at technical schools (7½ per cent of boys, 2½ per cent of girls), and 75 per cent at secondary moderns. Ede, on the other hand, stated in his speech that 'I have gone through the Bill with a small toothcomb, and I can find only one school for senior pupils – and that is a secondary school'. The pedantic commentator may wonder what a 'small toothcomb' might be, but his point was clear – there would not necessarily be three types of school, he did not know where the idea came from, and a secondary school could be of any type which suited its area[19]. Gillard has pointed out that none of the words 'tripartite', 'selection', 'eleven plus', 'grammar schools' or 'secondary modern' appear in the Act at all.

Little has been said here about internal issues within the Labour Party. They have received attention from other writers[20], and are not often central to the life of James Chuter Ede. They did, however, sometimes impinge on him, including when the activities of Aneurin Bevan caused dissention within the Parliamentary Party. On 28 April 1944 Bevan had spoken against the government, when Ernest Bevin, as Minister of Labour, had issued orders restraining instigators of strikes. Bevin had received some support from the unions, but Bevan had proposed the motion against him in the House. On 2 May Ede was told by the Chief Whip, Whiteley, of the recommendation that Bevan should have the Labour whip withdrawn. At a meeting of the Parliamentary Party on 3 May, there was a challenge by MPs supporting Bevan. It was unsuccessful, and he was expelled, but Ede was annoyed that the main criticism had been on Bevan's role in opposing the government; his own objection was to the language Bevan had used. This would portend later difficulties with Bevan. For the moment, Ede's conclusion was that 'the only cure for Bevan's frame of mind was office', which was out of the question then. Even when he reached the Cabinet, he would be a difficult colleague.

On 9 May, prior to the Education Bill being passed to the House of Lords, it was considered by the Commons at the Report Stage. Before they started, however, Mrs Cazalet Keir had asked the Prime Minister to make a statement on equal pay for equal work, and he confirmed a Royal Commission would be set up, which had a brief wider than just teaching. When it came to the Education Bill, Butler proposed a list of amendments, including one reinstating the original Clause 82 on teachers' pay, without the equal pay amendment, and Mrs Cazalet Keir was clearly satisfied by what her efforts had achieved. He also proposed consequential amendments arising from the decision to change the Board to a Ministry, while Ede dealt with a share of the amendments himself. They continued their work on 11 May, until Ede was able to move the Third Reading of the Bill – 'my privilege, and … a very high honour'.

He spoke at loquacious length, about history and education in the USA, until he was rebuked from the Chair for deviating from the matter of the Third Reading. He listed the Bill's achievements, finishing with a tribute to Butler, 'a very great man indeed'. He:

> represents one tradition of the educational life of our country – the tradition that passes from the public schools into the university – although I understand from private conversations with him that he is, at least, unique in this, since he chose his public school against the traditional wishes of his family and managed to impose his will on them. That only shows that he started on this job very early in life. I come from the other tradition – from the elementary school, through the secondary school to the university.

His message was one of unity – of those two traditions, and of a national system of education for all pupils. The first MP to speak in congratulation was Mrs Cazalet Keir, and she was joined by many others. This continued on 12 May, until eventually Butler closed the debate, giving due credit to his colleague. The Education Bill had passed its Third Reading, and Ede found a telegraph boy waiting

> at Ewell that afternoon, with a telegram: 'Ede Tayles Hill Ewell. South Shields Labour Party Congratulate you on your Great achievement we are proud of our Member. Gompertz'.[21]

Sadly, at this moment of triumph, Ede's life was disrupted by the health of his wife, Lilian. On 8 May 1944, she had been unable to get up, and a nurse was summoned to visit in the afternoon. Her husband returned to find her in great pain. Next day, the nurse came to give Lilian breakfast, just before Jim went to London and, when he phoned at lunchtime, the call was answered by their neighbour Mrs Wiltshire, who said a specialist was visiting that evening, and a nursing home was being sought. The specialist, Dr East, confirmed a thrombosis, and prescribed six to eight weeks' rest. After consulting their GP, Dr Wilde, about different hospitals and homes, they decided she should spend the time in Epsom Hospital. On getting there on 11 May, Ede found her in 'a large, airy private room', having arrived by ambulance in acute pain.

For more than two months, he was visiting Lilian in hospital daily, when that was possible, and when it was not, he relied on friends such as the Wiltshires to look in, while they often provided him with meals, either at their house or his. He found his wife very tired, but recognised that was precisely what her doctors wanted; she needed rest. He wrote with the news to Lilian's brother Dick and two sisters on 12 May, hearing back from Dick and sister Florrie four days later. It was a particular disappointment for Jim, because he and Lilian had planned to stay in New Brighton for those few days, while he was carrying out Board duties in the Wirral area. He still had to go, but left her behind to be visited by these friends.

When he went to the hospital, he took letters of congratulation, such as one from the Mayor of South Shields complimenting him on the progress of the Education Bill, which received its First Reading in the Lords on 16 May 1944, was debated by them on 6 to 8 June, and in Committee on 20 to 29 June. Meanwhile, there was plenty of work for Ede to do, as he made several journeys round the country to explain the Bill. On 1 June he took the train to Cornwall, noticing the US fleet docked in Plymouth Harbour. Staying near St Austell, he spoke to the staff and boys of King's Canterbury, who had been moved to the Carlyon Bay Hotel. The next day he addressed several more evacuated schools, and then went to the station in Truro, to see Lilian's niece, Joyce Buttersby, who lived in Falmouth. On D-day, 6 June, he was in Huddersfield, when he recorded that news of the invasion of France was making 'everyone … agog'. Additionally, other Parliamentary business was proceeding, with Morrison introducing a Town and Country Planning Bill, to permit local authorities to plan redeveloping areas which had been bombed. Ede was pleased to note that Morrison's conduct on the bill was unfavourably compared, by Bevin, to his and Butler's on the Education Bill.

A further pleasing development was the announcement in the King's Birthday Honours, that Ede had been appointed to the Privy Council. Without any false modesty, Ede had prepared his own press release, writing to warn the editor of the *Shields Daily Gazette* in May (subject to an embargo on the news), with a brief autobiography attached, and explaining that as 'the photograph you have recently been using of me excites my wife's steady condemnation, I am venturing to enclose one which taken (*sic*) in my robes as Charter Mayor of Epsom and Ewell which commands her approval'[22]. On Thursday 8 June a supplement to the *London Gazette*, dated the previous Friday, published the new honour (at the same time, as it happened, that Ede's old adversary, Viscount Halifax, now Ambassador to the US, was promoted to an Earl). According to Jefferys, this appointment was due in part to support from Butler[23]. Visiting Lilian in hospital each day, he would bring her and read all the letters of congratulation he received. He retained them all his life; they fill a complete file[24]. Amongst them is an intriguing letter from 'Muriel', at East Hill House, Mundesley, addressed to 'Uncle Jim', with congratulations from her and Norah, who were running Penelope's Café there, and from Eddie; they sent their good wishes to Auntie for her recovery. Mundesley would shortly be her destination for part of her convalescence.

On top of everything else, he learnt that Butler had had an accident on 11 June, falling off a ladder in the garden of Pembroke College, when he was visiting his parents in Cambridge. He had been knocked about, and was now in a nursing home. This added to Ede's workload, both with questions in the House and outside Parliament. On 15 June he deputised for Rab at a National Liberal Club lunch, addressing a meeting of members; he was able to tell them that he had once been a member himself, thirty years before, in his own Liberal days. Next morning, he rang Mrs Butler, who confirmed her husband had broken ribs, and was expected home at the end of the following week. It was a week of compliments and hardships. The *Times Educational Supplement* described the Privy Counsellorship as well-deserved, and *The Schoolmaster* wrote a piece with a friendly caricature, but his nights as well as days were under pressure. In response to the Normandy landings, the Germans started their flying bomb attacks on London and the counties to the south. Ede and his neighbours, the Wiltshires and Barbers, reinforced the shelter on his property, and spent several disturbed nights sleeping together there. He summarised the situation in his diary on 20 June 1944:

> How I had planned that my Privy Counsellorship should be the occasion for a celebration which would have enabled me to show LME how much I appreciated her help and encouragement

but instead the achievement had been clouded by her illness in hospital, the renewed attacks, sleepless nights, and extra pressure from Butler's absence.

On 29 June, he was sworn of the Privy Council at Buckingham Palace[25]. His work as alderman on Surrey CC continued when it could. He used his good offices to resolve a dispute there about the longstanding issue, teacher representation on the Education Committee; the SCTA would have two representatives there, and the Secondary Association one[26]. However, he no longer described himself as Alderman Chuter Ede; he was now Right Honourable.

After considerable pressure from Butler to set an early date, and printing delays caused by the flying bombs[27], Lord Fleming's Committee finally published its report on the public schools on 26 July, before the Parliamentary recess. This was, of course, too late to influence the Education Bill, which covered public schools only in regard to their registration and inspection arrangements, and it made little impact on Ede's work. It has been unkindly described as 'a report full of special pleading which had little influence on the course of events'[28], though that comment is no less accurate. Most of its proposals were ignored, both by the government of the time and its successors.

On 27 July, the Lords' amendments to the Bill were considered by the Commons. Most of these were accepted by Butler, sometimes subject to minor further amendment, Ede taking only a secondary role, though he seems to have played a larger part as the proceedings went on. One significant change made was to alter the term 'auxiliary school' to 'voluntary school', the phrase still in use today. On 1 August, the Lords accepted the final Commons version.

By this time, Ede had finally been able to take Lilian out of hospital on 22 July, and they immediately went by car to Minehead, where she stayed convalescing for four weeks. Jim based himself there, but moved back to London, Ewell or elsewhere as work required it. He kept in correspondence with her family, until on 19 August they left Minehead for Norfolk, stopping off in Luton for a night, and reaching Mundesley on the coast the next day. Once more Lilian stayed put, while he spent each week in Ewell and the office, with some trips to South Shields, trying to get back to Mundesley at the weekends, including a longer stay there for his birthday on 11 September. It was 25 September before he was able to bring Lilian back home, 140 days (as he noted) since her health first broke down.

On 3 August 1944, the Education Act had finally received Royal Assent, and Ede recorded in his diary that it 'ends the first stage of the great educational adventure on which I embarked in May, 1940'. G.A.N. Lowndes, who had written an authoritative history of education in the 1930s[29], produced a second edition thirty years later in which he analysed the influence of the Act, and concluded that:

> few Bills of such a length and such importance can ever have passed through all their stages in the House in less time and with less controversy and so small a residue of hard feelings.

The reason, said Lowndes, was that Ede and Butler were persuasive and were ready to listen to, consider and discuss proposed amendments, even when they disagreed, and in consequence 'few ministers have ever won such golden opinions in every quarter of the House'. It was a major achievement and the evidence shows that George Thomas was correct in his view that Ede was 'just as responsible as Butler' for it[30]. Indeed, Thomas would later write, even though he had not joined Parliament in 1944, that 'all Britain regarded him as one of the Joint Architects' of the Act[31].

So what did the 1944 Act achieve? The provision with which it is most associated nowadays – establishing secondary modern, technical and grammar schools for education after age 11 – was not one which it covered at all. That was an arrangement accepted by Ellen Wilkinson and George Tomlinson, Ede's Labour successors at the Ministry of Education, and followed from the ethos of the Spens and Norwood Reports, but even as fine a historian as A.J.P. Taylor describes the Act as making secondary education free – which of course is one of its achievements – and of three types – grammar, technical and modern[32]. This on occasion infected later supporters of comprehensive schooling; Tony Benn's diary for 25 October 1976 inveighs against 'the danger of divisiveness engendered by the 1944 Education Act with all its nonsense about different types of minds requiring different types of schools'[33]. Ede, however, had ensured references to the three types of school were removed from the statute.

One really major achievement was providing for the rise in school-leaving age to fifteen, which was set for 1947, and for which Ellen Wilkinson achieved approval that year, shortly before her own death, despite the problems of that difficult winter. The long-term aim of raising it to sixteen would eventually be met, though not for nearly thirty years. Along with this, free secondary education was achieved for all children up to that age, with abolition of the elementary schools.

I have covered the Bill's Parliamentary progress in some detail – perhaps more than some readers might wish – to illustrate the range of measures it embraced. Even a list restricted to the main ones is still quite long. Nursery schools and classes were established, along with provision for children requiring special educational treatment, for developing further education, for medical treatment, milk and school meals, and social and physical education. The 'county colleges' for young people were to be established, though that innovation was never seen through. Independent schools were put under a programme of inspection, the procedure for teachers' salaries was made statutory, and local administration through the LEAs (with their additional powers and duties) made clear. The compulsory act of worship and RI teaching, with power for parents to withdraw their children, was introduced (though this had been almost universal already). The Central Advisory Councils were set up. Over the years, many of these provisions have been amended or superseded, but the general structure of state education designed in 1944 remains. In the words of one commentator in the 1950s, Butler and Ede 'discarded the traditional concept of education' by showing it to be a continuing process, beyond the narrow confines of basic schooling and instruction.[34]

Some have commented that this was a 'Tory measure'[35], and certainly it was conservative in some respects. It altered, rather than abolished, the dual system, with its religious issues, and it did little in regard to independent schools, apart from requiring their inspection. Perhaps it was insufficiently ambitious in its target for raising the school leaving age to sixteen. However, in a Parliament with such a massive Conservative majority, and an elderly Prime Minister with traditional views who was reluctant to consider social legislation at all, its orthodox nature was unavoidable in some degree. A few Labour MPs and supporters (such as Laski) felt too many compromises were made, but Bailey has shown that they were in a minority. The Act has been differently appraised by commentators over the years since 1944, as educational thinking has moved in one direction or another, and the criticism of the Norwood Report has clouded some of that assessment[36]. The comment was made at the time, that what it provided was a challenge for future years. This particularly related to resource issues, when so many more teachers were needed, and buildings required to be constructed.[37] That, though, took place after Ede's career (though not, of course, his interests) moved away from education, and so is of less concern to us. We need only say that the list of the Act's reforms is long and, though many of its provisions have been amended over time, it is to the great credit of James Chuter Ede, working with Butler and their civil servants, that a measure of such a reforming nature was enacted – particularly during a time of national crisis, in the Second World War.

Another view is that the Act was largely the thinking of the civil servants rather than the ministers at the Board of Education[38], a claim which might put both Ede and Butler in their modest place. However, studies of the documents – principally correspondence and Ede's diaries – lead to the conclusion that Ede made many suggestions to the team at the Board, and was at least equal in importance in developing the provisions of the statute[39]. Even on the religious issue, where Rab certainly took the lead, Ede's understanding of the Nonconformist position was an essential balance to the Anglican stance; and in regard to the teaching profession and unions, his grasp of how the system worked was better than anyone's. Barber's comment was that 'Ede's role in the passage of the 1944 Education Act can hardly be overstated'.[40] As George Thomas would say, in his assessment of Ede's role, 'a whole generation is in his debt for the 1944 Education Act. On education he was a giant … full marks.'[41]

One change which the Act made, and which Ede immediately took up, was the alteration of the name of the Board of Education (with its President) to a Ministry. Up to August 1944 his diary constantly refers to Rab Butler as 'the P.' Once the statute was enacted, he is 'the M'.

Chapter 11

Change in Government

Churchill's coalition continued while the war in Europe lasted. On 30 August 1944 Ede was writing to Bevin, asking him to ensure that there should be early release of servicemen for educational purposes included in the proposals he was putting together for demobilisation at the end of the war. In fact, Bevin reported this to the cabinet, which decided nonetheless that it could not give preference on these grounds[1]. Ede was also concerned that, while science and medical students had not been called up, 'Humanitarians' had been, at a great loss to education. Unless they could return to the universities, this might be 'destroying the future of the civilization for which we are fighting'. Butler subsequently had a little more success in achieving these objectives.

In September 1944 Ede was having to deal with the report of the Committee on the training of teachers, which had been published in May. Teacher training had been an issue for the Board since Ramsbotham's time, and early in 1942 Butler had established an enquiry chaired by Arnold McNair, an academic lawyer who had become Vice-Chancellor of Liverpool University. In its report, the members of the Committee failed to reach agreement on the role of universities in training, and there followed much fruitless discussion with those representing universities and others. Ede was firmly of the view (shared by his colleague, Sir Fred Mander of the NUT, a McNair Committee member) that universities should take control of teacher training, as they could provide a richer education. This had been one of the Labour Party's seventeen points in 1943.

He wrote to Rab on 12 September[2], arguing that the universities should be exhorted to agree, despite their misgivings about being overwhelmed by more students of a different type from those whom they already educated. Ede was persuasive enough to provide Rab with a way forward, though he seems to have played a lesser role after this. The suspicion must be that by 'different type', some universities were indicating it was one thing to educate an élite of men (and, to a small extent, women) in their specialised subjects, some of whom would teach those subjects in the grammar and public schools to the older pupils, who would then form subsequent intakes of undergraduates; it was another to train those – more predominantly women – who would spend their careers teaching children of lesser ability in the elementary (or, as they would now be, primary) schools. That, as we have seen, is exactly the attitude Ede had always resisted, both in its élitism and its gender bias; teaching of all types was a profession demanding full and equal qualification for all its members.

There was immediate interest in the new Education Act. On 6 October 1944, Ede was invited to address a conference, at the Friends' Meeting House in Birmingham, put on by the British Association for Commercial and Industrial Education, after which he took questions[3]. He stressed the new duties on parents and the abolition of the elementary system, and raised as an issue the competition for places in secondary education. He retold the story that in 1895 he had sat the Surrey Junior Scholarship examination, when thirty-two out of sixty-four candidates were successful. Now, he said, there are 900 places for 9,000 applicants, so there was certainly more to be done to educate young people to their potential, and provide qualified recruits for commerce and industry, represented by the Association.

With Butler, on 24 November he met a delegation from the Governing Bodies Association, led by Bishop Fisher, and the Headmasters' Conference, to discuss the Fleming proposals. This meeting proved fairly unproductive, and resulted in an agreement to meet again in the new year, to concentrate on Fleming's scheme for primary school children to receive bursaries to join the public schools as boarders. Rab led most of the discussion, but Ede was able to make his contribution, dealing with the likely views of the LEAs on the various proposals about getting the public schools to take more pupils from the state sector[4].

On 28 November 1944, Churchill held a gathering for all the ministers, from all parties, at Downing Street. A V-2 raid was going on (though in the distance), while the PM read out, behind closed doors, the King's Speech to be presented to Parliament the following day, and then toasted the King. Attlee in turn proposed the health of Churchill, and assured the company that the coalition would stay together until Germany was defeated, but said he did not know if that would be another year. Churchill made some pleasant compliments to him in response, going on to applaud many of the Labour team. Morrison, with his special knowledge of London, had been tasked with dealing with the most difficult situations there, while Bevin had transferred men into jobs where they earned only half their previous pay, and had put millions of women into work. Cripps was credited with bringing 'a keen brain and wonderful organising abilities to his tasks'. Ede records no mention of himself by Churchill, though such a mention would have been surprising, bearing in mind his (apparently) junior role.

Bevin spoke next, pointing out the contrast between Churchill's words now and what he had said about the Labour Party in the past – a contrast which would be seen again in the election campaign the following year. Toasts were drunk all round, and the party seems to have ended on a note of jollity, although not all Ede's Labour colleagues in Parliament would turn out to be so pleased when the King's Speech was presented.

By this time, Ede proudly noted, he had been Parliamentary Secretary at Education for four years and 205 days, so becoming the third longest occupant of the post; on 6 December 1944 he had passed the period of office of the Duchess of Atholl in the 1920s. Herbert Lewis had held the position for some seven years under Asquith and then Lloyd George, while Trevelyan had done so for a similar period in Asquith's ministry. Ede would go on to complete five years and thirteen days in the job (according to his own statement to the Commons on 11 June 1945), with only Lewis and Trevelyan having a longer record.

On 8 December an amendment to the Address was debated, and heavily defeated, although Ede saw no Labour MPs other than members of the Government in the No Lobby, most of them having evidently abstained – 'by his looks the PM did not regard this as a very favourable vote'. The subject for the amendment was, perhaps improbably, British actions in Greece, where many Labour members felt the Government was supporting an oppressive monarchy against the forces of democracy whose resistance had liberated the country. During the week from 11 to 15 December, this point was picked up again at a Party Conference, which Ede attended, and which showed itself extremely perturbed about Greece, before it also passed a resolution on India, interpreted by *The Times* as calling for immediate withdrawal from the Subcontinent[5]. Though the Conference also decided overwhelmingly that the Labour ministers should remain in the government until Germany was defeated, it is clear a wide section of the party felt an increasing distance from the Conservatives dominating it.

On 12 December, Ede read the draft paper produced by the Ministry of Education on *The Nation's Schools*, which the civil servants intended should prompt the implementation of the Education Act. One issue he greatly disliked was its unsympathetic references to the multilateral school. On 18 December, having decided against going to sit on the bench in Epsom, he saw Butler in the office, learning that Rab too was not satisfied with the notes for *The Nation's Schools*, and had written criticising certain points. Ede told him he particularly disliked the 'dismissal of the multilateral school with a sneer', and Butler replied that he was more in favour of such schools than any of his team.

At the end of the year, Ede's summary was that 1944 had seen great achievements for him, not just because of the Education Act, which had 'given the education service a fresh start on improved lines', but also from his Privy Counsellorship, which 'represents the highest peak I am likely to reach personally'. In his view, he would from now on 'go downhill but in doing my share to unify the education system of the country I have realised my best hopes and fondest ambitions.' With this typical piece of modesty, clearly honestly meant, he closed the year, not realising what the next few months had in store.

On 2 January 1945, Ede was invited to a dinner party by Lord Kemsley, the proprietor of newspapers including the *Sunday Times*, whose editor was also there. Others round the table were Kemsley's son (the Conservative MP for Buckingham), the Dean of St Paul's, the Headmaster of Harrow, and the historian Arthur Bryant. Why Kemsley should have invited Ede, with whose politics he would have been broadly out of sympathy, can only be wondered. Though he had entertained him before, back in 1941 when Dorothy Thompson was in town, this time the occasion was a much smaller party. Perhaps the host was just interested in a lively discussion, which certainly took place. Much of this related to the premiership, R.W. Moore, the Harrow head, saying Churchill had been very tired when he had recently visited his old school. Ede said he believed Churchill 'would carry on until he had won the war and dealt with the peace', and all agreed he would get a majority when the election was held. Kemsley tipped Butler to become Foreign Secretary, a proposal Rab quickly scotched when Ede saw him the next day (he did get to the Foreign Office, in fact, but not till 1963).

While Labour concern for Greece continued, much of the discussion during the rest of the winter related to the outcome of the Yalta Conference, which had just taken place between Churchill, Stalin and Roosevelt. The Commons voted its support for Churchill, a proposal treated as a matter of confidence, with a Labour backbench amendment regretting the Yalta decisions on Poland being well defeated on 28 February 1945. Next day, the confidence motion was approved *nem con*, with the two tellers against it, John McGovern and Campbell Stephen from the ILP, having nobody to count through.

In March, the Conservatives held a Party Conference, at which Churchill, putting his hand on Butler's shoulder, announced that his government had passed the greatest Education Act in the country's history. When discussing this, Rab confirmed to Ede that everyone realised it was the result of the Coalition. For much of the time remaining to them at the new Ministry, administrative life was relatively humdrum, though on 16 March regulations were issued on awards of direct grants to secondary schools, broadly following the Fleming recommendations. A quarter of places in direct-grant schools would be free, and reserved for grant-aided primary pupils, another 25 per cent the LEA could fill (and pay for) from its own schools if it wished, and the remainder would be filled by examination, with fees for poorer children subsidised from Whitehall. Not all Labour MPs were enthused by this, but most were won round by Ede and by the part played on the Fleming Committee by the Labour nominees, G.D.H. Cole and Harold Clay.

At last, on the night of 31 March to 1 April 1945, Part II of the Education Act 1944 came into effect. Ede was well aware of the importance of that date. He stayed awake until midnight, so he would experience the moment that elementary education expired[6]. Next in his diary is the first verse of 'Now thank we all our God …', one of the great Lutheran anthems. He probably recalled the remark made by George Ridley, the NEC chairman, about the White Paper in July 1943, that he hoped to lay a wreath on the grave of the word 'Elementary'. Ridley had not lived to see the day, having died in January 1944, but Ede could lay that wreath on his behalf. It was Easter Sunday and, at the invitation of the Vicar of Epsom, he went to the town's parish church, to hear a blessing on the Education Act, on the Minister, and on the Parliamentary Secretary.

On 26 March, David Lloyd George had died, and Ede attended his memorial service at Westminster Abbey on 10 April. He 'arrived by the wrong door and sat with the ordinary congregation', when presumably he could have sat among the Privy Counsellors. That evening he went with other Labour ministers to see Attlee, who discussed with them his forthcoming visit to San Francisco, joining Anthony Eden for the UN Conference on International Organization, which would create the UN Charter. There had been some criticism in the Party about his involvement[7], but the decision was generally supported by his team.

May was the momentous month of that spring. VE Day occurred on 8 May, and Ede found Parliament Square packed with people. He noted that he rang Lilian up, as though phoning his wife was an exceptional action merited by such an exceptional event. Churchill was cheered in the Commons, and made a grateful speech, following which at his suggestion the House adjourned, so that its Members could go to St Margaret's Church to give thanks. The crowd was bigger than at the Coronation, and Ede processed with his colleagues through a space kept just wide enough by the police. Two days later, it was clear the future of Parliament and the coalition was under review. Rab told Ede he did not want an early election, but some Conservatives made it clear they did not see any grounds for delaying one, indicating a degree of optimism on their side.

That optimism was not well-founded. On 26 April, a by-election in the Conservative seat of Chelmsford had seen the Common Wealth candidate elected by a comfortable majority, and then on 17 May, the old Parliament's last by-election was held at Newport, when this time the Conservative candidate won, but with the ILP achieving 45 per cent of the vote. As agreed by the coalition pact, Labour did not contest either seat, whereas on 15 May at Neath the Conservatives had given Labour a free run, and Ede noted their candidate's vote was only six different from that in 1931, with this time challenges from a Welsh Nationalist and a Revolutionary Communist. On Whit Monday, 21 May, Ede discussed these results in his diary, but felt that using by-elections to speculate on a general election was likely to turn out badly – 'the continental situation may have deteriorated so far as to have created another Red Bogey'. He gathered, from the radio news, that Churchill had suggested his coalition colleagues remained in government together till Japan was defeated, but the Labour leaders declined; the defeat of Germany was as much as their Conference had agreed.

So, on 23 May, Churchill resigned as coalition leader, and was invited to continue with a caretaker Conservative Government. Parliament was to be dissolved on 15 June, with a General Election on 5 July. Ede finished his work at the Ministry of Education, speaking to Maurice Holmes, who did not think Labour would do badly, though he himself was less optimistic. His discussions with other MPs that week showed a wide divergence of views about the likely election result. Butler was sorry they were parting, but expected Ede would continue what they had started at Education if Labour won, commenting that 'the Tory Party's organisation was by no means good …Their only asset was Churchill'.

When Rab rang the Edes the next Sunday, 27 May, he spoke first to Lilian, and then to Jim, with the news that he was being transferred to be Minister of Labour, replacing Bevin. The Education portfolio went to Bonar Law's son, Richard, who had spent most of the Second World War at the War Office and then the Foreign Office, and Ede's job as Parliamentary Secretary to Mrs Cazalet Keir. Her appointment seems strange, in view of her opposition to Churchill on women teachers' pay, and the next day

Butler told Ede he disapproved. Wallace comments that 'Churchill's choice may be seen as an example of magnanimity towards an erstwhile thorn in his flesh, evidence of his sense of humour or testimony of his indifference towards education'[8]. He apparently commented that 'there were as many girls to look after as boys'[9]. That morning, 28 May, the PM had received Ede at Downing Street, thanking him for what he had done, though he could not resist referring to the episode of his refusing a promotion, and later that day he provided a 'tea party' for all the Coalition ministers. Churchill was effusive about the way the parties had held together, and in particular about Attlee's contribution. He stated they would go together to any international conferences which might be held before the election (as indeed they would go to Potsdam, where the conference was being held when the election result was announced). According to Ede's account, 'he intended to say no word that would disparage the great work Labour & Liberal Ministers had done', a statement which sits poorly with what he actually was to say a week later.

On 4 June, Churchill made a radio broadcast, in which he attacked the Labour Party, referring to 'some form of Gestapo' as the underpin for its aim to introduce socialism to the country. This went down badly in many quarters, newspapers including *The Times* the next day criticising the speech. Such extravagant language about the team who had been part of his government for five years, and who had joined him in destroying the Gestapo, might almost have been calculated to backfire. The Independent Labour member, D.N. Pritt, said in the Commons that the broadcast had given Labour fifty seats.

After attending to closing business in the House, Ede worked on his election address, completing it on 7 June. One of his election leaflets stressed his status as a Privy Counsellor, Rt Hon James Chuter Ede, with a photo of him in his Epsom robes and chain of office, and the messages 'A FRIEND SENDS A MESSAGE TO YOU', and 'Help To Make Your Own Future'. It asked the electors to 'work together to get the sort of country and the sort of world we want'. He posted what he had written to Ernie Gompertz in South Shields, who needed to arrange its printing, along with the usual small cards featuring a younger photograph of 'A Faithful Friend, true to the Borough, true to service men and women, true to the workers, true to the seamen', and details of when and where to vote, individualised for each polling station. Labour's ambitious programme for a new government included 'a high and rising standard of living, security for all against a rainy day, an educational system that will give every boy and girl a chance to develop the best that is in them', to quote the Party manifesto, *Let us Face the Future*. In fact the manifesto offered no new thinking on education, but merely gave support to the new Act, which should be implemented quickly[10].

Having sent his work off, he attended the House to listen to Richard Law take two questions, neither of which suggested he had yet mastered his brief. Butler spoke to Ede, complaining that Law was doing the job of Eden, the absent Foreign Secretary, and the Ministry of Education was not being adequately looked after. On 11 June, the Conservatives issued their election manifesto and, Labour having chosen education as a subject for a Supply Day, Law was again at the despatch box. He started inauspiciously by saying he had not had time to take stock of his new ministry, appearing to blame the opposition for choosing to debate the topic of education, and had had extra duties in Eden's absence. He admitted he was not on top of the specifics of the Education Act, so when Ede and others asked him questions of detail, he several times had to excuse his ignorance. The Labour MP Arthur Creech Jones paid tribute to Ede's 'very considerable contribution' to making the Act, and to the way both he and Rab had started implementing the Act while at the Ministry. His colleague William Cove, always critical of the Conservatives in education, berated the new government for *The Nation's Schools*, which had just been issued. As Ede had feared, this supported the tripartite system and advocated a reduction in grammar school places. Cove felt this failed to do justice to implementing what he already called 'the Butler Act', though Mrs Cazalet Keir responded that it was 'the Chuter Ede Act' also.

That was not intended as a compliment to Ede, but to join him in any criticism which MPs might make. Kenneth Lindsay suggested that the Conservatives were saying that the only thing which kept Butler safe was Ede's presence (indeed, one MP compared the two to Don Quixote and Sancho Panza, prompting Ede to ask who was who). Lindsay asked Ede how much of *The Nation's Schools* he had seen while in office, and was told he had read it all, and that Ede and Butler had suggested corrections and discussed them together. Before Mrs Cazalet Keir wound up, Ede made a long speech, saying he felt he was attending an inquest on himself, and was now being allowed to give evidence. He paid tribute to both Ramsbotham and Butler, and to the team which had created the Act, despite manpower shortages. Then he went on to ask about progress on divisional administration, LEA development plans, and school medical schemes. He also spoke about direct grant schools, stressing how important it was that they should not impose fees so high as to exclude poorer pupils, suggesting a new Labour Government might require all places in such schools should be free (in fact it did not do so[11]). He recorded that he 'had a sympathetic hearing'.

In fact, *The Nation's Schools* was an unfortunate incident in Ede's career. Wallace describes it in a chapter heading as 'Labour's Debacle'[12], illustrating an attitude to Ede always rather begrudging, though that refers as much, or more, to Ellen Wilkinson's subsequent loyalty to the document, issued a few weeks before she took over at Education. Wallace had probably not read the entries in Ede's diary which, as we have seen, make clear his support of multilateral schools. Once confronted on the issue, Ede found it hard to avoid ministerial responsibility for the pamphlet, and he must be accountable in part for the statements approving the tripartite system and reducing the number of grammar school places. It is easy to paint the civil servants at Education as the villains of the episode, committed to obstruct multilateral schools, producing a document immediately Butler and Ede had been replaced by ministers with little experience (Law knowing nothing of the tripartite issue, and Mrs Keir disagreeing but too new to influence publication), but Ede cannot escape involvement in it.

There is no doubt he was expecting to be, if all went well, Minister of Education within a few weeks, or failing that the shadow minister, and in that light he made a few minor contributions on education matters, before Parliament was prorogued on 15 June, and immediately dissolved. All the while, he had been in contact with Ernie Gompertz by phone, but had not yet visited South Shields. He was there by 25 June, opening his campaign with a meeting at the Marsden Miners' Hall, after delivering his nomination papers, and confirming that his only opponent would be a National Liberal (in effect, Conservative). He stayed on Tyneside, living as usual in a hotel (while Lilian stayed at home), speaking on 29 June in Jarrow on Ellen Wilkinson's behalf, while she returned the favour for him at the Mortimer Road School in South Shields.

Ede was still not optimistic about the election, despite what he described as 'neutral opinion' expecting Labour to do well. He toured the constituency with Gompertz on polling day, 5 July, taking in the east end of South Shields in the morning, including Westoe, the strongest Conservative area, and the west end that afternoon. He took the train home on 6 July, while the counting was suspended so that overseas votes from servicemen could be sent in. He spent the next days on Surrey business, on the magistrates' bench, or on family matters – Nell and Noel Ede were about to holiday in Cornwall, and asked their brother to send them a guidebook to Mevagissey[13]. He picked up rumours about the election results. Gompertz wrote to him on 11 July, concluding he had held the seat 'by no very substantial majority', and on Friday 13 his view on that majority was between 1,500 and 2,000. A few days later, Gompertz was reporting on the view in Jarrow, that Ellen Wilkinson had carried her seat by 4,000 votes. He had come up to London, and more speculation ensued.

All was made clear on 26 July, when Ede, having taken the train back the day before, went to South Shields Town Hall at 9.00 am, finding his team certain of victory, the discussion being by how much. By 11.00 the Mayor was able to announce the result:

Ede	Labour	22,410
Parry	Conservative	15,296

This was a 60:40 split, with a majority of 7,114, compared with 9,099 ten years earlier. This was in fact his smallest majority in any election between 1935 and his retirement, but it was comfortable enough, and soon it was clear it was part of a massive national victory for Labour. By 3.00 pm Labour had won 364 of the seats declared, enough to give a comfortable majority, including all the Tyneside and Durham seats. At Jarrow, the majority was not 4,000 but 11,000. It was, Ede said, returning to his old Liberal roots, 'as great as 1906'. He mentioned he had warned Butler that the nation would swing left, though he expected it to take one election more to happen, but this was the 'Red Letter day in the best sense of the term'. One of the Borough Council, Alderman McAnay, rang him during the evening to confirm Churchill had resigned, and the King had invited Attlee to replace him.

Next day, 27 July, he quickly packed and checked out of his hotel, asking the receptionist to ring Lilian with the news he would be reaching London at 6.30 that evening. On his train he was joined at Darlington by an RAF officer, who introduced himself as Geoffrey Cooper, the new Labour Member for Middlesbrough West. That had been a Liberal seat, held until his death earlier in the year by Harcourt Johnstone, Ede's old opponent. They swapped each other's papers to read (a *Daily Herald* for a *New Statesman*), Ede finding Cooper 'a very bright intelligent man … if all our Service members are like him we have secured a great improvement' in Labour MPs. In all, 393 Labour Members had been elected.

The reasons for the Labour landslide have been much debated, and are not central to a biography of Chuter Ede. It is clear that most servicemen voted Labour, though their numbers, at fewer than 1.5 million, were not sufficient to make the difference. Many others, like them, were first-time voters (the register had not been updated during the war), most of whom did likewise[14]. They felt that the National Government, in effect the Conservatives, had led the country into the war without due preparation and, while giving credit to Churchill, were unable to look upon him as a mainstream Conservative – something which from a modern perspective may seem surprising, but at the time reflected his (fairly recent) rebellious independence within the party. Some voters had been affected by the new experience of meeting those from less privileged backgrounds, as children were evacuated and work threw different sorts together. In general, the mood of the country was for something different, and Labour offered that much more than the Conservative Party, together with better Party organisation and a less complacent approach to both the election and post-war reconstruction. For Ede himself, this recalled his early days as a Liberal and one of his old heroes:

> As I had often foretold, the country desiring to give power to the Left had followed the precedent of 1906 when it installed the steady, faithful but uninspiring Campbell-Bannerman. Attlee is no firework but the country found that Churchill had produced just the appropriate background for our Party's set piece.[15]

In fact, the *News Chronicle* had been publishing opinion polls, supplied by Gallup, for more than two years, which put Labour's share of the vote at 45 per cent or more[16], greatly ahead of the other parties, but these were not widely followed in those days.

On 28 July, a Saturday, Ede attended a party meeting at Beaver Hall in the City, after Attlee had already announced the most senior ministerial appointments. Beaver Hall was the London headquarters of the Hudson Bay Company, where beaver furs were once auctioned, in Great Trinity Lane (the site was redeveloped in the 1980s), and presumably was the best location available for such a large meeting at short notice. He travelled by Underground, and was drawn aside by William Whiteley, the Chief Whip, who told him the new PM 'had something very big for you'. Education, which Ede wanted, was 'not nearly big enough for you'. Despite Ede's protestations, Whiteley continued by indicating he would go to the Ministry of Labour, and told him to think it over through the weekend. However, Ede felt Bevin, who had become Foreign Secretary, had planned this with a view to his being his stooge at the ministry. At this point, the seven ministers already appointed were still awaited, from meeting the King at the Palace[17], but they soon arrived to great applause. Bevin and Attlee came in last, and then went on their way to Potsdam, as the new British representatives, without Churchill and Eden in tow.

At this moment, Ede's diary concludes, to be taken up only sporadically during the rest of his political life. Presumably he found himself too busy during the next few years. On Wednesday 1 August, Attlee saw him, not to offer the Ministry of Labour, but the Home Office. The Labour portfolio was to go to George Isaacs, and Education to Ede's constituency neighbour, Ellen Wilkinson. This amazed Ede, bearing in mind that she had spent much of the War as junior minster to the Home Secretary, while he had of course been at Education. He is said to have accepted the invitation with a cricketing metaphor, which would have been close to the heart of both men: 'You are asking someone who has been a cover point all his life to suddenly become a wicket-keeper!'[18]

Ede's protégé John Strudwick commented later that he could have been the greatest Minister of Education of the century[19], and when his obituary appeared in his professional journal twenty years later, it was described as 'the great disappointment of his life'[20]. He said as much, again with a sporting comparison ('you must play where the captain directs') to his NUT colleague Ronald Gould, who also described him as 'much disappointed'[21]. It can be speculated that, had he taken over at Education, instead of the inexperienced Wilkinson, already in declining health and with less than two years to live, he might have given political direction to the ministry which would have set the subsequent debate on the 11+ and comprehensive schools on an entirely different course. George Thomas, one of the new Labour intake, recalled that

> In the ranks of the teaching profession there was not a little heartburning, for the Union had long since taken a special pride in [Ede, and] looked forward to him being the first Union Member to become Minister of Education.[22]

Attlee did suggest he remain a member of Surrey County Council for the time being[23], ensuring that his connection with education would not be lost entirely and, as we shall see, Ede linked the fields of the two portfolios together when he could. On 3 August, the appointment was announced, to widespread congratulation, but also widespread surprise, particularly in the media[24].

Why Attlee chose to swap the duties of his two ministers over was unclear. On taking up his diary again, Ede recalled he would have sooner had the Ministry of Education, but Attlee had said he was the only man with some knowledge of the work of justices as well as of local government[25]; that sounds fairly implausible, when several portfolios were being passed to those with scant experience of them. In his own account, after leaving office, Attlee gave one explanation:

> I needed a man (*sic*) of particular quality for the Home Office which is a post where mistakes can easily be made … Ellen had done well as a junior minister and I knew she was an enthusiast for education[26],

though many years later he hinted at different thinking. In interviews with Francis Williams, a journalist with Labour sympathies who had been his public relations adviser and helped him write his autobiography, he gave an account of life as Prime Minister.

Williams asked him about his 'principles of Cabinet-making', and Attlee answered that you must make your Cabinet as small as possible, and then look at the key posts, considering first the fitness of a person for a post and secondly his status in the party.

> You may have a man who is admirably fitted for one post but you may want him for another. Chuter Ede was eminently fitted to be Minister of Education, but a Home Secretary is a particularly difficult job and he was far the best man for that. He had therefore to leave Education, which was his special thing, and go to the Home Office. Again nowadays, if you can, you should have some women in and there are certain jobs like Education or National Insurance where a woman will fit better than others.[27]

That helps confirm the speculation that he felt it essential to have a woman in his cabinet, and that Education was a more suitable job, while the Home Secretary should be a man (not until 2007 did a woman hold the post, though since then, to date, one has done so most of the time). We may raise our eyebrows now at such gender stereotyping, but can go only so far in imposing today's standards on decisions taken that many years ago.

'Home Secretary is a particularly difficult job', said the Prime Minister and, in giving it to him, one of the points he mentioned was the Home Secretary's role in approving capital punishments. According to Ede, Attlee said, 'we are not bound to support any decision that you give in capital cases, and you are not entitled to come to us and ask for our view. You must make the decision yourself, and you must bear the responsibility yourself'. As a result, Ede told the Commons many years later[28], he was to 'know the awful loneliness of a Home Secretary', which would haunt him during and after the Timothy Evans case.

Chapter 12

The Untried Home Secretary

One of the striking features of the new Cabinet put together by Attlee was the age of its members. The youngest person round the table was Bevan, for whom Chuter Ede once thought office would cure his frame of mind. He was 48, and at the other extreme Addison and Pethick-Lawrence were well over 70. Ede was a little short of 63, and the PM himself just a few months younger, both slightly older than the median age. This was not the obvious formula for a reforming government, but that was what it became. Ede was not in what has been described as the 'inner Cabinet'[1] – Attlee, Ernest Bevin, Herbert Morrison, Hugh Dalton and Stafford Cripps – grouped by one writer as 'The Tortoise and the Hares' (respectively Attlee and the four others).[2] In some respects he was an additional tortoise, though no less useful for that. He was certainly in the next group of senior ministers; an important chairman of committees, to use Kenneth O Morgan's description. In fact, in strict seniority, as Home Secretary he was pleased that 'at Privy Council meetings, I take precedence over Ernie Bevin'[3].

Attlee held an evening reception for the new MPs and party supporters, receiving guests with his wife before the music and dancing started at 7.30, with a pause for half an hour of speeches between 8.00 and 8.30. The purpose of the event was to meet the members of the Government, and the programme, presenting 'The People's Choice', included photographs of all the Cabinet, with Ede on the top row between Ernest Bevin and Manny Shinwell[4].

Ede joined the Oxford and Cambridge University Club, which gave him more of a London base than he had had previously; Maurice Holmes was an influential member of the club and, retiring from the Ministry in 1945, subsequently became chairman. Ede also took his opportunity to speak about his priorities to the press, including even overseas journals. He reassured one Canadian correspondent[5] that the British Labour movement was not Godless or irreligious, and he caused amusement by the contrast between his theoretical powers as Home Secretary and his mild manner:

Reception to celebrate the new Cabinet's success. (© *Surrey History Centre*)

'If there is a Gestapo' he said whimsically, looking at me over his glasses, then I am its head" – and for the life of me, I couldn't help thinking of 'Mr Chipps' (*sic*).

As well as discussing the potential reforms in magistrates' courts and criminal justice in the interview, he linked the need to reduce child labour with the development of education. He mentioned how his predecessor Morrison had pledged action over employment of children outside school hours and, asked if his aim was to wipe out the last trace of child work, said:

> The Government has not considered it to that point, but it has a strong following among Labour people, many of whom went to work at very early ages. The system of family allowances … should relieve much of the necessity of making schoolchildren work.

He specifically said he regarded his move from Education to Home Affairs as a natural one, as 'my new job deals with the failures of the old'[6].

We shall see that Ede continued throughout his life to deal with the subject of education whenever the opportunity was right, and occasions arose very soon after the new government was formed. In Gateshead on 17 November, he made a speech defending Ellen Wilkinson, who had been criticised for her attitude to some of the direct grant schools which were increasing their fees as a means of becoming more independent of state-funding and control. Before joining the Board of Education, he had been aggrieved about how old endowments for schools had been diverted from their original purpose, and he had to raise this again. Schools had been set up with ancient trusts, to provide benefits for children of families with limited means but, now they were trying to increase their independence, the trustees were failing to carry out the wishes of their founders. It was right that the Minister of Education should have the duty to see the intentions of the benefactors were carried out, and that Parliament should place the responsibility on her. The endowed schools were not for a single social class.[7]

As Ede settled into the Home Office, he recognized the need to resign from his post as Assistant Secretary of the Surrey County Teachers' Association, which he had held since 1914[8]. This had been unpaid since he joined Churchill's government, and he no longer needed the money in any case, his annual salary being about £5,000. Clearly, there would be a potential conflict of interest if he retained the position. It is important, though, to stress that he had never left, and never would leave, his union background behind him. In 1941, Ernest Bevin likewise had merely taken leave of absence as general secretary of the Transport & General Workers' Union, continuing to interact with his union colleagues throughout the war, and afterwards, now that he and Ede held two of the great offices of state. This is stressed by Bevin's most recent biographer, Andrew Adonis, who argues that he succeeded where several other union leaders failed as Labour politicians, because he 'didn't change'. Adonis, however, does not mention Ede among his examples of failures; he gives him no mention at all. If we consider the point, we must surely join Ede with Bevin among the successes.[9]

Though reducing his commitments, as Home Secretary he had to take on some unexpected duties, and his long association with the British Museum now began. The Museum was a body, nominally independent of government, governed by trustees, nearly half of whom were *ex officio*. These included the Commons Speaker, the Lord Chancellor, the Archbishop of Canterbury and Bishop of London, the Lords Steward and Chamberlain, the Lord Chief Justice and the Master of the Rolls, and in this case the Home Secretary – twenty-three in all. Nine members of the body were 'family trustees', appointed by the families of former benefactors of the Museum – such as Lord Elgin following his gift of the Parthenon Marbles.

It was an unwieldy body – when reform was actioned in 1962 there were fifty-one trustees – and in practice management was delegated to a Standing Committee, traditionally chaired by the Archbishop, though even this might consist of twenty individuals. According to Ede's later account,[10] he learnt he was a trustee when he received a notice of meeting; he attended a couple of times, and was then told by the Speaker, 'I am glad to see that you take an interest in this work. It would be a very great advantage to the Standing Committee … if you would join them so that their views could be made known in the Cabinet.' He was on board.

At the Home Office he must have looked for 'quick wins', and within two months he speedily swept away many Defence Regulations. Barbara Castle claimed the number of these was 227,[11] though Ede's own report to the Commons[12] indicates that 180 had been revoked by the Coalition Government just after VE Day, with 50 more withdrawn, and 3 new ones made, by Ede and Herbert Morrison between them in September. That indeed equals a net total of 227, though Ede did not seek all the credit Barbara Castle gave him. Still, it showed an intention to make changes quickly, a more minor one being in his own office, where he removed an old copy of *Crockford's Clerical Directory*, and put in its place on his desk a volume of Milton's writings.[13] Then, in time for November, he wrote a Cabinet memo on 4 September, proposing to reinstate the Cenotaph ceremony on Remembrance Sunday, stopped during the war owing to the risk to public gatherings. He suggested the same date in 1945 for commemorating both wars, but for future years preferred a date such as 15 June ('Magna Carta Day'), unconnected with VE Day, VJ Day, and the 1918 Armistice, the various dates on which the wars ended. He was told to discuss this with the British Legion, the churches and others, and in the event had to report back on 24 January 1946 that November remained the overwhelming consensus[14] – and to this day it remains in November.

Churchill's Caretaker Government had done little by way of preparing legislation, and Ede was called upon to put a programme together speedily to get reforms moving. He spent the greater part of August and September in drafting Bills on Supplies and Services, on Emergency Laws, and on the Police. These all had their second readings before Christmas and, along with the Electors and Jurors Bill, for which he was also responsible, made the main provision for Parliamentary business in these early months. Whiteley told him more than once that without his help the Whips could not have kept the machine working.

On Ede's birthday, an article appeared in the Beaverbrook press[15] which made him 'somewhat gratified with the attention I received'. Some emergency powers had been prolonged by the previous governments and, with the new administration announcing they would be extended, the article complained that:

> Now the Socialists have come to power, and almost their first action has been to give Mr Morrison's baby artificial respiration at the hands of Mr Chuter Ede. But the revived child is an altogether lustier infant with far greater potentialities for mischief.

Ede believed this was quite justified, though his proposal to give the Supplies and Services (Transitional Powers) Bill a five years' life, instead of the two proposed by the Coalition, evoked strenuous opposition.

The purpose of the Supplies and Services Bill and the Emergency Laws Bill was to extend the Government's emergency powers, so that rationing in particular could continue. Ede's political case[16] was that Government powers would run out in February 1946 if fast action was not taken, while his economic one was that many goods would continue in short supply, and that inflation must be avoided. His speech covered rationing of clothing, furniture, fuel, building materials, agriculture and food, and price controls generally. There would be no additional controls, except on prices, and there would be extra Parliamentary supervision over any Regulations, but a five year period was needed to recognise the difficulties which would be faced, not least by places such as South Shields, and to avoid repeating the economic problems which followed the Great War.

At the Supplies and Services Bill's Third Reading, Anthony Eden, temporarily leading the Conservatives, implored Ede to reconsider the five-year period when the Bill was returned from the Lords. Ede:

> blandly inquired how [Eden] knew it would come back from 'another place' at all. He fumbled at this, for it was a clear indication that we were watching for indications as to the extent to which the Lords are to be given orders by the Tory machine. In the end the Lords only groused.[17]

The Supplies and Services (Transitional Powers) Act safely came into effect.

This was not an easy time to be responsible within government for law and order. Large numbers of young men were returning from the disciplined ranks of the services to their old haunts, released from the restraints of the previous years, and wanting to make the most of their freedom. While withdrawing Defence Regulations made during the emergency of wartime pressures was a self-evidently positive step, the changes did cause problems for the Home Secretary. On 20 December 1945 Ede had to answer a series of questions in the Commons about the activities of Oswald Mosley and his supporters. Mosley had been released from house arrest when the Regulations covering him had been revoked in May. The Fascists held a meeting on 15 December, at the Royal Hotel, Woburn Place in Bloomsbury, where it was reported a journalist had been manhandled, and several MPs wanted to know what action the Home Office would take. Ede pointed out it was no business of the government or police to maintain order at private gatherings, though the police would act if a breach of the peace occurred. He did not want to get involved in issuing new regulations, which would be hard to draft, and would run counter to the ideals of a free country. However, he was giving his mind to 'the control of truculent, armed minorities in a democracy'.

Then there was a 'crime wave', or such was its description in various newspapers, with stories of very serious offences, alongside more amusing ones. More guns were in circulation and, in Glasgow, a man had shot dead a woman railway clerk, and injured a porter and a boy at a station, apparently in an unsuccessful robbery. In Surrey, the police had chased a car containing a stolen safe along the Kingston Bypass and into central London, where it smashed into a tram and another car. The safe was recovered, the five men in the car escaped, one of them having thrown a bottle of gin at a motorcycle policeman – but missing. In Marylebone, burglars gathered up furs worth £300, but then stopped to cut out pictures of 24 pin-up girls from a magazine, and had to leave in a hurry, so overlooking much jewellery and a haul of £1,500. In Westmorland, hundreds of pounds' worth of Christmas turkeys had disappeared. The *Daily Mail* declared the crime wave was caused by the black market, originating in shortages – turkeys were fetching £10 each. Ede's measures in response included unannounced closing of specific areas, with roadblocks after 11.30 pm, so motorists and pedestrians would have to satisfy police of their identity and business. The police were considerably stretched, but in some places a rudimentary neighbourhood watch was formed, using former members of the Home Guard and civil defence. These events were significant enough to reach the press in New Zealand.[18]

The Police Bill was aimed largely at closing down some of the smaller police forces, by merging those, mainly of small boroughs, into their county force. There was some opposition to this at the Committee Stage, but the critics put too much effort into detailed argument about where the population limit should be fixed for closing forces run by municipal boroughs. In the end, the only non-county borough remaining with its own force was Cambridge, a large town in a less populous county, and some 45 forces were merged when the Police Act took effect in 1947. There were still about 130 separate police forces in England and Wales, including the Metropolitan Force, which consisted of about 20,000 officers out of a national total of nearly 67,000.[19] Ede was able to record with satisfaction that the Third Reading on 13 March 1946 was unopposed.

Ede started writing up his diary again in March 1946 – or more accurately, he wrote a brief memoir of five pages, including several press cuttings, on 17 March, and followed it up with one more entry on the next weekend, before putting it aside. He started with a review of his initial period in cabinet, up to the end of 1945, and then into the new year. He recorded some enjoyable social engagements. The one he found most spectacular was the first, when he and Lilian attended a Fire Force display at Reading, and she distributed trophies. They were met at Bracknell by a outrider from the National Fire Service, and at the Reading boundary by the Chief Constable. Policemen were stationed at all traffic lights, so they went through without delay. The Edes also attended a social event at 10 Downing Street, where Lilian had been to a gathering of Ministers' wives.

When a conference of Foreign Ministers took place in London, they attended a reception in the Royal Gallery. Bevin, the host, was late, so Ede had to start receiving the guests, who included the Soviet delegate, Molotov, with six security guards. When he advanced to shake hands with Molotov, his 'thugs', with their hands in their jacket pockets, crowded around. The dinner for the conference was held by Attlee in St James's Palace. Speeches were made by the US, British and French attendees, as well as by Molotov who, Ede noted, spoke in Russian but corrected the interpreter – confirming the view that he well understood English. Also at St James's Palace, the King presided at a gathering in connection with the United Nations, after which Attlee held a dinner in the Painted Hall at Greenwich, which Ede felt was a fine setting, but with so little heating that all were uncomfortable.

He and Lilian went to the 'opening of the ballet at Covent Garden', no doubt the event on 20 February 1946,[20] when Margot Fonteyn performed with the Sadler's Wells Ballet in *Sleeping Beauty* as the Royal Opera House was resurrected, having been used as a Mecca dance hall during the war. Maynard Keynes had been determined to see it reopened, using his connections at CEMA and the Treasury, and encouraged by his ballerina wife. He had become Chairman of the Covent Garden Trustees, and that night organised a great success, but he 'felt rather shaky in the evening and could not perform all my duties', Lady Keynes having to greet the King and Queen. He managed to entertain guests in the intervals, though, the Edes presumably among them. In fact Keynes had had a small heart attack. He went off to the USA four days later, on a fruitless attempt to negotiate a government loan, collapsed again on his travels, and within two months was dead, so that was the last time Keynes and Ede were together. Because of Lilian's own poor health, Jim enjoyed the occasion more than she, though knowing little of music, it was the spectacle which thrilled him most.

They also went to an informal dinner at the Mansion House, as well as the Jubilee Dinner of the Jersey Society at Grosvenor House (the Channel Islands being now within his duties). However, she suffered days of discomfort after each of these functions, and her health was becoming a significant concern to him. She was suffering from great pain in her left foot, caused by some vascular problem. She went into hospital in Epsom, and was then treated in Wimpole Street. In December she was taken into Hammersmith Hospital and, apart from a brief return home for Christmas, was there till 10 February 1946. She had been unhappy with some of her doctors, and was disappointed when the specialist at Epsom Hospital was called up for the services and posted to India, which Ede managed to get postponed for just a brief period.

Not everything was recorded in his written notes. In the course of a new year visit to Tyneside, Ede was involved in one incident he did not note – on 5 January 1946, he was a passenger in a sleeper train which crashed into derailed goods trucks at Ferryhill, just south of Durham.[21] He was, though, uninjured, and returned to London, where on 10 January he went with

Ede broadcasting 'Hand in your firearms' for the BBC. (© *Surrey History Centre*)

Newsam, his Deputy Under-Secretary, to Scotland Yard, to meet more than 30 senior police officers, at the invitation of the Metropolitan Commissioner; he 'spoke to each individual and then gave a short talk'.[22]

Then, on 14 February, he recorded a broadcast appealing for the surrender of firearms. This was circulated through the cinemas by British Movietone News, which had 'always been ready to lend space in the interests of the community. In this case … the story is "Hand in your firearms"'. Following pictures of small arms, rifles and much larger ordnance being loaded on to lorries for disposal, Ede was introduced, to give a message about half a minute long. This had been recorded in a BBC studio, before a large microphone and a movie photographer. The film shows his discomfort at this type of speech, with a rather stilted reading from notes:

> The Government wants everybody who has unlicensed firearms to give them up. Why? Because they cause nasty accidents in the home, and

enable criminals to get arms. These souvenir revolvers and guns and ammunition are a danger to all of us.

He asked the audience to hand their weapons to any police station, with a time limit of the end of March, six weeks later.[23] The wooden manner in which he asked 'Why?' and his juxtaposing accidents in the home with his real concern – armed criminals – betrays the novelty of this use of the media for him. Clearly, new methods were felt necessary to meet the increase in lawlessness following the end of the War. The campaign did get coverage; he kept a cutting from the *Edinburgh Evening Despatch* of 21 February, which reduced it to doggerel:

Slogan for the police fire-arms campaign:-
Chuter wants your shooter,
Take heed, hand it to Ede!

The greatest success in Parliament which Ede recorded happened after the events of 13 March 1946. At the Albert Hall a meeting had taken place that evening of the Vigilantes Action League, which he called 'a mild Fascist organisation', that had been disrupted by Communists. The next day he asked for reports to be sent about the disturbances, and they reached him when the cabinet was meeting in Downing Street, just before midday on 14 March. Attlee took up his offer to describe the events, and Ede read out both a long police report, and another account by the head of the Disturbances Department, Miss Nunn, of her impressions of the meeting, which she had attended. This caused such merriment around the table that he was advised to tell the Commons about it, and he arranged with the Speaker to make a statement that afternoon. He read out Miss Nunn's report, that none of the advertised speakers had attended, and only some 150 to 200 people turned up, who looked even fewer in the space of the Albert Hall. They looked ridiculous, as did the Communists who arrived attempting to make the organisers appear as a Fascist bogy. There was laughter in the House at each of these statements.

The Communists were some 200 in number, and had intended to occupy some of the 2,000 free seats advertised, but the organisers withheld the seats so

they eventually paid to come in. (Loud and prolonged laughter.) They were, almost without exception, very young. They were clearly out for an evening's entertainment, and the proceedings had the air of a student rag rather than a serious political demonstration.

The Communists heckled the speakers, complained about the lack of free seats, proposed a motion banning Fascism, and sang the Internationale. The original audience moved to another part of the Hall, to carry on another discussion of their own. When the police arrived:

> Their entry was greeted by the singing of 'While Irish Eyes are Smiling.' (Loud laughter.) … Eventually Mr Cruikshank [a Communist leader] announced that the police had undertaken that if the Communists dispersed the original meeting would not be held. Somebody shouted 'Three cheers for the police.' (Laughter.) These were given, and the proceedings came to a more or less amicable conclusion.

The Communists and others had then celebrated outside.[24]

Ede gave this account, in a voice which produced hilarity in the House; as the *Manchester Guardian* reported, 'the author of the report had found an artist to read it'. 'Mr Ede has a deceptively solemn air, which makes his wit more telling', said *The Birmingham Post*. To the *Belfast News Letter*, he was 'Government Humorist Number One'. Having done so, he was asked serious questions about the spread of right-wing extremism and anti-Semitism, on which he advised all to keep a sense of proportion. But the Communist *Daily Worker* echoed some MPs, pointing out there 'was once a time … when people were asked to laugh at Hitler and Mosley, with disastrous consequences'. Still, Ede pasted the cutting in his short-lived diary.

Social engagements around this time included Victory Balls, Epsom holding theirs on 15 March 1946 at the Municipal Hall. Although 8 June had been designated as the day of celebrations for London and elsewhere, as Ede had recommended to cabinet,[25] his own town had pre-empted this, inviting its famous new cabinet member, and the Edes were excused the price of admission. On their ticket,[26] the figure of 7/6d has been deleted; equivalent to about £15 today, the event was probably not intended to fund itself. He was still able to walk the Surrey countryside at the weekend, though now without the ailing Lilian. On Sunday 17 March he went with companions, one a police sergeant, on three walks, being chauffeured between them, checking new footpaths and locations where wartime huts and installations had been restored. He visited the church as Wotton, near Dorking, where the diarist John Evelyn is buried, an inspiration to restart his own journal, though only briefly. The next weekend Lilian was able to join him, as the expedition round the villages was by car, and he then went to a meeting and quiz at his old school 'for the resuscitation of the Old Dorkinians Assn.' He remarked that none of the younger quiz contestants knew Julius Caesar was a Surrey cricketer.

Among the official engagements he had to carry out, he addressed a meeting in Kingston on 24 March relating to the Surrey Federation of the League of Youth. Then he opened one Police Training Centre at Pannal Ash, close to Harrogate on 31 May 1946, and visited another at Plawsworth, north of Durham, on 15 June,[27] conveniently placed for a further visit to South Shields.

Being responsible for the Channel Islands, he flew to Jersey in May, the first anniversary of the liberation of the Islands from the Germans, who had occupied them during most of the war. On 11 May, he addressed a large meeting at Victoria College, the main boys' school in Jersey, and gave a 'fairly long speech', according to the press,[28] mainly on education. He made his frequently-repeated joke about having been a teacher for sixteen years until, at the wish of the profession, he left it for its own good. He also told the story of his father indicating he was off to school on the day his sister Nell was born, 'and in one capacity or another, I have been obeying that order ever since'. Next, he mentioned his first school in the superannuated racehorse stable ('I found it famous and made it notorious'), and recalled some of the stories about his elementary school. The incident when he received just a penny from his teacher who had been greatly enriched by Ede's knowledge of Cromwell, led him to work out the commission he had earned and, he claimed, started his doubts about the capitalist system. He went on to make more serious comments about England's educational advances, the role of education in taking children from indifferent homes and giving them a 'spark of hope', and his concern that a child going to a technical school might be considered inferior to one at a secondary (ie, grammar) school. He linked his views on education to the material reconstruction in which Jersey was engaged.

He was, therefore, still very close to the subject of education, and pressed it where he had authority, such as in the Channel Islands. He was aware that, in June 1946, there had been attacks at the Labour Party conference on *The Nation's Schools*, led by the usual critic, William Cove, which Ellen Wilkinson had defended. Disowning it 'would mean repudiating the work of my good friend Chuter Ede', she said, standing up for his legacy at the Board of Education.[29] However, she was unsuccessful, because the party was not able to accept the tripartite system for secondary schools, or in particular the assertion that the three types of school would be of equal esteem. A policy which Ede had never looked on with enthusiasm was now becoming an embarrassment to his successors.

Dealing with foreigners from enemy countries was a duty of the Home Office, and here the Home Secretary became involved in a legal case which created a precedent. The decision was taken to deport a German, Netz, who challenged the Government's right to do so without due process. Netz had been in the UK since 1931, had been interned during the War, and was told in 1945 he would be repatriated. The High Court decided, in the case entitled *Netz v Chuter Ede*,[30] that revoking an enemy alien's right to remain in the country was a Crown prerogative, the action being an 'act of state', under which the courts would decline jurisdiction. This was in line with a similar judgment about the Foreign Office's right to intern a German national as an enemy alien, with no recourse to *habeas corpus*, in which Ernest Bevin had been involved.[31]

One of the next problems to address was the outbreak of squatting in the summer of 1946. As there had been no housebuilding during the War, and considerable loss of property because of bomb damage, there was already a shortage of accommodation for those working and living in the towns, particularly in the south of England. To those people were then added some 3½ million servicemen and prisoners-of-war returning home, more children at the start of the baby boom, and other problems such as more than 100,000 Polish soldiers refusing to return to their own country. People were sleeping on landings and in kitchens, or were doubling up in poor accommodation. Many men, though earning good wages, were unable to find any homes to buy or rent for their families. The government had been elected to pursue a policy of considerable house-building, but the construction workforce had been dispersed, and the minister responsible, Aneurin Bevan, was concerned about the quality of houses which might be built if the job was rushed. Bevan, believing 'only the best is good enough for the working class', has been criticised for failing to grasp the urgency, and making quality his priority over speed.[32]

The response in August 1946 was that people started squatting in abandoned military camps. This was not generally considered threatening, even if it may have been unlawful in principle; the sites were not in use for other purposes, they were of low value, and it would have been unjust to penalise war heroes for actions driven by extreme circumstances. On 20 September Ede reported to cabinet that 1,073 camps were occupied by roughly 40,700 people.[33] Some squats were planned as a group, but many were not, and cinema newsreels gave them publicity which spread the concept around. The response of cinema audiences indicated they had much popular support. Next, however, squatters moved into luxury apartment blocks in London, a move planned by the Communist Party.

The Government was torn between sympathy for the plight of the homeless ex-servicemen, and the need to ensure the rule of law. It called upon the minister who saw his duty as being to balance civil rights with law and order – the Home Secretary, James Chuter Ede – to chair a cabinet committee to deal with the crisis. The government announced that those in army camps could stay until Christmas, and made payments to local authorities to help improve the homes, but took police action against some of the squatters in flats and houses. They decided to withhold water, gas and electricity from houses, flats and local authority property seized, but looked at possibilities for alternative accommodation. They decided to build prefabs, despite Bevan's misgivings.

It was in this context that *The Observer* published a profile of Ede on 15 September 1946. It started by asserting that the

outbreak of civil disobedience took the Government completely by surprise. Its handling obviously required political tact, as well as firmness … agility and acumen at Question Time.

After a summary of Ede's previous positions and personality, it went on:

the Home Secretary has established himself as an incisive Parliamentary wag. No doubt his party is looking forward to hearing him on the subject of squatters. At 64, Chuter Ede looks young for his age, but a little tired.

It spoke of the Albert Hall incident as an example of his humour, and concluded that he

will survive the Squatters' Revolt and may well advance his reputation by showing that he cannot be hurried into hasty repressive measure or outwitted by astute agitation. He may well achieve more enduring fame by reforming our antiquated prison system … he has a reasonable chance of winning the country's gratitude for the way he handles both the popular and the unpopular tasks of his high office.

So it would turn out, though there was considerable work to be done.

In all, 1946 was a year of triumph and sadness for Ede. He was making headway with his duties as a senior cabinet member, and also seeing some of his work on the Surrey environment reach fruition. Near Burford Bridge below Box Hill, close to the road he took to school and walked for pleasure, are some stepping stones across the River Mole. They had been damaged in the war, and Ede had encouraged the Dorking UD Council to see to their reinstatement. The local authority agreed to upkeep the stones, but they passed the estimate for the initial work (£156/19/6) to him; he agreed to pay it, though 'considerably higher than I expected',[34] as his tribute for what

Dorking had done for him as a boy. He asked Clement Attlee to reopen the stepping stones, at a ceremony on his own sixty-fourth birthday, 11 September, the fifty-first anniversary of his joining Dorking High School. He entertained the School's Headmaster, with others (including London's Lord Mayor, and Lawrence Chubb, who chaired the Commons, Footpaths and Open Spaces Preservation Society – Ede had sat on the Society's executive for many years) at the Railway Arms, Westhumble, that evening, and was promised a record of the event in the school magazine. After dinner, the toasts included 'The Open Spaces and Footpaths of Surrey' from the Lord Mayor, to which Attlee replied; Ede had ensured, through a note to Chubb, in which 'I assume the guests would like to drink my health as host', that his contribution was recognised. The event attracted much press coverage, *Country Life* including a photo of the stones, while the *Daily Telegraph* and *Manchester Guardian* showed one with an attractive model strategically posed there. The *Daily Mail*'s contribution was of the Attlees walking hand-in-hand across them, and the *Surrey Advertiser* explained the PM 'stepped out resolutely, but Mrs Attlee appeared nervous of the quickly running water … Mr Ede was the next to cross, followed by the Lord Mayor … All made the crossing without mishap'.[35] Though a small achievement, it stayed in the public memory and, when the Open Spaces Society, celebrating its 150th anniversary in 2015, listed the successes over its history, replacing the stones was one, attributed to the Society's committee member, Chuter Ede.[36]

On the other hand, Lilian's health continued to deteriorate, and she suffered a coronary thrombosis, following which her leg, which had caused such trouble the previous winter, was amputated. Henceforth he would be looking after a wife confined to a wheelchair, and her prospects were not good. He went on, nonetheless, with his formal duties. He was back in Jersey in September,[37] along with Rab Butler, Lord Samuel and two other Privy Counsellors, chairing a Privy Council committee taking evidence about the proposed constitutional reforms there. They would report to Parliament, including changes for Guernsey also, in March 1947, which would be adopted the next year. Ede's papers for the autumn of 1946 also include records of a visit to the Isle of Man (for which, like the Channel Islands, the Home Office was then responsible) in October, inspecting another Police Training Centre, at Ryton-on-Dunsmore near Coventry, on 22 November, and opening a remand home for girls at Hammerwich House near Lichfield, the next day.[38]

The main achievements of the Attlee administration are well-known to those with an interest in British politics, but ones at the Home Office are often overlooked. However, as Ede would be able to show when he published his election address in 1950, he was concerned with a large amount of legislation, in particular guiding several major statutes through Parliament in 1948 and 1949, besides carrying out the administrative duties of Home Secretary. In doing so, he was well aided by his senior civil servants, the Permanent Secretary, and the Deputy Under-Secretary who would eventually succeed him. Sir Alexander Maxwell, an Oxford classicist, had spent his career at the Home Office, becoming Permanent Secretary in 1938. Two years older than Ede, he shared with him a Nonconformist background, being the son of a Congregational minister, and marrying the daughter of a Scottish minister (the wedding taking place in a Quaker meeting house). He was also of a liberal outlook in administering Home Office affairs, concerned with the welfare of the young and, it was thought, would have been content to see the abolition of capital punishment. Sir Frank Newsam, on the other hand, though with a similar academic education, had a different temperament, forceful and impatient, and was mainly interested in policing. In 1945 he had been for four years Deputy Under-Secretary covering security matters, and was working on restoring the Channel Islands after their ordeal under the Germans. He was a heavy drinker, which would have put him at a distance from Ede, and loved to bet on horses, which might have found sympathy from the (rarely gambling) man from Epsom, though may have caused him to question Newsam's judgement.[39]

Ede was not involved in the Trade Disputes and Trade Unions Act 1946, one of the Attlee Government's most significant measures of that year; it was sponsored by George Isaacs's Ministry of Labour and by Hartley Shawcross as Attorney-General. That would not, however, prevent him from claiming it as one of his achievements when he sought re-election. It aimed at changing the law under an Act passed in 1927 by Baldwin's administration.[40] That Act had made secondary action unlawful, as well as any strike whose purpose was to coerce the government of the day directly or indirectly, and mass picketing if it gave rise to intimidating a worker. Incitement to participate in an unlawful strike had become a criminal offence, and trade union members were required to contract in to any political levy which their union made on their behalf – since 1906 'contracting out' had previously been permitted. This resulted in significant fall in the income of the Labour Party, which was heavily reliant upon union funding. Although MacDonald's second government had introduced a bill to repeal various of these provisions in 1931, this was not passed, and the Act was particularly resented by the trade union movement and the Labour Party.

The Government was responsive to the mood of the unions, about 120 of its MPs being sponsored by them. Most of the cabinet were from a working-class background. Morgan interestingly lists Ede among the minority who were not, along with seven others who were all from a public school, titled or landowning origin. Ede's own background as a Nonconformist trade union man was more akin to that of George Isaacs, or even Ernest Bevin; though Bevin started in much more abject poverty, Ede had needed to sacrifice a first degree through lack of funds. He later resisted the suggestion that his home was middle-class ('it was certainly not well off ... my family was ... not bourgeois – they would have thought you were swearing at them if you'd said that).[41] His sympathy was naturally with the unions. Many Conservatives attacked the Trade Disputes and Trade Unions Bill as an invitation to intimidation, but Ede's former colleague, Rab Butler, was more reasonable, saying in the Second Reading debate on 13 February 1946:

> I have had the honour of being in close agreement with many trade unionists in the course of my public career, particularly upon the education proposals, ... without the trade councils and the trade unions, it would not have been possible for me to reform the law relating to education in the manner I desired. I feel sure that that co-operation will continue in the many fields in which we desire to bring about reforms of that character, and ... the long period of co-operation between the House and the trade union movement will continue on things which really matter.

This was a tribute to the efforts Ede had made when they worked together, which had not been forgotten.

In 1947, legislation was being prepared in the Home Office, but Ede was more concerned with administrative business, continuing with his formal functions, such as opening the new headquarters for his own local police force, Durham, at Aycliffe, along with its training school at Harperley Hall. Like the training centre at Ryton, this has been developed over the years, and they still operate as part of the College of Policing, which was set up (by the Cameron Coalition Government) with much wider powers than practical training alone, and independent from the Home Office. Ede did not, however, follow all advice about police training. The Hendon Police College, which had closed at the start of the war, could have reopened for special training of an 'officer class', but he decided against this.[42] While he believed in 'a Police College', for the higher training of the Police (above sergeant level), as he told Cabinet on 17 February,[43] there was no question of using Hendon for this; it was too small. More local colleges for all the force were his priority, in line with the Police Federation's policy against elitism. So he was taking some of the early steps towards making the police the professional operation it is today. Indeed, fostering the police into a solid institution, respected in a democratic society, has been identified as his dominant interest at the Home Office, a field where the Labour Party has often been portrayed as unsympathetic.[44]

His remit over foreigners in Britain sometimes had him lobbied by those with influence. In February 1947, a German named M.R. Irming wrote to several notable people, including two children of Prime Ministers – Lady Violet Bonham-Carter, Asquith's daughter, and Lord Cecil of Chelwood, Salisbury's son, who both forwarded his grievance to the Home Office. Cecil, we recall, had been in the Commons with Ede in 1923, and had met him again in 1941 at a function at the Polish Embassy. Cecil's papers show that he was using his weight to lobby the government widely, often with Bevin or with Attlee himself. Now it was Ede's turn.

Irming was complaining he had been asked to leave the country, at a time when Germany would not be a welcome place to return to. On 14 March, Ede replied to Lady Violet, copying his letter to Cecil, explaining that Irming did not need to go to Germany; if he left of his own accord, he could go to any country. He had been in the UK in the 1930s, until in 1938 the Home Office decided he should leave. He had stayed and, though he was abusing British hospitality, the Government was reluctant to deport him to Nazi Germany; he had links to the Spanish Republicans, having been secretary of the Friends of Spain during the Civil War there. He had spent the war years interned as an enemy alien and now, at large, he needed to make an effort to leave. Ede would give him three months, but otherwise he would reluctantly have to order deportation, which would certainly be to Germany.[45]

Deportation and extradition were a complex matter at the time, for Ede and the government. After the Nuremburg trials of the leading Nazis in 1945 and 1946, some further prosecutions were made for war crimes in the British Zone of Germany. Now, in 1948, it was decided to bring these to an end. Germany (or the western part at least) was being prepared for statehood again, and the policy of sending alleged criminals to the countries where their crimes had been committed ran up against the reality of many such countries being behind the Iron Curtain. As they were unlikely to get a fair trial, the government stalled at such deportations, no war crimes trials were held in Britain, and a number of war criminals found refuge in the UK (which, as it happened, caused problems many years later, in the 1990s). Then, in January

1947, the Polish Government applied for the extradition of Wladislaw Dering.[46]

Dering was a Polish doctor who, though not Jewish, had been imprisoned in Auschwitz by the Germans in 1940. In 1944 he had been released, to work for a doctor who conducted experiments on prisoners. By his account, he performed no experimental operations, and was called a hero on his return to Warsaw in 1945, but other medics in the camp, with whom he had differences, made accusations against him. So in 1946 he came to England. When Poland applied to get him back, the British Government confirmed that he was on several lists of alleged war criminals, and he was arrested. He claimed he had merely performed general surgery (which he was forced to do), had helped some Jews survive, and had reduced the number of victims being sent off to be gassed. As he had to turn some patients away, he had inevitably made enemies. He impressed his interrogators with his frankness.

As Home Secretary, Ede had to decide whether there was a prima facie case to justify extraditing Dering. In March the Home Office took the view that no such case had been made out, particularly bearing in mind that one of his accusers was alleged to be a doctor working for the Polish secret police who had herself carried out experiments on Jews. Alexander Maxwell himself, however, was less certain about this, as was the Foreign Office, while several MPs were lobbying on Dering's behalf, concerned about the effects of sending him back to Communist Poland. A report was requested from David Maxwell Fyfe and Elwyn Jones, both prosecutors at Nuremburg, now MPs on opposite sides of the House, each Attorney-General and Lord Chancellor in his turn. As we shall see, that was not the end of the matter.

While this was going on Ede, like all the cabinet, was mindful that 1 April 1947 was the date set in the Education Act for raising the school-leaving age to fifteen. This was now in the remit of Ellen Wilkinson, whose health had suffered for some years, and had recently worsened. Though there had been some doubt whether that date would be achieved, she had pressed ahead, and the cabinet agreed on 16 January, at the start of the bitterest winter weather in memory, to implement the change. Ede argued vehemently that any postponement would dishearten the more progressive education authorities,[47] and it was a triumph for him as well. She, though, did not see it through, as within three weeks she was rushed to hospital, where she died. She had been prescribed various drugs, and had taken an overdose, by accident in the view of the inquest. Ede did not record his sadness explicitly, but on the day she died he spoke on the BBC in appreciation of her[48] and, shortly after the age of fifteen was achieved in April, he paid a tribute to those involved in education, among whom Ellen Wilkinson must have been in his mind.

On 27 March 1947 Ede introduced the Fire Services Bill to fulfil a pledge, made by Herbert Morrison and others, to re-establish locally-managed fire brigades after the War. In 1938 all local councils were given the duty of providing their local fire services, but this was not satisfactory for wartime conditions, when explosives and incendiaries were causing widespread damage, and Morrison had set up the National Fire Service in 1941, controlled centrally. As a result, cities including Birmingham, Southampton and Plymouth suffered much less than they might, because fire crews could be directed from elsewhere to help them. The NFS was promised to be only a temporary measure, and Donald Somervell, who had been Home Secretary during Churchill's brief caretaker government, had reiterated the undertaking that fire protection duties should return to local administration. One question was which local authorities should be given the responsibility or, in Ede's phrase, 'where to draw the border line'. He had

> had two Bills before the House, one under the Coalition Government, in which I dealt with education authorities, and another in this Government, where I had to deal with police authorities, and any effort to draw the line creates more anomalies than it solves.

He had no doubt, however, that the promise must be carried out. It did not make sense to create again some 1,500 fire authorities, and his answer was to make the counties and county boroughs responsible for fire duties.

He paid warm tribute to the heroism shown, and the lives sacrificed, by fire-fighters during the War, and announced he would repeal Samuel Hoare's Fire Services Act of 1938, re-enacting those parts of it which were still relevant. He was flexible about the role of the local authorities below county level, and hoped they would find an arrangement which would help the county councils discharge their duties. In any event, fire authorities could decide to combine together. In fact, the final statute included provision for county fire brigade committees, with representation from district councils at the next tier down. The Fire Services Act received Royal Assent on 31 July 1947, after an easy passage through Parliament. As far as England and Wales were concerned, it came into effect on 1 April the next year, a day Ede celebrated by inspecting the London Fire Brigade, as it passed from his control to that of the local authorities.[49]

An interesting example of the Home Secretary's wide influence occurred while Ede held the post, probably at this time. He recorded later in his diary[50] a note about 'Mrs Topham, the autocratic owner of Aintree', the racecourse where the Grand National was run. With his interest in horse racing, he expressed the view that the race should be held on a Saturday, but she said firmly she would not allow it. Her attitude so incensed the stewards that they immediately accepted his proposal. He did not record which year this happened, but the Grand National had been on a Friday in 1946, but in 1947 was on Saturday 29 March; and it has normally been on a Saturday ever since.

Around this time, Ede increased his activities within the Unitarian Church, which would consume much of his energy when he had retired from front-bench politics. He attended the Assembly of the Unitarian and Free Christian Churches, speaking on 23 April 1947 to a public meeting on 'Individual Freedom in a Planned Society'.[51] He contrasted the times with the period of Whig supremacy, when Macaulay could justify excluding the working classes from government, and when a 'cultured and free society' existed for those at the upper level, but not for the 'mass of uneducated, impoverished people'. After 1832, society became free and 'unplanned' for the merchant classes also, but only recently, with the coming of universal suffrage, had craftsmen and labourers claimed their freedom. To make this freedom real, with equality of opportunity, there needed to be a duty to 'effect a revolution in our system of social values'. For that of course his prescription was education, and in particularly the requirements of the Education Act. The duty of parents, teachers and LEAs to give all children education suitable to their age, ability and aptitude was essential; and he put most stress on 'aptitude'. The task was to discover and develop personal endowments, in children with few talents as much as (or maybe more than) those with many. This makes for freedom, including of the intellectual kind, which he as Home Secretary was sometimes pressed to restrict when it involved doctrines disliked by some. Then the Whig claim that property should be the basis of freedom could be given the answer that 'He who invests his life in a calling has at least as much claim to be considered as he who invests his capital'.

Two days later, the Edes were at a concert in aid of the Royal London Discharged Prisoners Aid Society, at the London Casino. The Society is now part of NACRO, the National Association for the Care and Resettlement of Offenders. While its field of activity fell clearly within Chuter Ede's Home Office duties, their interest was not solely a government responsibility, Lilian being on the organising committee for the concert.[52] They were keenly aware of the work which needed to be done to rehabilitate criminals, and Ede would continue to be active for the association throughout his life.[53] The same mix of interests led him on 5 May 1948 to visit the approved school in Redhill run by the Philanthropic Society. This had been started as a farm school in the mid-19th century, becoming the model for many of the approved schools set up to prevent young people being sent to prison, and the Home Office had assumed control of these in 1938.

To add to his government duties, Ede was appointed Deputy Leader of the House of Commons, assisting Herbert Morrison in guiding business through Parliament. Morrison, though, held no administrative portfolio, his other responsibilities being Lord President of the Council and Deputy Prime Minister. To have this role in addition to the duties of the Home Office must have put additional pressure on Ede – particularly with Lilian's state of health – though in the long run it may have helped him pilot the legislation during the immensely productive next two years.

Among the concerns with which he had to deal was one which illustrates the sensibilities of the time. A film called *Good Time Girl* was produced by the Rank Organisation, about a girl who absconds from approved school, meets American criminals, and eventually ends in prison. Any audience would have known the story of Elizabeth Jones and Karl Hulten, convicted in 1944 of a robbery and killing spree, she a Welsh girl sent to an approved school for being beyond parental control, he a deserter from the US army stationed in Britain. The Americans let Hulten be dealt with under the English jurisdiction, and he was hanged, while his accomplice Jones, convicted of murder, had been reprieved by Morrison when he was Home Secretary early in 1945. She was now in prison, and her parents got their MP to protest that the film was trading on her story.

Although Rank argued that the film was a step in its move towards responsible social realism, Ede and his officials realised the court and approved school scenes were a travesty, and in August 1947 he wrote to Arthur Rank himself saying he would close down such a school, had it existed. They lunched together, and Ede thought they had agreed on improvements, but Rank then added a scene implying the poor teachers at the approved school were to blame for her crimes. Ede corresponded about the film with the official censor, who deplored it but said these were not grounds for refusing it a certificate; he seems to have achieved some changes to its dialogue, but not its presentation. So eventually the Home Secretary asked again that the offending parts be cut, and warned that he would denounce the film if any question about it was asked in Parliament. It was released in April 1948, and was more popular with audiences than critics.

The film remained in the public eye as it featured the young Diana Dors, who would go on to a career as an actress in undemanding films, and then a singer and celebrity in cabaret and on television. In fact, hers was the minor role of another teenage girl who treats the story as a warning. Interest in the crimes did not die down, and in 1990 another film, *Chicago Joe and the Showgirl*, was made about Hulten and Jones and their murder of a taxi driver, George Heath (Heath had once lived in Ewell,[54] which may have given Ede particular interest in the case). That film seems to have passed without remark from the authorities, as times had changed and, when the government files were released after nearly sixty years, press coverage[55] about *Good Time Girl* centred on the link with Diana Dors – Ede had probably not even registered her name.

In November 1947, the Commons considered the government's Parliament Bill, which reduced from two years to one, spread over two sessions instead of three, the period during which the House of Lords could withhold its consent to a Bill introduced in the Commons. That period had been enacted in the Parliament Act 1911, under Asquith's government, of which Churchill had been a member. The government was now worried that the Lords might reject some legislation, such as that covering nationalisation, at a point when there was insufficient time for the Commons to overrule the rejection before the next general election. So they wished to reduce the period of delay, and argued that the measure handicapped a Labour government more than a Conservative one, which of course benefitted from its permanent majority in the Lords. Over two days the House debated the Second Reading, and Ede played a major part, clashing with Churchill, who had come in from his sickbed to take part. There were many remarks at Churchill's expense, regarding his enthusiasm for provisions restricting the Lords in 1911, which had waned all these years later.

On 20 November 1947, Ede attended the wedding of Princess Elizabeth to Prince Philip, at Westminster Abbey. It had been privately agreed that they would marry, but Philip was Greek by birth, and by ancestry partly German. Despite serving in the Royal Navy, he had never formally taken British citizenship (though as a descendant of Sophia of Hanover he was probably naturalised as British by statute). Ede had been approached in 1946 by Earl Mountbatten, the young man's uncle, about ensuring his naturalisation, and on 5 December he gave a written answer to a Question, that Prince Philip of Greece

> has submitted an application through his commanding officer in accordance with the arrangements which … have been made to enable early consideration to be given to applications for naturalisation from foreigners who have served during the war in His Majesty's Forces.

The matter was accomplished some months before the engagement was announced in July, Ede being involved in Philip's choice of surname.

A German name was clearly best avoided and, as his German background was from the Oldenburg family, 'Oldcastle' had been suggested, but Ede felt 'something grander and more glittering can be found', advising the King to approve the name Mountbatten. Uncle Dickie Mountbatten, who had been steering the decision, was of course delighted.[56] The Edes got to know the Prince and Princess; he left among his papers a pleasant photograph of themselves with the young couple at a summer social occasion, with Lilian in her wheelchair. The event and date are not recorded but, as Ede was to be widowed in July 1948, it is likely to have been in 1947, when the Princess and Prince had just become engaged. Though he would only serve in the King's cabinet, as he was back in opposition before the Princess became Queen, their wedding was another ceremony which would provide experience for him to put to use as one of her Privy Counsellors working on her coronation.

On New Year's Day 1948, Ede made one final attempt to write up his diary as a Minister of the Crown. He went to it in his accustomed detail, an effort which doomed the project. In seven days, he wrote nearly six pages of a foolscap exercise book, in all 2,000 words. This was too much for an extremely busy man, carrying out a diversity of tasks, with a schedule of official and social appointments, and needing to read and comment on documents of several types. Yet, though he gave up after the entry for 7 January, these pages cast considerable light on his routine (if that is the word) in his work. They provide a representative slice of the life he led at the Home Office for more than six years, so they merit being summarised.

New Year's Day was not a public holiday then, so he went into London, but first visited the Ministry of Education in Curzon Street, where it had new headquarters, and received a warm welcome from his old staff. His business was as a Governor of the Whitgift Foundation, which runs schools in Croydon. He saw George Tomlinson, who had become Minister after Ellen Wilkinson's death, about a proposed increase in the schools' fees. They also took the opportunity to discuss a proposal for reforming the House of Lords. He went on to the Home Office, saying farewell to a retiring department head, lunched at the Oxford and Cambridge University Club, and was then driven to Chingford, to walk in the funeral procession of a policeman killed in a motor accident just before Christmas. He returned to the office, signed papers, went home, and had further discussions about the Whitgift fees on the phone in the evening.

The next day, a Friday, Ede discussed the tax on greyhound racing with an interested MP, and attended the Whitgift Governors' meeting. At the weekend, he called on some Epsom ladies and men at the Fire Station to arrange for their children to visit the circus at Olympia, visited a friend to return some borrowed property, went out with Nell (probably with a police driver) on a tour of much of Surrey, and also travelled to London and back, dropping off two official bags at the Home Office.

On 5 January 1948, he went to a magistrates' meeting at Epsom, where he sought views about how to deal with probation sentencing, and then to Kingston, to ask an officer at County Hall to deal with the case of a smallholder being evicted. After returning home for lunch, he went to London for a Labour Party committee meeting, and then had a discussion at his office with Newsam about various police problems, and also about their planned visit to the Channel Islands. After getting home, Ede chaired the annual dinner of Epsom Camera Club, to which he took the ailing Lilian.

Next day there was a cabinet meeting, which covered service estimates, the 'doleful' survey of the economy, regulations on midweek sport, and Lords reform. It was clear the House of Lords was the most contentious item. After lunching at his club, he met Lilian, and went off to Olympia, to meet Nell and the children and see the circus. (The circus was an annual event, at which they entertained children, often including some from a Surrey orphanage.[57]) He listened to the evening news, which mentioned Lords reform being in the cabinet's sights, even though Attlee had said it should not be mentioned.

On 7 January, he went to a committee of ministers discussing the political rights of civil servants, and then to the Home Office. Here he discussed with Maxwell and Newsam a murderer due to be hanged, and then with Anthony Nutting, a Conservative MP, his wife's conviction for shoplifting. She had been offended by the threat of prison, and by some words of the magistrate, to whom Ede agreed to speak. He had lunch at the Commons with Emanuel Shinwell, who lobbied him on a naturalisation case. Back at his office, he and his senior team discussed the Education Ministry's desire to have the cost of university education for children in care transferred to the Home Office. At a time when very few young people went to university, the number doing so from local authority care must have been miniscule, but the departmental dispute still occupied his time.

As to the condemned man, Ede set out his thinking, in this one instance of what would have been a frequent issue while he was in post. Every year, between about twenty to thirty murderers were convicted, all had to be sentenced to death, and the Home Secretary then considered whether to commute the penalty to life imprisonment.[58] On average, therefore, he was dealing with a case every couple of weeks. On this occasion, there were two murderers, a Spanish man and a woman, Martinez and Pavey, who had killed their new baby, born out of wedlock. Ede reprieved the mother just before Christmas, in view of the judge's statement that, if she had been able to afford medical evidence, her conviction would probably have been for infanticide, not murder.

Martinez's was a harder case, and needed an immediate decision, as his hanging was set for the next day. Some jurors had written in to say they had recommended mercy, but the foreman had not reported it, which seemed odd as the judge asked if there was anything they wanted to add to the verdict. Some journalists, stressing they were hardened men who were used to covering murder cases without intervening, had nonetheless pressed the case for a reprieve for him as well as Pavey. Ede discussed Martinez with his civil servants, and eventually decided to commute the sentence. He then learnt that the Spanish Government was also pressing for mercy, as was the Catholic Cardinal, so he would have felt he had decided right. However, home at 9.30 that evening, he was telephoned by a *Daily Express* journalist, asking why the man had been reprieved. Quite rightly, 'I told him I did not give reasons.'

With those words, this snippet of a diary ends, and only when he was in opposition four years later would he start again. This is unsurprising, as 1948 was to be the busiest year in Chuter Ede's legislative career.

Chapter 13

The Police, Criminals and the Electorate

On 15 January 1948 Ede returned to Jersey, where he saw the Jurats, the island's lay magistrates who, at the time, were members of the States Assembly. The constitutional reforms proposed in 1946 replaced them in the Assembly with more elected members, and he wished to confirm these would be carried through. The Jurats were judicial officers, and their legislative function was felt to cause a conflict in the separation of powers.[1] Next day he went to Guernsey, whose constitution was also being reformed, to discuss the problem of Alderney, which was suffering financial and administrative difficulties, the island having lost much of its population as a result of German occupation, when it had 'been converted into a fortress' and 'practically covered with concrete'.[2] Although falling within the Guernsey jurisdiction, its government had been separate from Guernsey's. He went to Alderney itself on 17 January, Newsam having told him he had received a letter about its administration from Sir Frank Wiltshire, a new judge in Alderney, saying he 'finds the machine creaky'. The outcome of his discussions was a link set up between the two islands, to streamline their joint administration. He subsequently made a further visit there, having already met the islanders in London.

On 6 February 1948, Ede introduced the Police Pensions Bill to the Commons. As he explained, arrangements for police pensions were complex and confusing, could be altered only by Act of Parliament, and were inconsistent with the state pension arrangements, which the government was introducing later that year as part of the National Insurance scheme. Things needed to be sorted out.

The Bill would reduce both contributions payable by new policemen, and the pension they would eventually receive, to take account of the state benefits. It would also remove some – though not all – of the circumstances in which a retired officer could be deprived of his pension, and would enable regulations to be made by the government to amend the arrangements. This last provision predictably caused criticism, as proposals to give a minister the power to make law by secondary legislation often do. The forfeiture provisions were also queried by some members, while others argued for more generous pensions for widows and dependants of the police. Ede, together with Kenneth Younger, who had been appointed as his junior minister in October 1947, dealt with the Bill in Committee on 20 February.

The question of widows' pensions was of particularly high profile at the time, because on 13 February 1948 a policeman in plain clothes, Nathaniel Edgar, had been killed in London by Donald Thomas, who was an army deserter and a suspected burglar resisting arrest.[3] Edgar had seen Thomas acting suspiciously and stopped him, only to be shot three times while Thomas escaped. Edgar was aged thirty-three, a married man with two children, and several questions were asked of Ede about the pension and other compensation his widow would receive. Ede attended his funeral on 19 February,[4] and Mrs Edgar's circumstances were much covered in the debate on the Bill next day. Thomas was arrested after a radio appeal for him, as a person 'who might be able to help the police in their enquiries' – believed to be the first time that phrase came into use – and in April was condemned to death for murder. In fact, Ede commuted this to life imprisonment, as we shall see, in view of the decision in the Commons to halt capital punishment.

While he was dealing with police pensions, Ede also had major work on elsewhere. In the debate, he despaired on 20 February that 'I am engaged upstairs in a Committee on which there are twenty lawyers. It does not lead to speed', and it was likely he was thinking of the Representation of the People Bill. Some of its provisions had been recommended by a Speaker's Conference which had reported in 1944, and which time had not permitted to be enacted. Among its objectives were abolishing plural voting, including the university constituencies, and increasing the size of the House of Commons, though it did considerably more than that.

When he opened its Second Reading, his initial remark was that the Bill

completes the progress of the British people towards a full and complete democracy begun by the great Reform Bill of 1832. From now on, every citizen of full age will have a vote, and only one vote. This Bill wipes out the last of the privileges that have been retained by special classes in the franchise of this country. It arranges for a complete redistribution of seats.

The country was to be divided into 608 single-member constituencies, in place of the previous 591. This embodied the work of the Boundary Commissions (one for each of the four countries of the UK), which had been set up under the House of Commons (Redistribution of Seats) Act, passed in 1944. As these were to be the only constituencies, the university constituencies were abolished, and graduates no longer had the right to vote in two places. Constituencies which had been represented by more than one MP were also abolished. The tiny electorate of the City of London, which returned two members, often unopposed, would cease to do so. British subjects aged twenty-one and over were eligible to vote, once registered in a constituency. Each voter was permitted to cast only a single Parliamentary vote in one constituency, even if registered in more than one. The arrangements which had given plural votes to electors who met a property qualification because of their business or shop premises were abolished.

Each constituency was to have an electoral registration officer (as was already the case), to compile an electoral register, to be published twice each year. Residence in the constituency on a specified date was the principal qualification for registration. Electors were to vote in person, other than in exceptional circumstances when a proxy vote might be permitted. The registration officer was to divide each constituency into polling districts, and designate polling places, subject to review by the Secretary of State. The appointment and duties of the returning officer were also laid down, as were procedures for recounts, for candidates who received less than an eighth of the total number of votes cast to forfeit their deposit, and for choosing the winning candidate by lot in the event of a tie. Much of this restated the existing law, but several points were brought up to date, such as the timetable for making nominations and holding the ballot.

Part II of the Bill defined the electorate for local elections. It would be larger than that for parliamentary elections, as it included a non-resident qualification where an owner or tenant occupied land with a rateable value of ten pounds or more. The electoral registration officer was to compile a local government register. There was no prohibition on voting in different local authority areas, but nobody could be registered more than once in a single local government district.

Part III brought up to date the provisions on corrupt and illegal practices. It significantly reduced the amount of expenses that candidates were permitted, as had been recommended by the Speaker's Conference. No supporter of a candidate was permitted to use a motor vehicle to bring an elector to the polls, unless the vehicle had been registered with the returning officer, and there were limits on the number of vehicles used. Each candidate was allowed to send an address to each elector post free, and was entitled to the use of a room in a publicly funded school in which to hold meetings. The broadcast of any programme relating to an election on a radio station, other than by the BBC, was prohibited; the BBC had a radio monopoly in the UK, so this was intended to prevent broadcasts from abroad. Churchill interrupted Ede's speech, to ask what punishment would be inflicted on British people listening to such a foreign radio programme and, on being told an election might be voided, he was reassured that an entire general election would not become void because people all over the country had listened in.

Ede wanted to repeal obsolete parts of election law, such as the ban on ribbons and cockades, and employing bands:

> 100 years ago, it appears that bands were provided mainly to drown the speeches of the other side, and not to cheer the supporters of the candidate who paid for them. It is doubtful if in these days, with the election expenses limited as they are, it would be possible to employ a band and, with the use of loud speakers, to drown the voice of a candidate if one were used.
>
> Mr Churchill: Does this prohibition apply to miners' choirs?
>
> Mr Ede: No, miners' choirs never were prohibited.

Other Parts of the Bill altered the dates for holding local elections in England and Wales, the conduct of parish council elections by show of hands was abolished, and the constitution of the LCC was modified, with various further changes relating to Scotland. However, much of Ede's speech on the Bill related to abolishing the university seats, which had been challenged by some of those holding them; this had not been proposed by the Speaker's Conference, and was one of the most contentious points. He ran through a list of prominent MPs – Newton, Peel, Palmerston, Gladstone – who had represented Cambridge or Oxford and then been removed from their seats as soon as they had tried anything radical. To suggest that these seats should be retained as they elected such great figures, was like arguing that, because Old Sarum chose the elder Pitt, there should still be rotten boroughs. At this Churchill, continuing in his facetious mood, called out, 'Like Limehouse', a dig at Attlee's seat, seriously depopulated because, as Ede rebuked him, of the sacrifices it made during the war. In any event, he could tell Churchill that the Limehouse constituency was being abolished; it became part of Stepney, while Attlee himself moved to represent Walthamstow West.

He ended his speech with a flourish, reminding the House that his proposals had been in discussion for centuries, quoting the Putney debates of 1647, when Rainsborough argued

> there should be universal suffrage without any property qualification …
> He said, 'The poorest he that is in England hath a Life to live as much as the greatest he.' We believe that that claim made 301 years ago is still

valid as the basis for the suffrage for this country. We hope through this measure to be able to complete the democratisation of this House.

At the end of the debate, the Second Reading was approved with opposition from only the Liberals, the Conservatives deciding to abstain.

On 16 March 1948, the House was debating the Bill in Committee, and Ede commented that, for the first time, he found himself replying to a speech made against him by Rab Butler, with whom he had sat side by side for about four years. Butler's subject had once again been the university constituencies, but Ede was able to cast his memory back to 1892, the first election he could recollect. Then,

> 'One man, one vote,' was regarded as one of the great war cries. At every election in which I have participated since, I have advocated this reform. I know of no outstanding constitutional reform which has been more insistently demanded than this one, and to suggest that this is something which has come unexpectedly upon university representatives is really to strain one's imagination.

There was much friendly sparring, with exchange of compliments, between the two. The debate went on for several days – during which, on 24 March, the Police Pensions Act received Royal Assent – with Ede defending the new constituency arrangements, and indeed increasing the number of seats, to deal with towns and cities where constituencies were too large. This raised objections from Churchill, Quentin Hogg and others, about seats being gerrymandered to favour the government.

In fact, the new constituency boundaries provided the main political and historical impact of this thorough updating of electoral law. It was carried out with Ede's usual efficiency, and not to the government's benefit. He conscientiously proceeded to redraw the constituencies regardless of any party political effect. He did this broadly in line with the recommendations of the Boundary Commissioners, but the result was to reduce significantly the number of seats Labour was likely to win. This outcome had been clear for some time. As early as the autumn of 1945, Ede and Morrison were in discussion about the redistribution, and on 10 July 1946 he had written to Morrison, noting that London was to lose 22 seats, while the 'adjoining counties profit considerably'.[5] Surrey MPs would increase from 14 to 19, and Middlesex from 24 to 28. Anyone in party politics would understand the implications of that. Hugh Dalton criticised the new boundaries, as initially proposed, and certain proposals were then moderated, saving some seats for Labour.[6] On 27 September 1946 the London Labour Party wrote to argue that the population had decreased when the government had encouraged dispersal from London during the war, but it had started rising again; the date of 15 October 1945, to which the Commission worked, was not a reliable one for estimating population figures. Three days later, Attlee himself suggested to Ede a review of the figures in 1947 before legislating, in view of shifting populations, but the Home Secretary replied the Labour Party had asked for the 1945 date and should stick with it.

He was also very clear about the independence of the Commissioners. When he wrote to nominees inviting them to join the Commissions, there was a proviso that they should not have taken an active part in politics. One barrister, MP Fitzgerald KC, so invited in September 1946, confirmed the point, but did not want Ede to 'appoint me under any misapprehension. I disapprove thoroughly of almost everything this government has done.' Fitzgerald was duly appointed.

Churchill himself, replying to the initial debate on this Bill, argued that redistribution was needed 'because of the present over-representation of the Socialist Party', so the issue was clear enough. Nonetheless, when the Boundary Commissions reported in 1947, the Cabinet accepted Ede's proposals about them on 18 December, and a further memorandum, on which it made its own conclusions in March 1948.[7] The Home Office continued to get representations from the Labour Party. On 11 May 1948 the Ashford Party argued that retaining the Romney Marsh area within their constituency helped the Conservatives with 6,000 of their electors (the requested change was in fact made, but did not effect the Ashford voting numbers at the next election). Once the Act had been followed by Ede's House of Commons (Redistribution of Seats) Act 1949, the new boundaries contributed to the party's near loss of majority in 1950, and its fall from government in 1951. This caused considerable comment later on, both in the memoirs of other politicians, such as Barbara Castle,[8] and from other commentators. Kenneth O Morgan, not an admirer of Ede, rather harshly described his redistribution of seats as 'self-destructive honesty'.[9]

While the Representation of the People Bill was becoming an Act, Parliament was also concerned with the Children Bill, which put further duties on the Home Office. Its aim was to establish a comprehensive child care service, at the same time as the National Assistance Act finally abolished the old Poor Law, which had been in existence, in one form or another, since Tudor times. Introducing the welfare state, one of the Attlee Government's main successes, was not directly Ede's own doing, but it created a need for new arrangements for children who were destitute or neglected.[10] The Home

Office had already taken over powers for these children from the Ministries of Education and Health, and the services available to these young people needed reforming. The Bill, started into the House of Lords by William Jowitt, now the Lord Chancellor, consolidated some existing legislation, including care proceedings, remand homes, reports to the courts, places of safety, fostering and adoption, but also required counties and county boroughs to establish a Children's Committee. The Committee had to appoint a Children's Officer, approved by the Home Office, and adequate staff in support. The parallels with the arrangements under the Education Act are clear and, as with education, this was to enable professional social work practice to develop in the field of child care.

Each Children's Committee took over management of the children's homes, reception centres, residential schools, remand homes and approved schools, which may previously have been the responsibility of education committees, or public assistance committees (which had been running poor relief since the workhouses and boards of guardians had been abolished before the war).

They took on the duty to receive into care children without parents or whose parents could not care for them, if it was in the interest of their welfare. One aim was to get childcare services working more closely with families, and the Act, once passed, provided in detail for how this relationship should work, both practically and financially. Fortunately for Ede, most of the work on the Bill was done by the Lords or by Kenneth Younger, but on 28 June 1948 he had to support Younger in a debate about controlling voluntary children's homes, and on ensuring that children encouraged to emigrate were given effective after-care. He made it clear he saw the Act as the means to a more professional approach towards childcare, viewing children as individual clients with their own needs. At the end, he was able to move the Third Reading of the Bill, which became the Children Act on 5 July.

Even more significant legislation was the Criminal Justice Bill, which had been heralded well in advance. Not only had Ede been involved, as we have seen, with Hoare's abortive Bill of 1938–39, he had announced as early as 1946 that it would be one of his major objectives while at the Home Office – the 'outstanding event of his present term of office', as the *Observer* forecast in his profile.[11] He had been under pressure from Labour backbenchers on the subject of penal reform. On 13 February that year George Thomas had pressed him in an Adjournment Debate about prison conditions – trials held secretly in prisons, and corporal punishment there, the lack of training with a view to reforming criminals, prison libraries, and youths sentenced to borstal training being detained in prison. Ede's answers show he agreed with most of Thomas's points. He had agreed most reluctantly to boys staying in prison and, while he felt the arrangements for trials against prison discipline were adequate, because sentences were passed to him for review, he was 'all against flogging except in cases where the brutality of the offender is such that common sense would be outraged unless adequate steps were taken to convince people'. The *Observer* had (slightly inaccurately) quoted those words in its profile.

The outstanding achievements of the Bill, for which it is best remembered, were set out in its first two straightforward clauses: to abolish penal servitude, sentences of hard labour, prison divisions (under which those convicted were classified into different groups according to the nature of their crimes and criminal records), and whipping. Where a statute provided for penal servitude or hard labour, an equivalent sentence of imprisonment would be substituted. These had been features of Hoare's Bill, and the case for abolition had become generally (though with exceptions) agreed. This was just as well because, as he said, in relation to the different issue of ending capital punishment,

> I doubt very much whether, at the moment, public opinion is in favour of this change, but I doubt also whether at any time during the past 100 years a plebiscite would have carried any of the great penal reforms which have been made.

It was in this context that he put his weight behind the Bill, which must be recalled when faced with those who belittle its effects. Morris says of Ede that 'the Home Secretary could hardly be described as a memorable incumbent of that office', and that the 'government, in spite of its steamroller majority, did not go about the business of penal reform with … either originality or greater enthusiasm',[12] but that is unfair. Ede, and Attlee also, with their experience of the fate of previous Labour governments, believed change should advance in step with what the public would accept and, as Morris admits, had to face down considerable pressure from established figures like Lord Chief Justice Goddard, whose obstructions in the Lords over the death penalty might have jeopardised the entire Criminal Justice Act. (Morris also wrongly includes Shawcross, the Attorney-General, as a supporter of capital punishment.)

Leon Radzinowicz, the founding father of criminology at Cambridge, knew and admired both Hoare and Ede, and drew some comparisons between them, though contrasting Hoare's education, aristocratic background and breadth of political experience with Ede's less privileged early life.[13] He believed that building up the position of the police, and maintaining respect for public order and the law, were Ede's main interests at the Home Office, rather than penal reform. Hoare, on the other hand, had a deep feeling for his (Quaker) family tradition, in which such reform had played a large part, and like Ede was an extremely hard-working and determined political innovator. Ede, though, was interested enough in the subject to be prepared to support Hoare in 1938–39, and of course as a magistrate he was familiar with many of the issues. Hoare in return willingly encouraged Ede in 1947–48, from his seat in the Lords, to which he had moved after a spell as wartime Ambassador to Spain. But Radzinowicz did say he noticed in Hoare a regret that it had not been he who became the 'formal father' of the Criminal Justice Act.

Ede introduced the Bill to the Commons on 27 November 1947, in a speech which took him an hour and a half. Although abolishing archaic and brutal punishments was the apparent initial purpose of the measure, that was not what he concentrated on. He discussed the increase in serious crime, and in prison population, which had occurred since before the war, and then first explained changes to the treatment of young offenders in the Bill. Young people on remand would be sent to local authority remand homes or Home Office remand centres, and once convicted, those under 17 could not be imprisoned by a magistrates' court, and those under 15 not at all. There would be an extension of probation homes and, as one change from the previous Bill's provision, detention centres would be provided for those who did not require a long spell in an approved school or Borstal. When given remission for good conduct, the more serious young offenders would be under supervision after their release.

He then went on to deal with changes to the probation system, which had been confusing and obscured by legal terminology. A probation order would now be available to the courts instead of sentencing an offender, and could be combined with a conditional discharge. The person convicted would be liable for a further penalty for the original offence if he committed another, and would meanwhile be under a probation officer's supervision for between one and three years. The finding of guilt would amount to a conviction – which had not always been clear in regard to probation – but would not in itself disqualify a person from other entitlements which might apply to a conviction. After this, Ede explained how the Bill would address the issue of persistent offenders. Preventive detention of up to ten years already existed as sentence open to a court, but it needed to follow a period of penal servitude and, he said, there were only thirty people currently serving such a sentence. There would now be sentences of corrective training (between two and four years) for repeat offenders over twenty-one, and preventive detention (between five and fourteen years) for those over thirty; they would be instead of any other sentence, not in addition. Setting the maximum of fourteen years for preventive detention was a further change from Hoare's Bill, which had proposed ten. This illustrates the government's concern about the increase in serious crime – though early release on licence would be available where the prisoner's conduct justified it.

Only after running through all these measures at length did Ede come to what he called miscellaneous reforms, changing the penal system and amending criminal law. He explained that, over the years, there had ceased to be much practical distinction between the conditions of hard labour, penal servitude and normal imprisonment, while ceasing to classify prisoners into first, second and third divisions would bring the law into line with contemporary practice. The 'ticket-of-leave' system, under which a person could be released early subject to restrictions, would disappear with penal servitude. Custodial sentences could now be only corrective training, preventive detention or straightforward 'imprisonment'. He confirmed that corporal punishment would be abolished, except in prisons, and ran through the changes needed in regard to administering fines and the bail system. Next, he announced that, for the first time in England, fingerprints of any suspects could be taken as soon as they were brought before the magistrates (as was already the case in Scotland).

This was a considerable list of changes to criminal and penal procedure – and there were many others in the Bill – which in due course became part of the Criminal Justice Act 1948. As one of his Labour colleagues, Dr Barnett Stross, said towards the end of the second day's debate, 'The Home Secretary has warned us that most of the discussion would range around the death penalty and flogging but, when he said that, he showed us his own mind, which was that the provisions relating to young offenders were perhaps the most important.' Ede used his experience on the bench to develop penal policy, with the Magistrates' Association having argued over many years for a new type of sentence for young offenders, keeping them away from older prisoners, and holding them for a shorter period than the old Borstals.[14] A period of between three months and a year was initially prescribed, and ideas about the régime developed through experience of military detention camps during the War. The Act eventually settled the question of the length of sentence at three months, or in exceptional cases six. The centres would provide, in the words of a later Home Secretary on his penal reforms, a 'short, sharp shock'. As Ede said, the 'régime would consist of brisk discipline and hard work'.

There was one significant further provision added to the Bill, for which Ede may not have been prepared, and another proposal over which there was much argument, which he knew was coming. The first was proposed in the House of Lords by Lord Simon,[15] the Lord Chancellor during the war, who wanted to end the 'preposterous anachronism' of peers charged with felonies (though not misdemeanours) being tried by the Lords themselves. The following day, the current Lord Chancellor, Jowitt, added his agreement, during the course of a long debate during which Lord Templewood, as Samuel Hoare had become, gave his forceful support to Ede's Bill. In due course, the Lords agreed an amendment to abolish the privilege of peerage, and this found its way into the eventual statute.

The other issue which became central during the Bill's course through Parliament was, as Stross had said, capital punishment. Right from the start of the Second Reading on 27 November 1947 Sidney Silverman, a longstanding Labour abolitionist, had referred to the amendment he was tabling, for a five-year suspension of capital punishment, and Ede acknowledged this at the end of his speech. The government had considered the argument, in a minute Ede presented next day to the cabinet, but felt there was no feasible alternative.[16] He recalled to the House the 1938 debate (in which he, of course, had voted for abolition), but up-to-date criminal statistics argued against any change. Since 1938, murders had increased by 40 per cent, wounding cases, burglaries and the like by more than a half, robberies with violence had trebled and rapes nearly so. More criminals were arming themselves, the police force was undermanned, and there was a real fear that miscreants would be more likely to take up arms if they had no fear for their lives. 'Were the circumstances the same as in 1938, I would vote for' Silverman's amendment but, as things were, the government could not recommend it. The proposal would be put to the House at the Report Stage of the Bill, for debate and a free vote.

To his admission that he had altered his view, he commented, 'My mind is not static on any subject', and Silverman interrupted, 'The Right hon. Gentleman will probably change it again.' Ede made no reply to that prophecy, which would turn out to be true, but it was clear he and his colleagues knew that public opinion, already being asked to swallow several changes in sentencing, was not yet ready to alter the death penalty. He was also aware of his duties in sustaining and developing the police force, which he took very seriously, and of their views on hanging.

In fact the position of the government was far more complex than he had suggested. The Attorney- and Solicitor-Generals, Hartley Shawcross and Frank Soskice, were firmly in support of Silverman, as were some in the cabinet, while Herbert Morrison, a former Home Secretary, was not. Neither was Jowitt, who would have to recommend the Bill in the Lords, and was mindful of the overwhelming support for the death penalty among the judges. Jowitt had even favoured retention of birching, though he eventually accepted he would not prevail on that. Initially, an agreement was reached that ministers who disagreed with the government line should stay silent in the debate, but could then vote as they saw fit. However, on 8 April Morrison argued that this should be looked at again, and convinced his colleagues that any dissenting ministers should merely abstain. Maxwell, Ede's Permanent Secretary, whose sympathies may have been with abolition, had argued that the government should take a firm view one way or the other, and either include abolition as a measure in its own Bill, or oppose the amendment and require support from all its MPs. As he foresaw, leaving the decision to Parliament would merely invite a battle between the Commons and the Lords, who would present themselves as upholders of public opinion.[17]

Though several MPs made their views on capital punishment known during the two days of the Second Reading, the actual debate took place only when the Bill returned to the whole House at the Report Stage on 14 April 1948. Sydney Silverman introduced his new clause, crediting Ede with having ensured its drafting would work in the event it was agreed, and spoke for less than half an hour, listing the inconsistencies he found in the arguments for retaining the death penalty – or at least doing so for the present, until the time was right for abolition. His proposal was seconded by Christopher Hollis, the Conservative MP for Devizes, a former President of the Oxford Union who treated the subject rather in the manner of an undergraduate debate. He ridiculed Bernard Shaw for supposedly arguing that some murderers can be reformed, but others can be medically identified as beyond reformation and should be killed 'as one would kill a mad dog'. He dealt with arguments that there were more firearms in circulation following the war, that it was unfair to ask the police to do their work without the safeguard of the death penalty, and that the hand of authority should not be weakened at a time when lawlessness was likely to grow.

Hollis contrasted the savage repression of Sidmouth – the longest-serving Home Secretary, whose time in office even Ede would not match – with his successor Peel, who saw lawlessness as a reason for reform, rather than against. Both Silverman and Hollis were able to remind the House of a time, not much beyond living memory, when death was the punishment for a range of crimes, which abolition of the penalty had not made more prevalent. It was a pity, to Hollis, that the present Home Secretary was unable to put himself in the great line of reformers from the past.

There followed six hours of argument from all sides before Ede delivered the government's reply. He could not recommend their support; though the debate was a 'credit to this great deliberative assembly', the time was not ripe for undertaking the reform. While subject to several interruptions, he gave his account of his discussions with ordinary folk around the country, who overwhelmingly took the same view. There had been an 'unusual run of successive reprieves' in the previous year, which itself had raised comment, though that was a matter of chance, as he applied the same principle to each individual case. With a new class of criminal the country, and the unarmed police in particular, had to be protected. He mentioned the Edgar murder, and was pulled up by Silverman as Thomas was awaiting trial. He repeated some of the statistics about increases in crime, and explained that, if imprisonment was made the alternative, the time served in the worst cases would need to be so long that running a civilised prison service would be impossible. He explained the circumstances any Home Secretary would see as reasons to grant a reprieve.

The Labour backbencher Reginald Paget concluded the debate on behalf of the abolitionists. Various speakers had commented on the extreme unlikelihood of an error being made in a murder verdict, and Paget discussed many cases, in Britain and the USA, where a mistake had come to light, sometimes too late to save the defendant. After he sat down, the House voted, and the amendment to suspend capital punishment was carried by 245 to 222. Three-quarters of the Labour members who took part voted for abolition, and 134 of Ede's supporters, a clear majority, were Conservatives. Nine Cabinet ministers voted with him, but many ministers abstained, including Stafford Cripps and Aneurin Bevan, who are said to have been disappointed by Ede's opposition,[18] as did the government law officers. The Bill's consideration went on, through the evening and the next day, 15 April, with several amendments discussed, and on 16 April when Ede proposed the Third Reading, he announced that, with the prospect of the law being changed to stop death sentences in that Parliamentary session, he would commute all such sentences.

That was a contentious decision. On its face, it made sense to decide that a murderer should not be hanged as a consequence of an accident of timing in his trial and the application of the new law, if indeed it was enacted. The House had taken a firm decision, not merely a resolution against the death penalty, and a short time might see it applied, once the Lords agreed and Royal Assent was given. Equally, it would be invidious to leave those condemned in an uncertain state about whether or not their sentences would eventually be carried out. However, the British constitution makes a clear distinction between the Crown exercising its prerogative of mercy, and the monarch or government generally dispensing with laws without Parliamentary consent, which was declared illegal by the Bill of Rights 1689. Consequently it was one thing for the Home Secretary to grant a reprieve in particular cases, and quite another to decide to commute every death sentence despite the law not yet having changed. Ede's policy was criticised at the time, including by Lord Goddard and Lord Simon on 2 June, and the following week the cabinet decided he would need to make a further statement in the House amending it. In practice, though, in each case for the next few months he decided to commute the sentence, and so a number of condemned murderers, including Donald Thomas, the killer of a policeman in the course of his duty, were reprieved. This continued until it became clear that the Lords would not countenance suspending capital punishment.

For the Lords were the main problem, both for Silverman and his supporters, and for the government itself. Jowitt had to present the Bill to the House, including the amendment on capital punishment, which he clearly did not support. On 28 April he told the House he was proposing it because he had agreed to stand by the result of the free vote, which was far from a convincing argument. The proposal was opposed by Samuel, a former Home Secretary, and Simon, who had also held that post before being Lord Chancellor, as well as Goddard, the Lord Chief Justice, and most judges and bishops. Templewood, having changed his mind on the death penalty, supported the Commons, as did a few others, mostly on the Labour side, but they were defeated on 2 June by 181 votes to 28. That same evening, the Lords took the opportunity to amend the prohibition on corporal punishment so birching was retained as a sentence; the majority for that was 29 to 17.

The government's initial reaction to the vote on hanging was to devise a compromise, which would retain capital punishment only for certain classes of murder. Although they convinced the Labour MPs, including Silverman, to support this, so that it was easily carried on 15 July, it was again blocked by the Lords five days later. Jowitt was still uncomfortable, and this time even Templewood, considering it unworkable, opposed it; the vote was 99 to 19 against. Ede and Morrison then convinced the Commons, to ensure the Bill as a whole was successful, to let the Lords have their way on the death penalty (though the Lords had to stand down on birching). Most Labour Members abstained. On 30 July, the Criminal Justice Act was one of more than fifty measures to gain the Royal Assent. At the end of the year, Ede appointed a Royal Commission to consider the question of capital punishment, and what changes or qualifications should be made to the law – though not whether it should be entirely abolished. Among its members was Alexander Maxwell, who in 1948 had retired, handing over the post of

Permanent Under-Secretary to Newsam. It was said that, although Ede 'did not altogether trust Newsam's judgement', he 'concurred in his promotion' but 'saw to it that he [Ede] remained firmly in charge'.[19] Then the Home Secretary started again to approve executions.

The nature of the Home Secretary's duty in relation to capital punishment is one which is hard to grasp nowadays, or to liken to any other ministerial task. The 'awful loneliness' about which Ede commented, after Attlee had told him he would need to take each decision without help or comment from any of his colleagues, was reflected by the experience of Rab Butler at the Home Office between 1957 and 1962. By his time, the Homicide Act 1957 had reduced the class of murders which were capital, but Butler still described the Home Secretary's responsibility as 'hideous'.[20] Each decision meant shutting himself up for two days. This does not mean he had no source of advice – Butler sought counsel from his officials, the judiciary and Lord Chancellor Kilmuir (David Maxwell Fyfe, who was himself at the Home Office from 1951 for three years), as Ede had consulted his office in the Martinez case. There was also lobbying from different sources, as for Martinez. On one occasion even Churchill wrote 'as a former Home Secretary' to Ede on behalf of three convicted soldiers.[21] But in the end, the decision was the Home Secretary's alone.

It was unfortunate for Ede that he had these duties at a time when there had been an increase in crime generally, and when there were several high profile murders, naturally covered by the press. As well as the murder of PC Edgar by Thomas, there was the case of Neville Heath, who in 1946 killed and mutilated two women. John George Haigh killed at least six people in the mid-1940s, destroying their corpses in acid. In April 1947, an armed raid on a jeweller's shop in London, led to a passer-by who tried to stop the robbers, Alec de Antiquis, being shot dead. Walter Rowland was convicted of killing a prostitute in Manchester with a hammer, despite having a good alibi, whereupon another man, David Ware, confessed to the murder. It transpired that Rowland had been convicted of murdering his young daughter in the 1930s, but reprieved and eventually released, while Ware's confession was dismissed as false, so the conviction was upheld – though Ware was in 1951 convicted of a hammer murder. In circumstances like these, it is not surprising public opinion was heavily in favour of the death penalty, though this applied more particularly to those cases which were particularly foul. It was a problem to distinguish the worse from the lesser cases and, despite attempts to classify murders into different types, the Home Secretary had to look at each case on its merits and reach his decision. Of the murderers

I have mentioned, Thomas was lucky that his timing fell during the pause in hangings while the Criminal Justice Bill was debated; Ware was deemed insane and committed suicide; and one of the de Antiquis killers was under age.[22] All the others were hanged.

When he summed up his case in the debate on 14 April 1948, Ede explained some principles on which he reached those decisions. At one time, virtually the only issue was whether the murderer was technically insane, a relatively easy decision, as a medical report would direct the Home Secretary's mind. But matters had become more complex as, without insanity, mental abnormality might now, in borderline cases, be accepted as lessening the killer's responsibility. In some cases, extreme provocation might mitigate the murder, and in others the judge and counsel may agree the wrong defence was advanced, so that some circumstances were not considered at the trial. His July 1947 Cabinet minute[23] added to these issues the age of the murderer (some, though old enough at 18 to hang, might be young enough to receive mercy), the effect of public opinion (such as where the agent who kills is working for a principal who, for whatever reason, would not hang), and the relative degree of responsibility where more than one person was convicted. There was also the certainty of evidence; if there was any doubt about the guilt, despite the jury's verdict, the sentence would be commuted. About half of all were reprieved, and Ede was typically having to consider a case every two weeks or so.

When Michael Noakes painted his portrait many years later, what stayed most in his mind was Ede's discussion of capital punishment, and his fairly relaxed attitude about these decisions, taking the view he was merely applying the law as his duty required. Noakes's recall was of Ede as the last Home Secretary to have to decide capital cases; in fact (though the last from the Labour Party) there would be four more. However, he remembered Ede saying he had to deal with some 120 cases (which sounds a fair estimate over six years), and to begin with was given a few precedents to suggest which circumstances might or might not be right for a reprieve, after which he had to reach his own conclusion in each case.[24] That ties up with Ede's own explanation to cabinet, and his remark, in the debate on the compromise proposal on 15 July 1948, that he imagined

that every Home Secretary, on taking office, receives the book which was given to me, recording instances in the past where hon. Members … have attempted to question Home Secretaries and the way in which the issue has generally been avoided of forcing anything which would be uncomfortable for the Home Secretary.

He could not, though, escape the conclusion that

> there is no responsibility which falls on any Minister of State which gives greater personal concern to the man who has to discharge it alone than successive Home Secretaries feel in the discharge of these duties,

and the events of 1949 and 1950 would come (as Noakes recalled) always to disturb him.

Others of Ede's duties towards maintaining law and order caused him to sanction a three-month ban on political marches in London during 1948.[25] He was entitled to do this under the Public Order Act 1936, a statute passed (against opposition from Labour) mainly as a response to demonstrations by Oswald Mosley's Fascists. Frank Newsam, earlier in his career, had been a leading mind behind the Act, which the Home Office was now able to use in circumstances where police numbers were depleted.

Deportation and extradition cases were also a heavy responsibility, but at least with these the Home Secretary had others to assist him. The arguments over Dering had continued throughout this time, without any conclusion.[26] In July 1947 Maxwell Fyfe and Elwyn Jones had decided there was a prima facie case against Dering, but wished to see more evidence, which had eventually been sent from Poland in February 1948. Ede then asked for a view from Jowitt, who did not believe Dering had been fully frank in his interviews and, aware how anti-Semitic were many Poles, raised the possibility that he might have behaved well to other Poles but badly to Jewish prisoners. By June Ede agreed the prima facie case had been made out, but then a further statement from Dering himself was obtained, and a group of MPs visited the Home Office to press the case against extradition. His Government colleague George Strauss, who had himself suffered because of his Jewish background, argued there would be no possibility of a fair trial in a Communist country. Still more evidence was taken, and the possibility raised that the case might have relied on mistaken identity. Eventually, in August 1948, Dering was released, after more than eighteen months, Ede having taken the decision not to extradite him.

This was an unsatisfactory episode. The government had agreed with its allies, at the end of the war, to surrender alleged war criminals for trial, and at the start of the saga the Home Office had recognised the case would set a precedent, so that the procedure and policy needed to be settled early on. The reverse had happened, and it is clear from one comment by Ede that an application for extradition to France (where one of Dering's accusers was based) would have been easier to accept that one from the Communist bloc.

Extradition and deportation remained awkward issues for the Home Office. On 23 September 1948, Ede told the Commons:

These matters give me the greatest concern, and I can assure the House that if there should be another case I shall act with the most scrupulous care and I shall have learned something from this case.

As for Dering, he started practising as a doctor in the UK in 1949, became a British citizen, and received the OBE, but in the 1960s he sued the author and publisher of the novel *Exodus* for libel over a reference in it to medical experiments performed by him. Though he won the case, the jury awarded him only a halfpenny in damages; they were unconvinced of his total innocence.

As well as the Criminal Justice Act, 30 July 1948 saw the Royal Assent given to the British Nationality Act. This measure had not really been planned, but was rather forced on the Government by a decision taken by Canada in 1946. Canada resolved to established a separate Canadian citizenship, independent of the common citizenship status of British subject, which covered nationals of the United Kingdom, the dominions and the British colonies. Ede had seen early on that this would be followed by other dominions, alerting the cabinet to the consequences on 16 November 1945,[27] and he recommended that the UK legislated in parallel with them.[28] In May 1946 the Prime Ministers of the Commonwealth Dominions had met in London, and Ede had joined them; they had called a conference of experts in nationality law, which met in February 1947 under Alexander Maxwell's chairmanship. It was agreed a few months later that each of the Commonwealth states might legislate for its own citizenship, while still retaining elements of a common status. That status was to be British subject or 'Commonwealth citizen', terms that were interchangeable, the latter being introduced to satisfy the new Dominions of India, Pakistan and Ceylon, and perhaps the Afrikaners and Quebecois, who might find difficulties with the concept of subjection to the British crown.

The British Nationality Act 1948, the United Kingdom's response for itself and its colonies, has been described as having two opposing aims – 'to give quiet consent to the changing nature of social membership in the colonies and shifting forms of state sovereignty', and as 'a desperate attempt to hold the Empire together'.[29] The Bill had started in the Lords and, when Ede moved the Second Reading on 7 July 1948, he explained the background, stressing that the newly-created status of 'Citizen of the United Kingdom and Colonies' would be a single one, for all born or naturalised in the United Kingdom or one of its colonies, covering all races:

there are … some who feel that it is wrong to have a citizenship of the United Kingdom and Colonies. Some people feel that it would be a bad thing to give the coloured races of the Empire the idea that, in some way or other, they are the equals of people in this country. The Government do not subscribe to that view.

That seems forward-thinking and liberal enough, but in common with most of his contemporaries, his position sprang from an outlook now regarded as embarrassingly patronising. While the objective in regard to the colonies was clear:

we cannot admit all these backward peoples immediately into the full rights that British subjects in this country enjoy; but wherever the British Dominions are, what Lowell called 'the homespun dignity of man' is at least recognised to the extent of the denial of the right of anyone to have a chattel slave. By linking the United Kingdom and the Colonies, we must give these people a feeling that on that homespun dignity of man we recognise them as fellow-citizens and that our object … is to hope to raise them to such a position of education, of training and of experience that they too shall be able to share in the grant of full self-government which this House has so generously given during the last few years to other places.

To say that the UK at least objects to slavery is scarcely a reassuring position. Nonetheless, Ede made his objectives clear, that this was a further step in the path towards independence of the colonies, expressed by Ede in the quotation from Lowell, one of his favourites which he would repeat in many speeches until his last years. The theme was echoed by Maxwell Fyfe for the Conservatives, in equally condescending terms:

let us say … we had much to offer the people of the Dominions, and more to people of the racially distinct and smaller countries of the Commonwealth, because … we were proud in this country that we imposed no colour bar restrictions, making it difficult for them when they came here. These people … found themselves as privileged in the United Kingdom as the local citizens.

This was in line with the UN Charter of Human Rights, and was perhaps an expression of pride that Britain did not have the race problems of the USA, though recently we have needed to recognise that, even if to a limited extent that is so, it is not for any lack of racial arrogance in the country's history. Difficulties would soon arise when the fellow-citizens took up the offer of migration to Britain, which, as is well-known, occurred from 1948, with the *Windrush's* arrival a couple of weeks before this debate, and subsequently.

The Bill importantly also provided that marriage would have no effect on a British woman's nationality, which followed measures adopted in Australia and elsewhere, which had given rise to inconsistencies, and it clarified circumstances for citizenship to be acquired by descent from a citizen of the UK and Colonies. Ede participated in a Women's Hour broadcast on the BBC, which covered the 'victory dinner' celebrating women's right to independent nationality.[30] The Act resolved the position of Irish citizens, who in many cases had dual citizenship, and dealt with the jurisdiction of English courts over crimes committed overseas. In those cases where British criminal law applies to things done overseas, such as murder, the Act generally restricted the scope of this to citizens of the UK and Colonies. The last point is the only significant part of the British Nationality Act still in force, as controls were gradually tightened on immigration from other parts of the Commonwealth between 1962 and 1971.

It is easy to be cynical about the purpose of this Act. Kathleen Paul[31] describes it as 'remarkable for the way in which UK policy makers turned a perceived necessary evil' – that is, the challenge from Canada – 'into a proactive tool of imperial policy'. She describes how citizenship of the UK and Colonies was advocated most strongly by the Colonial Office, to ensure the colonies did not get any sense of inferiority, but at the same time to encourage them to delay independence from the British Empire. Some Conservatives were more grudging than Maxwell Fyfe in their attitude to those in the colonies but, from Labour's perspective, it is hard to see how the measure could have been more generous, short of granting independence immediately. That of course is largely what happened in the next twenty-five years, but it was not yet on the agenda for most countries. In the meantime, Ede and his colleagues, including Alexander Maxwell, while undoubtedly subject to the paternalistic attitudes of their age, took as enlightened a position as they could about the status of Britain's colonies, and about racial equality, the opportunities for immigration, and the ultimate direction towards a Commonwealth of independent countries.

Chapter 14

Working Alone

While the conflicts around the Criminal Justice Act and Dering's case were going on, Ede suffered a major crisis in his personal life. On 1 July 1948, Lilian Ede died. She had been unwell for several years, though her death does not seem to have been expected. Latterly she had been confined to a wheelchair, following her leg amputation, but this had not totally restricted her, as her husband used to take her to Westminster and push her about the terrace at Parliament – 'a familiar sight', according to his own *Times* obituary years later. Her funeral was held at Epsom Parish Church, with her coffin carried by six policemen under the command of a seventh. He kept a photograph of the procession, led by himself, out of the church and down to the Rolls-Royce cars, including the hearse, blooming with flowers.

Maxwell Fyfe had given him the condolences of the House of Commons when debating the British Nationality Act the week after her death.[1] There is no record of Ede's own thoughts, but her death was called 'a crushing blow'[2] for him, and he was described as 'much affected by the loss',[3] as can be well believed. They had been married for over thirty years, working together in political, educational and other activities, preserving and walking the countryside of Surrey as a devoted partnership. It is not surprising they had no children, she being nearly forty-two when they married, while for most of their first year together they were separated by the war. She had encouraged him on, probably helped his conversion from Liberal to Labour, and supported him several times as he moved from one field to a new, less familiar one. Some of those who knew him detected a loss of spark in his character after her death, though he carried on with his task. From now on, his usual companion when one was needed was his sister Nell.

Regarding his marriage, enquirers sometimes ask whether there was any type of scandal in Ede's life, wondering perhaps whether secrets might be there to uncover. Well, none have been found. Like everyone in politics, he surely knew that sex and money are the major causes of disgrace which can undermine a career, even if their profile was lower than in today's world, and even if the risks were not spelt out to aspiring candidates as they are nowadays.

During his last parliament, he would play a small part in uncovering (or, some might say, fabricating) a sexual and security scandal, but in his own life there is nothing to suggest anything untoward. After thirty-five years a bachelor, he was a loyal husband till his late sixties, and a virtuous widower after that. As far as can be seen from his tax returns, he lived off his parliamentary and ministerial income, together with his union salary and sponsorship, and later his teacher's and union pensions. He carefully declared a few pounds earned each year from a hoarding on land in East Street, Epsom, let out for advertising. Any surplus he had to invest went into solid funds like Surrey County Council Stock and British Electricity 3 per cent Stock, both investments which related to his own experience, and which would cause no conflict of interest. The 3 per cent stock produced an income of nearly £80 from the late 1940s onwards, so must have been worth over £2,600, equivalent to between £50,000 and £100,000 today. He stated he did not follow the Stock Exchange, as either investment or gamble, although

> a person with a genius on those lines … could have made quite a considerable fortune, but I live a happy life and I am not anxious for more money than enables me to live the ordinary sort of … life that I enjoy.[4]

He was a cautious investor, in line with the prudent and restrained manner of his life – 'a man renowned for his integrity', in the words of a historian of the Education Act.[5]

Ede's work, of course, went on after his bereavement. He was piloting Bills through Parliament, and was by now recognised as a practical, non-doctrinaire member of the cabinet, very willing to work with political opponents to further his aims. Francis Williams wrote a piece in *The Spectator* on 30 September 1947, choosing him as the second in his series on 'Ministers as They Are' (Bevan was the first), evidently because, though avoiding publicity,

> when the history of the Labour Administration comes to be written it will not, I think, be found that his impact upon its fortunes is any less than theirs [ie, many of his colleagues], or that his contribution … was in any way subsidiary to that of several more colourful figures.

That judgement has not really been upheld; many accounts of Attlee's time hardly mention Ede, and none yet has centred on him. At the time, though, it was clear he was considered an essential member of the team, with his 'career of a Socialist in a predominantly Conservative area', Surrey, giving him the experience to co-operate with his opponents to get any job done.

Unfortunately, while Williams gave a good account of his biography and his work with Butler at Education, he gave no examples of what he was achieving at the Home Office, a gap I hope I am filling.

A new session of Parliament started on 26 October 1948, and the King's Speech promised a further flurry of legislation, including 'a measure for the future organisation of Civil Defence'. In the debate on the Speech, Attlee mentioned the Bill, saying he could not yet give a date for introducing it, but that there had been discussions between the government and local authorities on the general nature of future Civil Defence arrangements. Creating a new Civil Defence organisation would require cooperation from the local authorities and the general public. In fact, the Bill took no time to be presented, and on 30 November Ede was guiding it through the House. He explained he did not want to re-establish a Minister of Home Security, which the wartime Home Secretaries (Anderson and Morrison) had become, but a team of ministers, working together to cover their own respective areas, led by him as Home Secretary. Much of the effort would be placed on local authorities or on police authorities, and would get government funds to carry it out. The powers given to the Government included compulsory purchase of land, setting up shelters, entering property, and training those involved in civil defence. This was a short Act, which nonetheless added to Ede's workload. He managed to get it through to Royal Assent before the Christmas recess, on 16 December.

Attlee had interrupted the King's Speech debate to announce that a tribunal of enquiry was being set up to investigate corrupt relationships between Government ministers and businessmen, in the context of shortages and rationing. Ede appointed Sir George Lynskey, a High Court judge, to head this.[6] The case centred on Sidney Stanley, a Jewish Polish immigrant who went under several different names, who was found to have been friendly with John Belcher, a Board of Trade minister, and George Gibson, a Labour Party nominee to the Bank of England board. Shawcross presented the government's case, and interrogated those involved. When the Tribunal reported in 1949, it found that Belcher and Gibson had been influenced in their conduct, mainly regarding a football pools business which had exceeded its paper ration but was not prosecuted. They both resigned, and Stanley quickly disappeared to Israel. Others involved, including Hugh Dalton, were cleared. Ede's actions in instigating this brought about considerable public alarm, but the conclusions are now looked upon as very minor revelations. The 'affair enabled the government to preserve its white sheet, to continue as the unassailable, if somewhat dull, apostle of public virtue'.[7]

All the while, Ede was combining his constituency and religious work with that of Government. In November 1948 he had paid one of his regular visits to South Shields, and a few days later was speaking at the Priestley Hall in Leeds,[8] the educational arm of the city's Mill Hill Unitarian Chapel, where Joseph Priestley himself had been the minister in the eighteenth century. His notes describe the occasion as the Chapel's centenary, which would mean the building, as the congregation had been in existence far longer than that. Joining science, religion and education together, in Priestley's tradition, was a subject of concern there as well as to Ede himself, and his talk was titled 'Knowledge, Wisdom and Freedom', and included once more a reference to John Milton and 'Areopagitica'.

A constitutional innovation was made on 14 November, when Princess Elizabeth gave birth to her first son, Charles. For centuries there had been a tradition that the Home Secretary should attend any royal birth, supposedly to witness that no impostor was introduced, as had been alleged at the birth of James II's Prince of Wales in 1688. Ede considered this 'archaic', and obtained advice that there was no constitutional requirement for it. It seems the King and Queen wished nonetheless that the tradition continue, until they realised that each of the King's Dominions would be entitled to a representative present. On 5 November the King was told it was 'advisable for Your Majesty to put an end to the practice now'. Ede won the argument and, though he did sign the notices to be posted in London announcing Prince Charles's birth, did not attend on the Princess.[9]

The Home Office was the ministry concerned with the position of Northern Ireland within the UK, a matter which became critical in the winter of 1948–49 with the decision of the Irish Government to declare its country 'The Republic of Ireland', outside the British Commonwealth, on 21 January 1949.[10] The Unionists in Northern Ireland felt threatened by the development, which removed the last formal powers of the King in regard to the Republic. Frank Newsam took a major role, supporting the request from Belfast that Northern Ireland be renamed 'Ulster', and recommending a law to provide that no Westminster Parliament could remove Northern Ireland from the UK without the agreement of the Parliament in Stormont. On 6 January, Ede took part in a meeting chaired by Attlee with a delegation from Belfast. Attlee and his team rejected the proposal about 'Ulster', but there was considerable debate about names, and it was eventually agreed that 'the Irish Republic' was a term to use, where possible, in preference to 'The Republic of Ireland', which would need to be in any UK legislation, but which the Unionists felt was a threat to them.

The politician and his papers. (© *Surrey History Centre*)

After the cabinet had discussed these and other questions, mainly about the voting franchise, arising out of the action from Dublin, Attlee and Ede met Basil Brooke, the Northern Ireland PM, in London again, on 18 January. Brooke continued to argue against 'The Republic of Ireland', other than in the initial reference in any Act of Parliament, suggesting his supporters would not accept this, and might reluctantly demand separate dominion status for the North. Ede's reply indicated that, if it was a separate dominion, the North would not be assured Great Britain would come to its defence. Brooke had to stand down on this point, but secured agreement for a three month residential qualification for the voting franchise in the North, to prevent creating 'faggot voting' – obtaining an vote through a dubious property holding. When Dublin indicated its Republic of Ireland Act would not come into force on 21 January, but on 24 April, Easter Monday (a day resonant for Irish independence, which the British took as an unfriendly choice), Attlee and Ede postponed any action. Eventually, the Ireland Bill was presented to Parliament, and on 16 May Ede took part in the debate. The Ireland Act received Royal Assent in June, but was backdated to 18 April, to avoid any link with the Easter Rising, but so the provisions of the two countries coincided. The parts of Ireland were named 'The Republic of Ireland' and 'Northern Ireland', while necessary changes were made to the British Nationality and Representation of the People Acts 1948, but the Republic was declared not to be a foreign country.

On his travels while this was going on, Ede returned to the Channel Islands, attending the first meeting of the newly constituted States of Alderney on 18 February 1949, where his speech was broadcast on the BBC.[11] He was then in Nottingham on 23 April addressing a Parent Teachers' Rally at the university. His subject was the importance of designers and craftsmen.[12] Although his days in education were behind him, he would never cease from making the case for technical training, using his own background in science and teaching, and aware of the conflicting demands of the different types of secondary schools which the local authorities were setting up in the wake of the 1944 Act. In July 1949 he was visiting Holloway, the largest prison for women, to discuss the state of prisons with the women officers there.[13] The general view was that they were unsatisfactory; Holloway would eventually close in 2016, several times criticised for its condition. Ede probably agreed, and he was always prepared to listen to those working there. Then, between 19 and 25 July, he visited Amsterdam, to speak to the Congress of the International Association for Religious Freedom. This claims to be the oldest international interfaith group, with congresses held since 1901. They had ceased with the War, but started again at Amsterdam, where the theme was 'The Mission and Message of Liberal Religion', and his own address was 'The Fight for Freedom in the Human Spirit',[14] maintaining the central idea of his speeches at religious gatherings.

In September, nearer to home, he reviewed the Thames River Police.[15] This happily combined his Home Office functions with one of his abiding interests, boating on the Thames. We know this had been restricted by the petrol shortage during the war, but he had more opportunity, if less leisure, to pursue it now. Among his papers was a receipt for mooring from the Brown Duck at Day's Lock, between Reading and Oxford on the river, and membership papers of the Thames Motor Cruising Club, both from his years as Home Secretary. On 18 April 1949 he had been on the river downstream, taking photographs of the Tower of London and Tower Bridge, from whatever craft he was travelling on; these, like others, he would carefully stick into one of his albums, marking each with the location, date, and his initials in a monogram he had designed.

In 1949, the Government took advantage of initiatives from its own MPs, with Private Member's Bills, to encourage reforms beyond those it was making itself. The Married Women (Maintenance) Act aimed at enabling magistrates to increase maintenance paid to wives and children. At the same time, another Private Member's measure, the Adoption of Children Act, put local authorities in charge of placing children for adoption, and gave adopted children inheritance rights. It allowed the identity of an adopter to be concealed behind a serial number, so a child's mother would not know who was adopting the child. The Home Office response on this was largely done by Kenneth Younger, rather than Ede himself, and it took some months to find its way through Parliament. Both these Acts received Royal Assent on 16 December 1949 and, though not government proposals, would be seen as important enough for Ede to include them among Labour's achievements in office, when he sought re-election.

A further measure enacted that day was the Justices of the Peace Act, on which Ede took a more active role, having considerable experience as a magistrate. He knew there were problems with the way the local courts of summary jurisdiction were administered, and his Bill was a joint project with Lord Chancellor Jowitt, who first introduced it in the Lords.

Arrangements for magistrates' courts were covered by an Act of 1906 but, in 1944, a Departmental Committee had been chaired by Lord Roche, a retired Law Lord, to which Ede had given evidence. It recommended setting up Magistrates' Courts Committees to run the courts in each county and large borough but, as magistrates had long been involved in local administration as well, leaving the membership of these committees, and responsibility for their administration, to magistrates themselves. To obtain 'further guidance', as Jowitt told the Lords on 12 July 1949, the government appointed a Royal Commission in 1946 under Lord du Parcq, a current English Law Lord, originally from Jersey. Ede as Home Secretary had dealt with him in Jersey, and he had presided at the Jersey Society dinner early in 1946, which the Edes had attended. Du Parcq had just died in April 1949, so Jowitt paid tribute to him, and presented the Bill as the outcome of the Roche and du Parcq recommendations.

Ede had worked hard on preparing the Bill, not least in negotiating about the parts which covered the City of London with its Corporation. It came to the Commons on 28 November, when he went through its provisions at length. Magistrates would be subject to a residence qualification (of within fifteen miles of the area for which they were appointed, du Parcq having suggested seven miles). Ex-officio appointments of local authority chairmen would continue (despite du Parcq's doubts), though they would not automatically chair the bench. In line with du Parcq, JPs who were local authority members could not sit on cases involving their authority.

A retirement age for justices was set at seventy-five. This was an arbitrary age, decided after some debate in the Government. When Ede himself subsequently reached it, he told his colleagues in Surrey that Jowitt had preferred seventy; the decision was a compromise. Other provisions restricted solicitors who were JPs from acting in their own court areas, and permitted expenses to be paid to magistrates. The separate benches for small boroughs, set according to population, would be abolished, and special arrangements made for the City of London. The retirement age for those on the juvenile bench would be sixty – a precept Ede had himself followed seven years before.

The most significant parts of the Bill were probably the measures relating to Magistrates' Courts Committees for each county, county borough and those non-county boroughs retaining their benches, as recommended by Roche. Previously, the benches were largely independent bodies appointing their own justices' clerk, often a part-time appointment from among the local solicitors, though Roche had found that there were ninety full-timers, of whom only thirty-two were solicitors. Their running costs were partly funded out of fines and fees that they paid to their local authorities, which Roche criticised as it gave the authorities an interest in the amount of the fees and fines. Their court buildings were usually provided and maintained by the local authority, but the authorities were making up increasing deficits in funding their local courts. With loose oversight of the Home Office, each court was administered by its own magistrates in their own way, with the justices' clerk acting as legal adviser and court administrator.

The new committees were to be made up of magistrates chosen from each county, or large county borough, and they would staff and run their own courts. They would appoint the justices' clerks, professionally qualified, who should be full-time employees of the committee, with their staff being employed by the committee also, rather than by the Clerk, and there would be pension arrangements for them. The Committees would have a new duty of ensuring that JPs were properly trained, as proposed by du Parcq. The local authorities were to be responsible for the court accommodation and the expenses of court business, the committees having to consult with them about how the courts operated. The fines and fees would be paid to the Home Office, which would then pay the local authorities an amount equal to the fines, plus two thirds of the difference between them and actual expenditure.

Stipendiary magistrates were also being brought into the scenario. They could be appointed for counties, as well as for towns, and their pay (though coming from each local authority) would be set by the Home Secretary. Their appointment would be made by the Lord Chancellor, rather than the Home

Secretary, whose responsibility for policing required any potential conflict of interest with the police authority to be avoided.

There was much special pleading, in both Houses of Parliament, on behalf of specific towns and boroughs which were losing their own local bench, but the Government generally held firm. Just as with education, fire and police authorities, Ede understood the need to ensure that local administration did not extend to being operated, in a manner which was not cost-effective, by very small authorities, which might not have the manpower to do so efficiently.

On 6 and 7 December 1949 he was dealing once more with the Bill, this time regarding amendments which had been proposed. To his surprise, some Members were suggesting that the retirement age of seventy-five was too low, when he had expected arguments that it was too high. He then had to make up a rearguard action against a few Labour MPs who wanted the expenses payable to justices to cover loss of earnings as well as travelling and lodging allowances. Next, there were more calls in support of smaller towns who wanted to retain their benches, and several amendments proposed to vary the size of the places which might, or might not, have their own bench. Ede made a final amendment to permit assistant justices' clerks to become solicitors through specified experience rather than articles, so providing more qualified people to become clerks Shawcross, the Attorney-General, helped him deal with these and other amendments and, after a further day's business on 13 December, the Bill became an Act three days later.

During 1949 he had at last given up one of his duties, leaving Surrey County Council after service of thirty-three years. Most of that time had been as an Alderman, so he had not had to keep seeking re-election as a Councillor, but the role had nonetheless added to his workload, and in the early years had been the basis for advancing his career. The Prime Minister, we know, had wanted him to continue on Surrey, to maintain his breadth of activity, but the time must have come when the burden became too much. The duties of Government were great enough, sometimes going against the grain of a Labour minister. As far back as May 1947, Ede had chaired a cabinet committee, set up following a road haulage strike.[16] Now, in July 1949, he was having to exercise his rights under the Emergency Powers Regulations against the dockers and stevedores in the London docks, who were on unofficial strike.[17] This replicated problems in the docks from the previous year, when the Emergency Powers Act 1920 had been invoked. This time, though, there was particular evidence of Communist involvement, the strike being called mainly in support of Canadian seamen, members of a union under

Communist leadership, in dispute with their employers. Even ministers with strong union ties, like Ernest Bevin and Nye Bevan, condemned the strikers, but there was great discomfort in the Labour movement.

Ede would never cease to be a Surrey man, but leaving the County Council indicated local government was no longer his field, even though he still used his experience there to promote good practice, and prevent bad. In October 1949, Aneurin Bevan, a strong advocate of government close to the population, proposed a plan for reforming English and Welsh local authorities into some 300 single-tier ones, covering anything from 50,000 to a million people. As Minister of Health, Bevan was responsible for local government, but Ede put his foot down about this. He said people approved of the parish and county structure which had applied for centuries, and any change would reduce active participation, not increase it. He won the day, not least because the government's time was running out.[18]

Late in 1949, the NUT's journal, *The Schoolmaster*, started a series of articles by George Thomas, 'the most brilliant' of the 'teachers who like to represent the profession on the floor of the House', on 'Teachers in Parliament'. Whatever Thomas's view of his own brilliance, he was certainly an admirer of James Chuter Ede, like him a Nonconformist preacher, teetotaller and teacher, from one generation earlier. Thomas had become an MP in 1945, and Ede was the colleague who had made most impression on him, as 'the great teacher Parliamentarian of the day', whom he selected for the first profile in the series.[19]

Ede, Thomas said, had a threefold purpose in Parliament – to ensure his department functioned successfully, to fulfil his cabinet obligations, and to respond to the challenge of office as Deputy Leader of the House. The first two sound fairly trite, but the third reminds us of Ede's dual roles in the government. There followed a description of the respect he had gained from all backbenchers, as the record-holder among Ministers for staying for late sittings. In fact, now a widower, he may well have found it congenial to remain in Westminster long into the night, though it sounds as though this reputation had predated Lilian's death, when Ede must have been split by divided loyalties. Thomas, though, did not go into his personal life at all, merely describing the character he saw – 'witty, affable, friendly and keen' in the Chamber, while keeping himself to himself in the lobbies, with unyielding qualities of firmness developed in his early teaching years.

The physical description he gave is useful to us. Ede would stand at the Treasury bench, holding the box with both hands, looking over his spectacles, and boom forth, resembling a schoolmaster prepared for any contingency.

He would often show his humour and repartee. He had been responsible for the Licensing Act earlier that year, which permitted London clubs to remain open to 2.30 am, and had heard many criticisms about this. But

> I say to all my fellow total abstainers in the House that it is quite wrong of us to think that we can impose our views on other people in this country otherwise than by arguments and conviction –
> An MP interrupted: 'And example.'
> Ede continued: I did not include that in considering my honourable friends, for they are such outstanding examples of the clarity of expression that comes from total abstinence.

This, Thomas said, provoked a roar of laughter.

Under his watch, a report[20] on Sunday entertainments enabled cinemas to open, and music and theatres to be permitted, with restrictions between 2.00 am and 12.30 pm. Many sporting activities were allowed, and there were more exemptions to the ban on Sunday trading. Much food and drink, medicines, fuel and newspapers could be sold. Employment was permitted on Sundays, subject to specific conditions. By current standards, Britain was still a fairly dull country on the Sabbath, but things were moving forwards.

The Home Secretary's role in regard to alcohol licensing was sometimes the subject of comment about Ede. He himself remarked that his position made him the biggest licence-holder in the country, as he was responsible for 178 pubs run by the government in the Carlisle area. This was a consequence of a decision to take them over during the Great War, to prevent drunkenness among workers in a local munitions factory. The arrangement lasted until 1971, and no Labour Government was likely to disturb that improbable example of nationalisation, but it was incongruous enough for a newspaper article[21] reviewing his career when he retired in 1964 to choose as its headline 'MR EDE TEETOTALLER CONTROLLED 178 PUBS'. He, naturally, kept to his principle of 'live and let live', mutual tolerance between those who drink and those who abstain.

On this subject, *Punch* magazine in 1949 published a satirical Latin poem (with a loose English translation), contributed by Reginald Punnett, a former Cambridge professor, now in his seventies and with time on his hands to practise the classics which had been his forte at school (Clifton), before he had turned to science with a view to a medical career. In fact he became a founding father of genetics at Cambridge. The entire five stanzas are in an appendix at the end of this book,[22] but one verse is of particular interest:

tu severum oppidis novis regimentum
vel Carliolensium das Experimentum,
teetotalitarie Domus – Secretari!
Ede, bibi; cras tempus suffragari!

which was translated as:

Laws for new towns you may devise with Chuter Edean guile
Or such as have been foisted on the burghers of Carlisle
Teetotal-bureaucratic-wise with all that this denotes:
Come – eat and drink – tomorrow will be the time to think of votes.

Classical scholars will appreciate the pun on the name, 'Ede' meaning 'eat' in Latin, and so the last line implies 'eat, drink and vote' (rather than be merry), as well as instructing Ede to drink, having described him as the teetotal 'Domus – Secretari' – Home Secretary. 'Domus' itself carries a double meaning, suggesting Ede is the home of the severe régime – 'severum regimentum' – both for new towns and the Carlisle pubs.

Ede continued to support walking in the countryside while he was at the Home Office, and on 9 November 1949 he was at the Home Counties Ramblers Coming of Age Dinner.[23] He also took holidays within the country, though he now went further afield. That summer he travelled to the Scottish Highlands, choosing to illustrate his Christmas card with a photo taken by him, dated earlier that year, of the Bridge of Dulsie. This is a remote spot in the old county of Nairn, where a Hanoverian military road crosses a gorge of the River Findhorn. He wrote a couple of paragraphs in the card describing the site, from which it is clear he was accompanied ('we came after a long drought, the river was swift-flowing, and deeply dyed with peat, as if a vat in Guinness's Stout brewery had been discharged'), though whether by Nell or another is unclear. The card now was from him alone, with a rather formal, solitary message, less jaunty than in the past: 'The Rt Hon J Chuter Ede MP (Home Secretary) sends you his Sincerest Christmas Greetings and his Earnest Good Wishes for the Coming Year. Tayles Hill, Ewell, Surrey. December 1949.'

By that Christmas, the 1945 Parliament had reached its end. On 8 November Ede had given a short radio broadcast on the need to register to vote, which he followed up with another on 9 January 1950. The first broadcast was the subject of considerable correspondence with the BBC, as he was giving another talk on 14 November 1949, about recruitment for civil defence, and at one point it seemed they might be on subsequent days. The BBC suggested it might be better to arrange a Parliamentary Question on registration, to be covered in the news without the Home Secretary speaking himself; they felt the Home Office had little grasp of effective public relations. But the government was determined, and dates a few days apart were fixed.[24] The general election was due in 1950, and Attlee decided to call it for 23 February, as soon as the new electoral registers were published. So it was timely that, first thing in the new year, on 4 January 1950, Ede was awarded the Freedom of the Borough of South Shields, a sign that he had been accepted as a Tynesider, despite his southern roots. Without any business in the Commons, he was still addressing his old audiences around London. On 31 January he spoke at a dinner given by the Lewisham Teachers Association, in which he recalled his early days in teaching, and how the NUT had fought its campaigns in education.[25] He was then off to South Shields, to fight to retain his seat there.

Chapter 15

Last Steps in Government

As for previous elections, Ede and Gompertz issued small cards with the message 'VOTE FOR EDE – X' to be handed out in South Shields, but this time the photo was of an older and greyer man, rather than the middle-aged character in a wing collar and Mayor's chain of office. The message on the reverse was 'A Man of Character – A Fighter for Right – A Humane Reformer – JAMES CHUTER EDE – THE BEST MEMBER YOU'VE EVER HAD'. He was now able to call on his time in office when seeking votes, and his main election address described him as 'HOME SECRETARY, Privy Counsellor, Justice of the Peace, Deputy Lieutenant, Freeman of Wimbledon, Mitcham and Epsom & Ewell.' He could not yet add his Freedom of South Shields to his title, as its presentation had not been made, but they saw no problem in listing just his achievements in the South, a long way from Tyneside. The address proudly recorded that fifty-two Acts of Parliament had been carried though the House by him, or been prominently associated with him. Nine were listed by name – The Trades Disputes and Trades (*sic*) Union Act, Children Act, British Nationality Act, Representation of the People Act, Criminal Justice Act, Justices of the Peace Act, Married Women (Maintenance) Act, Parliament Act, and Adoption of Children Act.

In fact, of these last three statutes, two were Private Member's measures, which the Home Office had supported, though hardly carried through, while Ede was merely one of many Ministers who spoke for the Parliament Act. He was claiming himself 'prominently associated' with them, as part of Labour's team in office. Though the Parliament Act was in essence a technical measure, reducing the abilities of the Lords, it was considered significant enough to appeal to Labour voters of South Shields, and so was put into the list.

His letter to the electorate emphasised what was being done for their own area – new industries, improved conditions for seamen, and coal nationalisation, so that South Shields would never again become a distressed area. This was illustrated with a photograph of the Jarrow March, contrasted by another of 'TODAY'S FULL EMPLOYMENT', men and women rushing as if into or out of their workplace. Food rationing was made a virtue, as 'We insist on sharing fairly the food available in a time of world shortage.' The National Health Service and new homes being built were naturally given prominence, with a promise to keep on building, and to continue to improve education, especially higher technical training of skilled craftsmen.

Ede had three opponents in February 1950, for the only time in his elections at South Shields, a Communist joining the Conservative and Liberal parties in the ballot. In fact, the Communist candidate received very few votes, while John Chalmers, the Conservative who would oppose him in every future election, attracted little more than his party had done in 1945, though the presence of a Liberal reduced both his and Ede's share. Nonetheless, Ede once again achieved comfortably more than half of all the votes cast:

Ede	Labour	33,452
Chalmers	Conservative	15,897
George	Liberal	9,446
Smith	Communist	415.

Insofar as a swing can be calculated, it was some 5 per cent towards Labour. In the country as a whole, however, the swing went the other way, unsurprisingly in view of the landslide five years earlier. The Conservatives won ninety seats, and Labour lost 78, reducing the Government's majority to five, even though they received more than a million extra votes. Attlee made few changes to his team, and none at all to the senior Cabinet ministers. Ede remained Home Secretary, though Kenneth Younger was transferred from his Department to become Bevin's deputy at the Foreign Office. Younger's replacement as Under-Secretary of State was Geoffrey de Freitas. When the cabinet met on 25 February, immediately after the results were clear, it was evident they would have to hold back from some of the more controversial pieces of legislation in their programme, such as further nationalisation.

While these Westminster developments were happening, the criminal case which most affected Chuter Ede's entire later career had taken place. On 30 November 1949 Timothy Evans, a man just turned twenty-five, with very poor education and a drink problem, reported to the police that his wife Beryl had died. During the next few days, he made several inconsistent statements (according to the police), suggesting her death occurred while she was seeking an abortion, and was either his responsibility or that of his neighbour, Reginald Christie, whom he had agreed should carry out the illegal operation; and that he had also killed his baby daughter, after her body was found with her mother's. The police investigation was not carried out well. It seems clear they were convinced from the start Evans had killed both his wife and daughter, and little additional evidence was sought. Some confession evidence may have been fabricated. On 11 January 1950 he was tried for the murder of his daughter, Geraldine, and within three days was convicted and condemned to death. Evidence was brought that he had also murdered Beryl, though he was not tried for that, one conviction being enough. Evans had attempted to implicate Christie, but without success; Christie's evidence was considered reliable, as his other activities at the time were not known.

Evans appealed, but on 20 February, three days before the general election, his appeal was rejected. One of Chuter Ede's first decisions after being reconfirmed as Home Secretary was to rule that the sentence should not be commuted, and the hanging took place on 9 March. To Ede it seemed an entirely routine case, of the type he had to deal with month by month. Unlike some *causes célèbres* in the next fifteen years, which drove the case for abolition, it 'attracted no public attention while it was going on. I had no letters from Members of Parliament. There was no sensation in the press.'[1]

By chance, the Home Office was asked a Written Question on 22 March, about the statistics of murders for 1949. Ede's answer was that there were 135 known murders that year and, 34 suspects having committed suicide, 65 were charged. Of those, 25 were insane, 6 were acquitted, 31 convicted, and 3 awaiting trial at the year end. Of the 31, two were under age, 13 were executed, 12 reprieved, and a final decision was awaited for the other 4. So Evans was one of the 3 awaiting trial, his wife and daughter being among the 135 victims.

Thus Evans's chances of a reprieve had been fairly good, but his case was aggravated by a murder additional to the one for which he was convicted (it was usual for a multiple killer to be tried on only one charge), and had no mitigating circumstances. As an unattributed and undated cutting which Ede retained in his files stated, after the real circumstances had come to light:

> The most worrying aspect of the Evans case is precisely that Evans's guilt appeared so clearly proved. No criticism can be directed at the judge, jury, counsel or police … His trial proves once and for all that a case that appears absolutely clear may yet be a false one.

This was a rough quotation from comments by Reginald Paget, one of the abolitionists who took up the case, which Ede later quoted to the Commons.[2] In fact considerable criticism of the police was made subsequently, though it would take three years before the true circumstances became known, and by then Ede was out of office.

Among the Labour workers at the election had been the Rev John Kielty, the secretary of the General Assembly of the Unitarian and Free Christian Churches. His candidate at Hendon North had lost her seat to the Conservative, and in March he exchanged letters with Chuter Ede, the one congratulating the other, and the other giving condolences. Kielty had good reason to be grateful to Ede's work at the Home Office, for among other things he had managed to arrange for the Unitarians to be invited to join the Cenotaph service each Remembrance Sunday.[3] In fact his main motive for keeping in touch with his influential follower was that the Unitarians were wanting to send a group to the USA, to join the meetings in Boston celebrating the 125th anniversary of their church there. They needed dollars to fund the visit, but the Bank of England had refused them under the exchange controls in operation, and Kielty hoped Ede could get Stafford Cripps, as Chancellor of the Exchequer, to reverse the decision. Cripps, however, was adamant; he could not permit such an exception, and Ede was unable to help.[4] This started considerable correspondence between the two men, which would continue throughout Ede's life.

The short Parliament of 1950–51 saw much less legislation than its frantic predecessor, and Ede was himself involved in little. The small majority put particular pressure on all Labour MPs, and the strains of attending the Commons sometimes told. In May 1950 he was asked to dine with a visiting American Unitarian called Clarence C. Dill, who was interested in the public ownership of power; Ede was a good contact, from both his religious and electricity backgrounds. He had to let Dill know that, while he could be available for lunch, any dinner arrangement would be unpredictable when the House of Commons was sitting. In July, though, Ede did help steer the Maintenance Orders Bill, a measure started in the Lords, through the Commons. This had cross-party support, reforming the arrangements for granting affiliation and maintenance orders against fathers. In 1951, the uncontroversial Fireworks Act would be the final measure he sponsored.

The Home Secretary's troubles regarding foreigners in Britain, and in particular the influence of the Communist states, continued in 1950, with the proposal to hold a 'World Peace Festival' in Sheffield that November. It was clear the 'British Peace Committee' organising it was under Soviet influence. His colleagues held different views about Communist influence. Ede generally took the view expressed by Morrison in 1947, when disagreeing with a hard-line Conservative, Waldron Smithers, asking for Parliament to set up an 'Un-British Activities Committee'. 'The other political parties', Morrison had said, 'can take care of the Communists. We are not afraid of them, and I cannot understand why' Smithers was.[5] Ede often made clear that his duties for policing and civil liberties included permitting Communists to speak, and he had replied to the much-corresponding Lord Cecil of Chelwood in 1949, who asked for details of Communists in a union, that he was aware there were some, but could not give details. On the other hand, Ernest Bevin at the Foreign Office wanted the Conference 'crippled', if banning it entirely was unfeasible.

Bevin's view was echoed by many other MPs, and on 19 October 1950 Ede was asked 'what steps he intends to take to prevent aliens from coming to this country to attend.' But he held his ground:

> The self-styled British Peace Committee have been informed that applications from foreigners to attend the Congress will be dealt with on their individual merits and [we] reserve the right to refuse admission to any foreigner who is *persona non grata* ... I have some resentment myself at the holding of the Congress, but I do not desire to destroy the reputation of this country for free speech.

He told the cabinet he could not announce a refusal to admit entire categories of applicants,[6] and Bevin, who had less than six months to live, did not have the strength to challenge this further. Ede made a statement to the House on 14 November, to forestall a Private Notice Question, and was questioned from all sides. He stuck to his principle, that he could not declare the Conference illegal without an Act of Parliament, on which he was not prepared to legislate, as public assembly for British citizens should be free, while foreigners abusing the UK's hospitality could be excluded. He quoted figures of 431 foreigners either granted visas or admitted without one (though some with visas had not used them), and 287 refused visas or entry. The Home Office was active in discriminating between welcome and unwelcome aliens. It seems that the Peace Conference was eventually transferred to Warsaw.[7]

When Churchill's government was later criticised for taking a less tolerant view on admitting Communists, Ede made a joke against himself to prove he had kept to his principles. In 1950, he had admitted Picasso to the country, but excluded Shostakovich. 'I could explain ... why I admitted the painter and rejected the musician – it was possibly because I am tone deaf.' In fact, it may have been a question of their nationality, while he did appreciate how serious his role in dealing with aliens had been:

> I regard the duties falling on the Home Secretary under the Aliens Act ... as being the most responsible that he has to discharge ... matters

of life and death may not be involved here, but there are residents of this country who, if deported to certain countries on the Continent, would have a very short life after they walked down the gangplank. A deportation order would be a sentence of death, probably preceded by torture.

This seems inconsistent with his 1948 remark that there is no responsibility causing greater personal concern, to the minister who has to discharge it alone, than capital punishment. Perhaps the difference was the emphasis, in the latter case, on having to do it 'alone'.

There is perhaps an irony in the fact that two of the foreigners affected by Ede's decisions were the wife and daughter of Samuel Miliband, a Jewish Belgian who had reached Britain at the start of the war, along with his son, who took the name Ralph and served in the Royal Navy. Ralph's son, David, would in 2001 become MP for South Shields himself. In his maiden speech, David Miliband said of Ede:

> as Home Secretary in the 1945 Government – probably the greatest reforming Government in our history, one of his hardest tasks was to make decisions on immigration applications from millions of refugees around Europe. There were many hard cases … Despite long correspondence, the then Home Secretary felt compelled to deny his application. There could not, he wrote, be exceptions. My father had previously been given leave to stay, and later, I am pleased to say, my grandparents were allowed to join him.[8]

Within five years, David Miliband would be in the cabinet, and two years later Foreign Secretary, giving South Shields the distinction of having two MPs who held one of the four great offices of state.

Another issue regarding migration into the UK was the position of settlers from the British colonies, in particular the Caribbean. Just after the British Nationality Act had been passed in 1948, the *Empire Windrush*, a military transport ship sailing from Australia to Britain, stopped in Jamaica and, to help fill the ship and fund the voyage, an offer was made of cheap transport for those who might want to work in the UK. Nearly 500 black people ('coloured' as they were then known) came. When they arrived, however, there were immediate comments against organising migration around the British Empire, which had not been the aim of the Act, and during the government's remaining time in office, between 1,000 and 2,000 such immigrants arrived.[9] In 1950, the estimated 'coloured' population of the country was about 25,000, most of whom were seamen or servicemen who had remained after each world war. These numbers do not seem high by current standards, nor probably relative to those at the time who had come from the old Dominions or Europe, but there is no doubt this was a matter of race, and to an extent of education and qualifications for work.

On 20 March the cabinet discussed the matter, identified it as a problem, and asked for a note on it from Arthur Creech Jones, the former Colonial Secretary who had just lost his seat in Parliament. On 19 June they asked 'whether the time had come to restrict the existing right of any British subject to enter' the UK. All Ede's work to designate 'citizens of the United Kingdom and Colonies', which he had cited in his election address as one of his achievements, was being thrown into doubt, and he was appointed to chair a confidential Cabinet Committee on the question. Eventually, on 6 February 1951, he wrote a memo for the cabinet,[10] offering three options, all unsatisfactory – of applying to British subjects the controls which applied to aliens, of deporting some categories of British subjects, or of returning those who arrived as stowaways. The last was most acceptable, but hardly touched the main issue. It would be invidious to discriminate on grounds of colour, which might be implicit in any action taken, and he recommended no new legislation, which would break with the traditional policy. Also, amending the British Nationality Act would effect relations with the colonies and independent Commonwealth countries, and give the appearance that the Irish might be more privileged than others in access to the UK, as Ireland had just been declared 'not a foreign country'. A significant concern was immigration from south-east Asia, which might have a Communist aspect to it, but the Government merely noted that this must be watched. In the end, there was no further legislation about immigration until the 1960s.

For the remaining few months of Attlee's Government, much of Ede's activities involved a wide variety of departmental and other routine, either within Whitehall or without. The ministers made the most of their privileges. After inspecting the London Fire Brigade again on 15 July 1950, he was at Chequers next day, at a gathering of his colleagues and their wives, at which the Australian PM Robert Menzies seems to have been a guest, which Ede faithfully recorded with photographs mounted in one of his albums. Also in 1950, the Home Office issued a pamphlet *Atomic Warfare*, using the experience of the atom bombs on Japan to explain what might be in store, and Ede recorded another short film for showing on Movietone News,[11] aimed at recruitment for civil defence. On the first weekend of September, he made one of his regular weekend visits to South Shields, reading the lesson at the Unitarian Church there on the Sunday,[12] but staying on for the ceremony of becoming a Freeman of the Borough, to which he had been elected in January, on Tuesday 6 September.[13] On 16 September it was the Surrey environment which occupied him, as he became President of the Friends of Box Hill, a new organisation being set up to preserve the area he knew so well.[14] Then on 6 October he gave the Dr Williams lecture at the Presbyterian College in Carmarthen, his subject being once again 'The Fight for the Freedom of the Human Spirit',[15] as it had been in Amsterdam the previous year.

Union problems recurred in 1950,[16] with a strike at Smithfield Market of lorry drivers. Troops were used to get the meat in and out, under the control of the Home Office. In September the London bus employees were striking, this time with union support, against the employment of women conductors. There had been a wage freeze for two years. Some of the emergency powers, which could involve imprisonment for those who went on strike, ignoring arbitration, caused added resentment. Ede found himself receiving many complaints about these powers, but they were used later in the autumn against gas employees, many of the cabinet being in a panic about the Communists, particularly after the start of the Korean War. Although the emergency powers were altered the following year, this was all very difficult for a precariously-poised Labour Government, trying to impress its supporters, and the country as a whole, that it deserved a larger majority.

A further subject which came before the government late in 1950 was the proposed European Convention on Human Rights, and Ede was also involved in this.[17] On 1 August the cabinet had decided[18] the proposed Convention was inconsistent with government policies on a planned economy, such as regarding powers of entry to private property, and argued for a 'declaration' of rights instead, to put on record the differences between the democratic and Communist countries. The concept of the country's law being subject to an international court was 'intolerable', said Cripps. Jowitt, as Lord Chancellor, was asked to speak to David Maxwell Fyfe, one of the Conservative shadow cabinet, about it.

On 18 October Ede joined a meeting with Attlee, Bevin, Jowitt, Shawcross (the Attorney-General) and others, to discuss whether to agree to the Convention's terms. Jowitt had been scathing about the lack of precision in the document, its compromise between different legal systems leading to 'vague and indefinite terms … used just because they were vague and indefinite', and the impossibility of determining what finding a tribunal might reach on its provisions. This was unfortunate, because there was a strong political imperative (which Jowitt recognised) to support the Convention, which had been drawn up by the Council of Europe under Maxwell Fyfe's leadership. It would not have been to anyone's benefit if, after the experience of the 1930s and the war, human rights in Europe appeared to be contentious between the political parties. It was the first achievement of the Council of Europe, setting up of which had been agreed in London, after years of encouragement by Churchill. Rejecting it would undermine the Council. On the other hand, Maxwell at the Home Office had been wary of its apparent power to weaken Parliamentary sovereignty, and it overlapped with work the United Nations was doing on human rights. In the end the ministers agreed to support the Convention, while not accepting the right of individuals to petition under it, or the proposal for a Court to enforce it.[19] The government signed the Convention on 4 November, but the Court was not established until 1959 – although, over the course of the years after Ede's death, the Labour Party's approach to the Convention would change significantly.

At the end of 1950, the Home Secretary's mind was again directed to the problems of getting prospective electors to register to vote. The misgivings of the BBC a year earlier, about the right way to get the message over, were rather confirmed, as Ede had received significant complaints from people unable to vote in the general election. However, he went about publicising the issue in the same way, giving broadcasts on the subject on 11 November 1950 and 8 January 1951 – the first the day after he had featured on Women's Hour again, giving a speech on the Women's Voluntary Service. It is hard to avoid the feeling that, inspired by Churchill's radio addresses to the beleaguered country during the war, the government was too optimistic about the public attitude to the BBC in the following years.[20]

The year 1951 started with a small Unitarian group meeting at Watford on 12 January, where Ede's address was interrupted by hecklers. He looked on the matter with resignation, feeling it was the objectors who had lost out:

> I can well understand that some of those who came to interrupt did not understand what it was all about, as we were of course, discussing a way of life which they are carefully prevented from contemplating.[21]

That way of life then became all the more significant when Attlee appointed him Leader of the House of Commons on 9 March in place of Morrison. Kielty sent him his congratulations, and Ede replied that he was 'facing new and heavy responsibilities'. He was now responsible for managing government business through the House, and on several occasions was contributing to debates about breaches of Parliamentary privilege. On 5 May he wrote a memo for the cabinet, about preparation for legislation for the 1951–52 Parliamentary session.[22] Thirty Bills were to be introduced by Christmas 1951, an ambitious target, which eventually came to nothing.

That year, foreign affairs were consuming a considerable amount of the government's time, and in particular the stand-off between the USA and China, which had turned into the Korean War. In January, the Americans moved a resolution in the UN describing China (which had no seat there) as an aggressor, which it put pressure on its allies to support. The Foreign Secretary, Bevin, who was in his last illness, tried to argue that they should not offend the US, but his deputy, Younger, disagreed, and Ede (who had previously been Younger's chief at the Home Office) supported him, along with Dalton and Bevan. Gaitskell described Ede as anti-American,[23] and this extended to his support for Aneurin Bevan in opposing US plans to re-arm Germany. The suggestion to oppose the China resolution deeply concerned the Foreign Office civil servants and the military. In the end, the resolution was altered on 29 January, in a way which enabled the government to agree to support it.[24] The episode was the end of Bevin's dominance as Foreign Secretary. Six weeks later he was replaced by Morrison, and in April he died.

As Morgan said, Ede had become an important chairman of committees, though his skills were sometimes lacking. In April 1951, Bevan's difficult behaviour came to a head. In one sense this continued the strife between him and his Parliamentary colleagues dating from the war years. He had long been in passionate dispute with them on several matters, but his particular concern was preserving the National Health Service, which he had done more than anyone to set up. Hugh Gaitskell, appointed Chancellor of the Exchequer when Cripps resigned through ill-health, was planning his budget, and was determined to levy charges on some NHS services. Bevan was no longer at the Ministry of Health, but he made his opposition clear enough. He was threatening to resign, and stirring up arguments in cabinet. Ede initially had doubts about the charges, but in February the cabinet had decided the matter, and he felt it would be intolerable for Bevan to override that.[25] His former sympathy for Bevan evaporated when Nye started lobbying against the budget in the House Tea Room. Attlee was in hospital for a duodenal ulcer operation, and Ede went with Gaitskell to see him, as other ministers did from time to time. In Morgan's view, Attlee was unable to contribute positively to dealing with the quarrel. It was left to his colleagues to do what they could, and in the end they failed.

Gaitskell presented his budget on 10 April, with charges for NHS glasses and dentures, and recalled that Ede congratulated him on his speech.[26] Bevan got his protégé Michael Foot to write an article against the budget in *Tribune* on 20 April and, when the cabinet united against him, resigned two days later, making a statement to the House on 23 April. The next day, the Parliamentary Party met, with Ede in the chair. What Bevan said about the budget, and his manner of saying it, caused so much offence that Ede told the meeting his speech reminded him of Oswald Mosley. Mosley had been a Labour MP for a while under MacDonald's leadership, and briefly a minister, but his impetuous conduct had alienated the Party, even before he had moved to form his New Party and then his Fascist movement. To compare anyone now with Mosley was tactless indeed, though others had made the comparison.[27]

Ede's activities, for the final six months of government, were not legislative ones. He travelled, speaking at the incorporation of the City of Cambridge, which had previously had borough status, and he proposed the toast to the International Federation of Newspaper Publishers on 25 May 1951.[28] On 16 June he visited the Liverpool City Police Training School, where he was presented with a photograph album of the force in action.[29] The next day, with the Festival of Britain off the ground, he took part in its river procession, an aspect of the celebrations close to his heart as a boating enthusiast. Even closer to home, he saw new byelaws introduced for Nonsuch Park. As to the Commons, however, in the words of one of his successors, Roy Jenkins, 'the phlegmatic but uncharismatic Home Secretary, who had taken over from Morrison as Leader of the House, battled on in a stubborn and grey-faced way'.[30]

By the autumn, the government was running out of steam. Bevin had gone, Cripps had resigned, and the Bevan affair had caused much grief. Attlee needed to regain a fair majority, if he was to carry on at all. On 19 September, during the Parliamentary recess, Attlee proposed to a poorly-attended cabinet meeting that there should be another General Election, and Ede and the others agreed. They hoped the sense of promise generated by the Festival of Britain, and the improved economy would see them successful. Parliament was dissolved, with polling set for 25 October 1951. Ede had last spoken in a debate on 27 July, on the Fireworks Bill, and the questions he had answered in the House on 2 August would turn out to be his last contributions as Secretary of State. Another proposed measure, the Pneumoconiosis and Byssinosis Bill, to ease the suffering of workers in mines and factories, would have to wait.

Almost the last thing Ede did while Home Secretary was on another subject close to his heart, but unconnected with home affairs or education. He was already President of the Epsom Camera Club,[31] and in October he was able to pursue this interest, by opening an exhibition of the Institute of British Photographers, called appropriately British Achievement in

Photography.[32] The Institute was fifty years old, having been founded as the Professional Photographers Association in 1901 (it still operates now, as the British Institute of Professional Photography). In his brief speech, he praised 'photographic science and art – and I want to emphasise that the two things have always to be borne in mind', fusing his interest across the disciplines, which was one reason why photography was of such interest to him. He spoke about its use in the armed services (several service chiefs were present with him), in medicine and in natural history. The IBP described it as its first 'three dimension' exhibition; it contained exhibits of museum pieces, some going back to Fox Talbot, the father of British photography, as well as 'the smallest camera in the world', which Ede was pictured holding between his thumb and middle finger.[33]

When the election took place, Ede slightly increased his vote, in what to this day is a record turnout, of 60,000, for the constituency. John Chalmers, his Conservative opponent from 1950, secured 4,000 votes more votes then he had then, and the Liberal vote was squeezed:

Ede	Labour	33,633
Chalmers	Conservative	20,208
Kitchell	Liberal	6,270

In the country overall, it proved to be the election in which the greatest proportion voted for the two main parties, with Labour's vote increasing by some 700,000, to more than the Conservatives', even with their National Liberal and Unionist allies. Labour's share of the vote also went up, but mainly at the expense of the Liberals, and the government's majority disappeared. They had 295 seats out of 625, and Churchill was able to form a majority Government. Next day, 26 October 1951, Attlee, Ede and their colleagues resigned, almost all of them leaving government for ever.

Chapter 16

In Opposition

So what do we make of this Home Secretary? At the end of 1951, Chuter Ede was able to take pride in having maintained 'the traditional liberal policy of the great department for which I was responsible for a longer period continuously than any man since Sidmouth'.[1] He took care to say 'continuously'; R.A. Cross's two spells, under Disraeli and Salisbury, together surpassed Ede's six years and twelve weeks. But he was right; only Lord Sidmouth's nine-and-a-half years, as far back as 1812–22, have to this day exceeded his single spell – though longevity, of course, is not the most cogent consideration. It is what he achieved which matters.

Distinguishing between real results and political puff, we need not take much notice of the election claim that fifty-two statutes were at least 'prominently associated' with him in the five years 1945 to 1950. A senior cabinet minister, with a wide purview, will clearly be associated with many measures. However, a short list of the Children Act, the Justices of the Peace Act, the Criminal Justice Act, the Representation of the People Act, the British Nationality Act, the Civil Defence Act, the Fire Services Act, the Police Act and the Police Pensions Act summarises a considerable achievement, particularly set alongside the administrative work required (especially in those days) of any Home Secretary. Ede inherited child care services and magistrates' courts operating piecemeal throughout the country, and drove through the provisions which set up consistent procedures and standards. Many of the changes to the system of criminal justice were long overdue, and Ede, when making them, ensured those that grabbed the headlines – abolishing hard labour, flogging and so on – were accompanied by real steps to improve how young delinquents were dealt with. His own experience on the bench told here. Unlike some Home Secretaries, he knew the subjects he was dealing with.

The changes he implemented to the electoral system were those which, as he himself said, finally established the principles of 'one person one vote' and single member constituencies, for which there had been pressure from the Civil Wars, through to the era of the Chartists and beyond. Abolishing the university seats – against considerable opposition – as well as the business vote, two-member constituencies and the privileged position of the City of London, turned the House of Commons into the elected chamber we recognise today. At the same time, he accomplished the first thorough redistribution of seats, and changes to constituency boundaries, since 1918.[2] That Ede did so with little regard to the party political effect was consistent with his standard of integrity, whatever misgivings others, who sought a less impartial outcome, may have felt about it.

As to establishing the single status of 'Citizen of the United Kingdom and Colonies', without regard to colour or race, this step would doubtless be considered forward-looking, were it not that we know how events in the subsequent decades turned out. The decisions, initially to create this status, and then to retain it in the face of the early resistance to the concept of all British and colonial citizens being equally able to live in the UK, illustrate well Ede's attachment to a 'liberal policy' at the Home Office, even if we challenge his description of that policy as 'traditional'.

What might reduce the credit accorded to Ede from these innovations, is that some of them were dictated by necessity, or by the circumstances he inherited in 1945. The work on the British Nationality Act was an expedient to deal with decisions by Canada, and to a lesser extent Ireland and the countries of the Indian subcontinent. The Criminal Justice Act revived a measure from before the war, while the redistribution of Parliamentary seats had been set off by Morrison in Churchill's Coalition. However, the reality is that, in each case, Ede carried out the changes in his own constructive way. He found a solution to the threat to the status of 'British subject', and he took the opportunity to add his personal improvements to penal policy and representative democracy.

The same is true regarding the Fire Service, and perhaps Civil Defence and the police also. Returning fire brigades to local management was a pledge he had inherited from Morrison, but the way Ede did it showed he could make a virtue of necessity. He used his experience in local government and the Board of Education to decide the right level of local authority control for the reconstructed service. With the police too, his efforts were directed to designing a better organised, more professional force, with the right number of police authorities operating at the right level of local government. This was complemented by the system of police training centres which he fostered, to develop consistent professional standards in the redesigned service.

In regard to policing and penal policy, his libertarian principles made him firm not to use his powers to restrict free speech or private gatherings. These often involved extremists from one side or the other, but he was secure in his belief that the ideals of an open and free country, which in his mind Britain had been struggling to become since the seventeenth century, required tolerance to outweigh political control. In these respects he was upholding a 'liberal tradition' far more than some of his colleagues. At a time when economic and political controls were widely accepted as a consequence of the war, and in a government elected to introduce measures requiring them, he was able to keep a beacon of openness shining in his own field.

All this Ede did while taking the daily decisions required of a Home Secretary, sometimes dealing with life and death, and often with the safety and security of individuals or families separated from each other. He had also to react to incidents which happened, whether mass squatting, a perceived threat to the status of Northern Ireland, a sensitive film production, or an alleged crime wave. He had to re-establish organised administration in the Channel Islands, after the battering they had received from their German invaders. These were time-consuming tasks, which might have devoured all the energies of other, less proactive, ministers. He, however, carried them out while pursuing his far-reaching legislative programme, and while pressing the case for rehabilitating offenders and for reforming what he could control. Hindsight discloses areas where he might have done more, and shows he did not get every decision right, of course, but that would be too much to ask, and he certainly at the time was seldom caught in traps set by unexpected events. Many Home Secretaries fall from grace when matters go wrong on questions to which they have not been alert, but that did not happen to Chuter Ede, and in this respect his longevity in office may indeed be to his credit. He mastered the job, and while in government his affairs went right.

Finally, it is worth stressing how much the issues covered by him remain important today – among them, penal policy and prisons, British national identity, immigration and refugees, the environment, civil liberties, policing, and Parliamentary representation. Even while this book was being prepared for publication, issues of Britain's colonial heritage and racial attitudes, and how they should be recognised, became unexpectedly a major issue in the national debate. Discussions about policing and criminal justice have been part of this, as the country has looked back at its imperial past. As regards to Ede's work before becoming Home Secretary, there is of course how best to provide opportunities in education. To appreciate how Britain reached the position in which we are now, it is essential to understand the part he played. The rôle of Attlee's team in the mid-twentieth century is commonly cited as essential to understanding current issues, such as the health service, international relations, and the public utilities; Ede's contribution was as significant as any.

Now, for the first time in more than eleven years, he was neither a government minister nor fighting an election. He had become a senior figure in the Commons, and on the Labour front bench about fourth in seniority. A shadow cabinet election took place, and he came fifth in the ballot. According to his friend George Wigg,[3] he was reluctant to believe the Conservative victory would be spoilt by the 'rabid Tory right', but rather that the reforming ethos would continue. A positive sign was the reintroduction of the Pneumoconiosis Bill. The Conservatives had published an *Industrial Charter* four years before, which indicated they would not reverse most of the Labour reforms. Whether or not Churchill supported that, his influence on the new government's style was less (said Wigg) than Rab Butler's. Butler had become Chancellor of the Exchequer, and would become closely associated with the 'post-war consensus'. His influence was one of the reasons why Labour's expectation, that the new government might soon collapse, did not materialise.

Duties on an Opposition at the start of a new Parliament are not great, and much of Ede's time now involved his wider interests. Four days after the election, John Kielty from the Unitarians was writing to congratulate him personally, and sympathise on the government's defeat, and the next day, 30 October, he replied asking for an early opportunity to discuss ways to use his 'restored leisure' for the benefit of his causes:

> It is good to know that the spirit of my administration has been understood by those like-minded … it has sometimes been difficult to get a hearing for the voice of reason and goodwill, … to prevent it being entirely drowned in the noise of discordant and authoritarian creeds.

Kielty responded by return, suggesting they meet in November; this started a fruitful, active relationship between Ede and his church. Before Christmas, he had received an invitation from Dr Fred Eliot, of the American Unitarian Association, to visit the USA. Ede suggested the Whitsun vacation would be suitable timing, but funding was a problem. He could not contemplate paying the cost, particularly of flying both ways; Kielty replied that the 'Americans think of politicians as being like their own people, people with money', so the AUA would not be willing to finance the visit.

Though the trip to the USA had to wait, Ede was offered honorary membership of the church's Assembly, a privilege he valued. There could not be more than seven honorary members at any one time. He trusted those inviting him realised how hard he had tried in difficult circumstances to maintain the Home Office's 'liberal policy'.[4]

Then, on 14 December 1951 he was awarded an honorary Doctor of Laws degree at Bristol University, where Churchill was the Chancellor. A photograph shows the PM, newly-reappointed, looking very pleased with himself, in a line with Ede and seven other honorary graduates, including

Receiving an honorary doctorate from Churchill, Bristol University's chancellor (Ede 4th from left, Vaughan Williams 2nd, and Field Marshal Ismay 7th). (© *Surrey History Centre*)

Stafford Cripps, Lord Ismay (Churchill's chief military assistant in the War), and Ralph Vaughan Williams, another Surrey man, awarded a Doctorate of Music.

In 1952 he also joined the BBC's General Advisory Council, an appointment which gave him some difficulty. He had been approached in December about it, by Lord Simon of Wythenshawe, another Labour politician with a Liberal background, who chaired the BBC Governors, and whose wife Shena he knew from their mutual educational interests. The General Advisory Council's chair was Lord Halifax whose efforts, Ede told Simon, 'to establish a Catholic bloc against Russia' were 'largely responsible for the present split in Europe'. He did not relish serving under him. Few modern historians would blame Halifax for the Cold War, whatever his other shortcomings, and it surprised Simon when they lunched on 18 December, but Ede went on, that the BBC had an illiberal and unduly orthodox attitude towards religious broadcasting. He also felt Herbert Morrison would represent Labour better than he could. Ede confided all this to John Kielty.[5] who encouraged him to accept, not least because a wider point of view than a purely Party one was called for. In the end, he did so, attending his first meeting on 23 January 1952.

The GAC consisted of a large number of influential people from the British establishment, many of whom were too busy to attend regularly; it enquired into, and expressed its views on, the range of activities relating to the BBC, meeting four times a year. At this first meeting, Ede joined a discussion on commercial broadcasting, a possible future development, saying the younger Labour MPs were not generally attracted to the idea, while he thought it would be disastrous for freedom of expression if commercialisation became an established fact.[6] This started a seven-year association with the committee on which, in October 1952, Halifax was replaced by a senior judge, Lord Radcliffe, whose Deputy Chairman Ede himself became in 1953.

At the end of January 1952, Ede was appointed in his own right to another post which greatly interested him, one of the British Museum trustees, no longer being one *ex officio* when he ceased to be Home Secretary. He had been on the Trustees' Standing Committee, and they wanted to retain his input, so he was co-opted back to the board, and in May to the Standing Committee itself. He recorded that he was congratulated on this, in the final diary he kept, which was for only four months, the first entry being dated Tuesday 5 February 1952 – an arbitrary date on which to restart his journal? Probably not, as one suspects he actually commenced it a day or two later, for on 6 February George VI died. Ede was living through significant events.

A Parliamentary Labour Party meeting was going on when Attlee was called away, and he returned with news of the King's death. Attlee's immediate tribute to the King was, 'he was always very nice to me.' Sidney Silverman had been speaking to the PLP, and Ede commented to Richard Crossman that it took the King's death to stop Silverman in full flow.[7] In Parliament Churchill made a very brief announcement, and the sitting was suspended. The Privy Council met at 5.00 pm, with a large attendance, in contrast to the small numbers at routine meetings. Princess Elizabeth, in her absence abroad, was proclaimed Queen, and the proclamation was signed by the Privy Counsellors in turn, Ede noting he signed next after the Bishop of London. As the members of the council were circulating, he was approached by Mountbatten, who reminded him of their first meeting, in 1947 to discuss Prince Philip's naturalisation. 'I said his nephew had done very well', Ede recorded.

The MPs returned to the House at 7.00, when the Speaker and senior Members took the oath of allegiance to the Queen. Ede was fourth from the Labour benches to do so, only Attlee, Morrison and Gaitskell preceding him. The next day, after having spent the morning in Kingston on the bench, he received the summons to a further Accession Council on 8 February, and heard Churchill eulogise the King in a radio broadcast. When the council met, just before 10.00 am, the Queen addressed them, and subscribed to the oath to maintain the Presbyterian Church of Scotland. Ede said she described herself as 'Queen of Great Britain, Ireland', which he said was clearly wrong. After the meeting ended, they returned to the Commons, though it was hard to get through the crowds. Little further business was done for over a week, and the House attended the King's lying-in-state on 11 February. This was an impressive ceremony in Westminster Hall, conducted by Archbishop Garbett of York; Ede felt it was 'a thousand pities that Garbett was not advanced to Canterbury when Temple died'. He much preferred the 'saintly and stately' Garbett to Fisher. On 13 February he was among the Privy Counsellors at Buckingham Palace presenting the House's address to the Queen, and two days later attended the King's funeral (he had paid for his silk hat to be ironed for the occasion). He then went to South Shields for the weekend.

His next trip was to Devon and Cornwall. On 7 March he took the train to Exeter, attending various functions there. Next day he went to Torquay, where those who met him were Ivor Fromow and Winnie Merrett. Ivor, married to Mollie, lived at Lucius Street, with their daughters Janet, Theresa, Julia, and baby Helen. Winnie's family were Robert, five-year-old Susan and Charles; her mother also lived with them. Mollie and Winnie were the daughters of Dick Williams, Lilian Ede's brother, and, as we shall see, he and Nell would take a holiday nine years later with two of the Fromow girls, now close to adulthood.

On 20 March he took tea with the researcher, Sophia Weitzman, whose brother David was a Labour Parliamentary colleague of his. She had been commissioned by the government to write the section on education of its history of the Second World War (a project which eventually lapsed with her early death, shortly before Ede's, in 1965[8]) and he had evidently lent her the diaries he had kept during the War. When she questioned him on them, he told her 'the Diary was so libellous I thought it safe to burn it!' She was horrified at that, and told him he 'ought to leave it to the British Museum'. And so, gratifyingly for us, he did.

As 30 March was Nell's birthday, they held a small tea party for her, to which their brother Noel came, along with another couple. The following weekend he was back at the British Museum, where he found himself appointed to a sub-committee tasked with dealing with accusations made by the head of the laboratory and his assistant against each other. While Home Secretary, his attendances at the Museum had been sporadic, but the Standing Committee minutes from 1952 onwards show him to have become a regular attender of the meetings, which were usually on a Saturday, once every couple of months. The committee took decisions on all purchases and loans from the Museum collections, on property matters, and in great detail on employment arrangements of staff to a remarkably junior level. The minutes do not illustrate much about his personal contribution, but it is clear he served for a time on the Finance Committee, and by 1955 was one of the Trustees considering the production of a general catalogue of the Museum's printed books.

Education occupied much of his time at this stage. In the midst of the 12 February ceremonies he had addressed the Speech Day at Walpole Grammar School, Ealing, and during the weekend of 22 to 25 February he visited the Lake District, including various schools in Cockermouth, where South Shields children had been accommodated during the war. He had already warned the Unitarians in December that his obligations to the NUT would prevent him being active outside Parliament, and on 18 February 1952 he repeated the point. He would be unavailable during much of April, as he had to attend the Union conference, such was the seriousness of its problems. He went to the conference in Scarborough on Maundy Thursday, 10 April, and was there for a week. The new government was retrenching, and expenditure on education was under threat. To add to the load, George Tomlinson, who had remained the Labour spokesman, was unwell; in fact, though only just sixty-two, he died within six months. So on 25 March it was Ede who proposed a motion in the House condemning proposed cuts to LEA funding. They would undermine the operation of the 1944 Act, which Butler, now at the Treasury, should want to promote. His speech toured round England, citing what economies each LEA was having to make. He had clearly been briefed by the local NUT branches. In the end, Labour was defeated by 29 votes, the Liberals supporting the government.

One of the counties he mentioned in his speech was, naturally enough, Surrey, where he took pleasure in finding it granted proportionally more university scholarships than any other LEA. Though a Conservative county, he rightly claimed some credit for its education service, and soon after, on 17 May, he spoke at a conference on the History of Surrey Education, held at Tiffin Boys School in Kingston.[9] He was an expert on the subject.

A unique opportunity then arose for Ede, when he was appointed to the Coronation Committee of the Privy Council. He was one of a small group of councillors, under the leadership of the Duke of Norfolk, who would take charge of the arrangements for the Queen's coronation the following June.[10] Having written about King George's coronation, and then attended it, he knew the form.

If one takes Ede's diary at face value, much of his time was now consumed with sport and other recreation, while his health was weakening. On 5 April he listened to 'a poor broadcast of the Grand National', for which he blamed those employed by the 'autocratic' Mrs Topham, owner of Aintree racecourse, but by 19 May his eyes were giving him pain, and he was 'finding writing distasteful'. Perhaps that was why he would finally cease his diary three weeks later, on 8 June. He went with his sister and brother to watch Surrey play cricket against Sussex at the Oval on 19 May, however, and on 28 May enjoyed the main event in this side of his life, Derby Day at Epsom. Nell was hosting a party in a box in the Grand Tier at the course, where he called in before joining the Jockey Club for lunch. There he spoke to Lord Rosebery, the son of the Prime Minister whose attitude to Lloyd George's Budget had once infuriated him. The younger Rosebery had owned two Derby winners, was an accomplished cricketer for Surrey, and had been an MP and a member of Churchill's Caretaker Cabinet in 1945. He suggested that next year's Derby should be on a Saturday, which Ede approved; we have seen his support for a Saturday Grand National, and he would have been thinking of how working people could get to these entertainments. In fact the Derby remained midweek for many years.

As for his interest in horses, and in view of the belief of some that Ede did not bet, it is worth noting to see that 'I had no luck on the Derby ... but was not much down on the day.' On 29 May he was £1/16/8 up on the day, while the next day he backed some winners and ended only 17/6 down. These are not big amounts – £25 to £50 in today's money – but they show he could enjoy a small bet on occasion, and that the Derby meeting was one he would attend throughout. He confirmed this later: 'I make small investments ... I do not, if I lost every bet I made ... lose more money than I would spend in taking my sister to a London theatre.'[11]

Other sporting interests which he noted down included motor racing, and several more visits to the Oval, generally with Nell and sometimes Noel, when he recorded the play and the scores in fine detail. Then, on the final weekend of writing his diary, he travelled to Lincolnshire, and while there had the new experience of watching a test match on the television. This he described as 'very interesting'.[12]

The IARF – International Association for Religious Freedom – whose congress he had addressed at Amsterdam when he was Home Secretary, held its next congress in Oxford in August 1952. He was asked to speak to the members again, and this time his subject was 'The Threat to Freedom by Authoritarian Powers'.[13] The theme of individual freedom in his talks now linked to the common concern for what was taking place in many parts of Europe, even after the war had been won. We have seen how, as

Home Secretary, he had to deal with Communist governments such as that in Poland, and at the time he had also been approached on behalf of a Hungarian nationalist, E.J. Sebestyen, who had become stateless, and was living in England, while his wife and daughter were in Egypt. Kielty wrote to Ede on 9 September, explaining that Sebestyen wanted to take British citizenship but that, when he visited the Home Office to apply for visas for the family, he was not only told he would have to wait, but also had his labour permit taken away; he had successfully found himself a job, which was now in jeopardy. The outcome of the case is not recorded, but it is typical of the problems being faced because of Europe's 'authoritarian powers' at the time.

The year 1953 has gone down as one of British glory, with Hunt's expedition reaching the summit of Everest, and the young Queen being crowned. Having been part of the committee arranging the coronation, Ede happily attended it on 2 June, and retained his mementos about it.[14] A particular distinction came with the announcement of the Coronation Honours List, in which he was made a Companion of Honour. The grant of this privilege was dated 1 June 1953, and immediately Ede was flooded with letters of congratulation, enough to fill a further folder, which he kept in his papers, along with those received when he became a PC in 1944 and Home Secretary in 1945. They came from his contacts in many fields, including one from Brian Downes, the Master of Christ's, so there was no doubt he was now a distinguished member of the college. The following week Ede was cheered in South Shields, there for a ceremony at the Marine and Technical College, where he cast the base of a new telescope.[15] A further honour came, when he was elected President of the County Councils Association.

There was a darker side, however, to these months. On 31 March 1953 Reginald Christie, whom Timothy Evans had blamed for the murders of his family, was arrested, after a number of women's bodies were found in the house where they had all previously lived. Christie had moved out, after his wife had disappeared. When the police questioned him, he confessed to killing seven women from 1943 onwards, including his own wife and Beryl Evans, though he denied murdering her daughter, the one crime for which Timothy Evans had been convicted. In June, soon after the Coronation, Christie too was tried for a single murder, that of his wife, was convicted, and was hanged on 15 July.

Naturally, this raised deep discomfort about what had happened to Evans. Even if two murderers of women had independently happened to occupy neighbouring rooms, and Evans had blamed Christie without knowing this – all intuitively unlikely – the fact was that a jury had convicted Evans on the basis of evidence from Christie, the principal witness, held out as of good character, but now known to be a mass murderer. The Home Secretary, Maxwell Fyfe, appointed a QC, John Scott Henderson, to investigate, and he, holding his inquiry in secret, interviewed Christie and others before Fyfe confirmed the execution should proceed. In quick time, and two days before Christie died, Scott Henderson reported; Evans, he decided, had killed both his wife and daughter.[16] The case for the prosecution was overwhelming – as Ede was to reflect himself – and Christie's statement about killing Beryl Evans was untrue and unreliable, probably prompted by an attempt to show he was insane and thus should not hang.

That was too much for many MPs. They failed to get a debate on the case while Christie was still alive, but on 29 July 1953, Geoffrey Bing, a Labour backbencher and barrister, who had supported Sidney Silverman's attempt to abolish the death penalty in 1948, initiated one on the Scott Henderson Report. Bing argued the coincidences in the cases were incredible, and ridiculed the Report for implying that, if the police had established all the evidence that was available, a miscarriage of justice may have occurred, because Evans would have been wrongly acquitted. There was evidence from workmen in the house where the Christies and Evanses lived, which undermined the case against Evans; not only had it been suppressed at his trial, but Scott Henderson had seen but ignored it in reaching his conclusion. Bing criticised the entire procedure of the inquiry, and asked for the evidence to be made public.

His argument was taken up by Michael Foot, a future Labour leader, by Nye Bevan, by Silverman himself, and by Reginald Paget, one of Silverman's closest allies. Paget and Silverman had just collaborated in a book about miscarriages of justice, the greater part of which was devoted to the Evans case.[17] There were no speeches of substance in support of Scott Henderson's conclusions, other than Maxwell Fyfe's rejoinder that the inquiry had been properly carried out, had reached a fair conclusion, and was not going to be reopened. Nothing further would be published. Ede took no part in the debate. He was absent, as he explained later,[18] having not been given notice it was to take place. It was left to Paget to undertake that, to satisfy the Evans family that one day his body would be buried in consecrated ground, it would not be 'the last that this House ... will hear about the case ... We shall not leave this matter, whatever government is in power.'

Sure enough, on 5 November it was raised again, in an Adjournment Debate, by Fred Willey, another Labour barrister, who sat for a constituency near Ede's, in Sunderland. By this stage, the validity of the statements Evans supposedly made was in question. This time, Ede spoke. His main concern was to defend the Metropolitan Police, for whom he had been responsible at the time. He did not accept the criticism of the police about how statements had been taken or dealt with, and he quoted Paget's comment that there was no 'criticism against judge, jury, counsel or police … and yet the apparently cast-iron case was unquestionably a false one'. But he was starting to be concerned about the events:

> I hope that … all … concerned in considering whether this matter can now be regarded as closed will have regard to the necessity of giving full assurance to the public of this country that the police forces are not guilty of the kind of things with which they have been charged.

His reward was an angry letter from Evans's sister, Mrs Ashby, calling him both a coward and a Labour MP who disgusted her.[19]

In 1954, Ede presided over the North of England Education Conference in January,[20] addressing the delegates on higher technical education, on the administration and finance of education, on education in other countries, and on the three Rs. Then, on 26 February, he delivered the Biennial Lecture in Criminal Science at Cambridge.[21] He was lodged in what Radzinowicz called 'our most distinguished guest room' in Trinity College, but he asked who had recently slept in the bed. He was told it had been Lord Chief Justice Goddard, and jokingly objected 'I am not going to spend the night in Lord Goddard's bed', though presumably he did. Then, before the very large audience, he also joked that the University had previously shown little interest in him: 'It needed Dr Radzinowicz to come from Warsaw to bring me back to Cambridge', hardly a grateful response to the degree and congratulations he had received over the years.

On 7 May he gave a five minute talk on the radio,[22] in a series *Meet an MP*, for which he received five guineas (including his expenses, the BBC insisted), perhaps worth £140 today. Then, on 2 July, he added to his honorary degrees a Doctorate of Civil Law from his local university, Durham.[23] He was still regularly involved in educational functions. For example, later in the year, he opened the Ethel Wainwright School in Mansfield,[24] and presented the prizes at Workington County Grammar School.[25]

Politics was still important, of course. German rearmament, which had troubled Ede when he was in the cabinet, remained an issue through these years, and the Paris Agreements in the autumn of 1954 included a provision to allow West Germany to rearm, as part of the arrangement for ending the Allied occupation. The shadow cabinet approved this, but Ede joined with Hugh Dalton, Harold Wilson and another rising star, Jim Callaghan, in opposing it. Similarly, he had, earlier in the year, opposed the decision of the shadow cabinet, and then the PLP, to back the European Defence Community, which would have brought Germany within the same structure

With Prince Philip in South Shields (Chuter Ede second from right). (© *South Tyneside Council*)

as France, Italy and the Benelux countries.[26] He remained suspicious of Germany as a power.

It was significant that, throughout this Parliament, Ede had remained in the shadow cabinet, having been re-elected year by year – in 1952 he had come as high as second in the ballot. He retained his popularity, despite being clearly a man of Labour's past, and a good age. If, as many expected, the party regained power at the next election, due by the autumn of 1956, he would be seventy-three or seventy-four, and it was hard to think of him then continuing in office till his late seventies. By 1955, nine of the shadow cabinet were aged over sixty-five, and with hindsight the Parliamentary Party has been criticised[27] for refusing to force these old men into retirement, when they would not volunteer to go.

Clem Attlee himself had intended to hand over the party leadership in October 1955, but the question was brought to a head in April when Churchill eventually resigned and Anthony Eden, the new Prime Minister, immediately called an early general election. Chuter Ede was still continuing with his engagements outside Parliament. On 18 March 1955 he opened Denton Edgerton Park Secondary Modern School, in Leicestershire, where he was presented, not with the usual photographs or scroll, but with a plaster cast of three flying ducks.[28] At another school, later that year, he agreed to attend the speech day, and was warned that the headmaster was a Communist, and so he should have declined the invitation. However, he wrote back that he spoke to schools when he was asked, and had to accept that most heads were 'unregenerate Tories'; he considered 'the Tory Party as a bigger menace to the future of this country than the Communist party'.[29]

For by then it was clear the Conservative government would last much longer than Labour had hoped. Attlee stayed on to lead the party in the election on 26 May, and Ede was caught up in the fight in several places. After his adoption meeting on 1 May, he went to Hartlepool, a labour marginal seat, to speak in support of David Jones, the sitting MP. The next week he was speaking in Derby, then back home in Epsom on 9 May, and on to Mitcham the next day. He kept in correspondence with Ernie Gompertz, who noted that, to add to the pressure, Jim's brother, Noel was unwell.[30] The Mitcham Labour Party evidently felt he was still a useful voice, even though it was over thirty years since he had been their MP. Apart from the one election in 1945, the seat had returned a Conservative ever since Meller had beaten Ede in 1923, and the Member now was Robert Carr, himself to become Home Secretary in the 1970s.

The party also used him to argue its education policy in the press. He and David Eccles, the Minister of Education, wrote articles published side by side,[31] in which Ede put the case for abolishing the 11+ exam which, he said, was contrary to the 1943 White Paper. He also rejected the government's scheme to limit grammar and technical school places. Labour would build more schools (which would be comprehensive), extend playing fields, give grants to encourage more trainee teachers, and give special emphasis to technical and scientific education. The young people's colleges, provided for by the Education Act but never implemented, must now be carried into effect.

The contribution from Eccles covered many of the same points, but threw scorn on the policy of requiring LEAs to draw up plans for comprehensives, particularly on grounds of their size. The Conservative aim was selection. The Labour Party, he said, would be unable to keep its hands off the independent schools, whereas the government's intention was 'to win approval for carrying out the Butler Act'. So the Education Act for which Ede had worked so hard was now irrevocably identified with Rab Butler, and it had become tied into the debate, which would continue for decades, over comprehensive schools. Labour, after the experiences of Ellen Wilkinson and George Tomlinson at Education – neither still alive – was now committed to the comprehensive system, where Ede's sympathies had lain all along. It is impossible to tell whether, if he had been Minister of Education, the 11+ system would never have taken off. Certainly now he was starting the political pressure to end it.

From his comments at the BBC's General Advisory Council, it is clear Ede was attached to the old-fashioned view of electioneering. On 9 December 1953 the GAC had discussed politics in broadcasting, and he told the meeting he doubted if general election broadcasting was good – it destroyed the role of the local meeting. He was also against televising party conferences. During the next Parliament, he would tell the GAC (where the chairmanship had been passed by Radcliffe to Norman Fisher, an educationalist who chaired the BBC's Brains Trust) that the selection of MPs for broadcasting led to the danger of some members building up a reputation for themselves which did not correspond with the value set on them in the Commons. The years since may have confirmed his misgivings, but the comments show how Ede was moving out of sympathy with inevitable developments.[32]

As for the current election, he was able to put his efforts into work outside South Shields, as the outcome of the election there was hardly in doubt. The message on the small cards he distributed as usual was 'A FAITHFUL FRIEND – TRUE TO THE BOROUGH – TRUE TO THE WORKERS – TRUE TO THE COUNTRY – THE BEST MEMBER YOU EVER HAD'. His old opponent John Chalmers stood again as a Conservative, in a two-horse race, as the Liberals did not join the contest. The turnout was much lower than the extraordinary polling in 1951, and there was a small swing against Ede, but he still won with a nearly 60/40 margin:

| Ede | Labour | 31,734 |
| Chalmers | Conservative | 21,482 |

The small swing to the government was reflected in the country generally, and Eden had turned his slim Parliamentary majority into a comfortable one.

Ede took the decision at once to leave the shadow cabinet and, on 9 June 1955, he wrote to Clem Attlee. According to Richard Crossman, one of the younger men waiting for his moment, Ede and others were furious that Hugh Dalton had made public their intention to resign.[33] So, commenting on Dalton's own advocacy for a younger team, he told Attlee:

We have all recognised and deplored Dalton's failing physical powers and can sympathize with him. Fortunately, these signs of senility are not infectious. So far I have not found the burdens of parliamentary life insupportable ... and during a prolonged sitting I still feel my brightest at about 4 am ... however ... it would be an advantage to you as leader to have the opportunity of seeing some others than those who have been in office ... and before Dalton assessed others as possessing his own infirmities I had determined my course of action. From the day I made my maiden speech in 1923 your friendship and advice have been my most valued parliamentary assets.[34]

Attlee himself decided to stay on, despite his previous resolve, indicating initially he would lead through the next Parliamentary session. In fact, the government decided this would continue until October 1956, and Attlee stood down in November 1955.

Chapter 17

On the Back Benches

E de ended his letter to Attlee with the standard assurance that he would carry out whatever he was called upon to do, but his decision meant that, for the first time since the 1930s, he was now a backbench MP. In reality, he was free to take part in such matters in the House as he pleased, subject always to the party whip, and other activities outside. Never one to be unoccupied, on 2 June 1955 he wrote an article for *The Listener*, the BBC magazine, on 'The Policemen's Lot', for which he noted he was paid ten guineas.[1] This followed up two radio programmes in a series called 'The Policeman's Lot', discussing police recruitment and conditions, in which he had taken part just before the Election, being paid twenty guineas each time.[2] On 15 July[3] he was in South Shields, joining a civic reception for archaeologist Sir Mortimer Wheeler; both of them were supporters of the local Archaeological and Historical Society. He also became President of two organisations close to his heart, the Commons, Footpaths and Open Spaces Preservation Society, and the International Association for Religious Freedom.

Nowadays known as the Open Spaces Society,[4] the former was founded in 1865 as the Commons Preservation Society, and gradually extended its remit, rescuing various pieces of Surrey common land, including those at Wimbledon, Tooting Graveney, Coulsdon and Banstead, and village greens such as that at Ockley, south of Dorking, as well as footpaths, ponds and (elsewhere) beaches. It has encouraged the establishment of National Parks, which were enabled by a statute passed in 1949 while Ede was in government, and likes to claim the National Trust as its 'baby', which eventually outgrew its parent. In Ede's time, it was generally led by lawyers, who were taking up cases of encroachment and were presenting evidence to enquiries. One such was the Royal Commission on Common Land, set up by Eden's Government in July 1955, and the society was the first voluntary body to give evidence about how common land could be better used. Many of the Commission's eventual recommendations met with the society's objectives.[5] As we have seen, Ede had been a committee member for several years – though he seldom attended meetings – including while Home Secretary, when he replaced the stepping stones at Burford Bridge, which the society claims as one of its achievements. Arthur Hobhouse, one of the chief architects of the National Parks system, resigned from the society's presidency on 11 May 1955, and Ede was elected by acclamation. For the next three years or so, he attended executive committee meetings much more regularly, though he tailed off after that. He carried out duties for the society from time to time, such as speaking when the memorial to Sir Lawrence Chubb, its long-term official, was handed over at Kenwood,[6] or taking action when E.N. Buxton, its executive chair, died suddenly in September 1957 and needed replacing.[7] The society's aims certainly matched his own in regard to the countryside; he had been asking questions of ministers about commons and waste lands since before the War.[8]

Ede's election as President of the IARF (the International Association for Liberal Christianity and Religious Freedom) was at its Fifteenth Congress in Belfast, in July 1955[9]. As we know, he had spoken at its two previous congresses. It was founded by American Unitarians in 1900, and has existed under various names – it is now the International Association for Religious Freedom, having dropped the reference to Liberal Christianity, recognising that it includes members of most of the other major world religions. It is as international as its name suggests, but there has from the start been a significant British presence, and at least three Presidents of the international organisation before Ede had come from the UK, often setting an example of widespread travel among their duties in office.[10] Again, there has been a strong Unitarian component in the British support for the association; in the UK, it is based at Essex Hall, the country's Unitarian headquarters. In the 1950s, one of the main concerns of the UK group was to encourage the presence at their events of those from eastern Europe, where religion and independent thinking were discouraged. Ede is credited with using his political influence to further this work.[11] Appropriately, the theme of the Belfast congress was 'Liberal Religion in an Age of Anxiety'.

On 23 August he was in Cambridge, visiting various of his old sights, and using his camera to take them in. He was accompanied by a boy, whose name John is marked on several photos, but with no surname (though his initials were JP), and perhaps by Nell also. Many of the photographs, duly placed in one of his albums, are of Christ's College, in the garden or by the gatehouse, but others are in the familiar spots by the river. Also in 1955, Ede was happy to assist Ralph Harris, a young economist of Conservative leaning, in his first book, an appreciative account of Rab Butler's career to date. Harris's acknowledgement was to his 'amiable frankness' in casting light on how the

Education Act had come into being, and how its influence had developed since.[12]

An interesting opportunity arose later in the year, when Ede was appointed to the Parliamentary Delegation to the Round Table Conference on Malta. In October he and his colleagues travelled to the island, where they stayed at the Phoenicia, still one of the top hotels there, and were well dined by the Governor at his residence, the San Anton Palace, as well as at the Prime Minister's, the Auberge d'Aragon. Ede kept a record of it all. He went to the Trafalgar Day service of thanksgiving at the Anglican Cathedral in Valetta, on 21 October 1955, the 150th anniversary of the battle. The Maltese had been under British protection since they sought it during the Napoleonic Wars, so the celebration was significant, but the country's autonomous future had to be worked out. The conference would propose integration of Malta into the UK, though in the end this was prevented by political considerations on several sides, and it would be another nine years before it became an independent state. Ede maintained his interest in Malta, which transpired to be one of the last subjects on which he spoke in Parliament.[13] Meanwhile, he thought the subject significant enough to write an article in the *Shields Gazette* on his visit to the island.[14]

In Parliament, the issue of capital punishment would not go away. The Royal Commission, which Ede had set up after the conflict of the Criminal Justice Act 1948, had finally reported in 1953, though it was not until 10 February 1955 that it was debated by the Commons. It had been chaired by Ernest Gowers, best known to the public as an advocate of good English usage, but a civil servant of considerable experience (on which he had based his precepts on the English language), and now in his seventies. The commission had reached little by way of firm conclusions, deciding the death penalty should be retained in some cases unless there was strong public opposition, and that there was no more acceptable method than hanging. It recommended more scope should be given to the jury to mitigate the sentence, and a slim majority favoured raising the age for imposing the penalty to twenty-one. By 1955, Maxwell Fyfe had been appointed Lord Chancellor as Lord Kilmuir, and his successor as Home Secretary was Gwilym Lloyd George.

Lloyd George made it clear that the government's inclination was to reject the report's recommendations, such as they were. He felt there was no satisfactory alternative to capital punishment, though when in opposition he had supported the five-year suspension – in common with many Home Secretaries. Ede followed with the next speech, and Sydney Silverman then proposed an amendment renewing the suspension proposal. Ede's comments were ambivalent. He did not think giving the discretion to the jury was right, he was unsure about the deterrent effect of hanging, but he did believe that, with very few exceptions – he mentioned Haigh and Heath – no murderers would believe, on the morning before they committed their crime, that that night they would be in danger of the gallows. He then repeated the statement he made as Home Secretary, that no penal reform would have happened if the law had had to wait for public opinion, and next came to Timothy Evans. Repeating Reginald Paget's remark that the most worrying aspect of Evans was that his guilt appeared so clear, he concluded that, if Christie's activities had been known, Evans would not have been convicted, unless it was found the two acted together. The case showed a mistake is possible and 'I hope that no future Home Secretary … will ever have to feel … he sent a man to the gallows who was not "guilty as charged".' That was an ambiguous ending, not indicating how he proposed to see that hope realised.

Silverman was quick to point out that, if he had had his way in 1948, Ede's hope would have been fulfilled, regarding him and Evans. He said that the commission had at least decided that the present law was wrong and ought not to continue, which the government had rejected by proposing to do nothing. Since all the alternative modifications had their drawbacks, the only safe course of action was to stop the hangings. He was supported, as previously, by Christopher Hollis and several others from all parties, while there was cross-party opposition also. Paget summed up for the amendment, and the Attorney-General, Manningham-Buller, for the government. The amendment was voted down by 245 votes to 214, Ede voting for abolition.

Silverman and his colleagues would not give way, however. Before the end of 1955 they presented a Bill for abolition to the House, and more than 200 members asked the government to find time for it to get a Second Reading. That was declined, but it was agreed there would be a special debate on capital punishment. Then, on 21 November the Hunterian Society chose the subject for its annual debate.[15] By this time Ede was sufficiently on the side of abolition to be chosen to oppose the motion 'that capital punishment remains a necessity'. Sir Alfred Denning, some quarter of his way through his long judicial career, spoke for the motion, confining his support to 'murder most foul', rather than all cases, to show the community's denunciation of crime. Ede claimed that judges of old might have argued the same case for minor crimes which were once capital. The real problem, however, was the irrevocable nature of this punishment. He believed that Lord Chancellor Kilmuir still held, as he had in 1948, that no man not guilty of murder had been hanged, but after the Evans case he was now 'in a minority of one'. He repeated his comment from the Commons debate, that a man the morning before he committed murder would have laughed at the idea he would be in danger of hanging by the end of the day. Most murderers were not from 'the criminal classes', but ordinary humans unequal to emotional pressure. The seconders for each side were doctors, as presumably were most of the audience. Denning's motion was carried by a large majority.

The debate promised by the government took place on 16 February 1956. Lloyd George was proposing that the law on murder should be amended, to make changes to its definition and reclassify some killings as manslaughter, but that the death penalty should be retained. In the course of his speech, he said he believed Evans had been rightly convicted. Chuter Ede led for the opposition, by putting an amendment that the government should legislate to abolish or suspend capital punishment, and he stated firmly that he knew of nobody who thought Evans should have been hanged, or would have been if Christie's murders had been known. He believed public opinion had moved significantly, as had that of the churches, in the light of experience.

The belief in Evans's guilt was, however, supported by both Lionel Heald, who had prosecuted Christie when he was Churchill's Attorney-General, and by Rab Butler, who had just become Leader of the House. Whether or not Evans should have been hanged, they felt he was guilty of murder, quite possibly in concert with Christie. Ede was supported by Herbert Morrison, another Home Secretary who had changed his view after leaving office. At the end of the debate, Ede's amendment was carried by a comfortable majority, and he asked what the government's intentions might be. Eden, the Prime Minister, gave a delaying reply, but on 23 February he agreed the government would give time for Silverman's Bill to get a Second Reading, followed by a Committee Stage of the whole House, and a free vote. The Second Reading took place on 12 March, without any contribution of substance from Ede.

One point Morrison referred to in the February debate was the 'conversion of Sir Ernest Gowers'. For Gowers, who had chaired the Royal Commission, had since come to the view that capital punishment should be abolished, and had published a book arguing the case, *A Life for a Life?*, which Ede was asked to review.[16] Gowers said he had once been 'disposed to regard abolitionists as people whose hearts were bigger than their heads. Four years of close study of the subject gradually dispelled that feeling.' Ede described his verdict on the subject as 'guarded' and 'temperate'. The burden of proof on the matter, he agreed with Gowers, was now firmly on those arguing for retention of the death penalty.

Silverman's Bill passed successfully through the Commons on 28 June, Ede supporting the abolitionists on each vote. However, the Lords voted it down in July, and the government was not prepared to pursue it. Instead, it promoted a Homicide Bill, to limit the circumstances in which the death sentence could be passed, and broaden the defences which would reduce murder to manslaughter. Ede took an active part in the debates on the Bill, voting to restrict the use of hanging as much as possible, on 24 January 1957 arguing that the minimum age for the death sentence should be twenty-one, and five days later that all murder defendants should have their mental health examined. However, the government's proposals went through.

Perhaps the abolitionists could take comfort that a Parliament with a Conservative majority in the Commons now favoured ending capital punishment. By the time the Homicide Act 1957 was enacted, Lloyd George had retired, succeeded at the Home Office by Rab Butler, who described the new law as very odd. He had followed his duty to the Government by loyally opposing Silverman's Bill, but his sympathies were moving towards abolition, as he found his responsibility hideous. He also would in time have to deal with the fallout from the case of Evans and Christie.

Ede's photograph album shows that on 16 May 1956, when he made a small contribution to the debate on abolition in the evening, he spent the day watching the Australians playing cricket at the Oval, against Surrey. He did the same the next day. He now had more leisure time for his activities outside Parliament. In January 1956 he had spoken on 'Nonconformity in the Second Half of the Twentieth Century', to the London Board of Congregational Ministers, but confessed himself depressed at the reaction.[17] He felt the older members present understood the burden of his talk better than the younger ones. On 28 May, Mortimer Wheeler paid another visit to South Shields, where Ede joined the party in the Mayor's Parlour. In July 1956 he wrote an article for the *Congregational Quarterly*, on Nonconformity in the Second Half of the twentieth Century, quoting liberally from John Milton, Oliver Cromwell and James Russell Lowell, in terms which he used repeatedly in his speeches.

At the same time, he continued to be active for the BBC. On 20 June he told the General Advisory Council how much he supported schools broadcasts. They were an effective way for children to pick up information, though – supportive as ever of his own profession – the teacher was required to derive value from the programmes, and needed much preparation and follow-up work to achieve that. At the same meeting, he also spoke of a difficult problem which he recognised, that economics had become more important than politics in current affairs. He repeated this to the GAC on other occasions, this time adding that different economists were using words with different meanings, which hindered satisfactory broadcasting or discussion. Remaining as Deputy Chairman, he was chosen for a further three-year term of office when about half of its membership was reconstituted in October 1956.[18]

The Suez crisis was one of the main international issues that autumn and, after it had ended with British humiliation, Ede told his constituents what he felt about it.[19] At a local party meeting, he compared the Conservative Government's attitude to that of Lord North during the American War of Independence, and the Suez incident to the Boer War, touched off by the Jameson raid, 'a quick grab'. It would take years to eradicate the shock to the UK's allies and the Commonwealth. Anthony Eden had told the country at the election that it would be guided by UN principles, and had then taken action ignoring UN principles. There was also a racial element in his thinking, as those in Asia believed the words Eden had used to Nasser, the Egyptian leader, would not have been used to a white man, or the action taken against white people.

On 3 November 1956, Ede made the first of his long visits to North America, carrying out his duties with the IARF.[20] This had been in planning since the summer. In a sense, the idea developed the 1951 plan, from immediately after Labour had lost office, when Ede had written to John Kielty, offering to use some of his 'restored leisure' for the Unitarians' benefit. Then the invitation from Fred Eliot for him to visit the USA had foundered on the question of cost, but by June 1956, discussions on expenses had moved on.

Dr Dana McLean Greeley, the minister of Arlington Street Church in Boston, the headquarters of American Unitarianism, had spoken to Eliot, and to Ede and others, and was able to invite him 'for two speaking engagements in my church and such others as we can arrange from Montreal to North Carolina' – meaning several events, including two in Boston. Dana Greeley (in case of confusion about the name, a man, American Unitarians at that time having no women ministers, unlike the British) was a very influential member of the movement. He estimated the cost of the trip, including the return flight of $473, as some $700, and asked for a contribution from the UK of $100 to $150; in fact, $200 was agreed.

There was some question about whether the trip was under the auspices of the American Unitarian Association or the Arlington Street Church, which was resolved by Greeley and his church taking responsibility. Kielty issued a short résumé of Ede's life, mentioning his Amsterdam and Oxford papers, and his visits to various churches, particularly since being Home Secretary. He mentioned Ede was looking forward to the visit, but would Greeley 'please remember he is in his early seventies and cannot be expected to rush around as he did twenty years ago'. With little heed to that, the reply included a schedule from 2 November to 12 December, visiting fourteen locations, with multiple functions in many. Fred Eliot, who was unhappy about the request for a contribution from the UK, agreed to take charge of a visit to Chicago, and said that 'one major address a day is really as much as we ought to ask'.

Next, there were issues related to Ede's position as a Privy Counsellor. Should British diplomats in the USA be invited to meet him, and to events? In Canada, should local mayors and MPs be informed? By September 1956, after a trip Ede made to Holland, all these matters had been resolved. He would arrive at Boston on 3 November, leaving on 12 December, and a timetable was fixed. His own reaction was to 'feel the ordeal of the American visit with some trepidation, as the organisations to which I am scheduled to speak are more formidable than I had anticipated'.

He reached the USA immediately before the Presidential election, and attended a rally by Adlai Stevenson, the Democrat candidate (and himself a Unitarian) who was challenging President Eisenhower. Ede reported back to Britain his view that 'Ike' was impregnable, though not the Republicans as a whole. By the time his article was published,[21] the President had indeed been returned comfortably, and with only minor Republican losses in Congress. Ede noted also how shocked America was about the Suez incident a few months earlier. He saw the sights of Boston, and met the British consul and others, speaking on 4 November at a dinner at Arlington Street, and the next evening at an AUA dinner in his honour at the Union Club. Eliot hosted this, and various senior academics, including the President of Harvard, attended. One guest reported enthusiastically on the occasion, not least on Ede's reply when questions moved to Suez.

He then went to Canada, stopping off at Montreal, Ottawa and on 11 November Toronto, remarking how busy with cars they were. In Toronto a fund was set up, in response to his visit, to raise money for a gift to the rebuilding of Essex Hall, which had suffered badly in the wartime bombing. He spoke on most of his visits, in Ottawa for example giving the J.W. Ansley Memorial Lecture for the Ontario Secondary School Teachers' Association, at the Chateau Lorier.[22] After Quebec, he returned to Boston, going to schools and colleges, and speaking on 13 November at the Laymen's Night of the Arlington Street Church Preaching Institute. Then he moved on to New York and Philadelphia. He spent Thanksgiving, on 22 November 1956, in

Washington DC, giving addresses at three different denominational churches the same day. In Charlottesville, Virginia, he spoke at the Thomas Jefferson Memorial Church (a Unitarian foundation, in keeping with that President's own religious sympathies), and visited Jefferson's estate at Monticello. On 25 November he gave an address in Charlotte, North Carolina, where every seat was taken, and many were standing at the rear, some having travelled 100 miles to attend. The minister at Charlotte, the Revd Edward Cahill, an executive member of the IARF, praised 'his strong, powerful, prophetic voice'. Greeley by this time was reporting to Kielty that

> a schedule that most people would have thought or do think is too heavy … he has taken … with real courage and resiliancy (*sic*) … I have had thrilling reports from most of the places where he has been … He has done much good for us, and has given us lots of fun besides.

After returning to Boston, his next stop on 29 November was Chicago, in (as he explained to his readers in South Shields) a different time zone. Part of the discussion concerned arranging for the 1958 IARF Congress to be held there. He visited the University of Chicago, and then took a train to Cleveland, before flying back to Boston for a tour of New England. This took him to Providence RI, including Brown University, and in Massachusetts to the Unitarian churches at Plymouth and Salem, and then to Lowell, named after one of the State's main Unitarian families, one member of which he frequently liked to quote. In Boston to end the trip, he took part in a forum at Arlington Street on Education, and was finally given a farewell lunch at the Harvard Club. By the time he left for home on 13 December, he was able to say he had been in North America for six weeks, had visited 25 churches, given 48 formal addresses, attended 51 lunches or dinners, and travelled 6,500 miles (in addition to the Atlantic crossings).

To the modern reader, his reports have an air of ingenuousness about the way things are in the USA. As well as his remarks on the density of traffic and changing time zones, he comments with wonder on televisions in hotel rooms, the way advertisements interrupt the broadcast of American football games, the size of the cars, aircraft hopping between one city's airport and the next in the course of their flight, the spectacle of a city like New York from the air, and so on. Much of this, which would now seem unremarkable, was clearly novel in the 1950s to an educated and greatly-travelled elderly man like Ede, and so would have been all the more unusual to his working-class constituents on Tyneside. Once back in Britain, he spoke about the USA to the South Shields Labour Party early in the new year of 1957,[23] at about the time Eden was handing over as Prime Minister to Harold Macmillan, and wrote an article for the Unitarian *Inquirer* journal on 'American Unitarianism in 1956'.[24] On 16 January, at the BBC's GAC, he commented that American papers reported opinions rather than facts, and it was important that the USA received factual news from the UK. He repeated the point when acting as chairman at the meeting on 10 July; news broadcasts were important, as they concentrated on the news itself, not on comments on the news, as in the States.[25] These were fine statements of confidence in the BBC and its impartiality, but perhaps another sign that new developments were passing him by.

In addition to the Homicide Bill, his Parliamentary work in 1957 included a speech in Parliament on the subject of refugees on 8 March. A Jewish Labour MP, Maurice Orbach, had proposed a motion that restrictions should be removed on refugees persecuted for their race, creed or political beliefs. He was particularly concerned with those coming out of Hungary, where there had been an uprising against Communist rule in 1956, and those from Egypt – Jews and others – in the course of the Suez crisis. Ede took up the argument, recalling the six years when he had had to deal with the issue of refugees. In

> recent years there is nothing more appalling than the problem of the persecuted and the outcast in the nations of the world. From my personal experience in the years immediately following the war, I know that, if there had then been the same right of access to this country that there was in the nineteenth century, only the carrying capacity of ships and aeroplanes would have limited the number of people coming here. At a time when every additional person coming into the country was an extra mouth to feed, in that time of great shortage, the strain imposed upon one's feelings of humanity by the practical circumstances of the time was an agonising one. I hold the old Liberal tradition that this country should be the haven of anyone fleeing from persecution.

When he had preached in Salem in December, he had pleaded for help for the Hungarians, and recalled Milton's sonnet 'On the Late Massacre in Piedmont', about the persecution of the Vaudois, or Waldensians, by the Catholics in 1655. He applauded Cromwell's response to help those victims, and pleaded for a joint effort to be made by the liberal democracies now. He asked particularly that families should not be split up, but understood the problems. In his day he found that many refugees were professional people, rather than 'skilled artisans', which made them harder to settle into work. But the situation now was one where sympathy should override a government's natural caution. He considered his speech important enough to have it issued in print.[26]

With his affection for cricket, and in his own county, Ede joined Surrey County Cricket Club in 1957.[27] It is strange, in a way, that he should not have done so sooner, since the Oval, Surrey's main ground, is within walking distance of Whitehall and Parliament, whose clock is clearly visible from the upper floors of the pavilion. He had opportunities for many years to spend a few hours at county matches, as he had done in the early 1950s, and at test matches between England and touring teams from the Commonwealth, which in those days could be watched by members, without any requirement to book individual seats. That summer, the West Indies were touring England, and Ede could watch them being heavily defeated in the test match at the Oval in August, thanks in particular to the bowling of Surrey's spinner, Tony Lock.

On 8 June,[28] Ede spoke on the occasion of the foundation stone being laid for rebuilding Essex Hall. Near the Temple, this has been the centre for British Unitarians since the eighteenth century, now holding that role jointly with the Essex Church which moved to Kensington from the site of the Hall. It has an appropriately radical pedigree, having seen meetings of suffragettes and Fabians in the early twentieth century. His subject was the Unitarians' witness in upholding liberal principles in religion. In July, he agreed to speak in the Commons for the Nonconformist churches, about the tax treatment of church offerings. The debate was about the Easter collections in the Church of England, which were presented to the parish priest – was that part of his taxable income? Ede's point was that the Nonconformists depend entirely on their congregations to support their clergy, so concentrating on merely Easter did not address their problems at all. Often the tax effect on churches depended on the local tax inspector's attitude to a minister's expenses. He pressed for a clause to exempt collections from a congregation from tax, and secured an agreement from the Treasury to review the matter, which had often cropped up in debate.

The same month, he had recorded a radio discussion with others, on one of his favourite subjects – Freedom of the Individual – for which he had been paid twelve guineas. It was broadcast on 11 July, and the next day he received congratulations from the BBC for 'your masterly comments and very fine performance'. One listener had said, 'I thought Chuter Ede stole the show.'[29]

In July 1957, Ede decided he needed more secretarial help. It seems that until then he had relied solely on the party secretarial function in South

Shields for writing he did not do in person. At this time he was contributing about £400 a year towards the secretarial expenses in the constituency, but he now engaged a part-time assistant at five guineas a week.[30] The amount of work he was now taking on which was not related to South Shields, the Labour Party or the NUT was surely increasing, despite his advancing years. Mrs C.H. Saker, his secretary in the immediate period before his death, knew his affairs well, so may be the secretary he took on at this time, though the records are unclear whether she had any predecessors or colleagues.

At the start of September 1957, Ede's seventy-fifth birthday approached. On Monday 9, he spoke to the Epsom magistrates, bidding them farewell. He said he would reach the age of compulsory retirement that Wednesday, for which he could not complain, as he had fixed 75 as that age when he was Home Secretary. In fact, he hoped it would soon be lowered to 70. Though Lord Chancellor Jowitt had wanted it to be set at seventy at the time, the Government feared that whatever age was proposed, the Commons would set it at five years less. The age has since been lowered, including for a time to 65 and, though it is currently seventy, the argument is made intermittently that it should be increased again.

Pleasingly, on 1 October 1957 Part III of the Education Act 1944 finally took effect. This was the part which dealt with inspecting and disqualifying independent schools, and the occasion provided an opportunity for looking back. It was twenty-five years since the committee he chaired had presented its report on private schools, and he wrote in the journal *Education* an article recollecting the course of events.[31] He reprised the conditions identified by his committee in 1932, and suggested that to have lived long enough to see its recommendations brought into operation was a tribute to his stamina rather than his wisdom. Even since Kenneth Lindsay had complimented Ede on the measures when they were agreed in 1944 a further thirteen and a half years had elapsed. Though critical of Florence Horsbrugh as Minister of Education after she took over in 1951, he paid tribute to her for appointing October 1957 as the time to bring the provisions into force, and her three successors for carrying it out. He was satisfied at last that standards in private education would be enforced.

The evidence suggests that by now much of his activity in politics involved looking back. On 31 October 1957 it was reported[32] that Hugh Dalton, now in hospital, had received a barbed telegram from three of the 'Old Guard', namely Chuter Ede, Manny Shinwell, and Dai Grenfell, the Father of the House of Commons. Grenfell was a Welsh MP, but Ede, Shinwell and

Dalton all represented Durham constituencies, and there was a mixture of fellow feeling and competition between them.

There was, though, no doubt about Ede's continued commitment to freedom of speech. The BBC's GAC meeting on 6 October 1957 discussed the case of the high-profile commentator Malcolm Muggeridge, who had published a critical article about the monarchy. The BBC had cancelled Muggeridge's broadcasts for a week, but the GAC's review of the matter concluded that the ban should not be continued. Ede argued forcefully that it was good to hear views with which one disagreed; ever the royalist, he disagreed with Muggeridge, but insisted he should not be censored.[33]

By the end of 1957, Ede was preparing for his year of office as President of the General Assembly of Unitarian and Free Christian Churches, due to begin in April 1958. He had been to council meetings in London, and then to one in Kidderminster in October, at one of which he was nominated for election, and he was already making visits for the Assembly, having been to Richmond, to Lancashire, and to Manchester College, Oxford, the Unitarian college. While he took on the Presidency and devoted himself to it with his usual thoroughness, he was aware of his age and prepared for it with some trepidation. He wrote to Kielty, listing the number of engagements he was being asked to carry out, 'as I shall very soon have reached the limit of what I can do'.[34] His typical schedule was due to cover between two and four visits to congregations each month, most often at weekends. He pointed out to Kielty that he did have to fit in his political work, sometimes on Sundays (presumably a reference to his constituency visits), as well as NUT engagements on Saturdays. 'A few churches write saying that the President visits them every year ... a surprising violation of the principle of fair shares.' He was also concerned about his expenses; for example, when he went to Lancashire and took the sleeper back from Manchester, this cost £7 or more. He generally ended out of pocket, even with each church cheerfully contributing, but felt it must put a strain on some of the smaller congregations.

When the time came, he travelled from one congregation to another, having prepared a typed address for each occasion.[35] After attending the NUT Conference in Scarborough at Easter, he started his Unitarian duties at the General Assembly later in April 1958, where he spoke about the instability of an age where life is based on the fear of nuclear war,[36] and went to Taunton and Bridport for the weekend of 3–4 May. On 17 May, he spoke to the North Midland Presbyterian and Unitarian Association, giving a historical review of their heritage, full of quotations from Cromwell: 'the State, in choosing men to serve them, takes no notice of their opinions, if they be willing faithfully to serve them' – a proposition with more principle than accuracy – and, 'The Liberty I ask is to vent my own doubts, and my own fears, and my scruples', a well-formulated statement of Ede's own position. On 31 May he opened the Plymouth Unitarian Church, rebuilt after being bombed in the War, and compared the years of fighting with the city's blockades and siege of 1642–46. At the start of June, he was at Plymouth and Tyldesley, in Lancashire, on successive Sundays.

There were, from time to time, interludes to this schedule. On 7 March 1958 he opened Hemel Hempstead Police Station, in his capacity as former Home Secretary, which suggests the police still held him in good esteem.[37] On 25 March, he was invited to be the BBC Woman's Hour guest of the week, speaking about an anti-litter campaign.[38] Then, on 9 June, he attended the opening of Gatwick Airport's new terminal (now the South Terminal), and was able to take the first flight from there to the Channel Islands.[39] He also around this time accepted honorary membership of Ewell Rotary Club.[40]

For the Unitarians, he was often celebrating important (or less important) anniversaries. Thus on 11 June, he was marking the 250th anniversary of the Leicester Great Meeting, while in July it was Ditchling's 260th, and Kingswood Chapel was complimented on its 250th. Then on 26 July he made another visit to the USA, addressing the Arlington Street Church in Boston in August, with greetings from the General Assembly in the UK. He took the opportunity to quote one of the city's favourite sons, the writer James Russell Lowell, whose quatrain often found its way into his sermons and speeches:

> He had stiff knees, the Puritan
> Which were not good at bending.
> The homespun dignity of man
> He thought was worth defending.

Ede then told the story of Galileo, a martyr to honesty, truth and scientific enquiry, and noted the visit the young John Milton had made to the old man. That too would turn up in many of his addresses. From there he went on to the Chicago Congress of the IARF, which he had been involved in planning during his previous visit two years earlier. Fred Eliot, his host on his 1956 tour, had recently died suddenly, and he paid tribute to him in a way that 'all who heard it will always remember', according to John Kielty.[41] He was able there to end his three year term of office, and hand on the role as President of the IARF.

Home at the end of August 1958, he got back to his frantic schedule. He visited the chapel in Toxteth, giving it recognition as the oldest religious building in Liverpool, and also the congregation at Brighton. An event in Epsom on 9 September was a banquet at the Grandstand on the Racecourse, where he spoke on admitting new freemen of the Borough, of which he had become one as long ago as 1939.[42] On 13 October, he spoke at the Institute of Education in London on 'Local Democracy and Education', reviewing the history of the Education Act and what had developed from it. He was in his constituency on 22 October, opening the new factory of the Eskimo Slippers business in Jarrow.[43] His Parliamentary and denominational work overlapped on 24 October, when he hosted a lunch at the Commons for representatives of the American Unitarian and Universalist Churches. They had come over to join him the next day, when he took the chair in opening the rebuilt Essex Hall.[44]

On 26 October, he was at the 265th anniversary of a chapel in Leicester and, if the records are right, at a new one opening in London. Next day it was the 250th anniversary at Newington Green. In November, he was at Great Hucklow in Derbyshire, to speak to the Unitarian Young People's League, and then at the Elder Yard Chapel in Chesterfield for its 296th anniversary. At the end of the month he visited Dob Lane near Manchester, going on to Bank Street Chapel in Bolton, where he based his talk on Romans 12.2:

> be not conformed to this world: but be ye transformed by the renewing of your mind, that ye may prove what is that good, and acceptable, and perfect, will of God

and, in a historical survey of Nonconformity, he quoted John Milton and J.H. Plumb (another Christ's College man). In general at each of these churches he gave an address which, though tailored for the local audience, concentrated on the same theme. He would review the history of dissenters, and make special reference to Milton and to 'Areopagitica' in particular.

His original schedule included Manchester again on 7 December 1958, but he needed to decline that invitation, because Parliamentary business took him to Trinidad, to meet the newly-formed West Indies Federation; he was part of a delegation of three MPs and a Commons clerk presenting a Mace to their Parliament.[45] They flew out on 28 November, and the next day he was meeting members of the teaching profession in the island. The formal presentation was made by a Conservative MP, Sir Thomas Dugdale, on 1 December, and they attended dinners hosted by the Governor the next two evenings. They stayed at Government House and, when Ede returned on 7 December, he discovered he had missed 'the longest continuous foggy period in … history'. To Grantley Adams, the Barbadian PM of the Federation, he sent a copy of *The Valiant Stumper*, 'a history of the dangerous and honourable art of wicket-keeping'. Adams had once kept wicket for Barbados, and Ede was pleased when they met to find Adams shared his high opinion of Herbert Strudwick, the old Surrey and England keeper.[46] Adams studied at Oxford just after the Great War, and may then have seen Strudwick in action.

On his return from the Caribbean, Ede was laid low with what he called a bad bronchial attack, caused by the temperature difference between the West Indies and England. But in the new year, 1959, his health had recovered enough to get him to Sheffield Unity Church on 4 January, to Oat Street, Evesham a couple of weeks later, and then to others including the Men's League at Todmorden, addressing a further anniversary service. He had given his Presidential Address on the theme of the Instability of the Age – 'on the whole the great ages have been unstable ages' – and his references to the Civil War would illustrate that. By the start of February 1959, he was submitting his report to the Assembly's Council, listing this exhausting schedule. Still with the Caribbean in mind, however, he was able to join Dugdale to take part in a BBC radio broadcast, recorded at the West Indian Students' Centre in London, for a programme called 'Calling the Caribbean', when they answered questions about their visit and their thoughts on the new country.[47]

In Parliament, Ede had been active enough in 1958 to take part in the Select Committee on Obscene Publications, and on 16 December he spoke in the House to encourage early legislation on the subject. This was taken up by the young Roy Jenkins, whose father Ede recalled from their days in Parliament and Government together. Describing him as 'a worthy son',[48] in April 1959 Ede was able to support his Obscene Publications Act which came into effect that autumn.

Parliamentary procedure was an issue under debate at the time, taken up by the BBC. Enoch Powell, then temporarily out of office in the Conservative Government, had proposed a radio discussion about the changing nature of the role of the private member of Parliament. He suggested Chuter Ede as one participant, along with Tony Benn and Anthony Head, another Conservative previously in government, who represented Carshalton, as Ede had once done. The BBC took up the suggestion, with two programmes on the Third Programme in February 1959, though the personnel changed. Ede took part in both, earning each time 17 guineas, worth £400 or £500 today. In the first, he was joined by Powell, Lynn Ungoed-Thomas, once Attlee's

Solicitor-General, and John Foster, a Conservative lawyer with particular interest in human rights. The second panel comprised Sidney Silverman, the campaigner against hanging, along with Lionel Heald, who had been involved in the Evans and Christie case, and Lord Hinchingbrooke, another long-serving Conservative. These experienced Commons men talked at length about the new demands being placed on MPs, which Ede had experienced over more than thirty years.[49]

Although Ede had been unsympathetic to commercial television, he was prepared to perform for the independent broadcasters, when occasionally asked. In January 1959 he recorded a talk for Granada Television about the betting laws, which was broadcast as part of its *Searchlight* programme on 23 February. This was followed by a further interview, about street betting, with the journalist Kenneth Allsop, put out early in March. Then, his local broadcaster for South Shields, Tyne Tees Television, invited him to join its *Spotlight* programme on gambling in the north-east, on 28 April.[50] As we shall see, gambling would provide one of his main interests in the next parliament.

In April 1959 the BBC Chairman reminded the General Advisory Council that its members had been appointed for three-year terms, which would expire in September, when half would retire. As Ede's membership had covered more than seven years, and he had been among the half retained in 1956, it was time for him to cease his role as Deputy Chairman.[51] His last meeting would be in July.[52] Before then, on 29 May, he was able to speak about 'Fifteen Years' Experience of the Education Act of 1944'. It was, in fact, a few days after the fifteenth anniversary of the Education Bill completing its journey through the Commons, and he was invited to Olympia to give the Annual Sir Philip Magnus Memorial Lecture on the subject. He commented that the high birth rate in the late 1940s – what we now call the 'baby boom' – had caused problems in planning the new educational structures, but that these had been addressed. Then he concentrated on two of his frequent themes, insisting it was right that the tripartite system of grammar, technical and modern schools had not been mentioned in the Act, and that there was a need for more design and craft education for academic children. If there were to be secondary modern schools, he said, they needed to be ambitious for what their pupils could achieve.

Ede was becoming a regular broadcaster, much in demand on several subjects, and perhaps the most significant of the programmes in which he took part was a BBC discussion on 30 July 1959, entitled The Police and the Public. He was joined by the Chief Constable of Lancashire and a female JP from London, with Frank Byers, a former Liberal MP, in the chair. They covered a range of issues, including use of violence by the police, arming them (which all the panel opposed), forcing prisoners to make statements, corruption, bribes, and the qualifications and education of constables of both sexes. A 24-page transcript of the programme still exists,[53] so many of Ede's opinions are recorded. He believed the police sometimes reached their own conclusion about a case, and then found the evidence to support it – perhaps Timothy Evans was on his mind – and recalled that as Home Secretary he had been worried about one local constabulary which was shutting a blind eye to one bookmaker's operations, suggesting money was being paid. He wanted more police with a higher education background, and as to police women, they 'wear the best uniform of any of the services, and I chose it'!

Harold Macmillan, having taken over as PM at the start of 1957, decided to call the next general election on 8 October 1959, rather than wait till the following Spring. Ede was now seventy-seven, but he decided to stand again, announcing himself in his address as 'Faithful Man of the People'. He stressed the need for full employment as Labour's 'first care', and reminded the South Shields electorate what he had been doing for them regarding this. He also pressed for gradual nuclear disarmament, abolishing all NHS charges, taxing capital gains, reducing school class sizes, improving technical education, and removal of 'the anxieties associated with the 11-Plus examination'. Preparing Commonwealth countries for self-government and a higher standard of living was the main objective abroad. Then the central message was shown by a photo of Parliament captioned 'EDE watches over YOUR welfare – HERE'.

The election was again a straight contest against John Chalmers. Each of them slightly increased his vote, reflecting the larger electorate, though the percentage turnout was the same. There was a very small swing towards the Conservative candidate, reducing the majority by 1,300:

| Ede | Labour | 32,577 |
| Chalmers | Conservative | 23,638 |

This result reflected the two parties' performance in the country as a whole, and Macmillan's majority in the Commons increased to over 100.

Among the activities in the new Parliament in which Ede became involved in the spring of 1960,[54] was the Betting and Gaming Act. This permitted betting shops to open, so that gambling on horses did not need to be done, surreptitiously and illegally, through street runners. Ede, though scarcely a gambler himself, considered betting to be a folly, not a sin. He was proud as an Epsom man to support racing, and his particular concern was that people of wealth could get betting facilities legally, especially by phone, while many in the working class had to resort to illicit methods. He did not dislike the street bookie; he complimented him as someone many considered 'a good sport for taking … risks so that they can have a bet'. But he naturally preferred to put the business on a legal footing. His speech as the Bill went through the house was commended in *Sporting Life*.[55] Meanwhile, honours kept coming. In April, he added to his honorary degrees with a doctorate of laws from Sheffield,[56] and on 23 June he was elected an Honorary member of the Town Planning Institute.[57]

In April 1960, Ede was able to return the hospitality he had received in the USA from Dana Greeley, who visited the UK with his wife. Dr Greeley was returning home first, so Jim and Nell Ede arranged to take Mrs Greeley on a drive round the Surrey countryside on 25 April, and give her lunch and tea. As they had no car, this involved making arrangements with a friend for transport.[58] Following this, his visits to Unitarian Churches continued, even though he had passed the chair of the General Assembly. On 12 June, he was in Sidmouth, to celebrate their 250th anniversary, giving a talk similar in content to those he gave during his Presidential year.[59]

The year 1960 was in some ways one for looking back, and making plans for a quieter life. He would have been sad to note that, in March, his old comrade Ernie Gompertz had been removed by the ever-fractious South Shields Labour Party and had seen his post as secretary and agent abolished. He had promptly resigned from the local Council and all his other public offices; Ede kept the newspaper cuttings in tribute to him.[60]

In November Noel Ede died, aged seventy-four. Noel, who worked as a rating surveyor, did not feature much in Chuter Ede's life, and was a single man with no family, as far as is known. He had been living in Worcester Park, just north of Ewell,[61] but had suffered from a stroke five years earlier, which Chuter Ede said had kept him in hospital throughout that period. 'I have got one brother and we rarely meet without quarrelling over something', was his comment on Noel, made during the 'Frankly Speaking' interview on the radio – but deleted at his request before transmission, in view of the circumstances.[62] The International Friendship League, an organisation which still exists, describes Noel as its founder in the early 1930s, though Ann Godden, its current International Secretary, thinks it is more likely to have started in the 1920s, with more influential sponsors. Noel, she suspects, was one of the last survivors of its pre-war committee, who saw it disbanded in 1942, but then restarted it and kept it going, and has been credited with playing a larger part than he did.[63]

Ede was much closer to his sister, Nell, and they went on doing things together; on Saturday 23 July, his old friend and protégé John Strudwick, in his turn a county councillor and JP, came from his home in Banstead and took them to the RHS Gardens in Wisley.[64] By now, he had decided the time had come to give up his Commons seat, and he announced this to South Shields that month, making it clear he was handing over a task which had still to be worked on: 'There are still fights for justice and freedom to be waged. Locally and nationally full employment has still to be secured and maintained.'[65]

A newspaper tribute the next day was headlined 'A RARE BIRD – THE POLITICIAN LIKED by ALL'.[66] It traced his career from a teenage speaker addressing labourers on Surrey village greens, to a senior MP, and emphasised his humour:

he was once asked why he did not stop people 'making fun' of the Government on radio programmes. He replied: 'When we cannot enjoy healthy laughter about ourselves and our acquaintances we have become very advanced cases of mental disease … democracy … can tolerate a sense of humour whereas dictatorships cannot.'

Ede was prepared to use his authority as an elder statesman. In August and September 1960 he protested against the jailing of Patrick Neary, who had led a strike of seamen. Neary had been imprisoned under the Merchant Shipping Act 1894. This is a massive statute, originally of more than 700 sections, which consolidated the wide range of law on the merchant fleet, and included ancient provisions against desertion, absence without leave, and combining to disobey lawful commands. Ede joined the cause to get Neary released, and to have the relevant sections repealed.[67] Then, in October 1960, he was approached about Henshaw's School, in Oldham, where it was alleged there was a religious test regarding admission of pupils. The school, now known as the Bluecoat School, was an Anglican foundation, which became voluntary aided, and has faced this type of criticism over the years, but Ede dealt with it in very quick fashion. He advised those complaining to rely on section 25(3) of the Education Act 1944, with which he was of course very familiar. This provided that there should be no requirement, as a condition of any pupils attending a county or voluntary school, that they attend, or abstain from attending, any place of worship.[68]

Although Ede had given up his role at the BBC, he was still in demand to make broadcasts. In February 1960, he spoke again about the police in 'The Arm of the Law', and on 2 August he was interviewed by a Conservative journalist, T.E. Utley, regarding a recent study, Government by Appointment, on the need for a proper system for making appointments to some 40,000 public posts. He was concerned about the amount of patronage involved, without proper procedures. The next day he received a letter from an academic at Bristol University, asking how he could get on committees dealing with public affairs, or become a JP, in the light of the comments on the programme, and his own experience of voluntary work. Ede replied that such a short programme (sadly, only seven minutes long) had not been adequate to deal with how society uses 'unorganised goodwill'.[69]

Of particular interest is an interview chaired by journalist George Scott, who would go on to edit *The Listener*, in which he answered questions on his career and beliefs.[70] Broadcast on 21 December 1960, it was part of the 'Frankly Speaking' radio series, a programme which had been running through the 1950s, with two or three interviewers putting unscripted questions to a single interviewee. Many of the subjects were not in politics – earlier in the year the guests had included the actress Flora Robson, made a Dame that summer, and the singer Gracie Fields. When the BBC rebroadcast some of the interviews in 2015, none of those chosen was a politician. Ede must have considered this an honour in itself, retaining as he did a cutting about it among his photographs.[71]

The BBC produced, from an unnamed author, notes in advance of the programme, listing much of Ede's career, but also with interesting comments about him, evidently gleaned from a preliminary chat, as prompts for questions. So he 'has a lot to say to the question "What do you consider to be the basis of politics?"'. He was 'quite violent in his views on the educative merits of National Service', with 'of course, strong views on capital punishment'.

> If one makes the assumption that his great achievement was at the Home Office he launches straight into the Ministry of Education period which was his real love. I understand also that he is something of a feminist and can be drawn in this field. I suspect him of having views on the younger generation which might be got at through questions on juvenile delinquency.

In the interview itself, Ede began by emphasising his mother's impact on his career – 'in both my religious and political opinions, my mother's was the formative influence'. He recalled that, in the 1892 General Election, his family were disappointed by the Conservative victory in Epsom, 'and I resolved at that time I'd put it right'. He went on to discuss his education and career, saying that his 'greatest contribution to Socialism' was indeed his part in drafting 'the Education Bill of 1944', whereas 'at the Home Office as a ex-teacher, I was only like a doctor turned undertaker, burying the mistakes of my former profession'. He felt the 1944 Act had made a difference to aspirations, though the schools had not turned out as he hoped:

> every parent now thinks his child has a right to a Grammar School education, no matter how unsuited for … the dead languages he may be … the parity of esteem is not there,

for as to equality,

> We're a long way off … My chief disappointment is that we have not yet been able to create the social atmosphere … that will say the eleven plus examination is a social disaster.

He also spoke about the role of the police, about delinquency, and about the Evans case and the need for the death penalty to be abolished.

It was shortly after this, in February 1961, that Ede was approached by Alan Bullock, seeking a conversation about the period when Ede and Ernest Bevin had been associated together. The first published volume of Bullock's biography had taken Bevin through his years as a trade union leader up to 1940. Bullock was now working on the second volume, while the third would not be completed until, after thirty years from Bevin's death, his papers became available. As I started this book by saying, it was an immense project. Ede lent Bullock some of his diaries, and they spent time together, though it does not sound as if he disclosed much. Anecdotes about Bevin are copious, and Bullock repeated many, from the dozens of witnesses he interviewed, many of them dead by the time he was writing, but little from Ede. He did record, however, Ede's one judgement on Bevin:[72] 'Was he the biggest man I met in the Labour Movement? He was the biggest man I met in any movement.' This was a generous tribute to a man who had used his influence to help Ede achieve so much, and from someone who had also known Maynard Keynes and Winston Churchill. In the 'Frankly Speaking' interview, his view had been that Bevin, 'a great man', would in the future have become 'a distinguished ornament of one of the ancient Universities' instead of a self-educated Union man – though 'he was no Parliamentarian', and so would not have made a good Prime Minister.

As President of the County Councils Association, Ede was able to visit counties around England for a variety of activities. In October 1960 he had been asked to address the prize-giving of the Commonweal Grammar School in Swindon, as 'I have some great-nieces who are pupils there.' The event took place on 3 March 1961, with Nell Ede handing out the prizes, and he making the speech. He had explained to the school that he did not charge for giving that type of address, but would need their expenses covered, including a hotel and first-class train fare. He could claim his own from the CCA, but asked the school to meet Nell's. On 22 March he sought his expenses from the Association, having deducted the charge for breakfast for 'four of my nieces resident in the town'. With no apparent children of any of his own siblings, these were no doubt Lilian's nieces, the Fromow daughters; on the lists of prizewinners and exam achievements, there were no pupils called Ede.[73]

That year's AGM of the County Councils Association was the last over which he presided. He had had to get the date fixed so it did not coincide with the Derby at Epsom, which he explained he could not miss; he lunched with the Stewards of the Jockey Club annually on Derby Day.[74] Having dealt with that, he then gave up his presidential role of the CCA after eight years. Also in 1961 he resigned as President of the Open Spaces Society, after six years, though he would still support its activities; he attended a Footpath Conference on 28 September 1963, chairing one session.[75]

For he needed to concentrate on the most pressing priorities. One of these was justice for Timothy Evans. A book *Ten Rillington Place* had been published in January, called after the house where the Christie murders had occurred. Its writer, Ludovic Kennedy, a less-known figure today, had a high profile in the 1950s and 60s as a television personality, Parliamentary candidate (without success), journalist and author, with a particular interest in the navy (in which he had served in the Second World War) and miscarriages of justice. In strong terms Kennedy put together the case that Christie had murdered both Beryl Evans and her baby, her husband being entirely innocent. He quoted Ede's remark, from the 1955 debate, that 'a mistake was made',[76] in an open letter to the Home Office. He gave a firm, though one-sided, account of the story, much of it based on Reginald Paget's book from eight years earlier.[77] He challenged the statement that no criticism could be made of the police, arguing they had falsely concocted several confessions attributed to Timothy Evans, and had failed to carry out a thorough investigation. About the same time, Norman Birkett, a highly respected judge and former Liberal MP, now in the Lords, wrote an article stating that no jury could possibly have found the case against Evans proved beyond reasonable doubt, had the full facts been known in 1950.[78]

Butler, the Home Secretary, was asked to grant a further enquiry. He and Ede spoke on 14 February 1961; Ede's practice was never to intervene in any decision to be made by his successor Home Secretaries, but Rab asked for his advice. He gave it in writing the following day: Evans should get a posthumous free pardon. Ede, who had been corresponding with Kennedy, cited several issues raised in his book. He met Butler again on 9 March, and the next day wrote to him that their conversation 'caused me great distress of mind'.[79] He went through the arguments, conceding that Rab's position was unprecedented, but was able to quote Milton to assert that Parliament ought to act without precedent when the circumstances required it. The Milton quotation is from an unfortunate, ambivalent source – the *Tenure of Kings and Magistrates*, his justification for the execution of Charles I. However, on 16 March Butler declined the request, on the grounds that no new information would be forthcoming, and so much time had passed, and discussion held, since 1949, that the evidence would be confused. Through her solicitor, Morley Lawson, who lived on Epsom Downs, and was acting at Kennedy's expense, Evans's mother had petitioned Butler for consent for the body to be transferred to ground consecrated by the Catholic Church. He refused this also, as well as the suggestion of the free pardon, on the grounds of lack of precedent.[80]

By now, Ede's radio work was running down, and he took it on only when it did not impose too much inconvenience. He declined an invitation in February 1961 to visit Cardiff for a Television Wales and the West programme, even though it was on capital punishment. However, on 27 March, he recorded one of his last radio programmes, on the subject which was consuming him, though for the Canadian Broadcasting Corporation. He had first been asked to contribute to a discussion on the contrast between the accusatorial and inquisitorial methods in murder trials. Though a lifelong magistrate, Ede was no lawyer, and this was so far outside his range that he wrote to Dick Mitchison, a Labour Parliamentary colleague, for advice. In the end, he and the CBC settled for an interview about the Evans case.[81]

On 15 June, after Ede and Kennedy had lunched together, a debate in the Commons was introduced by Ede's former Cabinet colleague, Patrick Gordon Walker. He described the remarkable coincidences in the previous account of Geoffrey Bing, who was no longer an MP, and mocked Butler's arguments. 'The case will not lie down. This case cannot be stifled by authority.' Among those who argued against reopening the case was Sir Hugh Lucas-Tooth, the junior Home Office minister when Christie's murders had become known in 1953. In a speech much interrupted by MPs, he asserted that 'there was no impropriety' at the Scott Henderson Inquiry, which was 'common ground, and accepted by hon. Members on both sides'. 'Not accepted by me,' Ede interrupted. The House had to be called to order to let Lucas-Tooth finish and, when he did, Ede took the floor. He was heard almost in silence.

It was one of the most impassioned speeches he ever made in the House, or that some members had ever heard from anybody. He said he could have abstained from taking part, but that would have been an act of cowardice. He had not intended to raise the Scott Henderson Report but, since Lucas-Tooth had done so, he needed to recount what had happened. Then he recited Kennedy's account of how the lawyers for the Evans family were excluded from the enquiry:

> I was first appointed a magistrate in 1920, and I have had some experience of the conduct of judicial inquiries of many kinds … an inquiry so conducted — into which both counsel and solicitor had the greatest difficulty obtaining admission until they went straight to the Home Secretary to get that permission — is a travesty — [Interruption] — of anything in judicial procedure recognised by the law of this country hitherto.

He described the conversation he had had with Butler on 9 March – as a 'friend', to whom he had a 'deep obligation' for his support during the Education Bill – advising him what to do. He was alarmed that Rab had said, 'I am advised that I cannot say that this man Evans was innocent', but that was the wrong question, because nobody has to prove his innocence. He should ask instead, 'In the light of all the evidence, can you regard this man as guilty beyond all reasonable doubt?' What would happen today if such a case went before the Home Secretary, who decided not to commute the sentence but then, before it was carried out, learnt of six other victims of similar murders? – a rhetorical question, which he did not need to answer. Birkett, with no personal interest in the case, had said no jury could convict on the facts as now known, and Parliament should accept that Evans should get the benefit of the doubt. There was no need to declare him innocent.

Ede mentioned Evans's mother and sisters, who believed his soul would be in Purgatory while his body was in unconsecrated ground:

> I do not accept that view … But by my own claims to have my religious beliefs respected I am compelled to respect the beliefs of every other person … this is a state of spiritual anguish for these three women who took the utmost care themselves to question the man in his last hours whether he was guilty or not and received throughout all their inquiries a stout denial.

Even if it took an Act of Parliament, their wishes should be respected. There were 121 Acts from the past relating to those convicted of treason, whose good name it was then decided to restore. One, Alice Lisle, has her picture in the Members' Lobby; she was executed for helping defeated soldiers after Sedgemoor, but her conviction was annulled by statute as soon as William and Mary came to power. The list of dukes whose good names were posthumously restored was too long to read out. Even if there was no precedent for a pardon, the urgency of the situation demanded one be set.

His friend George Wigg had confirmed with the Catholic Church that they could rebury Evans's remains, as his mother wished, without any public demonstration. This would give the House the chance to end a story which Ede had started. He disclosed that Frank Newsam said to him when he confirmed Evans's death sentence, 'you must not forget that this man has stuck to his story that he did not do it and that Christie did'. Legal opinion, however, thought Ede had taken the right course, on the evidence as it was, and now Butler should do likewise in the light of the current evidence.

The debate continued for nearly two more hours. An interesting contribution was from George Rogers, whose constituents both Evans and Christie had been, and who knew them both 'superficially'. He said Evans's mother had come to him while her son was awaiting execution and, though there was little he could do, he had intuitively formed the view that he was innocent. When the later murders became known, he had visited Christie in the death cell, though he was disappointed they were not alone, and so he could not ask questions in the detail he would have liked. He was one of the first to call for the Scott Henderson Enquiry, but it had disappointed him, and a new enquiry was needed. He felt that, while Kennedy had not written anything new, there was more evidence to be uncovered.

It concluded with Butler paying tribute to those who had spoken, including Ede for his 'exceptional' speech, and referring to Ede as 'my friend', in response to his own description of Rab. He expressed how difficult he had found taking part, but nonetheless refused all that was requested. A further inquiry would not bring the truth any nearer. A free pardon is not granted simply in the circumstances that a jury might not now convict; that might justify a reprieve, but a pardon is different, and there must be certainty of innocence. Consequently, he was barred by statute from authorising the removal of Evans's body.

It was clear that a Private Bill would be needed to override the Capital Punishment Amendment Act 1868, which required each body after hanging to be buried in the prison grounds. So Ede and his colleagues proposed the Timothy John Evans Bill for that purpose, but its progress was stopped a few days later. As Butler had told him, the government could not support such legislation.

In the summer of 1961, Ede went on holiday to Switzerland, taking with him Nell and two women, Julia and Theresa Fromow, described as his 'nieces' (in fact, as we know, great-nieces of Lilian Ede).[82] The arrangements were made by travel agents organised by John Kielty at the Unitarian office, so the visit may have been made to permit him to attend a final Unitarian Congress that August.

It was at this point that the Surrey County Teachers' Association, with which he had first become involved more than fifty years before, decided to commission a portrait of Ede, which they wished to present to Surrey County Council. On 10 June 1961 they decided to issue a circular[83] to his 'many friends and colleagues', asking for subscriptions, as the 'Association owes more than they can ever repay to the genius of Mr Ede and to the inspiration and devotion of the lady who was his wife from 1917 to 1948'. They asked for the collection to be made by October, so the artist could proceed with the commission.

The portraitist selected was Michael Noakes, a young Surrey artist, starting a career which would include painting the Queen and Duke of Edinburgh, Queen Elizabeth, Bill Clinton, Margaret Thatcher and many others, probably totalling over a hundred in all. His pictures also include landscapes of the Surrey countryside, but it is portraits in oil which came to dominate his work. He was then aged twenty-eight, and living in Reigate, where Ede sat for him. A book he wrote on oil painting a few years later included an unusual photograph of Noakes in front of the Ede portrait on his easel, pipe in his mouth, with Ede himself sitting solidly in a hard armchair. In the photo's caption, he stated he tried to show 'a man who had retained a basic simplicity and humanity in spite of having held a very burdensome office'.[84]

The portrait was presented to Surrey in February 1962, and now hangs in the corridors of County Hall in Kingston, with a description written below, listing Chuter Ede's name, title and honours, his dates as Home Secretary, Surrey CC member and chairman, and SCTA president, together with 'MP for Mitcham 1923', the one occasion he represented his own county at Westminster. When shown a photo of this more than fifty years later, Noakes was keen to take a copy, for he had not forgotten him. Then in his eighties himself, a few months before his own death in May 2018, he was able to recollect Ede as a cooperative sitter, interested in talking about his work. He remembered his belief, as a Unitarian, that 'God did not play mathematical tricks'. He also recalled Ede's story that, when happening to be in Windsor, he contacted the Castle and arranged to call in and visit 'the Queen'. Whether

The Michael Noakes portrait in County Hall, Surrey. (*By permission of Surrey County Council*)

that was the Queen herself, or perhaps her mother Queen Elizabeth, or even grandmother Queen Mary, is impossible to say. What stayed most in Noakes's mind, though, was their discussion about capital punishment. The Evans case in particular disturbed Ede, especially as the family thought his soul could not be saved if he was in unconsecrated ground. Noakes would have understood; he had had a Catholic education himself. He felt the case 'tortured' Ede.[85] It is a good window into his state of mind close to the time when his efforts to do justice for Evans seemed to be failing.

At the same time, Ede was of course also occupied with Parliamentary concerns. After Aneurin Bevan had died in 1960, his Commons seat had been taken by Michael Foot, who had soon caused difficulties, with four other MPs, by opposing the defence policy of Gaitskell and his team. They had the Labour whip withdrawn in March 1961, but there was considerable concern on the back benches about this. Ede was one of a large number of Labour members who wrote to Gaitskell asking for the whip to be restored, and ensured that the press in South Shields covered this.[86] He was also asked by Butler to involve himself in a couple of other Home Office matters. In July he was appointed to a committee to review the law on Sunday entertainments.[87] Then in October, he heard that Rab proposed to call together various people, including representatives of churches, to discuss juvenile delinquency. Ede lobbied the Unitarians to be included among their nominees, and duly took part in the discussions. On 20 November, he was invited to take part in a conference on crime prevention.

In September 1961 he collected a file of newspaper cuttings on the subject of the public schools, which would result in an article, some 4,000 words long, published the following January in the *Hibbert Journal*, a quarterly religious magazine.[88] He had been invited by the editor to write this, in reply to an article submitted by a former headmaster. Ede spoke to the Head of Epsom College, and to the Whitgift Foundation – the two public schools of which he was a governor – in preparation for what he wrote. However, this activity in his old fields of interest was darkened by the health of his sister Nell. She had suffered from a scalding accident, and ended in hospital, with him reporting in November that her recovery was very slow. In the new year, they took a holiday together, in Devon as usual, but she had still not recovered.[89] Eventually, she managed to accompany her brother to a function a couple of months later.

In addition to commissioning his portrait, Ede's union colleagues arranged for the NUT to institute

> an annual lecture to be given by a prominent person not actually engaged in the field of education but able to speak on the contribution of education as he sees it from his particular field of activity, be it politics, business, commerce, industry or some aspect of the cultural life of the nation … a very appropriate way to honour the outstanding services rendered to the Union, the education service, and the nation, by the Rt Hon James Chuter Ede.[90]

The inaugural Chuter Ede Lecture was given by Rab Butler on 22 March 1962.[91] The occasion was to be chaired by Clem Attlee but, owing to his ill health, he was replaced by a Labour colleague with a similar background to Ede's, Jim Griffiths, who said he had entered Parliament in 1936, when he had come to know both Butler and Ede. He had been told of Ede, 'You watch that man. He knows Parliamentary procedure inside out. He knows the rules so well that he can play offside, because he knows when the referee is not looking.'

In the presence of both Jim and Nell Ede, Butler gave an account of the 1944 Education Act, and paid tribute to Ede's part in it. He claimed they had much in common from the start, being both at Corpus Christi College, Cambridge, and had worked together to get the Act agreed, not least by Archbishop Temple and the churches. When the audience discussed the talk, Ede made a gracious reply, putting Butler right about which was his college, and saying he felt as though he was attending his own funeral and the wake afterwards. On the religious question, he recalled one talk he had given in Chicago, where he had given an account of his English schooldays. He compared the school's act of collective worship with the US custom of saluting the flag – 'among the heathen that is a collective act of worship'. He told some of his regular anecdotes – the news he would start school the day after his sister (now sitting with him) was born, and his response to being introduced as one who started life as a teacher: 'I started life as a pupil, and I have been on the side of the underdog ever since.' To finish he described himself as a 'congenital Nonconformist. How ... I have remained in the Labour Party without being chucked out, is a mystery.'

Among his Unitarian duties in 1962 was a visit to the Scarborough Church on 22 April, when he spoke about Charles II's Act of Uniformity, 300 years before. The Act had caused large numbers of clergy to become Nonconformists, when they refused to adhere to the Anglican Church and Prayer Book, and Ede gave a historical review of those and subsequent events. One of the ministers he cited was Richard Frankland, another member of Christ's, ejected from his ecclesiastical post; he had been directed towards a position at the New College in Durham, established by Cromwell as a university for the North of England, but that had not survived. Ede's conclusion of the history of the time was a plea for scientific, as well as ecclesiastical, tolerance.

As an indication of his ecumenical approach, he also engaged with the Catholic bishops during these years, about their educational concerns. Many of the issues dealt with by the 1944 Act kept recurring, in particular pleas about the funding Church schools should receive. The free churchmen would then express their doubts. Having used his good offices with the Ministry of Education in July 1962, he then showed a party of American Ursuline nuns around the House of Commons.[92]

His constituency retained their affection for their departing member. Over the years he had been on several excursions with the South Shields Archaeological and Historical Society, and had been elected their president. In October 1962 the members elected him president for a second time.[93] His activities in the House of Commons included further debate on ecclesiastical matters on 14 December 1962, when he explained, 'Ecclesiastically I am a Congregationalist'. He was vexed that the *Daily Telegraph* abbreviated this to a statement of his just being 'a Congregationalist', since he had gone on to say he was a Nonconformist, in contrast to his old colleague George Thomas, a Free Churchman. This distinction, which he had made before, seems to be that, while he mainly attended a Congregationalist Church, he did not adhere to any faith, but insisted on being able to think and find his faith for himself.[94]

The following week, he spoke about the proposals to reform the British Museum, of which he had been a trustee for nearly twenty years, first *ex officio*, and then co-opted for life. On 13 October Ede had been at the Standing Committee when it received a report from the subcommittee considering a British Museum Bill, which endorsed strongly the view he advocated, that availability of the Museum's collections to students of whatever degree was a principle that, as in the past, should govern its administration. The Museum nominally included the Natural History Museum in Kensington, though this had its own trustees and director, and the Government decided it should have a separate identity, a proposal which had been debated since Darwin's time. In addition, the Museum library was overflowing, and a new building and repositories were needed (the subcommittee had stressed how dissatisfied the Trustees were about their limited storage capacity), while their powers to lend or dispose of Museum property required updating. Finally, the archaic structure of its Trustee board, with fifty-one members and a Standing Committee of twenty, was in need of reform. John Boyd-Carpenter, the Minister who introduced the Bill on 20 December 1962, thanked Ede among a number of those who had helped to develop the measure. Ede spoke, to confirm that a trustee appointment should not be for life, though he was uncomfortable about separating off the Natural History Museum, feeling it would add to the dangers of dividing the sciences from the arts. He was very encouraging about most of the changes, and also wanted the status of the employees at the Museum to be put on a formal basis.

By 1963, the mood in the Labour Party was changing. The South Shields party had acquired a new headquarters, to replace the offices they rented in Laygate, from which every election had been fought. The new building was to be 'Ede House', and Hugh Gaitskell, the Party leader, was to open it on 19 January. He had had to cry off because of illness, and then died the evening before.[95] The opening went ahead in a sombre mood. His early, unexpected death prevented Gaitskell leading the Party into the next election which it seemed likely they would win, and there was a leadership contest between Harold Wilson, George Brown and Jim Callaghan. Ede had done some work with Brown, whom he had known in Parliament since 1945; in March 1962 Brown had approached him on behalf of residents of Bisley, not far from the extreme western border of Surrey, who were opposing the suggestion that a prison should be sited there.[96] According to the account of George Wigg,[97] Ede supported Brown, the party's Deputy Leader, but the comfortable winner was his cabinet colleague from the 1940s, Wilson, who was nearly victorious on the first ballot.

One of Ede's last campaigns related to the London Government Bill, which Macmillan's government promoted to reflect London's huge expansion since it became a county in its own right in 1889. A Royal Commission had reported in 1960, recommending that 'Greater London' should become a local government area, and this had included a large tract of northern Surrey. Charles Hill, the minister responsible, published his own plan in 1961, and in May 1962 reduced this area after discussions, but continued to argue that the northern part of Epsom and Ewell (essentially, the Stoneleigh estate) should be part of a new Greater London borough. Initially, this had been Sutton (along with Cheam, Banstead, Wallington, Beddington and Carshalton); subsequently, in June 1962, the Epsom councillors argued that, if three wards had to be separated at all, it should be to the Borough of Kingston upon Thames (covering also Surbiton, Malden and Coombe), though they still opposed the whole plan. Ede joined many in Ewell and in Epsom in opposing the idea that their Borough should be divided up or absorbed into London. The local Labour Party told him they believed the entire London reorganisation was motivated by political malice to the Labour LCC.[98] 'I took part in all the preliminaries for the obtaining of a charter for the Borough of Epsom and Ewell, which has the great distinction of being the only borough to be torn in two parts by the Bill', he said on 23 January 1963, insisting on the special status of a chartered borough, different from that of some of the 'boroughs' which would make up Greater London.

He took part in the Standing Committee, and spoke several times on the Bill, which was widely opposed by Labour, concentrating his efforts on the effect on the Surrey local authorities. Coulsdon and Purley were strongly opposed to amalgamation with Croydon, and on 20 February he used his knowledge of all those places to support their opposition. His next speech covered Epsom and Ewell, which for years had been surrounded by natural barriers, with plans preventing them becoming absorbed into continuous suburbia. A survey of the residents of the three wards proposed to be included in Kingston had overwhelmingly supported remaining in Epsom and in Surrey. One of Epsom's features was that the Downs provided 'a great Cockney festival' each year, for London people to leave the capital, thanks to the Epsom and Walton Downs Regulation Act, to which he had contributed in 1936, and for which the ratepayers of the Borough contributed. Cyril Black, the Conservative MP for Wimbledon, who supported all the Surrey opponents to the changes, suggested the government was trying to expand Kingston to make it a viable size. Keith Joseph, who had succeeded Hill as minister, was not to be moved, and Ede's amendment was defeated, though Black voted with Labour in the division.

However, the story ended happily for Ede and the people of Epsom and Ewell. When the Bill went to the House of Lords, one of the amendments on which the Government was defeated was on the boundary of the Borough of Kingston, to exclude the three Epsom wards. On 25 July 1963, the Government proposed that the Lords amendment be agreed, and Ede received a telegram (on a congratulatory form) from the Mayor of Epsom, thanking him.[99] Ede, the first to speak in the Commons, was not gracious in victory, saying a great deal of time would have been saved if his proposal had been accepted on 20 February, that he could not understand the Minister stating he disagreed but had decided to accept the change, and assuring him that if 'this absurd proposal' were revived, it would be opposed by Epsom and Ewell more heartily than ever.

On 1 August he was a guest of the Mayor of Epsom, speaking at a cocktail party to celebrate the defeat of the proposal that all or any of the Borough should leave Surrey.[100] To this day, the map of Greater London shows a gap between Sutton to the east, and to the west the 'peninsula' of Chessington, part of Kingston, sticking out into Surrey. That gap comprises the northern part of Epsom and Ewell, which in fact acquired London telephone numbers, so close they are to the capital, when they went entirely numerical.

As for Kingston, it became the least populous London borough, apart from Kensington and Chelsea near the centre, with much the smallest population of any of the outer boroughs.

On party issues, Ede was of less influence with the leaders, but tried to play his part from the backbenches, especially covering Home Office affairs. In May 1963 he backed a motion of censure against Henry Brooke, the Home Secretary, for failing to reveal that Chief Anthony Enahoro, a Nigerian leader, would not get legal representation over an application by his government to have him extradited, a position well covered by his local paper on Tyneside.[101] This was a useful problem to throw at the government, bringing in human rights issues, and harking back to the difficulties with extradition which Ede had had himself, nearly twenty years earlier. He also remained active in the Royal London Prisoners Aid Society, which he had supported with Lilian many years before, taking part in its sponsoring committee.[102]

The greatest scandal at this point, however, concerned John Profumo, the Secretary of State for War, and his involvement with Stephen Ward, Christine Keeler and others. The matter involved three issues. First, there was sex, which naturally interested the press most; Profumo, a married man, had had a short affair with Keeler, who was living in Ward's home, and other men and women had had brief relationships which the media were keen to cover. Secondly, there was national security, as one of the men concerned was a Soviet diplomat; he might have posed a risk for security if he was sharing a mistress with a minister, particularly one with a defence role. This aspect of the case was largely fabricated to give it some weight, so as to justify politicians asking questions, and so the opposition could embarrass Macmillan and his Government. George Wigg was one of the main Labour Party voices pursuing this. Then, last, was the falsehood perpetrated by Profumo, when he was induced to make a statement to the Commons, primarily aimed at repudiating any suggestion of a security breach, potential or actual, but which included the statement that 'there was no impropriety whatsoever in my acquaintanceship with Miss Keeler'. That was completely untrue, and ended with Profumo's resignation, not just from the Government, but as an MP and from the Privy Council also.

A recent account of the Profumo affair[103] does not mention Ede's role at all. Perhaps that is just as well, because in hindsight almost everyone concerned comes out badly. However, he was involved enough to ask a Parliamentary Question of Brooke, as part of George Wigg's plan. A more junior Labour MP, Ben Parkin, had put down a question, but was encouraged to withdraw it, in favour of one from somebody with more weight. Wigg drove with Jim and Nell Ede to watch the Coronation Cup at Epsom on 30 May 1963, having decided that, as a former Home Secretary and held in high regard on all sides of the House, Ede was the right person next day to ask a question Wigg himself had drafted[104] – what information had Brooke received from Stephen Ward in connection with police enquiries into his own activities? In fact, it was well known that Ward was complaining that the police were making life difficult for his 'patients and friends' (he was an osteopath, and his 'friends' presumably included Keeler and other women), to cover up, he thought, the fact that Profumo had lied. No real answer was expected, but it did the trick; Profumo confessed his adultery to his wife the same day, and resigned the next week.

By the middle of June, Parliament was in a 'frenzy', according to the journalist Anthony Sampson, as recounted by Davenport-Hines, whose own phrase is 'parliamentary hysterics'. On 17 June, Ede experienced a 'lop-sided' debate, as he put it in a letter to Wigg, with too much prominence given to Privy Counsellors. He decided not to intervene, but felt Wigg's own contribution was 'vigorous and noteworthy'. In fact Wigg had briefed Wilson to speak, condemning the government, about running a 'system which pays a harlot 25 times as much as … the Prime Minister, 250 times as much as .. Members of Parliament, and 500 times as much as … ministers of religion'. For Ede it was 'the worst day I have ever spent in Parliament'.

Later that summer, an enquiry was held into the scandal under Alfred Denning, now in the Lords and Master of the Rolls, and Ede noted he had not been asked to testify. He was no longer significant enough to be asked to give evidence. However, the Denning Report did elicit one interesting reaction from him. He disagreed with its assertion that 'since 1952 the Home Secretary and not the Prime Minister had been responsible for the Security Service. When I was Home Secretary I always regarded myself as responsible. The Home Secretary must always bear responsibility for security', as the Special Branch is responsible to him. In 1945 there was a Ministry of Home Security, headed by the Home Secretary, he insisted.[105]

In 1963 Ede also became concerned about the reaction to an article written by Arthur Koestler in *The Observer*. Koestler was anxious about Communist infiltration into British politics in general, and in particular the Labour Party, and James Luther Adams, an influential Unitarian at Harvard and the Arlington Street Church, had raised it with some alarm. Ede's reaction illustrates the calm refusal to panic which was characteristic of him. Communists exploit dissatisfaction, he said, and concentrate particularly on trade unions, where there is considerable apathy, but they seldom make any political headway. He cited South Shields, which suffered most acutely during the 1930s, and again at present, but at 'an election in which over 44,000 votes were polled the Communist's share of that total was only 400'.[106]

There are signs here that his recall of events, once so exceptional, was beginning to falter. The only election when he had a Communist opponent was 1950, at neither of the periods he mentioned; the candidate did indeed poll about 400, but the turnout then was nearly 60,000. The election with 44,000 votes had been his first victory in South Shields, in 1929, and his opponents then had been a Liberal and a Conservative. However, Ede had lost none of his humour, concluding 'if this present Government doesn't make more converts to the CP nothing will.' Adams visited London that summer, and Ede was at pains to invite him and his family to the Commons.

By the autumn of 1963, he and Nell recognised it was time he moved from his oversized house at Tayles Hill to her home at 172 East Street. She had been living there for most of her life, though she doubtless stayed much of the time at Tayles Hill, acting as his housekeeper after Lilian's death nearly twenty years before. They circulated change of address cards, effective from 26 September, confirming the change of telephone number from Ewell 3300 or 5600 to Epsom 2969 – in February 1964 it changed to 22969.[107] They cleared out his papers, records and archives, with a significant amount being thrown away, though the amount retained was vast, and would two years later generate considerable work for his personal representatives. It was clear by this stage that he was in his last months in the Commons, and he gave up his membership of the Oxford and Cambridge University Club in 1963.

There was a long Parliamentary recess that autumn, and after the House adjourned on 2 August Ede made no further contribution for the rest of the year. Perhaps his health did not permit him to come back for the Queen's Speech in November or the next few weeks. The last speech he made was on the morning of the adjournment debate, and concerned another case of capital murder. James Hanratty had been hanged in April 1962 for the 'A6 murder' committed in August 1961, on the evidence in particular of the victim's lover, who had been raped and shot in the course of the crime. Though there were a number of problems with the conviction, including a doubtful alibi and a confession by another criminal, Butler could not agree to commute the sentence; but within a few months a request was made for Henry Brooke, who had succeeded him as Home Secretary, to set up an enquiry into the case. Several MPs supported the request, and Ede was one. Brooke, however, was not to be moved. Ede had no connection with the case, but he was by now convinced that 'the traditional belief in the infallibility of the British legal system' no longer existed.

His support for matters educational did not flag. On 20 September he went to Eastbourne, to address a meeting of the Campaign for Education (an NUT exercise) on 'Educational Development to Meet Modern Needs'. The event was chaired by his old colleague, Hartley Shawcross, who told him, 'You really have not changed at all since' their days in government.[108] He spoke to a similar meeting at Aldershot on 14 November, and took Nell to the Campaign's Rally at the Albert Hall on 28 November.

During the recess, Macmillan resigned as Prime Minister, believing his health was failing, and it was widely thought that Butler at last would head the Government. In fact, the position went to the Foreign Secretary, Lord Home. He appointed Butler to the Foreign Office, renounced his own earldom and took a seat in the Commons. It was no more than a year before he would need to call an election, and Ede was preparing to retire. He kept in touch with his constituency, going there on 6 March 1964 for a visit of the Duke of Edinburgh, who was opening the South Shields Marine and Technical College, an educational interest he would not have overlooked.

He maintained to the end his belief in free speech. In January 1964 he received a letter from a doctor, Margaret Eastwood, who recalled him from his time at Surrey and her teenage years at the Wimbledon County School for Girls, about the bad influences of the BBC on young people. She was aware of a forthcoming debate in the House on BBC standards, presumably knew of his previous BBC connections, and complained the broadcasters promoted adultery, contraception outside marriage, and other evils. Ede replied that 'I do not think censorship … would do other than create a feeling that unofficial opposition … indicated that people were afraid of freedom of utterance. I … am not inclined to enter into any controversy on the subject.' He took no part in the debate.[109]

One of the final causes he took up as an MP was that of a resident in Carshalton, once in his own constituency, who wanted to use his home for religious purposes. In May and June 1964, he lobbied Keith Joseph, the Minister of Housing and Local Government, about a change in the planning decision to prevent this as a change of use. Surely it was a use incidental to that of a dwelling house? Joseph told him that the circumstances, as investigated, showed the lounge would be turned into a meeting room, with chairs of a church type, accommodating up to 35 people. That was not merely incidental. Ede was obliged to accept the decision.

It was around this time that Ede must have assisted Ronald Manzer in his book on *Teachers and Politics*. Although Manzer did not publish this until

1970, he acknowledged the help Ede had given him during his research. Though mostly about the role of the NUT in educational policy since 1944, and so covering a later period than his main involvement in the field, Manzer was able to establish the nature of how the Union operated, mainly depending on local organisations, dominated by an 'active minority'. All we know about Chuter and Lilian Ede, John Strudwick, AE Baxter and their colleagues supports this, and all we know about Ede himself shows his willingness to help those enquiring about the past.

Chapter 18

Lord of Epsom

The General Election of 1964 was held on 15 October, five years and one week after the previous election in 1959. Although it was sometimes said that (until 2011) an election must be held within five years of the previous one, the constitution merely limited the old Parliament to a life of five years. That had been the requirement since the Septennial Act had been amended in 1911, and so it was open to the Prime Minister to delay the dissolution until the five years had elapsed, and then call an election subsequently. Douglas-Home, having been PM for less than a year, did so.

Chuter Ede had made his final contributions to the Commons in July, on two disparate subjects. On 23 July, the subject was Maltese independence. He recalled he had visited Malta as a member of the Round Table Conference in 1955, and so understood the historical circumstances of the British presence there. The Maltese, with British help, had thrown out the garrison Napoleon had left there on his way to Egypt, and had then asked to become a British colony, with the proviso that they were permitted to retain their Catholic religion. While he felt that condition must be respected, he was alarmed that the draft constitution of independent Malta extended the principle to requiring that all state education must be Roman Catholic, and that only Catholic teachers could be employed anywhere in the country's education service.

That was, of course, in complete antithesis to the dual system which Ede had done so much to perpetuate in England and Wales, and in which he firmly believed. The Catholic authorities were strongly behind it in this country, and he expressed himself perturbed by how different their attitude was in a country where they were in a majority. He knew his views on this, and other points in the draft constitution, would have little influence, but all the same he was prepared to the end to speak in support of the educational principles he had always supported.

Finally, a week later, he made a short intervention on the Vestures of Ministers Measure, a seemingly esoteric matter referred to Parliament by the Church of England Assembly. The point he made was that, as a Nonconformist, he regretted that Church of England matters should come before the House at all, but that he would follow the wishes of his constituents who in large numbers had, remarkably, expressed strongly favourable views on it. In the course of his short speech, he implied that he opposed the country having an established church at all.

With that, he bowed out of the House, which on 31 July 1964 adjourned for the summer recess, until 19 October, a date set by the government, clearly an artificial date, as Parliament would have to be dissolved sooner, as it was on 25 September. In the *Shields Gazette* that day, a tribute put him second only to Churchill among the retiring MPs as 'a good House of Commons man', and concluded that a life peerage would be a fitting tribute to him. The journalist who wrote it, Cyril de Gruchy, interviewed Ede, who spoke about his time at the Home Office, and in particular his regrets over Timothy Evans, but confirmed that it was his time at Education which gave him most pleasure, his 'peak achievement', though the 11-plus system had given him dissatisfaction subsequently. As if to demonstrate his priorities had not changed, he went to Dartington Hall on 10 October, five days before the election, to speak to the South-West Area Conference for Young Teachers, of the Devon & Cornwall NUT.[1] His theme was the 1944 Act and the years following.

A group of forty-one Labour colleagues joined together to present Ede with an appropriate gift – *A History of the Derby Stakes*, which was found, signed by them all, after his death.[2]

The Labour candidate chosen to replace Ede at South Shields was Arthur Blenkinsop, an experienced Tyneside politician who had been a junior minister under Attlee, and a Newcastle MP for fourteen years until losing his seat in 1959. He shared his predecessor's love of the countryside, of conservation and of walking, being in his time President of the Ramblers Association. They had worked together on the executive of the Open Spaces Society. In Blenkinsop's case, his territory was the Borders, rather than Surrey. Indeed, he would die fifteen years later, still in his sixties, while rambling there.[3] Blenkinsop retained South Shields by 29,694 votes to 16,344, not achieving quite Ede's poll of 1959, but increasing the majority through a sharp fall in the Conservative vote. In the country as a whole, the Labour Party gained enough seats to reach a slim majority, Douglas-Home resigned in favour of Harold Wilson, and the Labour Party was in government once more.

Early in December, it was announced that Ede had been given a life peerage, to enable him to sit in the House of Lords. This was contrary to what he had said early in his career, but time had moved on, and he was now in retirement. When choosing as his title 'Lord Chuter-Ede of Epsom', he changed his surname by deed poll to Chuter-Ede, so becoming James Chuter Chuter-Ede.[4] While this may seem odd today, there was at the time keen resistance to peers incorporating their forenames into their titles. The form 'Lord Thomas Jones', though familiar enough nowadays as a colloquialism when Mr Thomas Jones is ennobled, has properly been reserved as a courtesy title for the sons of dukes and marquesses. A few earlier attempts to incorporate Christian names had succeeded. Field Marshal Sir Alan Brooke had been created Lord Alanbrooke in 1945, and the Cabinet Secretary, Norman Brook, had become Lord Normanbrook in 1963, but both had names which could easily elide together. The journalist Francis Williams, whose work has been cited in this biography, managed to hyphenate his names to become Lord Francis-Williams in 1962, Lord Ritchie-Calder did the same in 1966, Lord George-Brown in 1970, and Ede's former War Coalition colleague Lord Geoffrey-Lloyd in 1974. The last two at least, changed their surname in order to achieve this. It was said the College of Arms obliged Chuter Ede also to do so.[5]

On 10 December 1964, the *Epsom and Ewell Advertiser* took the opportunity to announce the peerage, with a description of Ede's career, and a list of the positions he had held over the years.[6] It reads rather like the core of a prepared obituary, modified for the occasion, which indeed the same paper would be publishing a few months later. Meanwhile, he received a large batch of letters, which together created a further file of congratulations. When thanking John Kielty, the Unitarian Secretary, for his letter, he said that in discharging his duties in the Lords, he hoped he could continue to be of help to the work of the General Assembly.

He also hoped he could go on assisting the NUT, and carefully worded a request for his Union sponsorship to continue. He pointed out that his MP's salary had been £1,750 and, with £350 from the Union, he was now facing a reduction of £2,100 a year. His only income would be a £200 annuity, £24/8/8 teacher's pension, £179 from investments, and £30 from rental. It seems the NUT agreed to continue the £350 allowance, so he could speak for them in the Lords, though his educational contribution was now limited.

On 21 January 1965, Ede was able to pay tribute to an old friend, at a dinner in Kingston marking John Strudwick's retirement as General Secretary of the SCTA, a post he had held for twenty years. Together, they had managed the Association for effectively half a century. Ede had to decline an invitation to the SCTA's AGM on 30 January, as he was attending Churchill's State Funeral. However, having continued to attend the NUT Conference, in Margate and Blackpool the two previous years, he managed to get to a final one, held in 1965 in the Isle of Man, which had once come under his supervision.

He did not play a large part in the Lords. In July 1965, Attlee recorded that he himself was the only one of his generation of Labour politicians who still attended the House, apart from Ede.[7] However, only two speeches by Ede are recorded.[8] On 9 February 1965, he spoke on the Commons Registration Bill, recalling his time as President of the Commons Open Spaces and Footpaths Preservation Society, which was celebrating its centenary year. The Bill aimed to get registers of common land, and town and village greens, drawn up, together with claims of rights of common or ownership of the land, and the Society was at the forefront of promoting it, following a report of a Royal Commission on the subject.

The main point he made was that getting those with rights of common to register was extremely difficult unless, he felt, 'the people in the big house' were such bad neighbours that villagers took the opportunity to provide information against them. He had experience of promoting Bills to regulate Walton and Epsom Downs, and elsewhere, and even after advertising for claimants, no replies were received. The commons had become an amenity for recreation of urban dwellers, and all connection with their original agricultural purpose had disappeared. Future governments would need to repeat the exercise of updating the commons' registers as a routine task. Lord Chorley, who had succeeded Ede as the Society's President, identified this as a maiden speech, and congratulated him on it. The congratulations were echoed by other peers.

Ede probably thought that his broadcasting days had ended with a five-minute BBC talk, 'Voice of the People', recorded conveniently in Newcastle in March 1962, but on May 1965, he spoke on the radio one final time. For the Open Spaces Society he made an appeal on the BBC's 'Week's Good Cause' programme. He was unsure about doing so, as 'my experience on this type of production is a very unhappy one and I do not regard myself as a very suitable person to make an appeal'. His reticence is a mystery, as he was a frequent broadcaster. He had once before made an appeal, while Home Secretary in May 1949 for the memorial fund for the penologist Alec Paterson; perhaps he felt that had not been a success. In fact, he managed this broadcast, which raised about £500, including £100 from the Ramblers Association.[9]

In view of the warmth in which his maiden speech was received, it is strange that, when he made his final intervention in the Lords later in the year, he claimed to be addressing the House for the first time, the speaker following him identified his address as a maiden speech, and it was the subject of further commendation.

This was on 20 July 1965, during the debate on abolishing the death penalty, on which of course Ede could speak with concern and authority. The abolition Bill had come to the Lords from the Commons, and was now in its Second Reading. This time, it was supported by the Lord Chancellor and the Lord Chief Justice. Ede did not mention Timothy Evans, though other peers did. It was a short and rather unimpressive speech, but he followed it with his vote in favour of the Bill, which was passed by 204 to 104, on a free vote, and sent to Committee. On 21 July, Ede was one of a delegation which went to see the Home Secretary, Frank Soskice, who, having previously supported the Evans campaign, had himself declined in February to reopen the case, and had been criticised for changing his mind. Unsuccessful, the campaigners formed a Timothy Evans Committee, launched at a press conference on 28 July, which Ede and Kennedy attended.[10] In the words of Kevin Jefferys in the *Dictionary of National Biography*, his campaign for Evans was 'the last struggle of a liberal nonconformist of the old school'. When the Murder (Abolition of Death Penalty) Act was passed, capital punishment for murder was stopped for a trial period of five years, subsequently to be made permanent, and so never carried out in the country again. The Act also repealed the Capital Punishment Amendment Act, which Rab Butler had said prohibited the transfer of Evans's remains to consecrated ground.

So Chuter Ede lived just long enough to see one of his causes achieved. The Act received royal assent on 8 November 1965, and came into effect the following day. On 10 November, Soskice authorized Timothy Evans's body to be removed from the Pentonville graveyard, transferred to his next-of-kin, and then reburied in Leytonstone.[11] The press had believed the burial would be at Greenford but, to put them off the scent, the solicitor in charge got the Home Office to authorise a decoy car to leave Pentonville first, thus avoiding an unseemly media circus while the ceremony took place.[12] The reburial was much less than the Timothy Evans Committee sought, but Soskice did also agree to a further enquiry.

It is unlikely Ede knew much of these successes. According to Michael Noakes, his lost his mind towards the end.[13] His health certainly deteriorated, he suffered a fall at his home in September 1965, hitting his head, and moved from the house in East Street into a nursing home at Wilmar Lodge, Epsom Road, Ewell, after a week in hospital, where it had been discovered he had prostate problems.[14] The home is very close to Tayles Hill, where he had lived until shortly before, and still operates, under the name The Elders Care Home. It is a large Victorian house, used previously as a maternity home, and has been extended over time. Nell Ede wrote to John Kielty about it, saying 'you will have noticed how rapidly he has aged lately'. When Kielty wrote back with his concern, Nell got their secretary, Mrs Saker, to ask if he could make a visit, and explain that the doctor was unwilling to let him have an operation, in view of his age. Kielty, however, was out of the country, and Ede died at about 6.30 am on 11 November, Armistice Day.

The following day, the newspapers were quick to issue his obituary. According to *The Guardian*,[15] 'he was a steadying voice on the right' of the Labour Party, second only to Churchill (who had died ten months earlier) in his ability to entertain the House. To *The Times*, he 'was one of the most sensible politicians of his generation', bringing to the House 'the finest qualities of the best type of schoolmaster – patience, good humour, tolerance, and an acute instinct for detecting humbug and woolly-mindedness'.[16] Most of what was written is an account of what you may have read here in more detail, but *The Times* obituary is striking by the amount of space it devotes to the issue of capital punishment. Kielty wrote to *The Times*, adding remarks about Ede's contribution to Unitarianism, and his pride in occupying the former pulpit of William E Channing – a founding father of Boston Unitarianism and champion of religious freedom. He said Ede had greater admiration for the men of Marston Moor and Naseby, 'who stayed at home and fought it out', than for the Pilgrim Fathers, but their friends in Boston took the point generously.

Local papers, such as the *Epsom and Ewell Advertiser* and the *Surrey Comet* issued their own obituaries later in November.[17] The *Advertiser* was particularly pleased to report that he had never missed the Derby, and reported on his local activities, including the Epsom and Walton Downs Regulation Act, and preserving Epsom and Ewell Borough intact from local government reorganisation. Louis White, the vice-chairman of Surrey CC, added some words, referring to the portrait of Ede in County Hall, and to his statement that his service on the County Council gave him the greatest pleasure of any part of his public service. It also included a warm tribute from John Strudwick, who had long worked with him as a Labour councillor and alderman in Surrey, and at the SCTA, under the headline 'one of the Giants of Local Government'.

In Strudwick's view, Ede's contribution to local government ranked with that of Joseph Chamberlain and Herbert Morrison, or even eclipsed theirs, as he did not lead the majority party in his area. So, as well as recounting his national career, he described the new hospitals built in the inter-war period, management of flooding on the Wey, eight by-passes originating with his planning, and his environmental concerns – Norbury Park, Newlands Corner and Ranmore, and Leith Hill. Strudwick was unsure whether Morrison or

Ede had coined the phrase "Green Belt" in 1935, but he gave them both credit for creating the open space between London and Surrey, though at the same time Ede led the development of estates in Carshalton, Banstead and St Helier. The St Helier estate was described as 'controversial', as where 'there had been a stretch of farm lands, the massed houses of the descendants of those people who could find no separate homes in London now stand'. Nonetheless, after that slightly ambiguous compliment, he finished with an echo of the famous tribute to Christopher Wren in St Paul's, '*si monumentum requiris, circumspice*': 'if in Surrey you want a monument to Chuter Ede, look about you'.

The *Surrey Comet*'s obituary,[18] under the headline 'Surrey is Deeply in his Debt', covered two columns and more, listing Ede's life, achievements and interests, adding to it a 'Comment' column, remarking 'it is difficult to know where to begin a humble tribute'. It described him as 'the policeman's friend' while Home Secretary, and one of the draftsman of Surrey CC's long-lasting standing orders. As to the Green Belt, it resolved Strudwick's hesitation by confidently stating the phrase was coined in correspondence between Ede and Morrison (in fact, the concept was much older, being used by Octavia Hill, founder of the National Trust, early in the century, though in the sense we now understand it the phrase may have come into use in the 1930s). It concluded

> he would rest content if he felt that what he had done in numerous fields in years gone by had provided the sound foundations on which subsequent generations of administrators could continue to build with confidence.

In the case of the Unitarian movement, John Kielty wrote an obituary[19] in its journal *The Inquirer*, applauding Ede's success in including a Unitarian representative among those at the Remembrance Day service, and that 'unlike so many, when he became a national figure he strove to emphasise rather than hide his Unitarianism'. He recalled his hard work in visiting churches around the country and on his trip to America, and quoted from his address to the Chicago Assembly in 1958. As for his attachment to Epsom, Kielty added 'though he considered gambling a mug's game he had a deep love of horse-racing ... Often on Derby Day, possibly because he was indifferent to the gambling side of it, he often "picked the winner".' To illustrate the man, it included a photo of him and other European delegates at the 1955 Belfast Congress of the IARF. On 11 December, *The Inquirer*'s London Diary reported a note from the Revd J. Reece Walker, who became a pupil teacher at the same time as Ede, some 60 years earlier. 'Truly a great Unitarian', he said. 'Between us, Chuter Ede and I had 120 years' unbroken membership of the National Union of Teachers'.

The NUT's own tribute,[20] headed 'The Union's Greatest Man', called him a distinguished Home Secretary, for whom 'the monument to his disappointment' at never being Minister of Education 'still stands in the children's committees being connected with the Home Office rather than the Ministry of Education'. Ede had said Education was 'the one Ministry that deals in hope', but quoted his remark about leaving every Surrey Education meeting frustrated at the lack of progress. But as for progress 'towards giving every child the opportunity to develop its talent to the full', nobody 'has made a bigger contribution ... That, and the unspoilt state of some of his beloved Surrey hills, are his true memorial.' That obituary was attributed to 'a Special Correspondent', and one suspects the hand was that of John Strudwick again, or else his Union colleague Edward Britton.

By the time the local papers (other than the *Comet*) and the journals had issued these obituaries, Ede's funeral had already been held. With a speed uncharacteristic of today's funeral directors, the service was organised, under the supervision of Epsom's Town Clerk,[21] for Tuesday 16 November 1965, three working days after his death on Thursday 11. Despite his nonconformist convictions, the funeral was to be held at St Martin's Parish Church, Epsom.

By 9.00 the Town Clerk has been told of the death by the doctor, had rung the Mayor and the Deputy, and was speaking to Nell Ede. He then told the press, arranged to go early that afternoon with the Deputy Mayor to visit Nell, who confirmed she wanted him to take over the arrangements, and then saw the undertaker. He was soon speaking to the Vicar of St Martin's, confirming the arrangements to the Mayor, and finalising arrangements for a Government minister to give the address.

He got funeral notices into *The Times* and other papers on Friday 12 November, while more details of the service were being finalised. By Monday 15, arrangements were being made about seating. Nell stated that the personal mourners would not exceed six, in the first row on the right of the nave. Interestingly, she indicated that, as well as members of Chuter Ede's secretariat, there could be 'a number of others who claimed to be kinsmen of his'. On the Thursday she had said she was the last surviving member of the family, so who could these claimed kinsmen be? A clue may lie in the 1952 visit to the Fromow and Merrett families in Devon, the 1961 visit to the Swindon school where his great-nieces were pupils, or the trip that summer, taken by 'you, Miss Ede and your two nieces, Julia and Theresa Fromow'.[22] Perhaps Nell was thinking of the wider family of Lilian Ede. Whatever the answer, a further fifteen seats were to be reserved, in the third pew, behind Ellen Ede and her party at the front, and the Queen's representative in row two.

The Town Clerk contacted his former Chief Clerk to come in to supervise the ushers and allocate accommodation in the church. When the occasion arrived, there was a procession of dignitaries, but the Town Clerk noticed that Surrey's Lord Lieutenant, the Earl of Munster, was sitting near the back of the church. He twice had to send a message to Lord Munster to get him to sit next to the Queen's representative in the second pew.

The service was conducted by the vicar, with the minister of Epsom Congregational Church also present.[23] Six Epsom policemen carried in his coffin, a tribute which not all Home Secretaries would achieve. This was Ellen Ede's suggestion; she recalled the police had acted as bearers at Lilian's funeral. It was a short service, comprising three hymns ('The King of love my Shepherd is', 'Sing we of the golden city', and Bunyan's pilgrim hymn, 'Who would true valour see'), one lesson (read by the Congregational minister), one psalm, prayers and an address. The lesson was the first seven verses of *Revelation*, chapter 21 – the new heaven and earth, and the new Jerusalem coming down with God from heaven. The psalm was 'I will lift up mine eyes unto the hills' (Psalm 121), perhaps to recall Ede's work in what we would now call environmental causes, and his love of the Epsom and Walton Downs.

Arthur Peacock, a Unitarian minister who had watched the procession and then joined the service, recalled[24] that the first election in which he himself took part was the 1923 Mitcham by-election, which he described as 'sensational ... it was then that I got to know Ede. I wonder if his orthodox sister knew they sang a hymn by a humanist ...!' That presumably referred to 'Sing we of the golden city', the least well known of the three hymns, written by Felix Adler, a Jewish German-American of highly unorthodox religious views.

The address was given, as suggested by the Town Clerk to Nell, by George Wigg, Ede's associate in a number of endeavours. Wigg was still in the House of Commons, and at the time Paymaster-General in Wilson's new Government, where he acted as the Prime Minister's factotum in various projects. He was given a portable microphone to put round his neck, and his obsequies for Ede were as glowing as would be expected, referring to a forty year association between the two men.

We have a detailed account of this tribute, from Wigg himself. The memoirs of retired politicians often suffer from a degree of self-importance, and Wigg's live comfortably up to that – he quoted at some length a generous selection of what he had written or said over the years. We know that Ede himself refused to write a memoir, regarding such publications from his colleagues with contempt, because 'these people prove that they never made a mistake'.[25] In the case of such as Wigg, the benefit is that a direct and detailed quotation can in turn be made when the occasion calls for it. He said:

> James Chuter Ede was described by *The Times* as one of the most sensible politicians of his generation. That statement is true. A man does not serve the community as he did, both locally and nationally over so many years, without having his feet firmly planted on the ground. It is certainly true that he had the capacity to get to the heart of a problem. He never made quick, harsh judgments. He thought in terms of men and women and not in terms of statistics. He was at home with all sorts and conditions of men, women and children. He could make them laugh, for he had a joyous sense of humour.
>
> Perhaps his greatest gift was his capacity to understand. He could anticipate a need and often see a difficult situation before it occurred. He had an almost superhuman instinct for what ought to be done and how to do it. He preferred action to speech. He was ever on the watch for those who needed help. He was always gracious. He entered a humble dwelling with as much respect as he entered a lordly mansion. He could not patronise if he tried. He was always generous and yet strong in controversy. He was sometimes angry, for there was nothing sickly or sentimental about him. He knew how easy it is to sin, how difficult to live nobly.
>
> Yes, he was a sensible person, but the secret of Jim Chuter Ede, surely, is that he loved his fellow man. A man who lived as he did has gone right to the heart of things. He was no theologian but his faith in God was massive. My words this morning come from many discussions I have had with him. Indeed, I have gone for inspiration to a wonderful sermon preached by Dick Sheppard forty years ago, a sermon the essentials of which Jim and I often discussed. I can say of Jim today he would have me urge you not to mourn but to thank God for the wonders he performs.
>
> It is an essential part of humanity that we sorrow and it is right that we pay our respectful sympathies to those he loved, but we shall not have read aright the lesson of Jim Chuter Ede's life unless at this moment we thank God for it and try to profit for the example he gave us. Of one thing we can be sure, that the message he leaves with us is that for him, as for us, today is not the end but the beginning.[26]

Wigg said that he used as his source Sheppard's *The Human Parson*, a book published in 1925, a short collection of seven sermons given in Cambridge. It is hard to identify a particular one as the inspiration, but they are well in keeping with Ede's own style of preaching.

Nell Ede, with whom her brother had been living at 172 East Street, placed a single wreath on the coffin. There were about seventy floral tributes in all, many no doubt from the wide group of dignitaries with connections to the deceased's many activities. The Earl of Westmorland (promoted to a Duke in one local paper's report) represented the Queen, and Clem Attlee managed to attend, formally dressed under his silk hat.

Clement Attlee and Alice Bacon leaving the church after Ede's funeral in Epsom. (*By permission of the* Surrey Comet)

He looks frail in the press photos, escorted by Alice Bacon, herself a Home Office minister, in whose official car they had travelled. By her account, he said the morning suit and hat were very old, and asked on his way, 'I've been to a number of funerals lately of my old colleagues – do you think I will be the next?'[27] He had been widowed eighteen months earlier, and in fact had less than two years to live.

Attlee was quoted as describing Ede as a 'first-class Home Secretary, a very good man on local government, and an extremely wise man of great character and wit'.[28] At the funeral, all the local authorities with which Ede had been associated were represented, including South Shields, whose mayor must have had to make a sudden, long journey, in view of the short timescale provided to him. Representatives of various schools, unions and associations, churches, the police and the magistrates' bench were there. The total number attending was not known, but the 800 service sheets ordered proved adequate. St Martin's is a substantial church, with a broad shape, having been largely rebuilt in the early nineteenth century, but a congregation approaching 800 would have been a tight fit, though they doubtless felt Ede deserved it. The *Surrey Comet* account of the funeral described it as a 'tribute to Epsom's greatest son', a description echoed by one local historian there more recently.[29]

Like most of his family, James Chuter Ede's body was buried in Epsom Cemetery. Unfortunately, his grave there cannot be found. I assume he was buried in the same plot as Lilian, now dead for seventeen years, but her grave is not marked. There are several family graves of Edes and Chuters there, but the only relatives with a stone which is at all readable (and that not very well) are his grandmother Elizabeth Ede and (buried with her) his little sister Lizzie (Agnes Elizabeth) who had died in 1899. Behind it, looking towards the little cemetery chapel, is an area of open lawn, with a couple of flat graves, and many plots completely unmarked. Somewhere in that lawn, we can assume, lie Lilian Ede and James Chuter Chuter-Ede.

South Shields held its own memorial for their former MP, in the evening of 20 December, at St Hilda's Parish Church. A conventional service, it included familiar hymns ('The Lord's my Shepherd' to the tune 'Crimond', 'How Sweet the Name of Jesus Sounds', 'I Vow to thee, my Country' to Holst's music, and 'Abide with Me') as well as the standard funeral sentences and an address. Then, on 9 February 1966, a further service was held for him, at Essex Hall in London. It preceded a meeting of the General Assembly of the Unitarian and Free Christian Churches, and was conducted by John Kielty,[30] with whom Ede had corresponded so much in his later years. Again Lord Wigg (now representing Harold Wilson, the Prime Minister), the Police Commissioner and the Chairman of Surrey CC attended, along with representatives of the Government and Parliament, and of course Nell Ede. The service comprised just two hymns, both less well-known ('From age to age how grandly rise the prophet souls in line', and 'Men, whose boast it is that ye come of fathers brave and free'), one lesson (not identified in the order of service), a few prayers, and an address from the Rev Eric Shervell Price, the President of the Assembly, the post James Chuter Ede had held eight years earlier. The time had come for a successor in office to pay tribute to his distinguished predecessor.

Chapter 19

Afterword

Probate was granted for Ede's estate on 23 February 1966, to a value of £7,702, equivalent to perhaps £150,000 in today's (2021) purchasing power. Later that year, his executor, A.F.S. Cotton, of Theodore Bell Cotton solicitors, wrote about his papers to organisations who might have had an interest in them, suggesting they be passed to Epsom and Ewell Borough, and asking if any embargo should be placed on making them public.[1] In fact, Cotton deposited many of his papers with Surrey County Council in Kingston, and Ellen Ede added to these in 1971,[2] three years before her own death. A few papers were removed[3] by the Cabinet Office, and at least three Home Office files were destroyed; correspondence with ex-prisoners may have been considered so confidential that it should not have been preserved at all. Other papers were returned to different government departments. Some correspondence with the County Councils Association (which was in 1974 succeeded by the Association of County Councils), the BBC and the British Museum was returned to those bodies.

Cotton sent other items from his personal collection to Epsom, the Borough being permitted to choose what it wanted. Together with his staff, John Dent, the Borough Librarian, produced a rough index of the collection of this material. The local newspaper noted the 1890 Sunday school prize, along with school prizes, an adventure story of 'storm and loss' at sea, his grandmother's membership card of the 'Twenty Pound Burial Society' and mother's *First French Course* book, his father's geography book from Ewell Academy, books and pamphlets on early Labour Party history, and innumerable records of Epsom from the past.

The Surrey archives in Kingston were subsequently transferred to a new Surrey History Centre in Woking, and in 2009 much of the Epsom collection was moved there also. Over the years, researchers have consulted these, though never for a complete biography, and they are of such quantity that no biography alone could sensibly cover all they tell us about Ede. He hoarded his papers and mementoes and, even with a considerable amount thrown out when he moved from Tayles Hill to his sister's at East Street in 1964, the job of transcribing, analysing and editing them would need to be the subject of a three-year thesis, particularly when studied alongside his diaries. The two short-lived diaries from the Home Office period got to Woking, while the much longer ones from the war years and 1952 had, as suggested to Ede by Sophia Weitzman when she consulted them, already been sent to the British Museum, with open access permitted only after his death.[4] When the British Library opened in the 1990s to take over the Museum's publications and archives, they ended up there. Again, researchers have consulted them, but generally for the light they shed on the Labour role in Churchill's Coalition, or on the history of education, or for a bystander's comment from Ede on the activities of others in politics. One expressed the view that the meticulous diary 'suggests a tidy mind, capable of mastering detail … important business … train journeys … social engagements. If they are tedious reading in parts, their very thoroughness makes them an excellent historical source.'[5]

In a way, it is a pity they have not been much used to study the writer himself, as it has not done him justice, but it has also been an opportunity for a biographer wanting to assess the contribution of this interesting man. For he was both interesting, and versatile in his own interests. As his NUT colleague Ernest Luery added, he 'believed in the future but retained his love of our heritage'. He studied for a science degree, joined the Royal Engineers, and took an active involvement in the electrical industry, while happily quoting Milton's 'Areopagitica' and other essays and poems, giving historical lessons on Cromwell and his successors, and instructing religion in the Unitarian tradition. He rejected any concept of a clash between the humanities and sciences:

> the idea that one set of people in the country are interested in the humanities and another set are interested in the sciences, and that the two live in quite different worlds, is one of the dangers we have to face in the age in which we live. While science plays a bigger part in our life than it did before 1860, and while it undoubtedly influences opinion more than it did then, there are still the great abiding humanities and the ancient civilisations which so largely still form our own way of thinking. That ought to be borne in mind by the scientists and some of the people who appear to have lost interest in humanity somewhere just after the fall of Rome, and who have constantly before them some of the questions which are raised by the predominantly scientific outlook of the present age.[6]

His comments about the complementary roles of the Natural History and British Museums were reflected by his passion for 'photographic science and art', to use his own phrase, which illustrated the unity of the two cultures, and a belief that the role of teaching children involved being able to speak with authority on them both. There have been few holders of the great offices of State who studied the sciences at university, but he is one of them.

He was unusual in these, and in other ways – Barbara Castle described him as 'one of the most quixotic ministers in political history'.[7] Her thoughts when she wrote that were on his 'sternly upright' approach to following the Boundary Commission to redraw the constituencies more in line with the size of the electorate, an act (she thought) of 'political suicide', losing seats in 1950, and putting Labour out of office a year later. She, though, was a pugnacious party politician through and through, while Ede described himself as 'never a very good Party man'; that was in 1918, when he was first moving unconfidently from Liberal to Labour, and to an extent the description applied for the rest of his career. In 1962, his musing was, as a 'congenital Nonconformist, how … I have remained in the Labour Party without being chucked out, is a mystery.' Whether his views were on the left or the right of the Labour Party is hard to assess; Kenneth O. Morgan describes him at one point as 'a left-wing schoolteacher',[8] and in his next chapter as one of the ministers who 'were outstandingly conservative in their departmental assumptions', and 'no innovator'.[9]

In his 1960 Frankly Speaking BBC interview, Ede described himself as

a reformer … an egalitarian. I trace both those back to the Nonconformist radicalism of my parents … I'm very doctrinaire. Nobody's ever been able to fault me on the grounds that I'm not a good Socialist pressing for as much as we can get,

while also saying, when asked if it was 'Socialism which attracted you straight off?'

No, No. Nonconformist Radicalism, and that is still my natural reaction to any question that's sprung on me

and that

I am still politically a person of a liberal turn of mind but I am a Socialist in economics.[10]

The distinction he liked to draw between politics and economics was important to him, and is accurate for us, particularly bearing in mind the view he expressed to the BBC GAC that economic issues were becoming more important.

He was persuasive in his approach to political questions, rather than dogmatic, a characteristic, shared by Butler, which came to the fore in 1944 when the Education Bill was being steered through Parliament. 'Few ministers have ever won such golden opinions in every quarter of the House'.[11] This gave him an authority, as a senior backbencher, beyond his own political group. So too, on Surrey County Council, he gained a respect which enabled him to achieve a considerable amount, particularly in education and rural conservation, despite Labour always being the minority party. Underlying it all was his objective when 'he set out in politics to fight injustice and poverty, and from that course he never wavered'. David Clark, who used those words, castigates an obituarist (whom he leaves unnamed)[12] who said Ede 'set too much store on individual liberty to be more than a cautious, pragmatist socialist'. Lord Clark is on the right side here. Ede was not the major advocate of corporatist socialism, despite his role in the great nationalising government; his ideal model of State control was based at the local level, as with the regional electricity authority. But, having looked elsewhere, he believed a single Labour Party was the means to promote liberty and justice, as well as to fight poverty and discrimination. He had no enthusiasm for a Popular Front to join socialists together, however much he would work with others towards the objectives he desired.

There was an element of conceit in his character, as we have seen from his love of title and his willingness to write self-congratulatory press releases, but more often he comes across as modest, because cooperation was more important to him than confrontation. When Francis Williams wrote his profile of Ede for *The Spectator*,[13] in which, since his previous profile had been of Aneurin Bevan, he was able to look at these two Labour men side by side, he drew the huge contrast between their approach to party politics:

> Where Bevan is pugnacious and flamboyant, with an impish delight in the pleasures of verbal excess, Chuter Ede is cool, unruffled, conciliatory; a master of the art of understatement. Where Bevan flourishes a battle-axe, Ede makes delicate use of a rapier whose point has been dipped in a wit as dry, as urbane and as satisfying to the palate as a glass of excellent dry sherry before lunch.

Williams compared Ede 'to a Surrey landscape on a day in June; serene, pervasive, friendly, cultivated and neat, yet holding in reserve, a little withdrawn and not for immediate show, qualities that demanded deeper acquaintanceship'.

The reference to the Surrey landscape is exactly right, of course, not only because of Ede's interest in it and contribution to preserving it, but also because his personality came out in the walks he took around the county. In 1992 his union colleague Edward Britton told Robert Evans that the two of them, in the teachers' walking club they ran, could walk for over an hour without a word coming from Ede's mouth, and then his whole manner would alter. He would speak to those around him as though they were a public meeting, in a most entertaining way – though he was at root a shy man.[14] In the words of Bill Blyton, another Durham MP with his roots in South Shields, he was a 'shy man with little small talk. He would pass you in the corridor of the House of Commons without speaking.'[15]

In consequence, there was a difficulty in forming close relationships which, though helping him get accepted as an impartial and reliable colleague, carried the disadvantage that it was hard to have close dealings with him, based on social contacts rather than professional ones. Wallace, in his doctoral thesis,[16] produces a coloured sociomapping chart, illustrating the links between the senior members of the wartime Board of Education and its expert outside advisers, in terms of school, Cambridge or Oxford college, and London club membership. Of the twelve men named, all had some such link with one or more of the others, excepting only Ede who, Wallace concludes, 'was the outsider'. It is hard to resist his conclusion that Ramsbotham, Butler, their officials and their advisers all respected him, and related to him, for his expert contribution on education, but not on any less formal, more social level, which may have restricted his influence. It was not of course his fault that his background was less privileged than many of these, but he could have chosen to join a club and socialise there. Though he claimed to have been a member of the National Liberal Club before the Great War, he would have ceased membership when he changed his party affiliation, and perhaps sooner when he went to fight in France. Although he became a member of the Oxford and Cambridge Club[17] while Home Secretary, and occasionally invited guests there and referred to the club in correspondence, it did not greatly interest him.

He preferred to lunch at a hotel near his office, and commute to and from Ewell (where he was confident enough to buy a large house) as quickly as work permitted. There is probably nobody left who knew him in his political context, but one Labour supporter in South Shields who was active in the 1960s said that, though he did not meet him personally, he recollects him as 'austere and remote' as an MP.[18] Bailey comments[19] that Ede did not communicate well, even with those with whom, over the years, he had common interests, such as the Nonconformist churches and the NUT, and so could not take advantage of the contacts those organisations might have provided. He was happy to address meetings formally, but less confident in more casual social circumstances. Morgan's description of him as 'a somewhat austere former schoolmaster' reads slightly dismissively in its context,[20] but there is an element of truth in it. Lord Clark, though, makes an important distinction:

> many in the 1990s judge Chuter Ede as they remember him personally: a rather severe, ex-cabinet minister who was eighty-two when he finally ceased to be MP … It is much more difficult, but probably more accurate, to envisage him in 1926 as a relatively young man, passionately fighting for the miners … Behind the austere, stern mask, there was kindness, tolerance and humility.[21]

So it was in the 1990s that Philip Ziegler wrote his life of Harold Wilson, where he mentioned that Wilson usually sat in Cabinet between Chuter Ede and A.V. Alexander, 'but had little in common with these unglamorous and slightly superannuated figures'.[22] We may accept 'unglamorous' – though might that not apply to Wilson also? But 'slightly superannuated' is unfair to Ede (and for that matter to Alexander, a slightly younger man), who in his sixties had finally achieved cabinet rank, and was energetically pursuing his goals.

Francis Williams went on to wonder whether the experience of having to leave university without a degree might have soured him – but no, he

> is the least sour of persons, the least class-conscious of Socialists … Chuter Ede has a mind essentially practical and concrete. Abstractions are seldom his concern. He is not given to overmuch contemplation of theories. What attracts his interest is not so much the ideal, although he bears that in mind, as the possible. He does not see either personal or public issues in the contrasted black and white of the Utopian or the doctrinaire. He is not one to sacrifice the possible to the perfect. He applies himself to what is within reach. He … has not, I think, any claims to being an original political thinker. He has little of the prophetic vision. He is the administrator of policy rather than its originator. But he has a deep humane passion. He cares for reform, for social justice, for more equality of opportunity, not just in the abstract but because he sees them always in terms of human beings. It is that humanity which accounts more than anything else, I think, for his popularity in the House.

He was clearly a person with a good sense of humour, and was liked for it. He had 'a pert turn of phrase', as historians of education have noted.[23] So, when he told the Commons that he had left the teaching profession in 1914, he claimed it was 'for its own good',[24] a joke he repeated on occasion, for example when in Jersey as Home Secretary. His diaries also show that feature, as when he commented in 1944 that the Derbyshire voters were convinced that leaving the Cavendish family required surrendering the family seat, because the MP resigned, having deserted the Duke's sister for another woman.

Williams's summary highlighted this. Ede had a

> quality of humorous sanity, a gift for deflating what is pretentious, for reducing whatever he confronts to its true life-size. He is … the epitome of thousands of other men in the corner seats of third-class carriages coming up to the City from the suburbs, who … give English middle-class life … its half-humorous tolerance, its idealism tinged with a scepticism that avoids sentimentality, its refusal to go to extremes, its determined belief that most things can be settled amicably if you don't let yourself get excited, its confidence in the solvent virtues of common-sense. He … is the kind of man it is invaluable to have not far from the centre of power when great social changes are afoot – the kind of man who has, fortunately for England, very often turned up in just such a place when large events are on the move.

It would be pleasing to quote this at even more length, but that temptation needs restraining. Ede did turn up when great changes were afoot, and he helped to form them. One of my family, with a particular interest in Clement Attlee from his student past, has commented on the *Spectator* article, that the traits described could be applied word-for-word to Attlee. The Prime Minister and Home Secretary were similar spirits working together, even though, to achieve what it did in those six years, the Labour Government needed other personalities to balance them. Though Ede may have been 'uncharismatic', to use Jenkins's description, a mild, self-effacing person must have been a calming presence, considering the number of men with a large ego Attlee was leading – Bevin, Morrison, Dalton, Cripps, Bevan – as well as others outside his government – such as Keynes and Churchill.

Clearly, much of his character derived from his Unitarianism, a tolerant and open creed which respects others and does not try to convert them. The early election leaflet which stated that, though an abstainer, he was as much opposed to compelling other people to abstain, as to their compelling him to drink, was typical of this approach. His admiration for Cromwell, followed closely by Milton, Fox and Bunyan, illustrates the tradition in which he saw himself. He once listened to a radio broadcast by the American commentator, Alexander Woollcott, about the revolutionary events of 1777, where Woollcott said Fox was the Englishman he would most like to have met, and Ede's comment was 'Cromwell first, Fox certainly second'.[25] Among the Surrey History Centre archives is a single sheet of paper, written in Ede's hand, with what is seemingly a quotation he had read and marked well, though unattributed by him:

> From Elizabeth's shrill protest that she 'made no windows into men's souls' to Cromwell's quiet dictum that 'Notions will hurt none but those that have them', was a long second stage in the steep and slippery ascent at the bottom of which the spirit of the Inquisition had been tending the fires of Smithfield less than a century earlier.

He believed he followed in a tradition of tolerance and free-thinking, featuring also Milton who, as we have seen, appeared so frequently (as a predecessor at his own College) in his talks and writings.

The points raised by this tradition still applied:

> this country has for centuries been a place where the alien and the outcast has been welcome to our great advantage ... the Huguenots came in: others, who were turned out by the Edict of Nantes at the same time and came with them, declared themselves to be Unitarians and so lost the benefits of the Act of Toleration. They were determined to be persecuted. It is a great and noble tradition which this country owes it to the world to see re-established as soon as possible,[26]

was how he summed up his attitude to toleration, based on his experience in office, when back in Opposition.

The belief that each person should think for himself, and develop his own relationship with the truth – whether divine or otherwise – was illustrated by the asides he would make in discussion and writing. So, in a letter to John Kielty at the Unitarian headquarters on 17 December 1957, about a tea party for Nonconformist MPs meeting a new Church group, he mentioned the Bishop of Gloucester's advocating:

> a group of wise men who were to guide all of us on economic affairs, which was expanded by the Archbishop of Canterbury into his particularly foolish pronouncement that seven people should be entrusted with the task of making pronouncements which we should all be expected to accept. These views were repugnant to the Members of Parliament

in attendance, who repudiated the notion of an authoritarian church pronouncement on economic matters.

The Archbishop, Geoffrey Fisher, did not suffer the same treatment as his predecessor, William Laud, had done during the Civil War. Nonetheless, with his deliberately formal language, the repetition of 'pronouncement', and final reference to 'authoritarian church', Ede made clear his distaste for any religion exerting its weight against what he would have felt was the grand, independent, Cromwellian tradition.

He even linked his admiration for Cromwell with his belief in the liberalising influence of education and the significance of teaching as a single profession. An unattributed extract in his papers records an account:

> 'The proper person to determine the concept of education', said Mr Chuter Ede … 'is the teacher, who has laid upon him the duty of fitting his education to the age, aptitude and ability of the child.' We have reached this position slowly and painfully after long years of struggle; and if it can be said that we owe the turn of the tide from uniformity to diversity to any one man, the credit for it should probably be given to Oliver Cromwell.[27]

The appeal to 'diversity' is surely part of Ede's nonconformist approach, in a tradition which he traced back to the Civil War.

Historians of the seventeenth century may comment that hero-worship of Cromwell involves turning a blind eye to some less savoury episodes in the Protector's career. Ede, however, was aware of the ambivalence of Cromwell's character, and how, in Andrew Marvell's conclusion on the man, 'The same arts that did gain/ a power, must it maintain', the end of his 'Horatian Ode upon Cromwell's Return from Ireland', where several atrocities had been committed. As early as 1904, when a Cambridge undergraduate, he gave a talk on Cromwell, in which he admitted he had his faults, and the 'trend of the events rendered his despotism the only possible outcome of the strife', a summary in prose of Marvell's judgement in poetry.

Ede's own experience in office illustrated the same point. Like all ministers, he sometimes had to act in an distasteful manner, and that may be particularly pronounced in the role of Home Secretary, with his 'double duty of upholding law and order, and safeguarding individual liberty vigorously'.[28] He was, though, pleased to bring about the abolition of many of the more archaic punishments. The biggest issue remaining, of course, was capital punishment, and it seems strange that he ever opposed the House of Commons when its mood was abolitionist. But his duty was to law and order, and to support the police; he would probably have been relaxed if the Lords had agreed with the Commons but, when they did not, he felt it was his responsibility to continue implementing the law as it was. Once he was out of the government, and the Timothy Evans case had added to the debate, he was prepared, as ever, to admit to a change in mind, and support the course he now felt was the better one.

Though he lived into the 1960s, he died too soon to become involved in most of the liberal developments, apart from censorship and capital punishment, of that (supposedly permissive) decade, but one guiding precept was clear:

> 'Is Labour fit to govern?'That question has been put to me a good many times at public meetings. My answer always has been 'No', because no man is fit to govern another. Self-government, like self-discipline, is the proper way in which this thing should be arranged.[29]

So it is interesting to speculate what view he might have taken on many of the other issues which arose in the 1960s. He would doubtless have been driven by his liberal principles, and those of his religion. As the website for British Unitarianism explains:

> Throughout our history Unitarians have stood for inclusivity, reason and social justice including gender equality (we've had women ministers for more than 100 years), gay rights (we've performed same-sex blessings for more than 30 years) and the abolition of slavery.[30]

On homosexual law reform ('gay' was not yet the term in use) he is likely to have voted to permit private, consenting adult activities. We do not know what he thought of his successor at the Home Office, David Maxwell Fyfe, setting up the Wolfenden Committee and then, when Lord Chancellor, opposing its recommendations, but he would probably have taken the view – common at the time – that he did not approve of homosexual behaviour, but what grown-up people did in private should not be the affair of the criminal law. He would probably have supported the Sexual Offences Act 1967.

As to abortion, the question is harder to decide. In general, reform here 'was an easier sell for a Labour government' than over homosexuality, to quote the biographer of a subsequent Home Office minister,[31] but there was a strong religious lobby, not confined to the Catholics, who were unhappy with relaxing the abortion law. In my view it is likely that, once the right was conceded for doctors to opt out of abortions on conscientious grounds – a concession agreed by the reform's main sponsor, David Steel, himself from a nonconformist background – Ede would have joined most of his Labour colleagues in supporting the change.

One of the difficulties is that we now tend to look upon abortion as a question of women's rights, and Ede's record as a feminist was somewhat mixed. Although in his own field he praised the work of women in English education from an early age, and campaigned against the poor pay women teachers received, he had few qualms about resisting the equal pay requirement added by the Commons to his Education Bill, joining his government colleagues in forcing a reversal of the provision. His early political leaflets addressed male voters, seeming to ignore the women who were now able to vote and, when it was clear they also had to be considered, it was Lilian Ede who was asked to make an appeal to them. Later on,[32] he asserted that girls dislike hard, exact subjects, and that 'if a woman is a good mathematician, she is no longer a human being', so science should not be too prominent in girls' education! Thankfully Shena Simon, with him on the panel of Any Questions in Education when he made that remarkable generalisation, made her disapproval firmly clear. So the statement, offensive and difficult by modern standards, was challenged even then, but perhaps he was merely being a man of his time; how far should we go in challenging his position on the issues of many years ago?

The debate on drugs is also one on which his position would be unclear. Logically, his position on alcohol – that he would not force others to abstain, nor have them compel him to drink – would have applied more generally, and it seems he did not use tobacco either, but took the same view on that. Most politicians at the time would have taken the same approach. The recreational drugs that were illegal, however, were generally viewed in a different light. In many cases, sale and supply of these drugs was an offence but unauthorised possession was not; and, during his last year in the Commons, the Home Office introduced the Drugs (Prevention of Misuse) Bill, creating offences of possessing amphetamines and other drugs. Ede did not speak in the House on this Bill, but it proceeded with very few MPs from any party opposing it, and it seems probable that he would have followed most of his colleagues.

What can be said, beyond speculation, is that he upheld the cause of liberalism, in which he grew up, within the broad coalition which is the Labour Party, and avoided falling prey to the tendency of so many Home Secretaries to become increasingly reactionary. He even claimed that his 'great Department' of State was one with a 'traditional liberal policy', scarcely a judgement all would make of the Home Office. He was perhaps looking back to Morrison and Hoare, the predecessors he knew personally, but he must have been aware that Lord Sidmouth, the longest-serving of them, had legislated against publishers and authors, suspended habeas corpus, and restricted public meetings. There was a limit to how far he could rely on 'tradition'.

Because of his manner of quiet authority, and the patient way he upheld his values, he became the figure described as the 'rare bird – the politician liked by all', when he announced his retirement. By then he had nearly thirty years' experience in the Commons, and a few more to go. He might almost have been the Father of the House; Churchill had achieved that in 1959, after thirty-five years continuous service. In fact, there were many long-serving MPs then, and service is counted only if it is continuous, while Ede had two breaks in his Parliamentary career. So Churchill, who had been an MP, with a short break, since 1900, was Father of the House at the end of Ede's time there. Only in 1979 did a member from the 1935 intake achieve the position. Ede, though well-liked, did not stand out by length of service.

Perhaps it is because he was an unostentatious figure that he has never been the subject of a full biography. His diaries have been mined for other purposes, John Strudwick devoted a hagiographic chapter on the life of his hero in his account of the SCTA, Ede's contribution to the Education Act 1944 has been the subject of papers by Bill Bailey and then Robert Evans, and a short article on his life has been produced for the Epsom and Ewell History website.[33] Despite the intentions of Evans and at least one other researcher, however, none of this has developed into a biography. Meanwhile, some forgot the part he played; when the NUT produced its pictorial history in 1970, Ede's name appeared, in passing, a single time, while credit for the 1944 Act was given to Butler and his civil servants, along predictably to Union officials.[34]

He has not, though, been entirely overlooked by posterity. Michael Noakes's painting of him still hangs in Surrey's County Hall in Kingston, and there is a bust of him in the Council Offices in Epsom, where the Labour Party's Borough and County Councillors placed lilies of remembrance in November 2015, fifty years after his death. A ward in Epsom Hospital bears his name, while a road off East Street, Epsom, a short walk from Hawthorne Place and Miles Road, is named Chuters Grove; though Evans said Ede 'is remembered' by this, it probably takes its name from being a development of James Chuter and his brothers, the Epsom builders. Mary Ede, James's daughter, remembered broods of white turkeys raised by her, her mother and sisters in the fields there before the street was developed.[35]

The Labour Party in South Shields remains based at Ede House, in Westoe Road, where several photographs from the past hang on the walls, and one of its spaces is called the Gompertz Room. In South Shields there was also a Chuter Ede Comprehensive School; the school closed in August 1989, but the site in Galsworthy Road is now the Chuter Ede Community Centre, where Lord Clark, at the time MP for the Borough, opened a photographic display in his memory in September 1999. There are Ede Avenues in both South Shields and nearby Gateshead. Epsom Council is trustee of the James and Lilian Chuter Ede Trust, which makes grants to university students from the Borough, under the terms of the will dated December 1948, which he must have made following Lilian's death – though it has made no outlay since 2014. This is probably the same fund which, according to one account, was set up to help Cambridge students from Epsom complete their studies at the university, established by such a bequest.[36]

Early in 1967, the Balderton Main Street Primary School, just outside Newark, established in 1964, changed its name to Chuter Ede Primary School. On 3 October, the renamed school was formally opened by the chairman of Newark RDC, and the headmaster, Frank Sperring, spoke about Ede's character and achievements, particularly in education. As a Unitarian, Mr Sperring said, Ede 'sought not personal aggrandisement, but improvement in living standards for all to share'.[37] Though it is unclear why a school in Nottinghamshire, far from Surrey or South Shields, should be the one to honour him, that tribute shows how well recognised Ede was following his death. Over the period since, the school has expanded in area, pupil numbers and subjects taught, and celebrated its fiftieth anniversary in May 2017 with Mr Sperring in attendance. To that school, perhaps incongruously, is where one is led by the web address chuterede.com.

On 5 September 1969, the Countess of Dartmouth, who was Chairman of the Greater London Council's Historic Buildings Board, gave a Chuter Ede Memorial Lecture to the conference of the River Thames Society, meeting at Culham College of Education near Oxford. It was a paean to the river, its development over the centuries, and its opportunities in the future, such as the footpaths by the river and the Thames Barrier. She thanked the society for all its work regarding the environment of the Thames, though she did not mention Ede by name at all, according to the press release of the lecture's text.[38] His contribution to conserving the Thames and its tributaries, his boating and walking activities in the river's basin, were understood by all present.

The NUT's Chuter Ede Lectures, of which Butler had given the first in 1962, went on at Hamilton House, the Union's headquarters, for several years. In 1963, Sir Harry Pilkington's subject was 'The Challenge of Change', and in 1964 the chairman of ICI, Paul Chambers, spoke on 'Education and Industry', explaining the skills of management in business.[39] In 1965, the violinist Yehudi Menuhin lectured,[40] at a meeting chaired by the composer Michael Tippett, which would have amused the 'tone deaf' Chuter Ede. After Ede's death, the NUT decided to ask the Prime Minister himself to speak in 1966, which he did in June, having postposed the event from March because of the general election which gave him a significant majority. Harold Wilson, accompanied by his wife and his sister (a teacher and NUT member), spoke to a capacity audience, including Anthony Crosland, the Secretary of State for Education.

In 1967 the lecture was given by C.F. Powell, a Nobel physics laureate, on 'Science, Education and the Future'. A Professor at Bristol (which had awarded Ede an honorary degree), he had worked particularly in the use of photography in atomic physics, so Ede might have been looking down with approval for many reasons. Now, however, the attendance was recorded by the NUT as 'somewhat disappointing'. The following year, a planned lecture by West Indian cricketer Learie Constantine, on 'Education and Human Rights' – again relevant to Ede on several grounds – was cancelled, owing to the speaker's ill health, and in 1969 no lecture was given, as it proved difficult to secure a suitable speaker. After that, it seems the lectures were discontinued.[41]

Ede is remembered by many, though fewer than he deserves. We are now able to celebrate his virtues and achievements, and recognise some of his shortcomings – though as he said with cunning when concluding the 1960 Frankly Speaking interview which I have several times quoted: 'I am a human being; I make mistakes. You know some of them. I know more; and I'm not going to tell you what they were.' With no marked grave, the best tribute is probably to extend the accolade given by John Strudwick that, as with Wren in his glorious cathedral, so for Chuter Ede in Surrey and elsewhere, '*lector, si monumentum requiris, circumspice*'.

Appendix

Latin poem (with English translation), contributed by Cambridge Professor Reginald Punnett to *Punch*[42]

Pro Bono Publico

Quotiens revisito Publicum Locale,
taediorum liquidans onus diurnal,
spero dis volentibus fore sempiternam
decus illud patriae, Anglicam Tabernam.

Thomas his cum Harrio sedet et Richardus
donec 'Tempus domini' clamat caupo tardus;
fundimusque innoxii lepidos sermones,
temperantes sobrias risu potiones.

hic jactando spiculo delectamur, namque
artis est ballisticae, mathematicamque
conservemus liberum ludum spiculorum.

tu severum oppidis novis regimentum
vel Carliolensium das Experimentum,
teetotalitarie Domus – Secretari!
Ede, bibi; cras tempus suffragari!

Cives, congregamini, poculum levantes
et pro Bono Publico fortiter cantantes
quoad vim sufficient guttura et nervi:
'Nunquam, nunquam, Britones nunquam erunt servi'.

Public Plea

As oft towards the local pub I plod my weary way
Intent on liquidation of the chores that crowd the day,
I pray that it will evermore endure through thick and thin,
The glory of our fatherland, the ancient British inn.

Here Tom, Dick and Harry sit partaking of their ease
Until the host raps out the ritual that always ends in 'please';
We bandy conversations of not too high-brow types
And temper our discreet guffaws with modest draughts of swipes.

'Tis here we take our pleasure in the noble game of darts,
For us the true foundation of all ballistic arts;
It helps to mathematicise the proletarian crowd:
We hold it as a righteous thing that darts should be allowed.

Laws for new towns you may devise with Chuter Edean guile
Or such as have been foisted on the burghers of Carlisle
Teetotal-bureaucratic-wise with all that this denotes:
Come – eat and drink – tomorrow will be the time to think of votes.

Come, citizens, with glasses raised replenished to the brim,
We'll toast the local public for all the times are grim,
And bellowing forth defiantly our patriotic staves
Assert once more that Britons never never shall be slaves.

Acknowledgements

Iam grateful that my initial enquiries were much assisted by Robert Evans, at Surrey County Council, who let me take his previous work forward, and showed me round County Hall in Kingston; and by Jeremy Harte and Peter Reed, at the Epsom & Ewell Local and Family History Centre, Bourne Hall, Ewell. I was fortunate to meet the late Michael Noakes, who welcomed me in to discuss his account of painting Ede's portrait, a few months before his own death. With his passing, I suspect there is nobody remaining alive who knew Ede apart from his wife's young family members; I certainly have not found anyone.

My thanks go also to Lester Crook, freelance editor, who gave me most valuable advice on how to present the work, as well as to Chris Wrigley of Nottingham University and John Bew of King's College London, who (as Lester arranged) read my draft as first reviewers, and provided many useful suggestions.

Chuter Ede has had four successors as MP for South Shields – Arthur Blenkinsop, David Clark, David Miliband and most recently Emma Lewell Buck. Blenkinsop died unexpectedly young, some fifteen years after Ede himself, but happily the other three are still with us, and all have aided me. David Miliband provided details of his own family connection to Ede, and referred me to others in South Shields who could help my work. Emma asked the team at her constituency office to assist, and Keith Palmer there took me on a tour of the town and to Ede House in Westoe Road. Above all, Lord Clark of Windermere has encouraged me, giving me a copy of his history of the Shields Labour Party, together with personal reminiscences and suggestions. My gratitude goes to them all, and to David Clark in particular.

I need also to mention with thanks the help given by the staff at the Surrey History Centre in Woking, the British Library, the National Archives and the London Metropolitan Archives. Information on particular subjects was provided at Christ's College Library by Charlotte Hoare (who has since moved to take charge of the Special Collections at Manchester University); Derek McAuley, of the Unitarian General Assembly at Essex Hall (from where the files have now been transferred to Dr Williams's Library, Gordon

Square); David Wykes, director of that Library; Howard Hague and Alan Ruston, the Unitarian Historical Society; David Steers, editor of that Society's *Transactions*; Matthew Chipping at the BBC Written Archives Centre; Kate Ashbrook of the Open Spaces Society, along with Annie Pinder, at the Parliamentary Archives, which hold that Society's records; Francesca Hillier at the British Museum Central Archives; and Rachel Baxter and Mariangela Pilloni, at the National Education Union (the successor to the NUT).

I am grateful to Janet Dawson (née Fromow) and Charles Merrett regarding the members of Lilian Ede's family; Ann Godden, of the International Friendship League, for her help regarding Noel Ede; Amy Howe at the UCL Institute of Education, for the Sophia Weitzman papers; Terry Reeves, for his Royal Engineers Special Brigade group within the online Great War Forum; Peter Clayton, for information on Octavia Hill and her use of the term 'green belt'; Lucy Shepherd and Thomas Gates, at the Oxford and Cambridge Club; David Blow and Sheena Digance, at Ashcombe School, Dorking; Vince Romagnuolo, former Borough Councillor at Epsom and Ewell, and Steve Davies, former employee there; and Julie Ford, at Chuter Ede Primary School, Newark.

Within South Shields, I was able to contact local historian Malcolm Grady, Adam Bell at the Museum and Art Gallery, and Jack Grassby, one of the few active Labour Party constituents who recall Ede, and thank them for their information, interest and comments. Elsewhere, Peter Godfrey, retired Unitarian minister, gave me his recollections of seeing Ede at conferences. Helen Batten (River Thames Society), Harriet Handsley (British Institute of Professional Photography), and Lloyd Langley and Stephanie Young (National Trust, Wallington) spent time investigating what they might have available on my subject.

My thanks go to them all, and to any others whom I may have overlooked.

Then, like all authors, I am grateful to my family for their support and encouragement. I thank my children, and in particular my son-in-law Tim Bennett, now like me a lawyer, but at Oxford an historian with a particular interest in political biography, for his suggestions and for the use of his substantial library. My brother John contributed his own recollection of seeing Chuter Ede when the stepping stones under Box Hill were reopened.

Above all, my wife Valerie read the proofs of this book, and was very patient, on the one hand pleased to have found an activity to occupy me, but on the other sometimes losing me to my researches, and even accompanying me down obscure trails. She and her sister Trudy encouraged me, and helped to finance my work. They did so from their inheritance from my mother-in-law, Joan Smith, who died aged 98, in the same week I finished the text, and whose estate I helped them wind up.

In the 1930s Joan had been obliged to leave grammar school at 16, when her scholarship ran out, and to give up any hope of sixth-form or university, owing to shortage of family funds. More than thirty years later she qualified as a non-graduate teacher. Chuter Ede felt it one of his great attainments that in the future no child with the right aptitude would, through lack of finance, fail to complete a university education – how far does that achievement still persist? It is to Joan that this book is dedicated.

Notes

Chapter 1: Introduction
1. Interview in The Telegraph, 1 August 2004
2. The Rambler, 60, 13 October 1750
3. *Frankly Speaking* (BBC Written Archives)
4. Personal conversation with Peter Godfrey

Chapter 2: The Early Years
1. *Observer*, 15 September 1946
2. Membership card at SHC 6408/1, quoted in *Epsom & Ewell Herald*, 23 September 1966
3. *Epsom Herald*, ibid
4. Handwritten note in Epsom archives, citing *The Surrey Advertiser*, 20 October (unknown year in 1890s)
5. *Epsom Herald*, obituary of Mary Ede, 19 May 1939
6. *Civic Progress in Epsom and Ewell 1850–1937*, note written by J.S. Underhill, Chairman of Epsom & Ewell UDC, for Borough Charter celebrations in 1937, quoted in the Borough 75th Anniversary Souvenir
7. Speech by JCE at Charter Luncheon, 29 September 1937
8. Caption to photo in *Advertiser and Observer Christmas Annua*l, probably written by Ede
9. Evans, *James Chuter Ede and the 1944 Education Act*, p 15
10. *Hansard*, 28 November 1949, at 799
11. *Epsom Herald*, ibid.
12. Handwritten note, ibid.
13. For example, the *Dictionary of National Biography*, and Jackson, *James Chuter Ede*, unpublished note, *Epsom & Ewell History Explorer*
14. *Hansard*, 4 April 1944, at 1952
15. Jackson, op cit, and handwritten note in Surrey Archives
16. Radio interview with JCE, *Frankly Speaking*, December 1960 (transcript at the BBC Written Archives), quoted by Jefferys, *Labour and the Wartime Coalition*, p 2
17. *Frankly Speaking*, ibid
18. *Epsom Herald*, ibid
19. *Evening Post*, 14 May 1946, when addressing Jersey teachers, and in his reply to RA Butler's Inaugural Chuter Ede Lecture for the NUT, 22 March 1962.
20. *Surrey Comet*, 4 October 1941, quoted in Evans, op cit, p 16
21. *Epsom Observer*, 6 March 1903
22. *Hansard*, 9 March 1944, at 44
23. *Hansard*, 29 March 1923, at 779
24. *Hansard*, 3 July 1923, at 245
25. *Hansard*, 15 February 1944, at 128
26. *Surrey Comet*, 4 October 1942, quoted in Evans, op cit, p 17
27. Evans, op cit, p 16
28. Lowndes, *The Silent Social Revolution*, p 25
29. *Evening Post*, 14 May 1946, address in Jersey when Home Secretary

30. *Evening Post*, ibid, and *Newcastle Journal*, 1 February 1943, quoted by Evans, op cit, p17
31. Evans, op cit, p 26
32. JCE diary, 25 December 1941
33. *Coulsdon Times*, 16 June 1944, quoted by Evans, op cit, p 17
34. JCE diary, 31 January 1942
35. *Hansard*, 29 November 1938, at 362
36. *Epsom Observer*, 6 March 1903
37. SHC 3690/2/1
38. *Epsom Observer*, 6 March 1903
39. SHC 3690/2/2
40. Obituary in the *Inquirer*, 27 November 1965, by John Kielty
41. *Epsom Observer*, 6 March 1903
42. SHC 390/11/5, cited by Jefferys, op cit, p 2
43. Ibid, cited by Evans, op cit, p 19
44. Peile, *Christ's College Biographical Register*, 1913
45. JCE diary, 4 June 1943
46. *Epsom Observer*, 6 March 1903
47. *Epsom Observer*, ibid
48. Shakoor, *The Training of Teachers in England and Wales*, unpublished PhD thesis, Univ of Leicester, 1964, p 84 ff
49. Gosden, *The Evolution of a Profession*, p 221
50. Burrow, *The Age of Reform*, in *Christ's – A Cambridge College over Five Centuries*, D Reynolds (ed), p 113
51. *A Cambridge Alumni Database*, http://venn.lib.cam.ac.uk, regarding Cartmell and Peile
52. Burrow, op cit, p 114
53. JCE diary, 4 June 1943, when in Cambridge to receive his honorary degree
54. Speech in Hartlepool, reported in *Hartlepool Northern Daily Mail*, 2 April 1957
55. Harrison, *The Character of Victorian Sport*, https://gassingabout. wordpress.com, 2013
56. *List of Members of Christ's College*, SHC 6408/7
57. JCE diary, 26 October 1942
58. Speech to Western Region 3 May 1958, SHC, 6408/17
59. JCE diary, 14 February 1952
60. 1903 Report of Union, SHC 6408/2
61. *Frankly Speaking*, ibid
62. JCE diary, 16 January 1942
63. Comment made to RA Butler, recorded in JCE diary, 27 February 1942 (Butler was wary of his forthcoming reception at Oxford's Conservative Association)
64. *Epsom Observer*, 4 December 1903, held at SHC 6408/12
65. *Epsom Observer*, 16 September 1904
66. Dinner seating plan, SHC 6408/13
67. JCE diary, 4 June 1943
68. *Surrey Comet*, 29 April 1933, on his appointment to chair that Council
69. Williams, *Ministers as they Are – Chuter Ede*, article in *The Spectator*, 30 September 1947
70. Obituary of Ede in *Epsom and Ewell Advertiser*, 13 November 1965
71. Speech delivered when President of the General Assembly, quoted in Jefferys, op cit, p 3
72. *Dictionary of National Biography*
73. *Frankly Speaking* interview, December 1960, in BBC Written Archives
74. *Country Life*, 25 May and 2 June 1936, at SHC 6408/10
75. Several photographs, magazines and letters are at SHC
76. Evans, op cit, p 20
77. SHC

Chapter 3: First Political Steps
1. Address to Sutton Association of the SCTA, reported in *The Schoolmaster and Woman Teacher's Chronicle*, 2 October 1941, cited in Evans, *James Chuter Ede and the 1944 Education Act*, p 20
2. Stated by Bailey, *James Chuter Ede and the 1944 Education Act*, in History of Education 26.3 p210, and Evans, ibid
3. *Surrey Comet*, 10 March 1923
4. In SHC collection
5. *Surrey Teachers' Quarterly*, April 1913
6. Evans, op cit, p 27, and SHC 6408/12
7. JCE diary, 3 August 1943
8. JCE diary, 26 January 1944
9. Taylor, *English History 1914–1945*, p 170
10. Article by JCE in *Surrey Teacher*, 1933, on *The Founding Fathers and their Successors*
11. Gosden, *The Evolution of a Profession*, p 28
12. *Surrey Comet*, 3 February 1962, quoted by Evans, op cit, p 27
13. Gillard, *Education in England: a Brief History*, chapter 4
14. *Hansard*, 13 November 1929
15. *Epsom and Ewell Observer*, 12 April 1906, SHC 6408/12
16. *Surrey Teachers' Quarterly*, April 1913
17. *Observer*, 15 September 1946
18. Jefferys, *Labour and the Wartime Coalition*, p 4
19. Cuttings in SHC 3690/2/3
20. Jefferys, op cit, p 3
21. *Surrey Teachers' Quarterly*, April 1913
22. In SHC 6408/2 CE 97.32
23. Jefferys, ibid
24. *Surrey Teachers' Quarterly*, April 1913
25. *Barnes and Mortlake Herald*, 30 July 1910.
26. *Epsom Herald*, 21 October 1911, cited by Jefferys, op cit, p4, and Evans, op cit, p 30
27. JV Strudwick, *The Story of an Association*, ch 6, typescript, SHC 6094/3/1
28. *Surrey Teachers' Quarterly*, ibid
29. Strudwick, op cit, and *Surrey Comet*, 29 April 1933
30. Evans, op cit, p 30
31. JCE diary, 27 January 1942, reminiscing on the occasion of Baxter's funeral
32. Strudwick, op cit
33. *Epsom Advertiser*, 18 November 1965, in a tribute after Ede's death
34. SHC 6408/2
35. *Surrey Comet, Epsom Advertiser*, both 13 May 1914
36. Strudwick, op cit, ch 1
37. Military papers in Epsom Museum collection
38. SHC 390/11/10, cited by Hyams at surreyinthegreatwar.org.uk/author/ jh0107/
39. Bailey, op cit
40. Some details from Lieut-General Terry Reeves, who coordinates part of the Great War Forum, dealing with the RE Special Brigade, on 1914–1918.invasionzone.com
41. In SHC, 6408/7
42. Postcards dated 24 May 1916, SHC 6408/29
43. Cited by Hyams, op cit, which gives a good resumé of Ede in the War
44. *Dorking and Leatherhead Advertiser*, 23 December 1916
45. *Hansard*, 12 April 1923
46. Programmes in various files at SHC
47. Bailey, op cit
48. *Observer profile*, 15 September 1946

49. *Frankly Speaking* interview, December 1960, in BBC Written Archives
50. *Hansard*, 12 April 1923
51. SHC 3690/2/6
52. *Dorking and Leatherhead Advertiser*, 10 August 1918
53. *Dorking and Leatherhead Advertiser*, 31 August 1918
54. Copy in SHC
55. Pamphlets in SHC, with bold and italic lettering as in Ede's original
56. Letter, 5 November 1918, in SHC
57. *Wallington & Carshalton Times*, 19 August 1920
58. Details taken from tax returns at SHC
59. Evans, op cit, p 31
60. Strudwick, op cit, ch 5
61. Committee minutes in SHC
62. Information variously from *Who's Who in Surrey* (1938), *The Surrey Comet* (10 March 1923), and unsigned handwritten notes in Surrey History Centre
63. Knight, *We are not Manslaughterers*, which gives a detailed account of the incident
64. Programme SRC 6408/2, dinner ticket 6408/1
65. JCE diary, 25 December 1941
66. Evans, ibid
67. Election pamphlet, December 1923, quoting the response to a PQ asked by Ede on 9 July 1923
68. Strudwick, op cit, ch 5, 8 and 25
69. Bailey, op cit
70. Britton in conversation with R Evans, in Evans, op cit, p34
71. *Surrey Comet* obituary, 13 November 1965
72. JCE diary, 16 August 1941, musing on his father's 101st anniversary
73. Its papers are at SHC 4455
74. Old Dorkinian Association Annual Dinner programme, 5 December 1936, SHC 6408/13

Chapter 4: The Member for Mitcham

1. Evans, *James Chuter Ede and the 1944 Education Act*, p 35
2. JCE diary, 27 January 1942
3. JCE's autobiographical note on becoming Privy Counsellor in 1944 (SHC)
4. A brief British Pathe newsreel of the event can be seen at https://www.youtube.com/watch?v=mypIvWzKrvI
5. Evans, op cit, p 19
6. Clark, *The Tories 1922–1997*, p 22

Chapter 5: A Surrey Tynesider

1. JCE diary, 11 December 1942
2. Strudwick, *The Story of an Association*, typescript, SHC
3. Manzer, *Teachers and Politics*, p 40
4. Clark, *We do not Want the Earth*, pp 68, 94–6
5. JCE witness statement as committee chair to Ministry of Agriculture enquiry, SHC 6408/1 CE97.56
6. Now in the Parliamentary archives, FCP/1/24
7. Gillard, *Education in England: a Brief History*, www.educationengland. org.uk/history, chapter 4
8. Taylor. *English History 1914–1945*, p 211
9. Bailey, *James Chuter Ede and the 1944 Education Act*, p 211
10. Strudwick, op cit, ch 20
11. JCE's autobiographical note on becoming Privy Counsellor in 1944 (SHC)

12. Simon, *The Politics of Educational Reform 1920–1940*, pp 137, 141–5
13. Details taken from *Shields Gazette*, 2 and 3 March 1960, when Gompertz was 'retired' by the party against his will, and from Clark, op cit p 31.
14. *Frankly Speaking* (BBC Written Archives)
15. Clark, op cit, p 30
16. Letters at SHC 390/2/2
17. *Shields Gazette*, 11 November 1965
18. Clark, op cit, p 25
19. Margaret Sutton, in personal conversation with David Clark, in Clark, op cit, p 60
20. *Newcastle Journal*, 21 January 1963, at SHC 390/2/2
21. Photographs at southtynesidehistory.co.uk
22. Lawton, *Education and Politics in the 1990s*, p 23
23. *Hansard*, 4 July 1929 at 365
24. *Hansard*, 13 November 1929
25. *Observer* profile of JCE, 15 September 1946. Quotation from JCE in Reynolds' Illustrated News, 29 June 1930, cited by Jefferys, *Labour and the Wartime Coalition*, p 6
26. Reported in the BBC's 'Archive on 4' on 14 July 2018, and by Chris Mason, its presenter, on the BBC website on 18 July
27. Strudwick, op cit, ch 6
28. *Epsom and Ewell Advertiser*, 18 November 1965, in Strudwick's obituary tribute
29. In SHC 6408/29 and other boxes
30. *Shields Daily News*, 30 January 1931
31. Ibid, 28 February 1931
32. Ibid, 6 March 1931
33. *Shields Daily News*, 9 March 1931
34. Ibid, 30 March 1931
35. *Observer*, ibid
36. Barker, *Education and Politics 1900-1951*, p 109
37. 'Twenty Five Years On', article by JCE in *Education*, 4 October 1957, from which all his quotations on this are taken
38. Strudwick, op cit, ch 13
39. Letter at SHC, 25 August 1931
40. Report of the Departmental Committee on Private Schools, 1932
41. *Surrey Comet*, 29 April 1933
42. *Shields Daily News*, 9 May 1932
43. Ibid, 31 October 1932
44. *Surrey Comet*, 29 April 1933
45. *Epsom Advertiser*, 11 May 1933; see also *Mitcham and Tooting Advertiser*, 18 May, and The Star, 12 June
46. *Surrey Comet*, 29 April 1933, and Advertiser, 27 April 1933
47. Southern Railway publications in SHC 6408/7
48. Still in his effects at his death – *Epsom and Ewell Herald*, 23 September 1966
49. JCE's autobiographical note, ibid
50. SHC 35/W3/53
51. Various cuttings at SHC 390/1/10
52. *Epsom and Ewell Advertiser*, 18 November 1965
53. *The Shieldsman*, 12 May 1933
54. On MacDonald as a pacifist Unitarian, see McCready, Blessed is the Peacemaker, in Transactions of the Unitarian Historical Society 27.2.97 ff, April 2020

Chapter 6: In South Shields to Stay

1. *Hansard*, 9 December 1935, at 653
2. JCE diary, 23 February 1942

3. Account and photograph in Jackson, *James Chuter Ede*, from SHC 6408/13, and at http://boyshighschool.co.uk/thepast/story.htm
4. Copy of petition at SHC 6408/2 CE97.33
5. Unattributed press cutting, SHC 6408/16
6. *Epsom and Ewell Advertiser* obituary, 18 November 1965
7. Speech by JCE at Charter Luncheon, 29 September 1937
8. Several press cuttings in SHC 6408/16
9. Article by JCE in Helios, July 1937
10. Strudwick, *The Story of an Association*, ch 2
11. Open Spaces Society files in Parliamentary archives, FCP/2/5
12. *Observer*, 15 September 1946
13. Various documents in the http://www.epsomandewellhistoryexplorer.org.uk website
14. *Surrey Comet*, 6 March 1937
15. Francis Williams in *The Spectator*, 30 September 1948
16. Speech by JCE at Charter Luncheon, 29 September 1937
17. 1 March 1937
18. JCE's autobiographical note on becoming Privy Counsellor in 1944 (SHC)
19. Summer 1937 edition, SHC 6408/17 CE89
20. April 1937 edition, SHC 6408/17 CE89
21. Detail in conversation of the author with Michael Noakes
22. Certificate at SHC 6408/9
23. SHC 6408/14
24. *Surrey Comet*, 2 October 1937
25. *Epsom Herald*, obituary of Mary Ede, 19 May 1939
26. *Per chevron vert and argent, in chief two horses heads erased or, and in base as many bars wavy azure*
27. Details from *The Evening News*, 29 September 1937; 75th Anniversary Charter Souvenir and issue of Borough Insight; *Surrey Comet*, ibid; and text of JCE's speech in Epsom and Ewell archives
28. SHC 6408/2 CE97.33
29. Hill, *Parks in the Past*, part 2, Bourne Hall Museum, Ewell, 2012
30. SHC 6408/2 CE97.65
31. Gillard, *Education in England: a Brief History*, chapter 4 – Barker, *Education and Politics 1900–1951*, Oxford, 1962, chapter V.
32. Report on comments from MPs to the Wilkinson memo, attached to a letter from A Creech Jones, at Manchester Labour History Archive, CP/IND/DUTT/31/03, cited in Mates, *The United Front and the Popular Front in the North East of England 1936–1939*, from which much of this account comes (pp 168–173, 202–3)
33. *Hansard*, 14 March 1938 at 130
34. Clark, *We do not Want the Earth*, p 76
35. Or 1939, according to the DNB, but 1938 is the date given in JCE's note on becoming Privy Counsellor, May 1944
36. Text of speech in SHC 6408/17
37. SHC 390/1/3
38. *Epsom Herald*, 19 May 1939
39. *Epsom Herald*, ibid
40. *Epsom Herald*, ibid.

Chapter 7: In the Coalition
1. SHC 390/2/6, quoted by Jefferys, *Labour and the Wartime Coalition*, p 7
2. JCE's own press release on his Privy Counsellorship in 1944
3. Strudwick, *Story of an Association*, ch 5
4. *The Schoolmaster and Woman Teacher's Chronicle*, 14–3–1940, quoted in Evans, *James Chuter Ede and the 1944 Education Act*, p 38

5. Barker, *Education and Politics 1900–1951*, p 75
6. See Simon, *Education and the Social Order 1940–1990*, pp 58–59
7. These are discussed in more detail by Simon, op cit, p 46 ff
8. Evans, op cit, p 45
9. Details from *Dictionary of National Biography*
10. PRO ED 136/216, quoted by Gosden, *Education in the Second World War*, p 230
11. *Daily Mirror*, 27 January 1941, cited by Evans, op cit, p 47
12. *Hansard*, 1 May 1941, at 631
13. Wallace, *The Origins and Authorship of the 1944 Education Act*, p 286
14. Jefferys, *RA Butler, The Board of Education and the Education Act, History*, October 1984, p 417, cited in Evans, op cit, p 49
15. *The Municipal Journal and Local Government Administrator*, 27 June 1941, cited by Evans, p 53
16. *Surrey Times*, 1 August 1942, cited by Evans, op cit, p 52
17. Evans, op cit, p 49, Jefferys, op cit, pp 417–8
18. Simon, op cit, p 58
19. Butler, *The Art of the Possible*
20. Jefferys, op cit, p 418
21. Butler, *The Education Act of 1944 and after*, speech at the University of Essex, 1965, cited by Evans, p 61.
22. Evans, op cit, p.8
23. Quotations from *The Art of the Possible*
24. Documents in PRO ED 136/228, cited in Gosden, op cit, p 272
25. Ibid, 138/20, Butler's personal note, cited in Gosden, op cit, p 487
26. Information personally from David Clark, Lord Clark of Windermere, a later MP for the constituency, and from his *We do not Want the Earth*, pp 94–96
27. PRO ED 136/228
28. Churchill, *The Second World War*, vol III, p 751

Chapter 8: A Strategy for Education
1. A more detailed analysis of these issues may be found in Middleton & Weitzman, *A Place for Everyone*, pp 246 ff
2. JCE's diary gives the defendant's real name and address in full, but I have called him Fred, and omitted his house number, *ex abundanti cautela*, as he may still be alive
3. PRO ED 136/597
4. PRO ED 136/294, quoted by Bailey, *James Chuter Ede and the 1944 Education Act*, p 217
5. That is, the subsequent Education Act – conversation with R Evans in 1992, quoted in Evans, *James Chuter Ede and the 1944 Education Act*, p 54
6. JCE diary, 30 March 1942
7. PRO ED 136/228, cited by Gosden, *Education in the Second World War*, p 277
8. Referred to in his speech, *Hansard*, 10 November 1938 at 409
9. Ede's personal file at the BBC Sound Archives. There is no text in the file, nor any further details of the subject matter.
10. Bailey, op cit, p 215
11. JCE diary, 16 January 1942
12. Skidelsky, *John Maynard Keynes*, vol 3, pp 286–7
13. Bailey, op cit, p 218
14. PRO ED 50/178
15. PRO ED 138/20
16. PRO ED 136/28
17. Meeting between Butler and Dr Weitzman, researching her history of education in the War, 25 May 1945, PRO ED 138/20
18. 18 June 1942

19. Text at SHC 6408/17
20. PRO ED 136/229, quoted by Gosden, op cit, pp282–3
21. Butler, *The Art of the Possible*, p 121

Chapter 9: Ready to Proceed

1. Simon, *Education and the Social Order 1940–1990*
2. *Hansard*, Lords, 12 July 1949 at 1133
3. *Hansard*, 28 November 1949 at 805
4. Reported in *Surrey Herald*, 16 October 1942, cited by Evans, *James Chuter Ede and the 1944 Education Act*, p 57
5. See for instance, Harris, *Politics without Prejudice*, p 76
6. PRO ED 136/351
7. PRO ED 10/285, cited by Gosden, *Education in the Second World War*, p 63
8. Simon, op cit, p 70
9. Butler, *The Art of the Possible*, pp 109–116
10. PRO ED 10/262
11. JCE to RAB, Board of Education papers ED 136/642, cited by McCulloch, *Educational Reconstruction*, p 106, and Gosden, op cit, p 78
12. PRO ED 136/229, 12 July 1943
13. PRO ED 12/518
14. JCE diary, 22 May 1943
15. Interview note and memoranda, PRO ED 136/356
16. Bailey, *James Chuter Ede and the 1944 Education Act*, pp 218–219
17. PRO ED 136/229
18. 20 Oct 1943
19. PRO ED 136/386, quoted by Gosden, op cit, p 301
20. Bailey, op cit, p 219
21. From paragraphs17–27, quoted in Maclure, *Educational Documents*, p 208
22. Well documented by Gosden, op cit, pp 370 ff
23. PRO ED 136/442, quoted in Gosden, op cit, p 425
24. Gosden, op cit, p 495
25. Butler, op cit, p 106
26. Howard, *RAB*, p 130

Chapter 10: The Privy Counsellor gets his Education Act

1. PRO ED 136/356
2. Butler, diary, December 1943, cited in G McCulloch, *Educational Reconstruction*, pp 31–32
3. Dent, *The Education Act 1944*, from which much of this commentary on the statute is derived. Though first produced in 1944, the book was updated by Harold Dent in 1969, to reflect changes over the intervening 25 years, which (though generally not relevant to considering the life of Chuter Ede) can be most useful in assessing the nature of its achievement.
4. Curtis, *History of Education in Great Britain*, p 381
5. Bullock, *Life and Times of Ernest Bevin*, vol 2, p 237
6. Inaugural Chuter Ede Lecture, 22 March 1962
7. JCE diary, 16 March 1944
8. Memo, 6 March 1944, PRO ED 136/480, cited by Smith, *The Womanpower Problem in Britain during the Second World War*, Historical Journal 27.4.925–945, December 1984
9. Maclure, *Educational Documents*, p 233
10. PRO ED 126/494, quoted by Gosden, *Education in the Second World War*, p 350
11. Dent, op cit, p 29
12. *Frankly Speaking* interview, December 1960, in BBC Written Archives

13. Gosden, *The Education System since 1944*, p 203
14. Gosden, *The Evolution of a Profession*, p 121
15. Howard, *RAB*, p 137
16. Recollection of Richard Pim, coordinator of War Map Room, quoted by Gilbert, *Winston S Churchill*, vol VII, p 721
17. Story told by Ede to Ralph Harris, in Harris, *Politics without Prejudice*, p 85
18. Adonis, *Ernest Bevin – Labour's Churchill*, p.183
19. *The Times* 14–04–1944, quoted in C Chitty & J Dunford (eds), *State Schools: New Labour and the Conservative Legacy*, and then in Gillard, *Education in England: a Brief History*, chapter 5
20. In particular, Jefferys, *Labour and the Wartime Coalition*, from Ede's perspective, and also in studies of other politicians, such as Reeves, *Alice in Parliament*, Thomas-Symonds, *Nye*, and Bew, *Citizen Clem*.
21. Telegram pasted by JCE in his diary for 12 May 1944 (capitals as in original)
22. SHC 390
23. Jefferys, op cit, p 202
24. File at SHC 390/2/8 and /9
25. *The Times*, 30 June 1943
26. Strudwick, *The Story of an Association*, ch 8
27. Gosden, *Education in the Second World War*, p 355
28. Maclure, op cit, p 212
29. Lowndes, *The Silent Social Revolution*, pp 242–3
30. Quoted by Evans, from his conversation with Thomas, in *James Chuter Ede and the 1944 Education Act*.
31. Thomas, *Teachers in Parliament*, in The Schoolmaster, 3 November 1949
32. Taylor, *English History 1914–1945*, p 568
33. Benn, *Against the Tide: Diaries 1973–76*, p 629, quoted in McCulloch, op cit, p 55
34. Lester Smith, *Education*, p 14
35. See this discussed by Simon, *Education and the Social Order 1940–1990*, pp 73 ff, and the cycles of changing attitudes to the Act by McCulloch, op cit.
36. McCulloch, op cit, chapter 4
37. See the WEA's Educational Pamphlet No 7, Shearman's *The New Education Act – a Citizen's Guide*, and 'Wanted One Hundred Thousand Teachers' in Giles, *The New School Tie*, ch VI
38. See Wallace, *The Origins and Authorship of the 1944 Education Act*, History of Education, 1981, 10/4, p 283ff
39. This is supported by, for example, by Jefferys, *RA Butler, The Board of Education and the 1944 Education Act*, History, 1984, p 415 ff, and Evans, op cit, pp11–12 and elsewhere.
40. Barber, *The Making of the 1944 Education Act*, p 43
41. In conversation with Evans, as above.

Chapter 11: Change in Government
1. PRO ED 136/315
2. PRO ED 86/109, cited by Gosden, *Education in the Second World War*, p 405
3. Copy in British Library
4. PRO ED 12/518, cited in Gosden, op cit, p 359
5. Jefferys, *Labour and the Wartime Coalition*, p201, citing The Times, 16 December 1944
6. Quoted from diary in Middleton & Weitzman, *A Place for Everyone*, p 312
7. Jefferys, op cit, p 208, quoting Harris, *Attlee*, pp 244–7
8. Wallace, *Labour, the Board of Education and the Preparation of the 1944 Act*, p 276
9. Keir, *From the Wings*, pp122–3
10. Lawton, *Education and Politics in the 1990s*, p 23; Barker, *Education and Politics 1900–1951*, p 79

11. See Ellen Wilkinson, 16 October 1945, Hansard 1070
12. Wallace, op cit, p 270
13. JCE diary, 21 July 1945
14. Jefferys, *The Churchill Coalition and Wartime Politics*, p 200 ff
15. JCE diary, 28 July 1945
16. Details may be found in PollBase at www.markpack.org.uk/opinion-polls/
17. Bullock, *Life and Times of Ernest Bevin*, vol 2, p 393
18. Account given by Edward Britton, NUT General Secretary, to Evans in November 1992 (Evans, *James Chuter Ede and the 1944 Education Act*, p 41)
19. Strudwick, *The Story of an Association*, ch 6
20. *The Teacher*, obituary 19 November 1965, cited by Evans, p 65
21. Gould in conversation, recounted by Betty Vernon, in *Ellen Wilkinson 1891–1997*, p 202
22. Thomas, *Teachers in Parliament, The Schoolmaster*, 3 November 1947
23. Strudwick, ibid
24. JCE diary, undated entry from March 1946; see, for example, *The Economist*, 11 August 1945
25. JCE diary, ibid
26. Attlee, *As It Happened*, p 153
27. Williams, *A Prime Minister Remembers*, p 80
28. *Hansard*, 15 June 1961, at 666

Chapter 12: The Untried Home Secretary
1. For instance, by Morgan, *Labour in Power 1945–1951*, pp 46–54
2. Radice, *The Tortoise and the Hares*.
3. *Observer* profile, 15 September 1946
4. Copy at SHC CE32; the programme gives the year and the timings but, oddly, not the actual date of the reception.
5. Interview in *Toronto Daily Star*, 22 August 1945
6. *Observer*, ibid
7. PRO ED 12/518
8. *The Schoolmaster*, 28 August 1945
9. Adonis, *Ernest Bevin – Labour's Churchill*, pp.182–4
10. *Hansard*, 20 December 1962
11. Castle, *Fighting All the Way*, p 183
12. *Hansard*, 9 October 1945, at 112
13. *Observer*, ibid, and *Times* obituary, 12 November 1965
14. PRO CAB 129/1/43 and 129/6/22
15. *Evening Standard*, 11 September 1945, quoted by JCE in the Commons on 9 October
16. *Hansard*, 9 October 1945
17. Undated extract from JCE diary, March 1946
18. Details summarized in *New Zealand Herald*, 12 December 1945 (cutting retained by Ede in his papers)
19. Harris, *New Police College Opened in Britain*, Journal of Criminal Law and Criminology, July-August 1949
20. Skidelsky, *John Maynard Keynes*, vol 3, pp 296–7, 462–3
21. Reynolds News, 6 January 1946
22. PRO MEPO 2/6954
23. At www.youtube.com/watch?v=LJmbvgDsUwM, the film can be watched online, and another video at https://www.youtube.com/watch?v=crrXNjCgC88 shows Ede making it.
24. Extracts and account from *Hansard*, 14 March 1946, as reported by *The Times*, 15 March, with cuttings pasted into JCE's diary
25. On 11 February 1946 – PRO CAB 129/7/7

26. At SHC 6408/1
27. Albums recording both visits at SHC 6408/16
28. *Evening Post*, 14 May 1946
29. Wallace, *Labour, the Board of Education and the Preparation of the 1944 Act*, pp 282–3
30. [1946] Ch 224, [1946] 1 All ER 628
31. *R v Bottrill, ex p Kuechenmeister* [1947] KB 41 (CA), [1946] 1 All ER 635; see Parry, *The Status of Germany and German Internees*, in Modern Law Review 10.4.403–410 (October 1947)
32. See Burnham, *The Squatters of 1946*, for this criticism, and a fuller description
33. PRO CAB 129/13/13
34. SHC 350/9/1
35. Cuttings in the Open Spaces Society papers, in the Parliamentary archives, FCP/2/390
36. On the Society's website, at www.oss.org.uk/what-we-do/our-150th-anniversary/tweet-of-the-day-about-major-events-in-our-150-year-history, listed as Day 222
37. Duret Aubin, 'Recent Constitutional Changes in Jersey', *International and Comparative Law Quarterly*, 1.4.491–503
38. Albums at SHC 6408/16 and illuminated scroll at SHC 6408/9
39. Details of Maxwell and Newsam from *Dictionary of National Biography*
40. Morgan, op cit, p 80
41. *'Frankly Speaking'* interview, December 1960, in BBC Written Archives
42. Morgan, op cit, pp 56, 315
43. PRO CAB 129/17/12
44. See, for instance, Radzinowicz, *Adventures in Criminology*
45. Cecil of Chelwood papers, British Library Add MSS 51192
46. Glees, *The Making of British Policy on War Crimes*, gives a more detailed account to the Dering case (though some of his chronology is incorrect)
47. Vernon, *Ellen Wilkinson 1891–1947*, p 207
48. 6 February 1947, in Ede's personal file, BBC Written Archives
49. Record at SHC 6408/16
50. JCE Diary, 5 April 1952
51. *Inquirer*, 26 April 1947
52. Programme at SHC 6408/6
53. File of papers at SHC 390/4/3
54. Jackson, at www.epsomandewellhistoryexplorer.org.uk/ CleftChinMurder.html
55. *Daily Telegraph*, 1 February 2006
56. Eade, *Young Prince Philip*, pp 184–8, citing Boothroyd, *Philip*, p 39
57. Recollection from Radzinowicz, op cit
58. Home Office submission to Royal Commission on Capital Punishment, August 1949

Chapter 13: The Police, Criminals and the Electorate
1. Duret Aubin, 'Recent Constitutional Changes in Jersey', *International and Comparative Law Quarterly*, 1.4
2. *Hansard*, 24 July 1947
3. Honeycombe, *Murder of the Black Museum*, ch 30
4. See a film of this at http://www.youtube.com/watch?v=3YYYfontzPo. A YouTube search for 'Chuter Ede' will provide several videos relevant to him, including one about the hanging debate (unsympathetic to abolition) at http://www.youtube.com/watch?v=EVa0ffuvZhQ
5. PRO HO 45/24248
6. Pimlott, *Hugh Dalton*, p 552
7. PRO HO 45/24249 and CAB 128/12, cited by Morgan, *Labour in Power 1945–1951*, p 406
8. Castle, *Fighting All the Way*, p 178

9. Morgan, *The People's Peace*, p 84
10. Younghusband, *The Children Act, 1948*, pp 65–69
11. *Observer*, 15 September 1946
12. Morris, *British Criminology: 1935–1948*, The British Journal of Criminology 28.2.20–34
13. Radzinowicz, *Adventures in Criminology*
14. Choppen, 'The Origins of the Philosophy of Detention Centres', *British Journal of Criminology*, 10.2.158–168 (April 1970), citing the Sixteenth Annual Report of the Association (1936/37), pp 16–17
15. *Hansard*, 27 April 1948, at 404
16. PRO CAB 129/20/47
17. A detailed analysis of these dilemmas is given by Bailey, *The Shadow of the Gallows*, in Law and History Review, 18.2 305–349.
18. By Morgan, *Labour in Power 1945–1951*, pp 54–56, though Morgan, generally critical of Ede, describes the entire Criminal Justice Act as a 'disappointment'.
19. *Oxford Dictionary of National Biography*
20. Butler, *The Art of the Possible*, p 201 ff
21. In August 1950, see Gilbert, *Winston S Churchill 1945–65*, vol VIII, p 1182
22. For more details, see Honeycombe, op cit, ch 37–42
23. See above, PRO CAB 129/20/17
24. Personal conversation with the author, November 2017
25. Undated press cutting (but from 1948) in SHC 3690/2/28
26. Glees, *The Making of British Policy on War Crimes*
27. PRO CAB 129/4/37
28. Paul, 'British Subjects' and 'British Stock', *Journal of British Studies*, 34.2.241
29. Shanahan, Different Standards and *Differences*, Theory and Society 26.4.434
30. 27 January 1949, from Ede's personal file, BBC Sound Archives
31. Paul, op cit, pp 243 ff

Chapter 14: Working Alone

1. Hansard, 7 July 1948 at 399
2. Obituary of JCE, *The Times*, 12 November 1965
3. Jefferys, in *Dictionary of National Biography*
4. *Frankly Speaking* interview, December 1960, in BBC Written Archives
5. Barber, *The Making of the 1944 Education Act*, p 38
6. Jackson, *James Chuter Ede*, pp 9–10
7. Morgan, *Labour in Power 1945–1951*, pp 298–9
8. SHC 6408/17
9. Pimlott, *The Queen*, pp 152–4, Eade, *Young Prince Philip*, p 222, Bradford, *Elizabeth*, p 141, and Holden, *Charles Prince of Wales*, p 46–49
10. Fanning, *The Response of the London and Belfast Governments to the Declaration of the Republic of Ireland*, gives more detail of this, quoting from minutes of meetings in the Cabinet Papers
11. Personal file, BBC Sound Archives
12. *Nottingham Guardian*, 25 April 1949
13. *Yorkshire Evening Post*, 30 July 1949
14. SHC 6408/6
15. Photographs at SHC 6408/13
16. Morgan, op cit, pp 374–7
17. Morgan, ibid, and the Observer News Service – Ede retained in his papers a cutting from the *New Zealand Herald*, 22 July 1949, copying this report
18. Thomas-Symonds, *Nye*, pp 160–1
19. *The Schoolmaster*, 3 November 1949
20. SHC 390/2/19
21. *Sunday Sun*, 2 August 1964, copy at SHC

22. Reprinted in The Caian, Punnett's college magazine, for 1949, and then in his obituary by FAE Crew in the *Biographical Memoirs of Fellows of the Royal Society*, 13.309–326 (November 1967)
23. Acceptance letter to Elsie Attwood, 14 September 1949, at SHC
24. Ede's personal file, BBC Written Archives
25. *The Schoolmaster*, 9 February 1950

Chapter 15: Last Steps in Government
1. JCE speaking in 1956, Hansard, 16 February 1956 at 2559
2. *Hansard*, 5 November 1953, at 454
3. Letter from Kielty to JCE, 29 October 1951, in Unitarian files, and supported by personal information from Derek McAuley, of the General Assembly
4. JCE's file at Unitarian headquarters, Essex Hall, from which comes most Unitarian correspondence cited
5. *Hansard*, 27 October 1947, at 503
6. Mahoney, 'Civil Liberties in Britain during the Cold War', *American Journal of Legal History* 33.1. 64 ff
7. *Hansard*, 13 March 1951 at 1309
8. *Hansard*, 25 June 2001. A more detailed account of Ede's role in the matter is given in Newman, *Ralph Miliband and the Politics of the New Left*, pp 42–44
9. Hennessy, *Never Again*, pp 442–3, cites the relevant cabinet papers
10. PRO CAB 129/44/51
11. It can be watched at https://www.youtube.com/watch?v=eIzsPMUBOUs
12. Letter at SHC 390/2/1
13. Burnett, *South Shields in the 1950s*
14. *Dorking and Leatherhead Advertiser*, 22 September 1950
15. Notes for the lecture at SHC, 6408/17
16. Morgan, *Labour in Power 1945–1951*, pp 435–441
17. Marston, 'The United Kingdom's Part in the Preparation of the European Convention on Human Rights, 1950', in *International and Comparative Law Quarterly* 42.4 pp 818–20
18. PRO CAB 128/18/12
19. Cabinet meeting, 24 October 1950, PRO CAB 128/18/28
20. Ede's Personal File, BBC Written Archives
21. Letter from JCE to Revd Wilfred Waddington, 3 February 1951, by personal information from Alan Ruston and Howard Hague, Unitarian Historical Society
22. PRO CAB 129/45/50
23. Williams (ed), *The Diary of Hugh Gaitskell 1945–56*, 2 February 1951, pp 231 ff
24. Morgan, op cit, pp 431–3
25. Williams, *Hugh Gaitskell*, pp 246–57 – the word 'intolerable' was that of Douglas Jay, Financial Secretary to Gaitskell, in conversation with Williams
26. Williams, *The Diary of Hugh Gaitskell 1945–56*, pp 242 ff
27. Thomas-Symonds, *Nye*, p 106
28. Notes on both at SHC 6408/17
29. SHC 6408/9
30. Jenkins, *Churchill*, p 838
31. Membership card for 1946–47, at SHC 6408/8
32. Unattributed cutting among SHC 6408/17
33. Details from the IBP's journal for October 1951, in JCE's papers at SHC 6408/17

Chapter 16: In Opposition
1. Letter to Kielty, 18 December 1951, in the files of the Unitarian General Assembly, Essex Hall

2. *The Times*, 27 and 28 October 1947
3. Wigg, *George Wigg*, p 161
4. Letter of 18 December 1951, ibid, and from Kielty to *The Times* on Ede's death, 12 November 1965, Unitarian file
5. Letter to Kielty, 19 December, and reply 21 December 1951, Unitarian file
6. GAC minutes in BBC Written Archives
7. Morgan (ed), *The Backbench Diaries of Richard Crossman*
8. Her considerable drafts failed to include any section on the 1944 Act, which would clearly have been central to the government publication, and it was abandoned. They were subsequently taken up by Nigel Middleton, and in 1976 *A Place for Everyone: A History of Education* was published, with authorship attributed to 'Middleton and Weitzman'.
9. *Journal of Educational Studies*, November 1952
10. *SHC 390/2*
11. '*Frankly Speaking*', December 1960, in BBC Written Archives
12. JCE Diary, 7 June 1952
13. SHC 6408/6
14. SHC 6408/2
15. Burnett, *South Shields in the 1950s*
16. Wigg, op cit, p 221 ff
17. Paget and Silverman, *Hanged – and Innocent?*, pp 115 ff
18. *Hansard*, 5 November 1953 at 454
19. SHC 390/4/1
20. Extract from *Education*, 15 January 1954, and photographs at SHC 6408/17
21. Radzinowicz, *Adventures in Criminology*
22. SHC 390/11/28, and Ede's Personal File, BBC Written Archives
23. SHC 6408/9
24. 2 October 1954, SHC ibid
25. 19 November 1954, SHC ibid
26. Morgan, *Crossman* op cit, 3 March 1954
27. By, for example, Dell, *A Strange Eventful History*, p 214, Edmund Dell in 1955 being in his thirties, a councillor with Parliamentary ambitions
28. Made by Alan Rowbotham in class 4A, and retained with Ede's papers, now at SHC 6408/21
29. Letter, 17 September 1955, at Working Class Library, Manchester, quoted in Mahoney, 'Civil Liberties in Britain during the Cold War', *American Journal of Legal History* 33.1.99
30. Various correspondence at SHC 390/2/2
31. Undated and unattributed press cutting, at SHC
32. GAC minutes, 9 December 1953, 9 March 1955, 7 March 1956, in BBC Written Archives
33. Morgan, *Crossman* op cit, 7 June 1955
34. *The Times*, 10 June 1955. Pimlott, *Hugh Dalton*, confirms Ede told other newspapers about his real concern for Dalton's powers

Chapter 17: On the Back Benches
1. SHC 390/11/28, and BBC Sound Archives at the British Library
2. Broadcast on 13 and 19 April 1955 (Ede's Personal File, BBC Written Archives)
3. Photograph at southtynesidehistory.co.uk
4. Details from Ashbrook, *Saving Open Spaces*
5. Ashbrook, op cit, pp 16–17
6. A photograph of Chubb's memorial plaque is included in Ashbrook, op cit, p 13
7. Open Spaces Society files, in the Parliamentary archives, FCP/2/8, and minute books at FCP/2/477 to /483

8. For example, *Hansard* 24 February 1936
9. *The Belfast News Letter*, 28 July 1955
10. Traer, *A Short History of the IARF*, iarf.net, p 22
11. Traer, op cit, p 23
12. Harris, *Politics without Prejudice*, page v
13. *Hansard*, 23 July 1964. Papers on the visit are at SHC
14. Undated copy at SHC 6408/17 CE89
15. *British Medical Journal*, 3 December 1955
16. *Shields Gazette*, 2 March 1956
17. Letter, 23 January 1956 in the Essex Hall files London
18. GAC minutes, 20 June and 17 October 1956, in BBC Written Archives
19. *Shields Gazette*, 9 January 1957
20. Details from correspondence, mainly between Greeley, Kielty and Ede, in the Essex Hall files
21. In the *Shields Gazette*, 28 November 1956, the first of four reports (with 10 December 1956, 3 and 4 January 1957), from which this account comes
22. Note at SHC, 6408/7
23. *Shields Gazette*, ibid
24. *Inquirer*, 26 January 1957
25. GAC minutes, 1957, in BBC Written Archives
26. Copy at SHC 6408/17 (CE89)
27. *Surrey CCC Yearbook*, 1958
28. Annual Report 1957, General Assembly of the Unitarian and Free Christian Churches
29. Ede's Personal File, BBC Written Archives
30. Income tax return, 1957–58, SHC 390/11/28
31. *Twenty Five Years On*, Education, 4 October 1957, from which several quotations have already been made in the chapter covering 1932
32. *Daily Herald*, cited in Pimlott, *Hugh Dalton*, p 628
33. GAC minutes in BBC Written Archives
34. Letter, 4 November 1957, in Essex Hall files
35. His report and written addresses are at SHC 6408/17
36. *Hull Daily Mail*, 16 April 1958, and several other newspapers
37. BBC Sound Archives index, under reference ANB2760N
38. BBC Written Archives, personal file
39. Invitation dated 4 March 1958, at SHC 390/1/4
40. SHC 7651
41. Obituary of JCE in *The Inquirer*, 27 November 1965
42. SHC, 6408/2
43. SHC, 6408/15
44. Annual Report 1958, General Assembly of the Unitarian and Free Christian Churches, and information from Howard Hague, Unitarian Historical Society
45. Report of trip at SHC 6408/15, photos at SHC 390/2/16
46. SHC 390/2/16
47. BBC Written Archives, file S6/1 (recorded 8 February 1959, broadcast 11 February)
48. *Hansard*, 24 April 1959. See also Campbell, *Roy Jenkins*, p 185
49. BBC Written Archives, File S6/1 and Ede's personal file
50. BBC, ibid
51. Hazlehurst et al, *Guide to the Papers of British Cabinet Ministers 1900–1964*, p 129
52. GAC minutes, 29 April and 8 July 1959, in BBC Written Archives
53. In file S6/1, in BBC Written Archives
54. *Hansard*, 5 May 1960
55. Copy kept by JCE, now in SHC 3690/2/28
56. Ceremony on 25 April 1960, scroll dated 4 May in SHC

57. Scroll in SHC 6408/9
58. Correspondence in Essex Hall files
59. SHC 6408/17
60. *Shields Gazette*, 2 March 1960
61. Jackson, *James Chuter Ede*
62. Letter from JCE to Helen Arbuthnot, BBC producer, 15 November 1960, in BBC Written Archives
63. Personal conversation with Ann Godden
64. Letter, 19 July 1960, at SHC 390/1/4
65. From obituary in *Shields Gazette*, 11 November 1965, cited by Clark, *We do not Want the Earth*, p 94
66. Unattributed cutting, 20 July 1960, perhaps from Newcastle Journal, in SHC 390/10/11
67. Press cuttings at SHC 390/2/4
68. Correspondence in Essex Hall files
69. Papers at BBC Written Archives, file 6/2
70. Hazlehurst et al, ibid, citing transcripts in the BBC Written Archives Centre
71. At SHC 390/2/4
72. Bullock, *The Life and Times of Ernest Bevin*, volume 3, p 93
73. Correspondence at SHC 390/1/5
74. Correspondence with CCA, SHC 390/1/5
75. SHC 390/5/2
76. Kennedy, *Ten Rillington Place*, p 15
77. Paget and Silverman, *Hanged – and Innocent?*
78. *The Observer*, 15 January 1961, retained by JCE (at SHC 390/4/1), quoted in Parliament, *Hansard*, 15 June 1961 at 650
79. The letters are at SHC 390/4/1, and the second is quoted in Wigg, *George Wigg*, pp 222 ff
80. Written answer, Hansard, 16 March 1961 at 142
81. File 6/2 in BBC Written Archives
82. Letter, 22 March 1961, in Essex Hall files
83. Copy in SHC
84. Noakes, *A Professional Approach to Oil Painting*, p 76 – photograph credited to The Times
85. Personal conversation with the author
86. *Shields Gazette*, 21 March 1961
87. SHC 390/2/18
88. File at SHC 390/3/2
89. Correspondence in Essex Hall files
90. NUT Report 1962, p 63
91. Report on lecture and discussion, British Library
92. SHC 390/3/3
93. *Shields Gazette*, 9 October 1962
94. *Hansard*, 14 December 1962, at 806–808
95. Clark, op cit, p 93
96. Correspondence at SHC 390/1/4. Coldingley Prison was eventually opened in Bisley in 1969
97. Wigg, op cit
98. SHC 390/2/20
99. SHC 390/2/21
100. Photograph at SHC 6408/30
101. *Shields Gazette*, 25 May 1963
102. RLPAS Annual Report for 1963, at SHC 6408/8
103. Davenport-Hines, *An English Affair*
104. Wigg, op cit, pp 276–7
105. *Shields Gazette*, 26 September 1963

106. Letters from JCE to Kielty, 29 April and 8 May 1963
107. Copies in Essex Hall files
108. SHC 390/3/5
109. File 6/2 in the BBC Written Archives Centre

Chapter 18: Lord of Epsom
1. SHC 390/3/6
2. *Epsom & Ewell Herald*, 23 September 1966
3. Clark, *We Do not Want the Earth*, p 111
4. *Dictionary of National Biography*
5. *The Inquirer*, 11 December 1965
6. *Epsom & Ewell Advertiser*, 10 December 1964
7. Letter to Jack Lawson, 11 July 1965, in Lawson papers, Durham UL, quoted in Bew, *Citizen Clem*, p 544
8. *House of Lords Hansard*, 1965
9. SHC 390/5/2, and JCE's personal file at the BBC Written Archives
10. SHC 390/4/1
11. Jefferys, *Labour and the Wartime Coalition*, p16, and DNB, and unattributed obituary of JCE 11 November 1965 (probably Evening Standard)
12. This was the subject of a question in Parliament, see *Hansard*, 25 November 1965 at 903
13. Information in conversation with the author
14. Letter from Mrs Saker to NUT, 18 October 1965
15. *The Guardian* 12 November 1965
16. *The Times* 12 November 1965
17. *The Epsom and Ewell Advertiser* 18 November, *The Surrey Comet* 13 November 1965
18. 13 November 1965
19. 27 November 1965
20. *The Teacher*, 19 November 1965
21. On 17 November the Town Clerk made a ten-page note of his activities, now in Epsom and Ewell Museum, from which most of these details come.
22. Letter from J Kielty, in Essex Hall files, 22 March 1961
23. Details from the service sheet, *The Surrey Comet*, 20 November 1965, and *The Epsom and Ewell Advertiser*, 18 November 1965
24. Letter to John Kielty, dated November 1965, evidently written on 16 November
25. 'Frankly Speaking' interview, December 1960, in BBC Written Archives
26. Wigg, *George Wigg*
27. Beckett, *Clem Attlee*
28. Unattributed obituary of JCE, 11 November 1965 (probably the London *Evening Standard*)
29. Jackson, *James Chuter Ede*
30. *The Inquirer*, 26 February 1966, and an undated cutting from *The Times*

Chapter 19: Afterword
1. Letter to Unitarian Churches, 10 May 1966, from Essex Hall files
2. Surrey History Centre introduction to Chuter Ede papers. One file (390/3/6) is marked 'DESTROY any correspondence of a very personal nature', dated 21 June 1965
3. Hazlehurst, Whitehead & Woodland (eds), *A Guide to the Papers of British Cabinet Ministers*
4. Strudwick, *The Story of an Association*, ch 6
5. Barber, *The Making of the 1944 Education Act*, p 43
6. *Hansard*, 20 December 1962, at 1503
7. Castle, *Fighting all the Way*, p 178
8. Morgan, *Labour in Power 1945–1951*, p 8

9. Ibid, p 55
10. BBC Written Archives
11. Lowndes, *The Silent Social Revolution*, p 243
12. Clark, *We do not Want the Earth*, p 94
13. 30 September 1948
14. Evans, *James Chuter Ede and the 1944 Education Act*, p 23
15. Told by Blyton to David Clark, see Clark, op cit, p 96
16. Wallace, *Labour, the Board of Education and the Preparation of the 1944 Education Act*, p 289
17. Information from Lucy Shepherd, archivist of the Oxford and Cambridge Club, and from a few references in letters and invitations at the SHC
18. Jack Grassby, in personal communication with the author
19. Bailey, *James Chuter Ede and the 1944 Education Act*, p 215
20. Morgan, ibid, p 54
21. Clark, op cit, p 96
22. Ziegler, *Wilson – the Authorised Life*, p 64
23. N Middleton & S Weitzman, *A Place for Everyone*, p 282 ff
24. *Hansard*, 15 February 1944
25. JCE diary, 4 November 1941
26. *Hansard*, 27 January 1954 at 1902
27. SHC 6408/Box 2
28. JCE, 4 October 1950, Dr Williams Lecture, Carmarthen
29. *Hansard*, 20 February 1963 at 510
30. www.unitarian.org.uk/pages/unitarianism-explained
31. Reeves, *Alice Bacon*, p 134
32. In Woking, 28 September 1956, papers at SHC 3690/2/28
33. At www.epsomandewellhistoryexplorer.org.uk/chuterede.html, by Linda Jackson, prevented unfortunately by her health from researching other than online
34. Bourne & MacArthur, *The Struggle for Education 1870–1970*
35. *Sutton Herald*, obituary of Mary Ede, 19 May 1939
36. Information from Steve Davies, former Council employee, and an undated note signed by Trevor Carrington White of Epsom, in Epsom and Ewell Museum archives
37. From information provided by Julie Ford, grants administrator at Chuter Ede School
38. Issued by the GLC (London Metropolitan Archives, GLC/DG/PRB/35/009/ 468)
39. *The Times* 3 June 1964, and *Courier* (newspaper of University of Newcastle) 24 February 1965
40. Cloake, *Pride, Passion, Professionalism*, p 23
41. Details from successive NUT Annual Reports, 1963–70
42. Reprinted in *The Caian*, Punnett's college magazine, for 1949, and then in his obituary by FAE Crew in the *Biographical Memoirs of Fellows of the Royal Society*, 13.309–326 (November 1967)

Bibliography and Sources

Considerable sources for this book come from the Chuter Ede archives, which are now in the Surrey History Centre in Woking – these are referred to by 'SHC' in footnotes to the text. Others come from the Public Record Office in Kew – referred to as 'PRO'.

The other main unpublished sources are Chuter Ede's diaries, most of which (together with various academic and manuscript works) are held at the British Library; the diaries are referenced Addl MS 59690–59703. The diaries from 1946 and 1948 are at the SHC.

The information relating to Parliament comes generally from Hansard (references are to the House of Commons Hansard, unless otherwise stated).

Other primary sources I have used are located at the London Metropolitan Archives, the Unitarian files at Essex Hall (recently transferred to Dr Williams's Library, Gordon Square), the BBC Written Archives Centre in Caversham, the Parliamentary Archives, and the British Museum Central Archives. Footnotes to the text indicate where these have been my source.

In addition the following unpublished studies have been consulted.

Evans, Robert, *James Chuter Ede and the 1944 Education Act*, MA Dissertation, Institute of Education, London University, 1993

Mates, Lewis H, *The United Front and the Popular Front in the North East of England, 1936–1939*, PhD Thesis, Newcastle University, 2002

Shakoor, Akhtar, *The Training of Teachers in England and Wales, 1900–1939*, PhD Thesis, University of Leicester, 1964

Strudwick, John, *Surrey Co Teachers' Association 'Story of an Association'*, Unpublished manuscript, held at Surrey History Centre

Wallace, RG, *Labour, the Board of Education and the Preparation of the 1944 Act*, PhD Thesis, University of London, 1980

The principal published articles and lectures I have consulted are:

Duret Aubin, C, 'Recent Constitutional Changes in Jersey', C. *International and Comparative Law Quarterly* 1.4.491–503, 1952

Bailey, Bill, James Chuter Ede and the 1944 Education Act, *History of Education*, vol 24, no 3, 209–220, 1995

Bailey, Victor, The Shadow of the Gallows, *Law and History Review*, vol 18, no 2, 305–349, 2000

Butler, R.A. Inaugural Chuter Ede Lecture, 22–3–62, (with comments from others), NUT, 1962

Choppen, Valerie, The Origins of the Philosophy of Detention Centres, *British Journal of Criminology* 10.2.158–168, 1970

The Economist 11–8–45, 1945

Chuter Ede, J., The Founding Fathers and their Successors, J. *Surrey Teacher*, 1933

Chuter Ede, J., Twenty Five Years On, *Education* 4–10–1957, 1957

Fanning, Ronan, The Response of the London and Belfast Governments to the Declaration of the Republic of Ireland, *International Affairs*, 58.1.95–114, Winter 1981–82

Glees, Anthony, The Making of British Policy on War Crimes, *Contemporary European History* 1.2.171–197, 1992

Harris, R.E., New Police College Opened in Britain, *Journal of Criminal Law and Criminology*, 40.2.217–222, 7/8/49

Hart, Stephen, James Chuter Ede – a Model Unitarian Overlooked, *Transactions of the Unitarian History Society* 27.2.67–96, 2020

Jefferys, Kevin, R.A. Butler, the Board of Education and the 1944 Education Act, *History*, new ser 69, 415–31, 1984

McCready, Thomas, Blessed is the Peacemaker – James Ramsey MacDonald, unitarian, *Transactions of the Unitarian History Society* 27.2.97–109, 2020

Mahoney, Joan, Civil Liberties in Britain during the Cold War, *American Journal of Legal History* 33.1.53–100, 1/1989

Marston, Geoffrey, The United Kingdom's Part in the Preparation of the European Convention on Human Rights, 1950, *International and Comparative Law Quarterly* 42.4.796–826, 10/1993

Morris, Terence, British Criminology: 1934–48, *British Journal of Criminology* 28.2.20–34, 1988

Parry, Clive, The Status of Germany and German Refugees, *The Modern Law Review* 10.4.403–410, 1947

Paul, Kathleen, "British Subjects" and "British Stock", *Journal of British Studies* 34.2.233–276, 4/1995

Punnett, Reginald, Pro Bono Publico, *The Caian*, 1949

Shanahan, Suzanne, Different Standards and Standard Differences, *Theory and Society* 26.4.421–448, 8/1997

Smith, Harold L., The Womanpower Problem in Britain during the Second World War, *Historical Journal*, 27.4.925–945, 12/1984

Thomas, George, Teachers in Parliament (1), *The Schoolmaster* CLVI, 3/11/49

Wallace, R.G., The Origins and Authorship of the 1944 Education Act, *History of Education* 10.4.283–290, 1981

Williams, Francis, Ministers as they Are – Chuter Ede, *Spectator* 30/9/1948, 1948

Younghusband, Eileen L., The Children Act, 1948, *Modern Law Review* 12.1.65–69, 1/1949

There is a considerable range of books, covering the history of the period of Ede's life, and also his particular interests.

Addison, Paul, *The Road to 1945*, Cape (paperback Pimlico 1994), 1975

Adonis, Andrew, *Ernest Bevin, Labour's Churchill*, Biteback, 2020

Attlee, C.R., *As It Happened*, Heinemann, 1954

Ashbrook, Kate, *Saving Open Spaces*, Pitkin, 2015

Barber, Michael, *Education and the Teacher Unions*, Cassell, 1992

Barber, Michael, *The Making of the 1944 Education Act*, Cassell, 1994

Barker, Rodney, *Education and Politics*, 1900–1951, Oxford UP, 1972

Beckett, Francis, *Clem Attlee*, Richard Cohen Books, 1997

Bew, John, *Citizen Clem: a Biography of Attlee*, Quercus, 2016

Boothroyd, Basil, *Philip*, Longman, 1971

Borough of Epsom & Ewell, *Borough of Epsom & Ewell 75th Anniversary Charter Souvenir 1937–2012*, 2012

Bourne, Richard & MacArthur, Brian, *The Struggle for Education 1870–1970*, Schoolmaster Publishing (for the NUT), 1970

Bradford, Sarah, *Elizabeth*, Heinemann, 1996

Bullock, Alan, *The Life and Times of Ernest Bevin*, vols 1–3, Heinemann, 1960, 1967, 1983

Burnett, Eileen, *South Shields in the 1950s*, Amberley, 2016

Burrow, John, *The Age of Reform* (in Reynolds, op cit), Macmillan, 2004

Butler, R.A., *The Art of the Possible*, Gambit, 1971

Campbell, John, *Nye Bevan*, Weidenfeld & Nicolson, 1987

Campbell, John, *Roy Jenkins*, Cape, 2014

Castle, Barbara, *Fighting All the Way*, Macmillan, 1993

Cazalet Keir, Thelma, *From the Wings*, Bodley Head, 1967

Chitty, Clyde & Dunford, John (eds), *State Schools: New Labour and the Conservative Legacy*, Woburn Press, 1999

Churchill, Winston, *The Second World War*, vol III, Cassell, 1950

Clark, David, *We Do not Want the Earth*, Bewick, 1992

Clark, Alan, *The Tories*, Weidenfeld & Nicolson, 1998

Cloake, Martin, *Pride, Passion, Professionalism*, NUT-NEU, 2017

Cosgrave, Patrick, *The Strange Death of Socialist Britain*, Constable, 1992

Curtis, S.J., *History of Education in Great Britain*, University Tutorial Press, 1948

Davenport-Hines, Richard, *An English Affair*, Harper Collins, 2013

Dell, Edmund, *A Strange Eventful History*, Harper Collins, 1999

Dent, H.C., *The Education Act 1944*, Unibooks, 1968

Eade, Philip, *Young Prince Philip*, HarperPress, 2011

Foot, Michael, *Loyalists and Lovers*, Collins, 1986

Gilbert, Martin, *Winston S Churchill*, vols VII & VIII, Hillsdale, 1986 & 1988

Giles, GCT, *The New School Tie*, Pilot Press, 1946

Gosden, Peter, *Education in the Second World War*, Routledge, 1976

Gosden, Peter, *The Evolution of a Profession*, Blackwell, 1972

Gosden, Peter, *The Education System since 1944*, Robertson, 1983

Harris, Ralph, *Politics without Prejudice*, Staples, 1956

Hazlehurst, Cameron, Whitehead, Sally & Woodland, Christine, *A Guide to the papers of British Cabinet Ministers 1900–1964 (revised ed)*, Cambridge UP (for the Royal Historical Society), 1996

Hennessy, Peter, *Never Again*, Cape, 1992

Hill, Carol, *Parks in the Past: Part 2*, Bourne Hall Museum, 2012

Holden, Anthony, *Charles Prince of Wales*, Weidenfeld & Nicolson, 1979

Honeycombe, Gordon, *Murders of the Black Museum*, John Blake, 1982

Howard, Anthony, *Crossman – the Pursuit of Power*, Cape, 1990

Howard, Anthony, *RAB*, Cape, 1987

Jefferys, Kevin ed., *Labour and the Wartime Coalition*, Historian's Press, 1987

The Churchill Coalition and Wartime Politics, Kevin Jefferys, Manchester UP, 1991

Jenkins, Roy, *A Life at the Centre*, Macmillan, 1991

Jenkins, Roy, *Churchill*, Macmillan, 2001

Jones, Ken, *Education in Britain: 1944 to the Present (2nd ed)*, Polity Press, 2016

Kennedy, Ludovic, *Ten Rillington Place*, Gollancz, 1963

Lawton, Denis, *Education and Politics in the 1990s*, Falmer, 1992

Smith, W.O. Lester, *Education*, Penguin, 1957

Lowndes, G.A.N., *The Silent Social Revolution*, Oxford, 1969

Educational Reconstruction, Gary McCulloch, Woburn, 1994

Maclure, Stuart, *Educational Documents*, Methuen, 1996

Manzer, Ronald, *Teachers and Politics*, Manchester UP, 1970

Middleton, Nigel & Weitzman, Sophia, *A Place for Everyone: A History of Education*, Gollancz, 1976

Morgan, Janet, ed., *The Backbench Diaries of Richard Crossman*, Hamilton and Cape, 1981

Morgan, Kenneth O., *Labour in Power, 1945–1951*, Oxford UP, 1984

Morgan, Kenneth O., *Michael Foot – a Life*, Harper Collins, 2007

Morgan, Kenneth O., *The People's Peace*, Oxford UP, 1990

Newman, Michael, *Ralph Miliband and the Politics of the New Left*, Merlin, 2002

Nicolson, Harold, *Diaries and Letters 1945–62*, Collins, 1968

Noakes, Michael, *A Professional Approach to Oil Painting*, Pitman, 1968

Paget, Reginald & Silverman, Sidney, *Hanged – and Innocent?*, Gollancz, 1953

Peile, John, *Christ's College Biographical Register*, Cambridge, 1913

Pimlott, Ben, *Hugh Dalton*, Cape, 1985

Pimlott, Ben, *The Queen*, Harper Collins, 1996

Radice, Giles, *The Tortoise and the Hares*, Methuen, 2008

Radzinowicz, Leon, *Adventures in Criminology*, Routledge, 1999

Reeves, Rachel, *Alice in Westminster*, IB Tauris, 2017

Reynolds, David, *Christ's – A Cambridge College over Five Centuries*, Macmillan, 2004

Shearman, Harold, *The New Education Act*, WEA, 1944

Sheppard, H.R.L., *The Human Parson*, Murray, 1925

Simon, Brian, *The Politics of Educational Reform, 1920–40*, Lawrence & Wishart, 1974

Simon, Brian, *Education and the Social Order, 1940–1990*, Lawrence & Wishart, 1991

Skidelsky, Robert, *John Maynard Keynes*, vols 1–3, Macmillan, 2000

Surrey County Cricket Club, *Handbook for 1958*, Boscombe, 1958

Taylor, A.J.P., *English History 1914–1945*, Oxford, 1965

Thomas-Symonds, Nicklaus, *Nye: the Political Life of Aneurin Bevan*, IB Tauris, 2015

Thorpe, D.R., *Eden*, Chatto & Windus, 2003

Tracey, Herbert, ed., *The British Labour Party*, Caxton, 1948

Vernon, Betty D., *Ellen Wilkinson*, Croom Helm, 1982

Wigg, Lord, *George Wigg*, Joseph, 1982

Williams, Philip, ed., *Diary of Hugh Gaitskell*, Cape, 1983

Williams, Philip, *Hugh Gaitskell*, Cape, 1979

Williams, Francis, *A Prime Minister Remembers*, Heinemann, 1961

Who's Who in Surrey, Baylis, 1938

Ziegler, Philip, *Wilson – the Authorised Life*, Weidenfeld & Nicolson, 1993

Finally, modern research relies on some sources only available online, and I have consulted the following.

Burnham, Paul, *The Squatters of 1946*, Paper presented to Tenants' History Conference, at libcom.org/files/ WWII-Squatters.pdf, 2009

Gillard, Derek, *Education in England: a Brief History*, www.educationengland. org.uk/history, 2011

Harrison, Stephen, *The Character of Victorian Sport*, gassingabout. wordpress. com, 2013

Hyams, Jill, *James Chuter Ede, Politician, Educationist and Soldier (1882–1965)*, surreyinthegreatwar.org.uk/author/jh0107/, 2016

Jackson, Linda, James Chuter Ede, *Epsom & Ewell History Explorer*, 2013

Jackson, Linda, The Cleft Chin Murder, *Epsom & Ewell History Explorer*, 2013

Pack, Mark, *PollBase*, www.markpack.org.uk/opinion-polls/, 2019

Rowe, Mortimer, *The Story of Essex Hall*, Unitarian.org.uk, 1959

Traer, Robert, *A Short History of the IARF*, iarf.net, 2005

A Cambridge Alumni Database, venn.lib.cam.ac.uk,

Great War Forum (Royal Engineers Special Brigade), greatwarforum.org/topic/547-royal-engineers-special-brigade

Index